S0-BIE-708

Religious Thought
in the
Victorian Age

Religious Thought
in the
Victorian Age

Challenges and Reconceptions

James C. Livingston

continuum

NEW YORK • LONDON

DISCARDED

NAZARETH COLLEGE

2007

T & T Clark International, 80 Maiden Lane, New York, NY 10038

T & T Clark International, The Tower Building, 11 York Road, London SE1 7NX

T & T Clark International is a Continuum imprint.

Cover design: Brenda Klinger

www.continuumbooks.com

Copyright © 2006 by James C. Livingston

All rights reserved. No part of this book may be reproduced, stored in a retrieval system, or transmitted in any form or by any means, electronic, mechanical, including photocopying, recording, or otherwise, without the written permission of the publisher, T & T Clark International.

Printed in the United States of America

Library of Congress Cataloging-in-Publication Data

Livingston, James C., 1930–
  Religious thought in the Victorian Age : challenges and reconceptions /
James C. Livingston.
     p. cm.
  Includes bibliographical references and index.
  ISBN-13: 978-0-567-02513-5 (hardcover : alk. paper)
  ISBN-10: 0-567-02513-6 (hardcover : alk. paper)
  ISBN-13: 978-0-567-02646-0 (pbk. : alk. paper)
  ISBN-10: 0-567-02646-9 (pbk. : alk. paper)
  1. Great Britain—Religion—19th century. I. Title.

BR759.L58 2007
230.0941'09034—dc22

                                                        2007003478

06 07 08 09 10   10 9 8 7 6 5 4 3 2 1

230.0941
Liv

Contents

To my wife and helpmate Jackie,
with love and abiding gratitude—
as always

Acknowledgments

This book covers a significant range of developments in scholarly fields of endeavor as they relate to religion in the late Victorian period in Britain. While well acquainted with the primary sources in the philosophy of religion, comparative religion, theology, and the philosophy of this period, and with aspects of the Darwinian controversies, I am, nevertheless, deeply obliged to several specialists in the history of British science and its cultural influences in the nineteenth century. This will be evident in the numerous citations to their works in the reference notes of the book. Special mention, however, must be made of Frank M. Turner, John H. Brooke, James R. Moore, Robert M. Young, and Robert J. Richards. They stimulated my own thinking and often guided me into areas I had not explored.

At the beginning of this project I was assisted by the support of the late Hans Frei, Frank Turner, Claude Welch, and Dale Johnson. Later John Brooke and Claude Welch read rough drafts of some chapters and offered invaluable advice about alterations, additions, and some corrections. I could not follow through on all their suggestions and, of course, the book as it stands reflects my own judgments.

Several institutions contributed to the completion of this book. The College of William and Mary offered me a generous research leave that was crucial. A fellowship from the Woodrow Wilson International Center for Scholars in Washington, D.C., allowed me uninterrupted time to write and to do research in the Library of Congress. The Wilson Center and my co-fellows there proved a great stimulant for my work, and my stay there was a memorable experience. Several months at Clare Hall, Cambridge, were also of great benefit, since the University Library is a treasure trove for scholars of Victoriana.

Staff at the Wilson Center, including student assistants, helped me in numerous ways, as did the librarians at the Library of Congress and the University Library, Cambridge. In the preparation of drafts and the final text, I am especially grateful for the generous assistance of three persons. Tammy Cooper, office manager in the Department of Religion at William and Mary, prepared several chapters on the computer while engaged in numerous other responsibilities. My daughter, Susannah, a professional editor, read most of the chapters and offered her expert advice. My wife Jackie, as always, was unstinting in her help with this project—in matters large and small—and to her the book is happily dedicated.

Introduction

The period of British religious thought covered in this book has not been neglected. Those familiar with the subject will be acquainted with the general overviews, as well as the many more specialized studies. This work, however, examines the thought of this period differently. Some of the standard histories adhere rather closely to traditional ecclesiastical interests and politics, and others attend principally or exclusively to Anglican theological movements or figures. These have proven highly valuable and instructive. Yet I believe that the intellectual history of late Victorian Britain requires that we view the religious thought of this rich era from a wider and thematic perspective.

By 1860 the religious discussion in Britain had significantly broadened in two important respects. First, the examination of critical theological issues had moved outside the bounds of the established Church of England and its three dominant parties. The discussion now engaged highly respected Roman Catholic, Nonconformist, and secular thinkers of impressive intellectual range. Second, and perhaps more significantly, the deeper and more consequential debates on matters touching on religion were no longer dominated by clerics and theologians. As the historian W. E. H. Lecky observed, it was the Victorian lay writers and sages, major and minor, who now were forming the opinions and fashioning the character of the age. They had, in some important ways, superseded or at least diminished the role of the clergy in the shaping of religious thought. The clergy no longer had the pulpits to themselves. The leading magazines and reviews—the *Fortnightly Review*, the *Contemporary Review*, the *Nineteenth Century*, to name only a few—had become powerful forums for the educated public. These periodicals carried extensive debates on, among other subjects, the ethics of religious belief; the theological significance of the new agnostic temper of mind; science and the reign of law as they were to bear upon beliefs concerning design, providence, miracles, theodicy, and the efficacy of prayer; and the debate over the origin and development of religion and morals. Between 1876 and 1881, numerous articles appeared in the new philosophical journal *Mind* on the mind, brain, and freedom debate, with explicit attention given to its moral and theological implications. To attend only or primarily to the theological writings or church publications of the period is often to miss the most sophisticated and rigorous discussion of the key theological issues of the day.

There is an earlier tradition of Victorian intellectual historiography that is reflected in the once influential books on science and religion written by J. W. Draper, A. D. White, J. M. Robertson, A. W. Benn, and W. E. H. Lecky. These "whiggish" historians interpreted the history of late nineteenth-century British thought as the victory of rationalism and scientific naturalism over theological dogmatism. They often viewed the period as a record of the failure of theology to address adequately the intellectual challenges of the day, and they chronicled the onset of secularization and religious enervation. Recent histories of the religious thought of the period seriously challenge these interpretations and claims.

It is true, of course, that by the turn of the century the hold of the churches over the institutions of society, for example over education, had been weakened, and there was a decline in worship attendance and other religious activities, especially in the cities. While ecclesial theology did cease to serve some cultural functions that it had filled earlier in the century, the intellectual discussion of religion actually flourished late in the century. A second purpose of this study is to demonstrate that the late Victorian decades were a time of vitality and creativity in the educated public's discussion of critical religious and theological matters. The texture of the scientific and philosophical debates after 1860 continued to be deeply interwoven with religious and theological issues. These concerns were constitutive, as, I trust, this study will demonstrate. It was an era during which a number of fundamental theological doctrines were examined and reconceived. This is true, for example, with regard to the broadening of doctrinal latitude, the wide acceptance of the historical-critical study of the Bible, the reexamination of natural theology and the nature and limits of theological knowledge itself. The era also saw critical reconceptions in the understanding of God and God's relation to the world, including new conceptions of teleology, providence, miracle, and theodicy, and Christianity's relation to other world faiths.

While it is beyond the purview of this study, I believe it could be shown that, while Britain in the twentieth century witnessed important theological developments, many of these were engaged and often substantively shaped in the debates of the latter decades of the nineteenth century. Contrary to some earlier assessments, the period was in fact a watershed in British religious and theological history. In the study of *religious thought*, it certainly would be incorrect to describe it as simply a time of secularization. The late Victorian period can best be viewed as a time of religious change—change that had profound and enduring influences.

I have not chosen to tell the story of British religious thought in the latter half of the nineteenth century by surveying again the major theological movements or schools of thought, or by examining the work of certain pre-eminent religious thinkers in chronological succession. Rather, I examine in some depth a number of the most critical theological debates or controversies that dominated the intellectual discussion of religion between roughly 1860 and the end of the first decade of the twentieth century. These issues are the subject of chapters 2 through 7. The choice of these themes is not intended to be comprehensive; I do nevertheless believe that they are among the most critically important and widely discussed religious questions of the period. One theological subject of great interest to the late Victorians—the developments in biblical interpretation and authority—is not dealt with in historical order and detail, but it is brought into the discussion in several chapters. Valuable studies have thoroughly explored this subject (Chadwick 1970, 40–111; Ellis 1980; Neill 1966; Rearden 1971, 321–59; Shea and Whitla 2000).

The central purpose of this book is to offer an account of crucial intellectual challenges to traditional British theology, challenges that provoked wide-ranging discussions and decisively shaped British theology. In several instances, they resulted in rather fundamental reconceptions of traditional doctrine and belief. Not all of the conclusions reached in these debates proved enduring, and some efforts to accommodate theology to advances in the sciences proved spurious or unnecessary. Yet even the ill-fated forays and speculations were efforts to respond to new, genuine questions that required answers.

Every historian of ideas must decide on what level of the discussion he or she is to settle. Many intellectual histories focus exclusively on the truly seminal figures. For the mid- and late-Victorian periods, that would include Mill, Darwin, and Newman, among others. Recently, however, historians have turned their sights on intellectual history "from below," on thinkers who, often for ideological reasons, were dismissed in their own time and largely forgotten. One thinks, for example, of the work of Adrian Desmond on the radical British evolutionists in London before the appearance of *The Origin of Species* and Roger Cooter's study of the popularity of phrenology (Desmond 1989; Cooter 1984). Others have canvassed the popular press to discover the various ways that ideas have been received, understood, and altered in the consciousness of the general public, that is, the diffusion of ideas at an unsophisticated but socially significant level (Ellegard 1958). This study does not attempt to explore deeply the socioeconomic context of the intellectual debates or their possibly important social determinants, as important as such an exploration might prove to be. While I take account of the religious and intellectual contexts of the period, I attempt what could be called a middle way, limiting my inquiry to the explicit discussion of religious ideas in the writings of the Victorian intellectual class. Historian of science Robert M. Young has referred to this as the "methodical," in contrast to the "unmethodical," trajectory of ideas (Young 1985, ch. 5). Such an approach, of course, includes the Mills and the Newmans but, more often, the so-called lesser figures who were important, since they often better represent the widely shared points of view of their time. I am thinking of figures such as the Duke of Argyll, George Romanes, Henry Drummond, W. B. Carpenter, and J. R. Illingworth. I believe that the historian Arthur Lovejoy was basically correct in saying that the tendencies of an age often appear more distinctly in its writers of lesser rank than in those of powerful genius. A George Combe or a George Romanes may be more characteristic of their time than are some of the greater minds of the Victorian Age.

A few words also are required with regard to the years 1860 and 1910 and the justification for beginning and ending where I do. History, obviously, is continuous, and periodization always involves some arbitrariness. Yet in retrospect I believe that we can see the years 1860 to 1910—conceding a few years at either end—as a distinctive and critical period in the history of religious thought in Britain. They were years of intellectual controversy and crisis and of efforts at resolution, and they hastened notable changes within British theological traditions without the loss of their crucial identity.

The years 1858–1863 brought to public notice a number of provocative works that challenged and even altered received religious beliefs. Henry Mansel's *The Limits of Religious Thought* appeared in 1858. Darwin's *Origin of Species* was published in 1859, the same year that Joseph Prestwick reported to the Royal Society on the antiquity of human fossil remains discovered in Devon and in France. In 1860 the controversial collection *Essays and Reviews*, written largely by progressive Anglican divines, was issued and caused an immediate scandal. In 1861 the philologist and comparativist Friedrich Max Müller published his *Lectures on the Science of Religion*, followed a year later by the Anglican bishop J. W. Colenso's *The Pentateuch and the Book of Joshua Critically Examined*. The works of two esteemed scientists—Charles Lyell's *Antiquity of Man* and T. H. Huxley's *Man's Place in Nature*—both appeared in 1863 to considerable notice. These were soon followed by influential anthropological works by John Lubbock, E. B. Tylor, and J. F. M'Lennan. Many of the ground assumptions of the older theological apologetic were severely threatened: notions of biblical inspiration and the vestiges of earlier arguments from miracle and prophecy; the understanding of humanity's place in natural history; traditional assumptions about God and the world that raised new questions about a particular providence, miracles, and theodicy; and claims regarding Christianity's uniqueness and absoluteness.

Before 1860 the Bible and natural theology remained the widely assumed contexts within which discussions about creation, anthropology, ethnology, geology, and even history were pursued. One is reminded, for example, of so-called scriptural geologists such as William Buckland, the ethnology of J. C. Pritchard, and the anthropological assumptions of most of the influential scientists. And rather suddenly—within a few decades, at most—there occurred a great reversal. The biblical world-picture and the human story now had to be corrected, revised, even radically reconceived in the light of other accounts cosmological, geological, biological, ethnographic, and anthropological. But the decades following 1860 did not result in J. W. Draper's or Andrew White's inevitable "conflict" or "warfare," which portrayed theology as surrendering unconditionally to the new science and naturalism. As I will attempt to show, theological prepossessions and concerns remained constitutive in the work of important scientists, for example, Richard Owen, A. R. Wallace, W. B. Carpenter, St. George Mivart, G. J. Romanes, and many more.

Until the 1860s the intellectual elite in Britain largely continued to share a common intellectual discourse. And few of the leading scientists, philosophers, theologians, and men of letters had qualms about addressing issues outside their special competence—whether they were issues of political economy, education, religion, or science. In the first six or seven decades of the nineteenth century in Britain there existed an intellectual "network," a "common intellectual context" (Cannon 1978, ch. 2; Young 1985, ch. 5) that reveals a rather typical approach to the relations between science and religion. Susan Cannon refers to it as the "Cambridge Network," although not all of those connected with the group were directly associated with Cambridge University. The group included William Whewell, Adam Sedgwick, William Buckland, and John Herschel. These men shared certain ideals and beliefs, and they were very influential. As Cannon shows, they were liberal in their theology and were devoted to freedom in the investigation of truth (1978, ch. 2).

This common intellectual context began to break down after 1860. The ever increasing scholarly compartmentalization is reflected in the disbanding of the Metaphysical Society, which was devoted to discussions of philosophy, science, and religion. It included many notable Victorians, such as Huxley, Gladstone, and Archbishop Manning. By 1880 it had become clear to the members of the Society that they no longer shared the basic principles that would allow a genuine discussion of ideas to flourish. The late Victorian era proved to be a time of increasing professionalization, with the development of specialized journals and societies. Now leading scientists, philosophers, and men of letters (Huxley and a few others were exceptions) were less willing to address questions beyond their professional sphere of competence. As a result, dialogue between theology and the sciences no longer remained intramural.

The increasing fragmentation of the earlier common intellectual context makes the years 1860 to 1910 an ideally limited period in which to examine the interplay of contending ideas. I suggest that by around 1910 there were certain achievements and positions broadly approved, though liberally drawn and demarcated, within which theological work would now be pursued. Differences persisted, of course, but if we attend to these core issues a century later we have the unmistakable sense that we have encountered many of them before, namely, in those years after 1860 when, as Owen Chadwick remarks, "Christianity entered another age of flowering divinity" (Chadwick 1966, 572).

In 1910 the annual meeting of the Church of England Congress was held in Cambridge. The focus of its theological attention was Albert Schweitzer's radical, and recently translated, *The Quest of the Historical Jesus*. The examination of Schweitzer's book, and with it the ex-Jesuit George Tyrrell's equally provocative *Christianity at the Crossroads*, published the previous year, nicely marks the far reaches of British theology's encounter with modern scholarship and criticism. Yet there was a growing sense that there was no turning back, no bold effort at restoration or a "repristination" of precritical ideas or apologetics.

CHAPTER 1

The Religious Background and Contexts of the Late Victorian Controversies

The Pre-1860 Background

Since the history of ideas does not unfold as abstracted segments, some knowledge of the background and contexts of these years of "flowering divinity" after 1860 is required. One significant feature of this earlier period is the rather parochial character of the British discussion in the early decades of the nineteenth century. The antipathy of the British toward Continental, and especially German, theology—"Germanism"—is often remarked. Only a handful of British religious writers and theologians—such as the poet Samuel Taylor Coleridge, the historian and later bishop Connop Thirlwall, and the Anglican priest Julius Hare—took any interest in German theology and the striking developments that were taking place there in the historical-critical study of the Bible and in the fields of historical and philosophical theology. Hare confessed to love the German writers, "among the greatest the world has ever seen," and yet, he lamented, "all my life I have seen them reviled in a mass by those who evidently know next to nothing about them" (Bodleian Library MS Eng. Lett., E86, f104).

The insular character of British theology is reflected not only in its isolation from Continental thought but in the domestic condition of the churches and the factiousness evident in the relations between the Dissenting churches and the parties within the Church of England. Two of the established church's parties were to have a profound influence in raising the spiritual life of both church and nation, infusing both with a new Christian devotion, ardor, and earnestness. But they also proved to be, with a few notable exceptions, indifferent to and professionally unprepared to meet the intellectual challenges to theology that were in the wind and that proved to be inescapable.

One group comprised the Evangelicals both within the Church of England and in the Dissenting churches. They often represented a rather narrow

7

biblicism, what Coleridge dubbed "Bibliolatry." The evangelical Anglicans looked to the "Protestant" Articles of the Church of England as the doctrinal articulation of their biblical religion, rather than to the liturgy, prayer book, or ecclesiastical tradition. Generally, the Evangelicals emphasized human sin and helplessness, Christ's one atoning penal satisfaction for sins, the necessity of a conversion experience, and the sanctifying work of the Holy Spirit. But doctrines were not the early nineteenth-century Evangelicals' defining feature; rather, it was the animating power of a religion of the heart, its directing force and moral discipline. It involved, as the writer G. W. E. Russell recalled from his early years, "an abiding sense of religious responsibility, a self-sacrificing energy in works of mercy, an evangelical zeal, an aloofness from the world, and a level of saintliness in daily life such as I do not expect to see realized again on earth" (Russell 1902, 232). This was its glory and the source of its spectacular influence on the whole of British life in the nineteenth century.

Early Nonconformist evangelicalism was shaped in part by its exclusion from the established church, and this is reflected in its estrangement from the wider culture and its often too peremptory expression of contempt for higher learning. This dismissal of critical scholarship was coupled—unexpectedly, one might think—with great confidence in the "evidences apologetic" of Bishop Joseph Butler's *Analogy of Religion* (1736) and Archdeacon William Paley's *Evidences of Christianity* (1794), which included the belief that revealed theology rested on the prior demonstrations of God in the natural world, as well as the testimony of fulfilled prophecies and Jesus' miracles in the New Testament. This apologetic tradition persisted longer into the century among the evangelical Nonconformists than it did with their Anglican kin. At mid-century the popular Congregationalist minister J. Guinness Rogers gave witness to its staying power as a theological strategy. Against theists who rejected Christianity, Rogers wrote:

> Bishop Butler has shown with unrivalled power of argument . . . that the man who admits that there is a God, and that in the works of nature we have a revelation of his character made to us . . . must admit that there are mysteries connected with the Divine mode of manifestation. If these, then, exist in the lower revelation [nature] and yet it is received and believed, despite them all, why is the higher revelation [the Bible] to be despised because it contains similar phenomena? (Rogers 1851, 143; also see Johnson 1999)

By the 1870s leading Nonconformist theologians recognized that the evidences apologetic was no longer credible among the educated public and that a reconception of the apologetic task was desperately needed (Johnson 1999, 130). Some held tenaciously to the older certainties, while others accommodated every wind of new doctrine, but the ministers and theologians who were gaining influence were those entering into critical dialogue with the new currents of late Victorian culture. These included theologians such as R. W. Dale (1829–1895), A. M. Fairbairn (1838–1912), and P. T. Forsyth (1848–1921), whom we will meet in later chapters. It would be quite wrong, then, to think of the history of theology in nineteenth-century British Nonconformity as a time of decline due either to an ever increasing fossilization or a wholesale accommodation to secular modernity. It is more accurate to speak of a "renaissance" of Nonconformist theology in the latter years of the century, one that involved significant developments in religious thought (Kent 1977; Johnson 1999).

The story of the Tractarian or Anglo-Catholic party in England is more complex, and many of its third-generation offspring, the Liberal Anglo-Catholics at the end of the century, were deeply engaged by the philosophical and scientific discussions of their time (Gore 1889; see also Wainwright 1988; R. Morgan 1989). Yet the leaders of the Oxford Movement in the 1830s and 1840s largely insulated themselves from the new movements in natural science and historical criticism. Men such as the historians Mark Pattison (1813–1884) and James Anthony Froude (1818–94), and the theologian Frederick Denison Maurice (1805–1872)—the latter perhaps the most important Anglican theologian of the midcentury—were initially drawn to the Oxford reformers John Keble (1792–1886), John Henry Newman (1801–1890), and E. B. Pusey (1800–1882). In time, however, they were repelled by their doctrines. Maurice remarked that the weakness of the Tractarian party—whose name derived from the series of papers entitled *Tracts for the Times*, published by the Oxford reformers between 1833 and 1841—consisted in opposing the spirit of the present age with the spirit of a former time, instead of trusting in and appealing to the ever present and active Spirit of God.

Like many, but not all, Evangelical scholars of the 1840s, the Tractarians were unprepared to tackle the issues newly raised by the geologists, by the "Germanized" historical critics, and later by Darwin (Livingstone 1987). Nor did they approve of philosophical theology. H. P. Liddon (1829–1890), devoted disciple of Pusey and an able but archconservative High Church theologian, spoke of Pusey as always taking "refuge in authority whether that of Scripture or of the Primitive Church" (1893, 1:83), and he concurred in his master's abhorrence of the philosophical handling of theology.

Looking back over his career in Oxford, Mark Pattison saw the year 1845, and John Henry Newman's conversion to Rome and his departure from

Oxford, as a crucial turning point in the history of the university. So did the Tractarian R. W. Church, but with a different verdict. "The 13th February, 1845," Church grieved, "was the birthday of the modern Liberalism of Oxford" (Church 1891, 340). While Pattison was smarting from the torrent of abuse heaped on the progressive theological ideas set out in the volume *Essays and Reviews* (1860)—to which he had contributed—he was, nonetheless, correct about the changed climate in Oxford and the educational reforms that were instituted there after the repudiation of Tractarianism. "We were startled," he writes, "when we came to reflect that the vast domain of physical science had been hitherto wholly excluded from our programme. The great discoveries of the last half century in chemistry, physiology, etc., were not even known by report to any of us. Science was placed under ban by the theologians" (Pattison 1885, 237).

There was, however, a progressive movement of considerable importance at work in Oxford before 1845, associated with Richard Whately (1787–1863), Thomas Arnold (1795–1842), R. D. Hampden (1793–1868), and other Oriel College "Noetics," as they were called. While open to the new learning, these liberal Noetics still owed much to the older "Evidences" apologetics that was soon to come under heavy fire. But the influence of the Cambridge-educated poet and religious writer Samuel Taylor Coleridge was increasingly felt. Both the Noetics and Coleridge were instrumental in the emergence of what came later to be called the Broad Church party, representing a greater liberality of mind. What this new generation of progressive theologians shared was a commitment to engage in discussion with the most recent findings of the natural sciences and in the historical-critical investigation of both the Bible and the history of the Christian church. One result of their influence was that intellectually the teaching of the Oxford Movement, based as it was on authority, was beginning to be antedated within a quarter century of its birth (Chadwick 1967, 59).

The new generation of progressive churchmen and scholars were seldom in full agreement on specific theological ideas, but they were joined by a common spirit and scholarly ethic. This was well articulated by Benjamin Jowett (1817–1893)—Oxford classical scholar and later influential Master of Balliol College—in his contribution to *Essays and Reviews*, titled "The Interpretation of Scripture." Among other subjects, the essay addressed the ethics of critical biblical scholarship. Some scholars had been insisting that the findings of biblical research should be confined to the scholarly few, since such inquiries would offend their weaker brethren and lead sensitive minds to desert their Christian faith. Jowett was aware of the solemn public responsibility of the scholar, but he offered two considerations in defense of his plea for scholarly openness. He argued that in the new climate of education and reading among the middle class, the historical and scientific difficulties were now well-known, "forced on the attention, not only of the student, but of every intelligent reader." Thoughtful persons continually were discovering that their own critical observations were shared by others; they lay "deep in the tendencies of education and literature in the present age." For scholars and leaders of the churches to remain reticent would therefore only lead to a "smoldering scepticism." Doubt simply would come in through the window if inquiry were denied entrance through the door (Jowett 1861, 372–73).

Jowett's second point was also shared by many of the new generation. The time had passed when it was possible to ignore the results of scientific criticism; therefore, it was imperative that Christianity should be seen to be in harmony with these results. It would be tragic if some critical objections to received ideas about religion should be widely acknowledged as valid, and that the leaders of the churches should continue to hold them up as only the objections of freethinking infidels. Jowett thought it would be a serious setback to the Christian cause. How incredible it is, he wrote, that the church "should now be opposed to one of the highest and rarest of human virtues—the love of truth. And that in the present day the great object of Christianity should be, not to change the lives of men, but to prevent them from changing their opinions." Jowett was, in fact, expressing a growing sense that Christianity was in a false position when the intellectual tendencies of science and knowledge were now opposing it. To continue along this path would "only end in the withdrawal of the educated classes from the influences of religion" (1861, 372–74).

Beyond the parochial disputes of the various churches and their too frequent dissociation from the new intellectual currents, there were other social and cultural developments that contributed to a heightened sense of intellectual crisis in the life of British religion after 1860. One factor was the improvement in education for the working and lower middle classes. It was not until Forster's education act of 1870 that England created a national system of education that increased the number of board schools beyond what were the dominant church-run voluntary schools. But even among the church schools there now were increasing numbers of those run by the evangelical Free Churches. More working-class children were able to read and write. Many of the Nonconformist publications directed to the working classes were radically anticlerical and critical of much for which the established church stood. In the decades after midcentury the educational level of the lower and middle classes improved markedly compared to their earlier situation.

Related to the improvement in education was the power of the press and the other print media. The Victorian era was the first age of mass communication. A momentous event was the repeal of the paper duty in 1860, which, with mechanized typesetting and other technological developments, greatly lowered the cost and improved the availability of newspapers and magazines. While the large city newspapers on the whole treated religious issues in a neutral way, they also gave religion wide coverage. Sunday sermons were not simply reported but regularly printed in their entirety or in long excerpted segments. More important for the ongoing theological discussion was the extraordinary extent to which religious subjects were featured in the weekly, monthly, and quarterly periodicals that were rapidly increasing in number in the 1860s and 1870s. They appealed to a better-educated readership and its interests, including religious questions that related to public affairs, science, and other intellectual currents.

An especially distinctive feature of the years just before and after the mid-century was the rising phenomenon of "honest doubt" and the attention given to works such as James Anthony Froude's *Nemesis of Faith* (1849), Francis Newman's *Phases of Faith* (1850), and especially Tennyson's *In Memoriam* (1850). W. J. Conybeare, a commentator on the ecclesiastical scene, reported in 1853 that many of the younger university-educated generation were now "influenced by sceptical opinions to an extent that twenty years ago would have seemed incredible" (W. J. Conybeare 1853, 342). This was related in part to the intellectual insularity of the churches. Owen Chadwick has remarked about the early Victorians' earnest efforts to oppose the inroads of revolution, freethinking, and apostasy and how these led to hasty attempts to ensure that religious doctrine was inculcated in the schools, that churches were built for the poor, that evangelical and missionary societies were established—in other words, that orthodoxy was preserved. But in all of this activity one can also observe a deep-seated insecurity:

> Confident of Christian truth, they wanted to be more confident. Grateful for their treasure, they felt nervous enough to want it locked from preying hands. You will end a sceptic unless you believe all the doctrines of the ancient church. You will end a sceptic unless you become a Roman Catholic. You will end a sceptic unless you believe that the Holy Spirit penned every comma of Leviticus. (Chadwick 1966, 528)

The theological context of this rising "honest doubt" and the church's fear of the loss of its educated classes is marked by two controversies prominent in the decades prior to 1860 but that proved to be ongoing and highly conse-quential in the years following. One had to do with the ethics of belief debate shaped by two conflicting aspects of Victorian life: the intense seriousness of religious belief coupled with the scrupulous moral difficulty in assenting to beliefs that now were open to question. It came to be called the *ethics of belief controversy* (J. C. Livingston 1974). The second challenge to traditional theology and its current apologetics was the agnostic controversy, a philosophical dispute about the sources and limits of any possible knowledge of God. Its origins are traceable to the convergence in Britain of the empiricist legacy of John Locke and David Hume with the late-arriving (in Britain) metaphysical skepticism of Immanuel Kant. The "agnostic principle" had become a respected, if ambiguous, handmaid in the service of Christian apologetics in Britain by the 1850s. But, as we will see, it would prove a risky, Janus-faced theological strategy. Despite that fact, it was to gain momentum and to inform most of the religious discussions in Britain in the second half of the nineteenth century (J. C. Livingston 1985; Lightman 1987). The ethics of belief debate began somewhat earlier, but it remained an enduring, contentious dispute to the end of the century.

The Controversy over the Ethics of Belief

The Victorian era is often spoken of as an age of faith, but by the middle of that era it had become a time during which the British experienced a great unsettling of religious belief. This new scrupulosity regarding religious belief is nicely represented in Anglican bishop J. W. Colenso's response when charged with religious heresy: "Our duty, surely," he responded, "is to follow the truth, wherever it leads us, and to leave the consequences in the hands of God" (Colenso 1862/1963, 8). It was in this rigorous moral climate that the Victorian clergy and educated laity had, week in and week out, to give both mental and verbal assent to the creeds and teachings of their churches at a time of intense religious criticism and unsettlement. In this context there emerged an extended, acrimonious, and divisive series of debates over the ethics of religious belief.

Much of the early debate focused on the ethics of conformity and subscription to the creeds and formularies of the established church. Laymen in the Church of England were not required to adhere to any particular doctrine, although it was expected that they could in good conscience recite the words of the liturgy. But those who would take holy orders, or those who would matriculate as students or hold fellowships and teaching appointments in the colleges in Oxford or Cambridge, faced stricter requirements. Prior to the mid-1850s young men entering the colleges were solemnly obliged to subscribe to the Thirty-Nine Articles of religion. It was not until 1871, when the Gladstone government passed the Universities Tests Act, that all degrees and appointments, excepting those requiring holy orders, were exempted from subscription to the Articles. And after the clerical Subscription Act of 1865, assent to the Articles and the Book of Common Prayer became general rather than particular, that is, an assent meant only that one accepted that the doctrine as set forth therein was "agreeable to the Word of God." This freed the consciences of some, but it became a cause of renewed controversy and an added burden to many sensitive minds who felt that the binding force of subscription was relaxed at the sacrifice of a scrupulous veracity. However, the movement for revision or relaxation had begun earlier.

Three years after Queen Victoria's (1819–1901) accession to the throne in 1837, the issue of liberalizing subscription was brought before the House of Lords. An 1840 petition presented by Archbishop Richard Whately of Dublin (1787–1863), earlier a member of the Oxford Noetics, asked for measures that would allow the Articles to be made consonant with the beliefs of the clergy. The archbishop of Canterbury, representing the traditionalists, saw the matter the other way around. If there were to be a bill, he would move that the Lordships make the practice of the clergy *more consistent* with the prayer book and articles (Hansard 1840, liv, 555). Probably not much would have come of the matter had it not been for a speech by Bishop Stanley of Norwich, who spoke of the "elasticity" of the Church of England, of the fact that not all clergy agreed with every part of their subscription, which "weighed heavily upon scrupulous and tender consciences." He pointed out that the Church's creed was Calvinistic, while its liturgy was Arminian, and that "the Church was founded on liberty of conscience and the right of private judgement." The speech offended almost everyone. The bishop of London reminded Stanley that the Catholic Church "was founded on truth," not private judgment. "If alteration were made for one tender conscience, it ought to be made for another. Where would it stop?" (Hansard 1840, liv, 557).

Thomas Arnold (1795–1842), the headmaster of Rugby School who in 1841 was appointed Regius Professor of History at Oxford, had signed Whately's petition. He favored a relaxation of subscription rather than a change in the Articles, because, as he argued, the Prayer Book exhibits the opinions of both King Edward's Protestant Reformers and the High Churchmen of James I's time. Therefore, a comprehensive subscription was required "unless the followers of one of these parties are to be driven out of the church" (Stanley 1845, 212). While Arnold did not want to drive out the Tractarians, he nonetheless felt that their subscription to the *present* Reformed Articles was dishonest.

The Anglo-Catholic Tractarian party, on the other hand, was not friendly to doctrinal liberality. Their response to Whately's 1840 petition for some measure of relief from the current subscription was John Henry Newman's Tract XC (1841), which sought to defend a Catholic reading of the Articles. Newman was then vicar of St. Mary's, the university church in Oxford. Tract XC more than awakened "the sleeping lions," for its effect was to overcharge the issue of religious belief and create a heightened climate of suspicion and doubt. Furthermore, it brought down on Newman a flood of charges of disingenuousness in his use of reserve and equivocation in his defense of the "Catholic" Articles. Tract XC appeared to many to evade the plain meaning of the Thirty-Nine Articles. Newman admitted as much. He asserted that the Articles were to be interpreted, not according to the meaning of the writers but, as far as the wording would admit, according to the sense of the Catholic Church.

Several bishops condemned Tract XC, and Bishop Bagot of Oxford was called upon to have it suppressed. Newman resisted such a move and threatened to resign as vicar of St. Mary's. It was finally agreed that publication of the Tracts would cease at the bishop's insistence but that Tract XC would not be censured. It was obvious, however, that the casuistry of Tract XC disturbed the bishop and, in a charge in St. Mary's Church in 1842, he voiced his objection to "a system of interpretation which was so subtle that by it the Articles might be made to mean anything or nothing" (Liddon 1893, 2:286). The importance of Newman as catalyst of a growing concern over sincerity of belief cannot be exaggerated. The special role that he played in the later Victorian debate over the ethics of belief is traceable not only to the Tract XC affair but, as we shall see, to his publication of *A Grammar of Assent* in 1870.

If Newman's Tract XC resulted in a climate increasingly rife with charges of intellectual dishonesty, it reached a crisis in 1860 with the publication of the book *Essays and Reviews* (Shea and Whitla 2000). Six of the seven contributors were priests of the Church of England. Several were men of real distinction, including Frederick Temple (1821–1902), headmaster of Rugby School and later archbishop of Canterbury; Mark Pattison (1813–1884), rector of Lincoln College, Oxford; and Benjamin Jowett (1817–1893), Regius Professor of Greek and later Master of Balliol College, Oxford. As Newman's tract was a manifesto of the Anglo-Catholic party, *Essays and Reviews* was a rallying call for the support of new developments in Continental historical and biblical scholarship and the broadening of the Church's interpretation of its doctrinal standards.

On publication, the seven essayists were roundly condemned, and the book was denounced by the bishops in convocation. The essayists were labeled *Septum Contra Christum*, the seven against Christ, and their moral integrity as clergymen was bitterly impugned. Samuel Wilberforce (1805–1873), the bishop of Oxford, charged that the seven, holding the views they professed, could not morally hold their positions as clergymen in the Church of England. He appeared to equate thorough, conscientious inquiry with "sinful doubt." In 1860 an English cleric was bound to "an unfeigned assent and consent to all and everything" within the Prayer Book, and to "all and every one of the [Church's] Articles"—but with one significant qualification, namely, that those doctrines be "proved by the most certain warrants of Scripture."

Legal proceedings were taken against two of the essayists on the grounds that their teachings contradicted the Church's Articles of Religion. However, on appeal they were acquitted by the Judicial Committee of the Privy Council. A pamphlet war erupted, and a Royal Commission was appointed to study the now ambiguous issue of clerical subscription. The commission recommended a simplification and relaxation of the forms of assent that the House of Commons passed into law on May 19, 1865. In place of "unfeigned assent and consent to all and everything" within the Prayer Book, clergymen now were to declare a general "assent to the Thirty-nine Articles of Religion and to the Book of Common Prayer" and to affirm belief in "the doctrine of the Church of England as therein set forth to be agreeable to the Word of God." This solution was not transparent, for the issue remained whether such latitude would allow clergy to put a "non-natural" sense on the words of the Articles and disguise their disbelief under the cloak of either a legal vagueness or a general assent. The *Essays and Reviews* controversy revealed a deep fissure in the Church between the laity and rural clergy on one side and the Church's clerical scholars and theologians on the other (Ellis 1980).

While by 1870 there was decreasing sympathy for penal proceedings against "errant" clergy, there was also great unease over the legalizing of what appeared to be radical latitudinarian belief and, especially, the condoning of a vague assent to what appeared to be "anything and nothing." The latter deeply troubled conscientious scholars such as philosopher Henry Sidgwick (1838–1900) and writer Leslie Stephen (1832–1904). Both men resigned their fellowships at Cambridge University because they no longer could subscribe to the Church's Articles. And both devoted their considerable talents in protesting against the clergy taking shelter under a broad interpretation that was lax and not perfectly conscientious (Sidgwick 1870; L. Stephen 1873; 1893). They abominated those clergy who could, for example, abandon belief in the virgin birth, hence the language affirming it, and to continue to recite the creeds day in and day out before their congregations. On the other hand, many liberal clergy saw in the demand for a rigorous and literal ethics of subscription a serious lack of historical perspective and a bribe against scholarly activity by the clergy. To opt out of the Church would be to fail morally to assist in the task of reforming the interpretation of the Church's ancient doctrine. For these clergy the moral issue was how to steer a way between an excessive reticence leading to suspicion of disingenuousness and moral insincerity, and a forthright, bold profession that might cause confusion and acrimonious division.

The dispute over the ethics of belief reached its crest in England in the 1870s. The leading periodicals of the day were full of discussions of the morality of belief. A rigorous philosophical debate on the subject was sustained for an entire decade, between 1869 and 1880, at the meetings of the Metaphysical Society, which included many eminent philosophers, scientists, and theologians. Numerous members of the Society were in the line of intellectual inheritance traceable to two of the seminal minds of the century in Britain: Samuel Taylor Coleridge and John Stuart Mill. In the 1870s the scientifically oriented empiricists were largely disciples of Mill and his *System of Logic* (1843). In the debate in the 1870s over religious belief the empiricists were represented through the writings of Leslie Stephen's *Essays on Freethinking and Plainspeaking* (1873), John Morley's *On Compromise* (1874), and W. K. Clifford's crucial essay "The Ethics of Belief," read before the Metaphysical Society and published in 1877.

Mill and his followers believed that the only method of inquiry that will yield truth and overcome error is the scientific method of experimental, inductive reasoning based on the uniformity of nature. Progress, they believed, depended on this belief and this method in overcoming error. And since erroneous ideas are a barrier to progress, a person's belief is a matter of the highest ethical concern. Beliefs are not merely personal matters, for they are that upon which a person is willing to act and, therefore, have enormous social consequences. The great enemies of the empiricists were, then, those who, like Coleridge, appealed to the distinctiveness of individual consciousness and to some form of cognitive "intuitionism."

In 1870 John Henry Newman published *A Grammar of Assent*, an explicit critique of the empiricists' ethic of belief based as it was on their formulation of it as "assent directly proportioned to evidence." Newman's essay argued that one can honestly "believe what you cannot absolutely prove" (Harper 1933, 120). The crux of Newman's argument was his distinction between real assent and inference and his rejection of the empiricists' notion that probabilities should never lead to certitude. He called it a "pretentious axiom" unrelated to real human experience. Newman argued that conditional inferences can move to unconditioned assent through the cumulation and convergence of "probabilities too fine to avail separately, too subtle and circuitous to be converted to syllogisms, too numerous and various for such conversion" (Newman 1870/1985, 207–8). And in all concrete reasoning, assent and certitude will have a crucial element of the personal, since it is an active judgment and will vary with the individual and according to the subject matter. "Judgment then in all concrete matters is the architectonic faculty; and what may be called the Illative Sense, or right judgment" (221). So, for Newman, concrete reasoning is not reducible to a formal logical or scientific demonstration, since it is based on converging lines of evidence and a personal judgment or perception of a legitimate, reasonable conclusion. For Newman such assent and certitude are not only reasonable but ethically right and imperative.

At the time, Newman's *Grammar of Assent* was the fullest and ablest critique of the scientific empiricist ethics of belief. It was not, however, without its critics, and many of the objections to his argument were telling. Almost to a person, Newman's critics focused on his conviction about the absoluteness of certitude and his rejection of the possibility of degrees of assent. While a belief may be unaccompanied by present doubt, such absolute assurance, the critics argued, is consistent with the possibility of future doubt and disconfirmation (see, e.g., J. F. Stephen 1872). They also made much of Newman's appeal to individual temperament and feeling and his emphasis on the inarticulateness of belief. They pointed out that it is painfully common for individuals to be absolutely convinced, yet unable to make explicit their reasons, and to be dead wrong (J. F. Stephen 1872). It is, therefore, essential that belief be proportioned to evidence that is open to or in the common possession of other reasonable persons. That is, the burden of proof lies with the individual who contends that his belief should be immune from such a common standard or rules of evidence (L. Stephen 1877). Basically, the empiricist critics were arguing that while Newman may have produced a brilliant description or phenomenology of belief—that is, how persons do, in fact, come to believe—he had failed to offer a compelling account of how one can be confident that he or she holds a true belief.

The Newmanians responded by convincingly demonstrating that the so-called common standard and rules of evidence assumed by the followers of Mill were founded on epistemological and metaphysical beliefs that were taken for granted rather than proven true (see, e.g., W. G. Ward 1878). Whatever the merits of the arguments on either side, it is clear that Newman's *Grammar of Assent* was *the* touchstone for the debate over the ethics of religious belief throughout the 1870s and beyond.

In the late Victorian decades, with the rapid development of the life sciences and the new social sciences, sympathy increased for those clerics, as well as the lay scholars, who were determined to stay in the Church and work toward reconciliation of Christian belief with the new findings in the sciences. In these latter years of the century, the ethical debate focused on the question of the legitimacy and limits of new nonliteral or nonnatural interpretations of the Bible and the creeds. More and more, clerical scholars were willing to test these limits in support of a forthright admission of liberal or progressive positions as consistent with sincere belief.

It was in this highly charged context that the Anglo-Catholic Charles Gore (1853–1922) in 1887 launched a quarter-century struggle against those clerics and scholars whose interpretations, to his mind, had openly rejected the natural sense of the New Testament writings and the Church's creeds (Gore 1887). Gore was at this time the first principal of Pusey House in Oxford, but he later was consecrated bishop of Worcester (1902) and later bishop of Oxford (1911). Gore claimed allegiance to two religious loyalties: a thorough intellectual openness and a forthright assent to the creedal standards of the Church. As in the earlier debates, this dual loyalty was to prove an unstable one. He was quite willing to recognize unhistorical myth and legend in the Old Testament, yet would argue on theological preconceptions—not on the basis of historical-critical results—that similar judgments could not be made regarding narratives in the New Testament without results disastrous to the Christian creed (Gore 1890, 354). For this reason he set limits on scholarly results when it came to research on the New Testament, and he imputed immoral motives to those who arrived at conclusions that might affect adversely the historical character of the miraculous events recited in the creeds. The old question, of course, was once again raised, although now in a context more insistent in questioning traditional so-called scholarly results or limits: If the creeds are the *terminus a quo* of theological scholarship, then are not the conclusions of research proscribed and precluded?

For the next twenty years this remained the complaint of the more progressive biblical scholars and theologians. Their response to Gore, and to others who were like-minded, is typified in the rejoinder of Hastings Rashdall (1858–1924) to the position taken by the philosopher Henry Sidgwick, who had joined Gore in drawing the line at the common "historical" sense of the Gospels and creeds as the "necessary position for the Anglican clergy." An Anglican clergyman and philosophy tutor at New College, Oxford, Rashdall asked Sidgwick the obvious question: Why should a clergyman be considered dishonest when he does not believe in a particular gospel miracle if it is admitted that he is not dishonest for not believing that Jonah was literally swallowed by a whale, giving both stories a spiritual meaning? Rashdall insisted that, in the case of the Gospels, it is a question "of what we may call general ethical or spiritual expediency, not of technical veracity" (Rashdall 1897, 148).

In the years that followed, the Anglican bishops, when meeting in convocation, left the ethical issue in ambiguous suspension. They both affirmed their "conviction that the historical facts stated in the creeds are an essential part of the Faith of the Church" but coupled this with recognition that "our generation is called to face new problems raised by historical criticism" and their anxiety not "to limit freedom of thought and inquiry whether among clergy or laity" (*Chronicle of Convocation* 1914, 260).

While the official pronouncements remained Janus-like, affirming what clearly appeared to be incompatible statements, the warning about the *denial* of any of the historical facts stated in the creeds soon was left behind. In statements regarding the incarnation, for example, the forms of expression shifted to an affirmation of belief in the doctrine of the incarnation and away from the mode of its representation in Scripture and the creeds. It was increasingly recognized that the ethical questions about assent to articles of belief was a dangerous red herring, and the ecclesiastical question inexpedient, when pursued in isolation from the theological question, which, it had become plain to see, was necessarily open to ongoing scholarly scrutiny and when a more general agreement could be reached (Rawlinson 1915, 204–7). Henceforth, subscription to articles of belief would be required only in general terms and would be susceptible to broad interpretation. Such a general assent and openness to a symbolic interpretation of certain biblical texts and creedal statements reveals one aspect of the late Victorian cultural and religious context. This debate both accompanied and, more importantly, assisted in the achievement of greater openness in the churches to historical and scientific inquiry.

The Agnostic Controversies after 1850

The controversies over the ethics of belief were closely related to a concurrent philosophical discussion about the limits of human knowledge of God that followed upon an advancing critique of both natural and revealed theology. This extended debate was later referred to as the "Agnostic Controversy," and the years between 1860 and 1890 were called the Age of Agnosticism, "the epoch of the creed *Ignoramus et ignorabimus*" (Seth 1894). These three decades were a time that declared both its confidence in the remarkable achievements of science and its profound sense of ignorance and doubt about metaphysical questions. By the 1880s, no philosophical question was more "in the air" or at the center of discussion, even in the popular press. The reviews were full of it.

While the philosophical origins of British agnosticism can be traced to the empiricist tradition from Locke through Hume and the late arrival of the philosophy of Immanuel Kant, its immediate sources are found in the writings of William Hamilton, H. L. Mansel, and Herbert Spencer. William Hamilton (1788–1856) was professor of logic and metaphysics at Edinburgh

University. He was profoundly influenced by his reading of Kant whom, it is now generally agreed, he did not fully understand. According to Hamilton, "The mind can conceive and consequently can know, only the *limited*, and *the conditionally limited*"—that is, the mind cannot know the Infinite or Absolute, which "can be conceived only by a thinking away from, or an abstraction of, those very conditions under which thought itself is realized. Consequently," he insisted, "the notion of the Unconditioned is only negative" (Hamilton 1852, 12).

For Hamilton, thought necessarily supposed conditions and relations—for example, space and time, mind and matter—and the knowledge of certain facts is always conditioned by our knowledge of other facts. "To think," Hamilton wrote, "*is to condition*; and conditional limitation is the fundamental law of the possibility of thought." Just as "the eagle [cannot] outsoar the atmosphere in which he floats; so the mind cannot transcend that sphere of limitation, within and through which exclusively the possibility of thought is realized" (14). What makes thought possible also necessarily limits it.

As the mind cannot transcend its conditionedness, so God as the Absolute or Unconditioned is not constituted by necessary relations, and thus, as Unconditioned, cannot be known. To think of God as Absolute *cause* is to conceive of the Deity in terms of some necessary relation to the world. Assuming such a hypothesis, one of two alternatives must be admitted: "God, as necessarily determined to pass from absolute essence to relative manifestation, is determined to pass either *from the better to the worse, or from the worse to the better*" (Hamilton 1852, 35). According to Hamilton, the dilemma of philosophical theology is unavoidable. Either God is independent of the world for his being and perfection, on which theory philosophical knowledge of God founders, or God is dependent on the world for his manifestation or perfection and all the difficulties concerning the divine passibility must be faced. Mill and the British Hegelians would grasp that nettle and usher in the late Victorian debate over panentheism. Hamilton concludes, however, that it is by revelation that we are made conscious of our inability to conceive of something that lies beyond the relative and finite. "True, therefore, are the declarations of a pious philosophy:—'A God understood would be no God at all';—'To think that God is, as we can think him to be, is blasphemy'" (15).

Hamilton's logical speculations were put to the test by Mill and others and *logically* found wanting. Nevertheless, his plea for a "learned ignorance" had a profound impact on men such as T. H. Huxley, who reported that as a young boy he "devoured it [Hamilton's plea] with avidity" (T. H. Huxley 1892a, 353). Hamilton's appeal lay then not in his speculations but in compelling passages such as the following:

The recognition of human ignorance is not only the one highest, but the one true, knowledge; and its first-fruit . . . is humility. Simple nescience is not proud; consummated science is positively humble. . . . The grand result of human wisdom is . . . an articulate confession, by our natural reason, of the truth declared in revelation—that *now* we see through a glass darkly. (Mansel 1866, 36–37)

It was H. L. Mansel (1820–1871), Waynflete Professor of Moral and Metaphysical Philosophy at Oxford and afterward dean of St. Paul's, London, who applied Hamilton's epistemological doctrines more directly to the problems of a Christian knowledge of God. He did this in his lectures of 1858 on *The Limits of Religious Thought*. Mansel saw Hamilton's "philosophy of the conditioned" as "the handmaid and auxiliary of Christian Truth" (Mansel 1856, 44) and boldly staked his case for Christian revelation on what came to be called, by both supporters and critics, "Christian Agnosticism." Mansel took his central postulate from Hamilton: "No difficulty emerges in theology, which had not previously emerged in philosophy," for the crux of the matter is that "the primary and proper object of criticism is not Religion, natural or revealed, but the human mind in relation to Religion" (1859, 61). Mansel saw the ground of the mind's impotence in relation to religion in Hamilton's "great principle," namely, that the Ultimate, being unconditioned, is incognizable and inconceivable.

Like Hamilton, Mansel argued that all human knowledge implies consciousness of relations, that is, of some thing, hence conditionedness. What a being or condition may be like *out* of human consciousness, our consciousness cannot tell us. The principle applies as well to the divine personality as to a future life. To speak of an Absolute or Infinite *Person* is inconceivable. "Personality, as we conceive of it, is essentially a limitation and a relation . . . but in God there is no distinction between the subject of consciousness and its modes, nor between one mode and another" (1859, 85).

Are we justified then in denying the personality of God? Far from it, according to Mansel, for we dishonor God by identifying him with the feeble and negative impotence of our thought, rather "than remaining content within those limits which He for His own good purposes has imposed upon us" (1859, 85). These limits of our positive thought cannot, Mansel insisted, be the limits of belief. We are, in fact, required to believe that a personal God exists and that he is also absolute and eternal. Our ideas and images may "not represent God as He is in Himself," but they "may represent Him as it is our duty to regard Him. They are not in themselves true; but we must, nevertheless, believe and act as if they were true" (1873, 113).

Mansel insisted then that our conception may be *speculatively* false and yet *regulatively* true. A regulative truth is but a guide to practice; it tells us how God wills we should think of him. If we are to know God, it must be by means of a representation of deity under finite symbols, drawn from the phenomenon of finite consciousness. Only a fool would claim that human reason can draw more than a human portrait of God. Mansel thus held that we must inevitably be reconciled "to a more or less refined Anthropomorphism," which, far from unsound, "is one that meets us in almost every page of Holy Scripture" (1873, 113). In biblical revelation, God graciously condescends to meet humanity's limits and its spiritual needs. But this accommodation to human needs admits of no explanation. Of our human ignorance and God's merciful revelation, Mansel concluded:

> It is not an adaptation to the ignorance of one man, to be seen through by the superior knowledge of another; but one which exists in relation to the whole human race, as men, bound by the laws of man's thought . . . as finite beings, placed in relation to and in communication with the Infinite. I believe that Scripture teaches, to each and all of us, the lesson it was designed to teach. . . . I believe that "now we see through a glass darkly" . . . that dark enigma that no human wisdom can solve . . . and which Faith can only rest content with here, in hope of a clearer vision to be granted hereafter. (1859, 262–63)

Many orthodox believers commended Mansel's *The Limits of Religious Thought* for its effort to cut the ground from under the rationalist critique of Christian theology. To others, however, it appeared that in applying the weapons of skepticism against atheism, Mansel had forgotten that it could be wielded with equal effect against biblical revelation.

T. H. Huxley (1825–1895), Darwin's disciple and the coiner of the term *agnostic*, had been greatly attracted to Mansel's Bampton Lectures and commended them to his friend the English geologist Charles Lyell "as a piece of clear and unanswerable reasoning." Huxley pointed out, however, that Mansel the churchman also could be compared to the drunken fellow in Hogarth's picture, the Contested Election, who sawed "through the signpost of the other party's public-house, forgetting that he was sitting at the outer end of it" (Mrs. Lyell 1881, 321–22).

Many of Mansel's *philosophical* contemporaries, including Mill, were as outraged by Mansel's book and its "morally pernicious" claim, namely, that it is not necessary to suppose that the infinite goodness of God "is not the same goodness which we know and love in our fellow-creatures, distinguished only as infinite in degree." Mill took his stand "on the acknowledged principle of logic and of morality, that when we mean different things we have no right to call them by the same name. . . . Language has no meaning for the words Just, Merciful, Benevolent, save that in which we predicate them of our fellow creatures." "What belongs to it as Infinite I do not pretend to know," Mill conceded, "but I know that infinite goodness must be goodness and that what is not consistent with goodness is not consistent with infinite goodness." "I will call no being good," Mill concluded, "who is not what I mean when I apply that epithet to my fellow creatures; and if such a being can sentence me to hell for not so calling him, to hell I will go" (Mill 1865a, 100–103).

Mill may not have thoroughly grasped Mansel's understanding of analogy, since Mansel's position did appear to steer between the pitfalls of a crude anthropomorphism and a pure agnosticism. Nor did he deny a resemblance between God and man. Rather, what Mansel maintained is that many things that to God are just, may appear unjust to humans. In one sense a phrase such as "the love of God" is, according to Mansel, utterly unimaginable. Yet the believer does trust that there is something in the ineffable mystery of God's providence that is the prototype of what humans experience as love in their encounters with their fellows. But Mansel wished to go further. For him Jesus' authoritative words are to be accepted on compelling external evidences—those of prophecy fulfillment and miracle: "Where the doctrine is beyond the power of human reason to discover, it can be accepted only as resting on the authority of the teacher who proclaimed it; and that authority must then be guaranteed by the external evidence of supernatural mission" (Mansel 1859, 155).

Mansel thus encouraged the clergy of his day to remain satisfied that the Bible and the whole tradition of orthodox doctrine were immune to historical-critical work. His uncritical biblical positivism was soon recognized by biblical scholars as naïve and not to be given serious attention. Yet despite his failure to take account of biblical criticism, Mansel's work proved influential. As Bernard Lightman has shown, Mansel was crucial to the development in the 1860s and 1870s of the movement of Victorian agnosticism that not only proved hostile to orthodox Christianity but, more significantly, contributed to an enduring agnostic cast of mind (Lightman 1987, ch. 2).

Mansel's connection with late Victorian agnosticism is traceable in large part to the enormous popularity and influence of Herbert Spencer's ideas in the last decades of the century. In the *Prospectus* (1860) to his multivolume *A System of Philosophy*, Spencer outlined the intellectual program that was to attract a large following in England. But it was in the précis of the *First Principles*, the book that was to become the "Bible of Agnosticism," that he sketched his conception of the "Unknowable." Spencer confessed that he was simply "carrying a step further the doctrine put into shape by Hamilton and Mansel." He then proceeded to show "that in this united belief in an Absolute that transcends not only human knowledge but human conception, lies the only possible reconciliation of Science and Religion" (Spencer 1862, v).

Where Spencer differed notably from Mansel was in his insistence that the Unknowable be conceived not only as a negation of the knowable but as something positive. While asserting that the Unknowable is *not* known, Spencer confidently proceeded to declare that it is "the fundamental reality which underlies all that appears" and that it is "the omnipresent Causal Energy or Power of which all phenomena are the manifestations" (1882, 91). How he warranted his knowledge of the existence and attributes of the Unknowable is unclear, and this muddle led him into numerous controversies.

Spencer's metaphysics deserved the derision it received. Yet to acknowledge that his work was not only derided but repudiated in his own lifetime is not to gainsay his cultural importance. Spencer's talent for joining an apparent scientific method with a deep, natural piety in an effort to discover a reconciliation of science and religion within an evolutionary worldview was enormously appealing to his age. His reverent humility before the mystery of existence largely explains the attraction of his agnosticism. In popular regard, Spencer's essays were the prosaic counterpart to Tennyson's *In Memoriam*.

Spencer's significance to modern religious history lies then in the crucial role that he played, primarily with Huxley, in the popularization and transformation of agnosticism from a rather arcane philosophical doctrine into a more inchoate but pervasive moral sensibility held by large numbers of people raised in religious homes but imbued with the scientific ethos and a new sense of the limits of religious and speculative thought. Not only militant secularists but numbers of ordinary laity and clergy saw in Spencer's *First Principles* an ally against dogmatism and a support for a Christian agnostic humility. As one clergyman expressed it in 1892, "We are all Agnostics. The term really expresses humility of mind rather than a stubborn pride of reason. . . . We may be bad theologians, and yet good Christians; Agnostics, yet believers. . . . The true attitude toward these mysteries is a reverent Agnosticism" (Dawson 1892).

While Spencer's agnosticism influenced a small segment of the Christian clergy in both the established and dissenting churches, his sphere of influence was much greater among those religious agnostics who had left Christianity but who wished to present agnosticism as a religious creed that had progressively evolved out of Christianity. It was this group that popularized theistic evolution in its Spencerian guise in the 1880s and 1890s (Lightman 1989, 285–309). Among the most effective popularizers of this moderate religious agnosticism was Richard Bithell (b. 1821), a banker also well educated in the sciences, who published numerous books, including *The Creed of a Modern Agnostic* (1883), *Agnostic Problems* (1887), *The Worship of the Unknowable* (1889), and *A Handbook of Scientific Agnosticism* (1892). It was Samuel Laing (1812–1897), however, who had the largest influence on the general public through his series of popular books, including *Modern Science and Modern Thought* (1885), *A Modern Zoroastrian* (1887), and *Problems of the Future* (1889). Laing was educated at Cambridge, for thirty years was chairman of the London, Brighton, and South Coal Railway, and was a Liberal member of Parliament from 1852 to 1885.

These religious agnostics not only were conciliatory toward liberal Christianity, but they also were politically moderate and opposed radical, socialist efforts to reform society. Again, their ideology was Spencerian, using Spencer's evolutionism to legitimate a conservative, bourgeois social order. They identified God with the reign of law, which they saw as guaranteeing progress through struggle. Using Spencer as their guide, they developed an optimistic theodicy similar to that of some contemporary Christian theologians, for example, the Scotsman Henry Drummond.

These religious agnostics often found themselves in conflict with the more radical scientific agnostics like Huxley and Leslie Stephen. They considered the agnostic creed of Bithell and Laing unscientific, and they deplored the ease with which the religious agnostics were able to draw theistic inferences from the evolutionary process. The difference in the two forms of late Victorian agnosticism is significant and is plain to see in Huxley's attack on Laing in 1889 in his famous essay "Agnosticism" (1892a).

What Huxley especially opposed was Laing's claim that agnosticism constituted a creed or distinct body of doctrine:

> [Agnostics] have no creed, and, by the nature of the case, cannot have any. Agnosticism is not a creed, but a method. . . . [It is] the fundamental axiom of modern science. Positively the principle may be expressed: In matters of intellect, follow your reason as far as it will take you without regard to any other consideration. And negatively: In matters of the intellect do not pretend that conclusions are certain which are not demonstrated or demonstrable. That I take to be the agnostic faith. (T. H. Huxley 1892a, 362)

This faith which Huxley held and preached with such zeal and success—and which he shared with Leslie Stephen and the physicist John Tyndall (1820–1893)—did, in fact, include three very basic tenets. These he summarized in a little-known article published in 1884. He wrote that the word *agnostic* involved (1) metaphysical nescience, (2) the application of scientific method to the study of all matters of experience, and (3) the rejection of much of Christian doctrine as unproven or unprovable (T. H. Huxley 1884, 5–6). These were to constitute the first principles and the faith of scientific, left-wing agnostics.

Leslie Stephen (1832–1904) was convinced that if men were guided by reason and experience they simply ought to be agnostic. This is what disturbed and disillusioned him about his Anglican clerical friends, whom he saw as having the greatest opportunity for influencing the minds of the younger generation. Instead, in his view, these liberal Anglican theologians were taking refuge in a most immoral form of skepticism that allowed them to assume "that as truth is unattainable it can do no harm to tell lies" (L. Stephen 1873, 40), or that if there is no "conclusive" evidence for a certain belief, one has a right to hold either the negative or positive creed. Stephen argued, against both the theologians and the philosopher William James, that such a man "has a right to hold *neither*." "By Agnostic," he wrote, "I do not mean a negative creed, but an absence of all opinion; and that I take to be the only rational frame of mind" (Annan 1951, 317).

For the stoical Stephen, the true deposit of faith was to be found in "that body of scientific truth which is the slow growth of human experience through countless ages, and which develops by the labour of truth-loving men, and under the remorseless pressure of hard facts" (L. Stephen 1893, 239). The principal legacy of the scientific agnostics was their championing, with W. K. Clifford (1843–1879), a powerful morality of knowledge and belief that came to be known as the ethics of belief controversy (Clifford 1877).

The fact remains, however, that the scientific agnostics oftentimes failed to recognize that not all questions are scientific questions and that it is not possible to answer all inquiries by a singular logic or method. This was one of the lines of argument of a host of critics from the 1880s to the turn of the century. Another critique, offered by some scientists themselves, was that men like Huxley and Clifford were not thoroughly agnostic about their own foundational beliefs. The Achilles heel of agnosticism proved to be its link with scientific naturalism. This is evident in the transformation in the 1880s of the biologist George Romanes (1848–1894), one of Darwin's colleagues, from a dogmatic scientific naturalist to its critic. Romanes came to believe that the scientific agnostics were not radical or agnostic enough. In his Rede Lecture at Cambridge in 1885, he called for a "pure agnosticism," one that would be applied equally by both the harbingers of the new science and the new theology and one that would silence *a priorism* of every kind. Romanes was especially critical of the dogmatic claims of men like Clifford. "If it be true that the voice of science must thus of necessity speak the language of agnosticism, at least let us see to it that the language is pure; let us not tolerate any barbarisms introduced from the side of aggressive dogma" (1896a, 37). Romanes came to insist that the claims of neither the scientific nor the spiritual mind could hold pride of place, especially since they so often coexist and alternate in the same person. Moral, aesthetic, and spiritual faculties "are of no less importance in their respective spheres" (1896b, 112–13).

The Victorian belief in the unity of truth and of intellectual method and inquiry was now and henceforth to be challenged. "My whole contention," Romanes wrote,

> has been that men of science, as such, have no business either "to run with the hare of religion," or "to hunt with the hounds of antitheistic negation." . . . If a man of science is profoundly interested in the great questions of religion, he should recognize that they have no more bearing upon his professional occupation than have the questions of politics, literature, art, or any other department of rational thinking. (1886, 333)

The epistemological and metaphysical assumptions underlying the agnostics' scientific naturalism were now resolutely attacked by an emerging, soon to be influential, school of British Idealists led by T. H. Green. Incisive criticism also came from Henry Sidgwick (1838–1900; see Sidgwick 1871; 1882), statesman and philosopher A. J. Balfour (1848–1930; see Balfour 1879; 1895), and, most thoroughly, from psychologist and philosopher James Ward (1843–1925; see Ward 1915).

James Ward's *Naturalism and Agnosticism*, first published in 1889, proved to be the dénouement of nineteenth-century British agnosticism as a philosophy. His critique of agnosticism focused on two themes that reflect continuing currents of thought in the twenty-first century: his philosophy of science and his conception of experience. Science, according to Ward, is by its very nature the realm of the abstract, disengaged from the immediacy of experience. Naturalism had come to accept this abstraction as final, *the* truth about reality. Yet experience in its concrete fullness forever defies the attempt at adequate scientific formulation, that is, abstraction. The two incommensurable realms that Leibniz called the necessary and the contingent, Ward designates as the realms of science and history. "Thought," Ward wrote, "gives us only 'science' not existence. . . . Thought gives us only the 'universal.'" But the particular is for science the "surd," or without reason, and yet it is the complex immediacy of this reality, "richer than thought," that *is* experience. "Science," Ward continued, "cannot originate experience;

for experience is the source of science, yet always more than its product, so surely as the workman is more than his tools. Science is but the skeleton, while experience is the life" (1915, 572–73).

In its process of conceptualization, science simplifies in that it must deal with conceptual entities less complex than real ones. Ward pointed to current molecular physics as an example. It tends to treat statistical means and hypothetical mechanism as concrete realities. Force, which is the description of the direction and rate of motion of a body, is reified as a thing. The truth of scientific simplicity can lead, then, to the falsity of simplification. Priority of interest, of attention, is transformed into metaphysics, that is, into priority of being. Because things are extended in space, we cannot, for example, assume, with Descartes, that reality is extension.

Ward's depiction of the philosophy of science, particularly its selective, symbolic, and instrumental (and, therefore, covertly teleological) character is one that is often recognized in philosophical circles today. It has implications for a deeper understanding of the role and meaning of experience. As Ward noted, "Our experience certainly does not embrace the totality of things, is, in fact, ridiculously far from it" (1915, 189).

The human consciousness consists of what Ward called "presentations," or the ways in which the objective world is presented to different individuals or to the same individual at different stages in his or her life. "Presentations" are not discrete atomic events; rather, they form a continuum. That is, new "presentations" are not mere additional items in a series; they modify the entire field of consciousness. Moreover, "presentations" are to and for an active subject, a self—not just a spectator. Just as the dualism of mind and body is a simplification, so is any dualism of subject and object. A real world and an active self are bound in a reciprocal relationship—related parts of a single reality, distinguished in thought but not in fact. For Ward the conative, subjective dimension of experience is an indispensable aspect of cognition. Every experience is somebody's experience, and it is determined by practical interests. Cognition is not conceivable without some motive to action (1915, 423ff.). Ward applied these psychological principles to the apprehension of space and time—and in this anticipated the French philosopher Henri Bergson.

With Ward, British thought had arrived at the threshold of the new philosophical world of voluntarism, *L'Action*, pragmatism, and existentialism— the world of the French philosophers Charles Renouvier, Maurice Blondel, Bergson, and the American William James. This intellectual shift is evident in the principal "concessions" agreed upon by members of the London Synthetic Society who met between 1896 and 1908. The Society's object was "to consider existing Agnostic tendencies, and to contribute towards a working philosophy of religious belief" (Balfour 1909). The Society included representatives of a wide range of philosophical and religious positions, including Roman Catholics, High Church Anglicans, and such independent minds as Henry Sidgwick, Arthur Balfour, James Ward, Oliver Lodge, and F. W. H. Myers, who were interested in psychical research.

The members of the Society were committed to the methods and main conclusions of science; they also, however, were convinced that there was no satisfactory scientific explanation of the development of rationality itself. And they wanted to restore the richness of human experience beyond the severe limits prescribed by the older empiricism. The works of Myers and Ward, and James's *The Varieties of Religious Experience* (1902), had revealed the richness and variability of human moral and spiritual experience.

There also was general consensus in the Society that while religion cannot be proven, cannot be an object of perfect knowledge or scientific certitude, it can justifiably fall back on the test of experience and the test of practice. George Tyrrell argued before the Society that "practice may well be the very condition of the faculty of discernment and therefore of 'theoretical justification'" (Tyrrell 1900, 287). The agnostic empiricist test was simply being expanded. The older empiricists had used the test of experience "to refine truth into a rather dry and austere question mark." The newer, more radical empiricism was "using the same test to make it a tropical forest of abundance, variety, and vividness" (Irvine 1959, 258). The work of the late-Victorian and Edwardian scholars of religion was concerned to rescue an increasingly secular society from the threats of scientific rationality and to unveil crucial elements of human life essential to the individual and society itself (Kippenberg 2002).

While the mission of the Synthetic Society was to humble the intellectual pretension of an impure and militant agnosticism, the fact remained that an agnostic temper of mind had, in important ways, largely won the day. In 1904 a member of the Society, the Christian theist and Oxford philosopher Clement Webb (1865–1954), reflected on Herbert Spencer's continuing appeal to his own time. It consisted, he thought, in the feelings of awe and even reverence in the presence of the ultimate mysteries of life. For Webb it was testimony to the fact that now genuine religion and an agnostic cast of mind were wholly compatible.

Another member of the Society, the prominent Roman Catholic scholar Friedrich von Hügel, was similarly struck by the fact that his contemporaries were confronted on all sides with a certain nescience. If this be agnosticism, then, he admitted, we must all be thoroughgoing agnostics. Moreover, he confessed, we are "such Agnostics in our better moments," because agnosticism "is but the sense of mystery, the consciousness of how much greater is the world of reality . . . than is, or can be, our clear, definable analysis and theory of it" (von Hügel 1931, 182). Von Hügel's agnostic temper regarding theological statement was widely shared by British theologians at the turn of the century. However, it was an agnosticism not hesitant about "staking belief" on a live hypothesis and testing that belief in experience itself.

The drawn-out arguments over the ethics of religious belief, coupled with the agnostic controversy that extended from Henry Mansel's *The Limits of Religious Thought* (1859) to James Ward's *Naturalism and Agnosticism* (1899), were critical in shaping the religious frame of mind in the late Victorian era. Concurrent with this context was an extraordinary quickening of the intellectual life in Britain after 1860, with the flourishing of the new social sciences and the increasing specialization in the natural sciences. This brought with it a flood of new, often threatening, knowledge and speculation that mark this period's distinct character. In reflecting on this new era, Oxford anthropologist R. R. Marett (1866–1943) spoke of it as a second Renaissance, one that had begun about 1858: "Immense vistas opened out on all sides, with philology, biology, archeology alike eager to break the dusty windows of the academies and let in light and air" (Marett 1936, 163–64). In the chapters that follow, we will see how religion, and Christian theology in particular, was caught up in and profoundly shaped by this new renaissance of ideas.

CHAPTER 2

God and the World—
The Reign of Law

Design, Providence, and Teleology

But with regard to the material world, we can at least go so far as this—we can perceive that events are brought about not by insulated interpositions of Divine power, exerted in each particular case, but by the establishment of general laws.

William Whewell

In order to avoid the too frequent, and consequently irreverent intro-duction of the Great Name of the SUPREME BEING into familiar discourse on the operation of his power, I have . . . followed the com-mon usage of employing the term *Nature* as a synonym, expressive of the same power.

Peter Mark Roget

The uniformity of Nature is the veil behind which in these latter days, God is hidden from us.

R. H. Hutton

The Background Prior to 1860

By the mid-nineteenth century the older warrants for both natural and revealed theology no longer seemed as self-evident or convincing as they had earlier. At the same time, questions about God's relation to the world, that is, the evidences of divine design, purpose, and providence in a world governed by natural law, also became more insistent and troubling. A new creative discussion of God's design and action in the world, including questions of a particular providence, evil and theodicy, and miracle began roughly in the 1860s.

The generation of clerical natural scientists in the decades just prior to Darwin had faced a formidable task. No longer could they approve of a theology that excluded large areas of natural history as exempt from scientific explanation. Generally, these thinkers embraced a progressive, developmental conception of natural history. They also were committed to a natural theology, yet increasingly found William Paley's influential *Natural Theology* (1802) wanting. Paley's design argument was utilitarian, emphasizing the usefulness of organs and physical characteristics in the adaptation of creatures to their environment. For Paley, each individual adaptation revealed God's providential design (Mahieu 1976). The next generation of theistic naturalists would require a wider and grander teleology, one that envisioned God as acting through general laws in a progressively developing natural world. This position is brought to the fore in William Whewell's Bridgewater Treatise on *Astronomy and General Physics* (1836):

> Events are brought about, not by insulated interpositions of divine power exerted in each particular case, but by the establishment of general laws. God is the author and governor of the universe through laws which he has given to its parts, the properties which he has impressed upon its constituent elements: these laws and properties are . . . the instruments with which he works. (Whewell 1836, 356–57)

God's creation and governance of the world were not in question; the issue was *how* God providentially creates and governs. Increasingly the answer was: not by special impositions but in the manner of law. Design by natural law was not, of course, new; it was a feature of Newtonian physico-theology. But the renewed scientific emphasis on the all-encompassing reign of law raised novel questions, and the issue focused especially on the reign of law in its relation to theism. As a result, newer forms of natural theology were proposed and debated (Brooke 1991, ch. 6; 1989a, 3–22; 1994, 47–65). At first these proposals gave theology a scientific respectability, since the argument from design and teleology was deeply ingrained in British scientific thinking. But this apparent gain was to prove precarious. Darwin noted that the post-Paleyian idealist vision of a wider providential design in nature was becoming increasingly opaque after 1859. R. H. Hutton (1826–1897), the prolific writer and editor of the *Spectator*, recognized this and the ironic fact that the reign of natural law had become a veil that more often than not *hid* God's personal presence in the world (Hutton 1885, 180).

To anticipate our story, we can say with John W. Burrow—and with due stress on his qualifier—that "much in nineteenth-century thought can be interpreted on the assumption that the Uniformity of Nature had acquired for many intellectuals a logical status and a numinous aura which made it a substitute for the idea of God" (Burrow 1966, 169). The pre-1860 theistic naturalists were, of course, unaware that their apologetic strategies regarding Providence would result in the development that Burrow describes. Moreover, the ways in which they envisioned the relationship between their theology and their belief in the reign of natural law, as a witness to the presence of God, were various and were fragmenting even before Darwin (Young 1985, chs. 1, 4, 5; Brooke 1977; 1979; 1989a; 1991, ch. 7). As J. H. Brooke suggests, this diversity, coupled with the increasing assimilation of theology to advances in scientific accounts of evolution, diminished the plausibility of the argument of natural theology. God was in danger of becoming increasingly remote. "A natural theology of the material world could easily become the Trojan horse of scientific naturalism if the boundaries between material and spiritual were not clearly drawn" (Brooke, 1989a, 57).

One position, associated with some of the authors of the series of Bridgewater Treatises written in the 1830s, conceived of God not only as original creator and planner but also as immanent governor, as an active Providence directly participating in nature's development through the law-abiding adaptation of means to wise ends. That is, nature not only reveals the Deity's original plan or mysterious law-abiding activity; it also reveals his particular, attentive providential interference. This is the position taken, in various formulations, by scientific men of eminence, including William Whewell, William Buckland, and Adam Sedgwick.

William Whewell (1794–1866) was the preeminent scientist-philosopher of his time and Master of Trinity College, Cambridge. He envisioned all historical causes as together forming a great progression from "the remotest nebulae in the heavens to those which determine the diversities of language, the mutations of art, and even the progress of civilization, polity, and literature" (Whewell 1840, 115). Addressing the issue of origins, however, Whewell wrote that it may well be that certain occurrences in the chain of events

> may be quite inexplicable by the aid of any natural causes with which we are acquainted; and thus the result of our investigations, conducted with strict regard to scientific principles, may be that we must either contemplate supernatural influences as part of the past series of events, or declare ourselves altogether unable to form this series to a connected whole. (116)

In such cases, Whewell maintained that the historical record is rationally more compelling than the universal operation of secondary causes; therefore, appeal to divine, miraculous powers acting in the role of efficient cause may be scientifically inescapable (see Hodge 1991, 255–88). Our present natural order, then, was begun by the actions of a creative power wholly other from any agency that has been efficacious since.

In later years, Whewell's revised natural theology included a repudiation of the older Paleyian tradition of teleology that conceived of God's design in terms of immediate, practical adaptation. Whewell conceded that there were seemingly useless and abortive features in creation that threatened the older optimistic natural theology and its cheerful theodicy. He acknowledged that in our endeavors to trace God's ways we often are lost and bewildered and fail to discern how the pain and the sacrifice of life fall in with the divine plan (Brooke 1977, 221–86; Yeo 1979, 493–516). Nonetheless, he defended a wider, grander plan in the mind of the Creator, a plan that included humanity's special place in the universe.

William Buckland (1784–1856), professor of mineralogy in Oxford and the university's most prominent representative of science, was the foremost English geologist of the 1820s. In his prolix and detailed Bridgewater Treatise, *Geology and Mineralogy Considered with Reference to Natural Theology* (1836), he sought to show that the earth sciences prove the Deity's law-abiding, continued guidance and superintendence (Rupke 1983). Buckland wrote:

> The evidences afforded by the sister sciences exhibit indeed the most admirable proofs of design and intelligence originally exerted at the Creation: but many who admit these proofs still doubt the continued superintendence of that Intelligence, maintaining that the system of the Universe is carried on by the force of the laws originally impressed upon matter, without the necessity of a fresh interference or continued supervision on the part of the Creator.

On the contrary, Buckland argued, the present structure of the earth's surface shows numerous violent convulsions following its original formation:

> When therefore we perceive that the secondary causes producing these convulsions have operated at successive periods, not blindly and at random, but with a direction to beneficial ends, we see at once the proofs of an overruling Intelligence continuing to superintend, direct, modify, and control operations of the agents which he originally ordained. (Buckland 1820, 18–19)

Buckland's vision of Providence's superintendence and grand design was cold comfort for many, however, demonstrating that not only individuals but whole species were mortal and destined to extinction. A commentator on Buckland's depiction of divine superintendence offers this striking verdict:

> In large part through the deliberate publicity efforts of Buckland himself . . . the English imagination was radically altered; it became populated by grinning monsters from the slimy swamps, and by a haunting realization that the earth is a great charnel-house of bones testifying to the transience of life-forms and is itself changing, melting away as in a dream. (Cannon 1960, 19)

Buckland sought to take the sting out of his melancholy developmental scheme by portraying earlier epochs as the preparation for the arrival of man, indeed, of Englishmen. As J. H. Brooke comments, "Buckland's God was an Anglophile who had arranged that iron ore, limestone and coal would be found in the same localities, providing all the ingredients of an industrial revolution" (1989a, 38).

In retrospect, we can see that Whewell's and Buckland's insistence that natural history is a law-abiding, gradual progression, yet subserving the changing needs of organic life by successive divine interventions, cried out for a simpler theory to explain the divine reign of law. Just such a challenge was proposed by the geologist Charles Lyell (1797–1875). He represents a second way in which God's law-abiding action in the world was then conceived. In his *Principles of Geology* (1830–1833) Lyell questioned the validity of any scientific work that presupposes miraculous interventions in nature. If the facts of natural history are to be explained by divine miracle, how, he asked, can science proceed? Science must assume that nature functions according to uniform natural laws. Lyell was not arguing for an exclusively naturalistic explanation of creation, for he was a theist; he insisted only that divine creation should be through laws.

Lyell was a determined proponent of what has been referred to as *actualism*, or the supposition that the nature of past events must be understood by analogy with processes observable in action at the present time (Rudwick 1976, 110, 185ff.). In an 1829 letter to his friend and fellow geologist Roderick Murchison on the plan of his *Principles of Geology*, Lyell affirmed that his whole endeavor was "to establish the *principle of reasoning* in the science . . . [namely] that *no causes whatever* have from the earliest time to which we can look back, to the present, ever acted, but those *now acting*; and that they never acted with different degrees of energy from that which they now exert" (Mrs. Lyell 1881, 234).

Lyell especially opposed those scriptural geologists who looked to other laws, to periodic miraculous interventions, to explain the past history of the creation. In the *Principles* he wrote that

> the more the idea of a slow and insensible change from lower to higher organisms, brought about in the course of millions of generations according to a preconceived plan, has become familiar to men's minds, the more conscious they have become that the amount of power, wisdom, design, or free-thought, required for such a gradual evolution of life, is as great as that which is implied by a multitude of separate, special and miraculous acts of creation. (C. Lyell 1872, 499–500)

Lyell continued throughout his career to believe in law-abiding, purposeful divine activity through rather mysterious "intermediate causes" or "delegated powers" of generation. He was prepared to hold that some modification of species could be produced by natural causes but that that was not sufficient to explain the origin of new species that reflect divine wisdom and design. Nor was he ever to believe that natural selection itself could account for the human mind. While insisting that the creation of new species is *not* the result of divine miraculous intervention, Lyell nevertheless held that the appearance of new species reflects distinct and particular acts of intelligent design. Providence is revealed in the seemingly coincident introduction of new species into physically supportive environments, all taking place by apparently synchronized secondary causes unknown to us, yet all in accord with natural laws.

A third form of natural theology at the time conceived of God's creative and providential governance as confined to the original plan and the laws that were established by God in the beginning. Each development in the evolutionary process thus represents the unfolding of the germinal seeds of the divine plan, which is manifest to our minds in the sufficiency and the majestic uniformity of the laws of nature. God's governance, however, does not require even law-abiding interventions, certainly not miracles. This rather deistic position was made popular by Robert Chambers (1802–1871) in *Vestiges of the Natural History of Creation* (1844) (see Secord 2000). However, similar views were held by the young Charles Darwin, by the comparative anatomist Richard Owen, and by Baden Powell—scientist, cleric, and contributor to *Essays and Reviews*—in his later apologetic works.

When Chambers speaks of the reign of divine law he is referring to that body of laws established by God in the beginning, by means of which new species develop. Chambers was a transmutationist. For him a law-abiding organic history meant *one* uniform law, not a series of ad hoc laws. "It is most interesting," he wrote, "to observe into how small a field the whole of the mysteries of nature thus ultimately resolve themselves." The passage concludes: "Nor may even these [laws of gravitation and development] be after all twain, but only branches of one still more comprehensive law, the expression of that unity which man's wit can scarcely separate from the Deity itself" (Chambers 1844, 360). How much worthier a conception is that which supposes "that all things have been commissioned by him from the first, though neither is he absent from a particle of the current of natural affairs in one sense, seeing that the whole system is continually supported by his providence" (153ff.).

The Paleyian tradition of natural theology, as that was carried forward in some of the Bridgewater Treatises, remained utilitarian, based as it was on a mass of individual evidences of adaptation of organisms to their environments. The "grander" vision of the reign of divine law that now had superseded it was increasingly perceived in terms of the unity of nature, of the harmony and beauty of the whole taxonomic system. It now was admitted that the efficiency of particular adaptions was often sacrificed to ensure the unity of the entire plan. This was the view of Richard Owen (1804–1892), England's leading biologist before Darwin. Owen believed in a providential evolutionism or progressionism. He saw the natural development of a species as the gradual unfolding, by secondary laws, of an ideal archetype of that species. The divine mind conceives and foresees all the modifications that will take place through time. Yet God's plan always proceeds through the agency of perhaps unknown yet knowable secondary laws.

Owen considered it a groundless fear that physical explanations of development might exclude evidence of divine wisdom and design: "On the contrary—the higher and more general are the laws regulating the structure of animals . . . the more will the Contemplative Mind be struck with the vastness of that designing intelligence which in originally ordaining them could produce such harmony and adaptation amongst their innumerable results" (Owen 1838).

While Owen opposed Darwinian natural selection to the last, his final great work, *On the Anatomy of Vertebrates* (1866–1868), shows how very close he came to the position of Chambers. Of the alternative, species by miracle or by law, Owen was adamant: "I accept the latter without misgivings, and recognize such law as continuously operating through tertiary time" (1868, 793).

It is slight wonder that several critics, including Darwin, assumed that Owen admitted the truth of the Darwinian theory. Owen was skating very close to Darwin's naturalism, but he refused to make the final move to a materialistic transmutationism. "Natural Selection," he made clear to the critics, "leaves the subsequent origin and succession of the species to the fortuitous concurrence of outward conditions." Owen proposed as an alternative what he called "Derivation." This involved an innate tendency to deviate from parental type, as "the most probable . . . way of operation of the secondary law" of the origin of species. Derivation recognized "a purpose in the defined and preordained course" of evolutionary progression (1868, 807, 818). This larger teleology, which emphasized God's preordained archetypal plan and the ambiguity of secondary causes, reinforced the idealist argument for design and was to prevail for some time. It also carried with it unrecognized fateful consequences, as we will see.

A quite different position on the reign of law and teleology prior to 1860 is that of the mature Darwin. In *The Origin of Species* (1859) and in other works, Darwin continued to use language that appeared to imply purposes and goals, but this language was devoid of explicit theistic reference. Nature, of course, revealed design and order, but logically these need not be directed to an *intelligent* end or purpose. Darwin had, in fact, naturalized the theological conceptions of design and teleology, but his teleological language was appealed to by scientists, philosophers, and theologians alike who continued to interpret evolution as purposeful and providential. The teleological argument remained surprisingly compelling in late Victorian scientific culture, especially among some physical scientists, such as Lord Kelvin (William Thomson, 1824–1907), who thought Darwin's theory deficient in exactly this regard.

The Context of the Argument from Design after 1860

In 1874 the American botanist Asa Gray wrote to Charles Darwin to tell him that he had done "a great service to natural Science in bringing back to it Teleology: so that instead of Morphology *versus* Teleology, we shall have Morphology wedded to Teleology." Darwin responded, "What you say about Teleology pleases me especially and I do not think that any one else has ever noticed the point" (F. Darwin 1887, 189).

That Darwin's own view of the natural world was imbued with features characteristic of British natural theology after Paley is now rather widely recognized by historians of science, although some would wish to minimize such an assimilation (see Cannon 1961; Young 1985; Ospovat 1981; Kohn 1989). W. F. Cannon has proposed the thesis "that the triumph of Darwinism is the triumph of a Christian way of picturing the world over the other ways available to scientists" (Cannon 1961, 109; for a critical view of Cannon's thesis see Hodge 1991). By this Cannon meant that in the natural theology dominant in the early decades of the nineteenth century there were a number of concepts that were similar to those that informed Darwin's own mature scientific work. These included the apparent randomness of raw nature, the need for an external organizing power, and natural evidence that the world is both purposeful and historical. Darwin perceived the randomness of nature as the fortuitous variations among individuals. The external organizing power became for him natural selection, and this "functions to ensure that only developments which have purpose will in the long run endure. Development is unique and irreversible" (Cannon 1961, 129). Of course, what Darwin added to the theistic world-picture was the fact that these postulates could be explained by natural laws as easily as by reference to God. This is what Cannon means by Darwin's "achievement"—the fact that he "'stole' the universe of the theologians from them" (129). Here is a relatively characteristic passage from Darwin's *Origin of Species*:

> To my mind it accords better with what we know of the laws impressed upon matter by the Creator that the production and extinction of the past and present inhabitants of the world should have been due to secondary causes, like those determining the birth and death of the individual. When I view all beings not as special creations, but as the lineal descendants of some few beings . . . they seem to me to become ennobled. (C. Darwin 1917, 396)

Baden Powell and an increasing number of British clerics and theologians could have written those words—in terms, of course, of a newly emerging conception of divine immanence. Charles Kingsley (1819–1875), Church of England priest and popular novelist, was convinced that Darwin's evolutionary naturalism had banished once and for all the idea of an interfering God. In 1859 he wrote to Darwin that he had "learnt to see that it is just as noble a conception of Deity, to believe that he created primal forms capable of self-development into all forms needful *pro tempore* and *pro loco*, as to believe that he required a fresh act of intervention to supply the *lacunas* which He himself had made" (F. Darwin 1887, 287–88).

For Kingsley, as for others, this teleology was by far the "loftier" view of the work of the Creator. One must ask then, in view of the theologians' capacity to accommodate and adapt Darwin's doctrine to a theistic worldview, whether it is accurate to say that Darwin "stole" the theologians' world from them (Brooke, private correspondence). The history of the theological responses to Darwin between 1860 and 1910 allows for some doubt on this score.

A study of the decades after 1860 in Britain reveals the rich complexity of its intellectual culture. It was the period of both the zenith and decline of scientific positivism. It was also the time when the influence of German

Idealism and *Naturphilosophie* continued apace in both British philosophy and biology. However, Kantian and later neo-Kantian metaphysical agnosticism, the latter derived from the German theologian Albrecht Ritschl (1822–1889) and his school, also invaded the British theological precincts during these latter decades. What is evident after 1860, however, is that there is a "fragmentation of [the earlier] context" (Young 1985, 126–63). Unlike the previous half-century dominated by the clerical naturalists, both science and theology became increasingly professional disciplines with their own sophisticated methods, highly specialized bodies of knowledge, and journals.

This intellectual diversity of the era is evident in the membership of the Metaphysical Society, which discussed a range of questions—from the grounds and ethics of religious belief, to animal intelligence and the logic of the physical sciences. The Society made a valiant attempt to maintain a common context of ideas, but after eleven years acknowledged that, despite a shared intellectual liberality of mind, their foundational working assumptions were irreconcilable. A concurrent change in the nature of periodical publishing reflects as well the increasing diversity within the intellectual culture. The "heavy" periodicals that had appealed to a broad, if comparatively small, intellectual constituency declined in circulation, or they were required to shift to a more popular style and subject matter. This trend was accompanied, indeed shaped, by the need for highly specialized journals for psychology (*Mind*, 1876), neurophysiology (*Brain*, 1878), anthropology (*Man*, 1901), and so on—all addressed to more limited professional audiences.

Scientific Naturalism:
Natural Law and Orthodox Theology Irreconcilable

The breakdown of the early and mid-Victorian common context is evident in a range of positions that emerged in the post-1860 era on the science and religion question and, more especially, with regard to the place of natural theology and the issues of divine providence, design, miracle, and theodicy. Contrary to some accounts, assurance in the efficacy of natural theology did persist, although its apologetic value was increasingly questioned and alternative positions were proposed. The decades of the 1860s and 1870s were, first of all, a time of growing confidence in scientific naturalism. Its disciples proclaimed, with Comtean zeal, not only the demise of providentialism but their new faith in both the application of natural law to the study of society itself and in scientific progress. This apparent victory of scientific naturalism often was heralded in the language of religious conviction and hope. It is discernible in the prose of such noted writers as John Lubbock, Leslie

Stephen, W. K. Clifford, Francis Galton, G. H. Lewes, John Tyndall, and the great apologists T. H. Huxley and Herbert Spencer. Looking back to the early years of her own intellectual formation, Beatrice Webb, the eminent Fabian socialist, described the intellectual and moral shift that was taking place in the immediate post-1860s years. She spoke of the "almost fanatical faith" that through the agency of science alone human misery would, ultimately, be swept away. And with this new faith in science, Webb observed the aware-ness of a new motive and the transference of the emotion of self-sacrificing service from God to man (Webb 1926).

George Eliot's growing faith in science was also indicative of the change. For Eliot the supremely important fact—again, a veritable shift in human consciousness—is "the gradual reduction of all phenomena within the sphere of established law," the consequence being the inevitable overthrow of belief in a particular providence and the miraculous. In her homage to natural science, Eliot spoke of natural law as "the most potent force at work in the modification of our faith and of the practical form given to our sentiments." It was a faith that could only be "urged upon the mind by the problems of physical science" (Eliot 1865, 54).

Many of the new apologists for science—Galton, Clifford, and Lewes—saw theology and science as irreconcilable. A few perceived an affinity between the more recent theological conception of Providence and the new scientific positivism in their common vision of an unshakable reign of law. Huxley, ironic and characteristically provocative, pointed to this congruence in what he called his "scientific Calvinism":

> If the doctrine of Providence is to be taken as the expression . . . of the total exclusion of chance from a place even in the most insignifi-cant corner of Nature; if it means the strong conviction that the cos-mic process is rational; and the faith that throughout all duration, unbroken order has reigned in the universe—I not only accept it, but am disposed to think it the most important of all truths. (T. H. Huxley 1892b, 567)

Huxley's notion of Providence would prove acceptable to few theological apologists—perhaps only to a Baden Powell, whose abstract conception of deity lacked appeal. Huxley did, however, focus on an issue that increasingly was central to the concerns of naturalists and theologians alike, and that explains in part the persistent interest in natural theology or some form of natural "pseudo-theology."

A number of prominent scientific naturalists did continue to insist that natural science and theology offered two rival, mutually exclusive—though not equally justified—worldviews and theodicies. In his presidential address to the British Association meeting in Belfast in 1874, John Tyndall called for an end to all evasion and equivocation on the question: "Two courses and two only are possible. Either let us open our doors freely to the conception of creative acts, or abandoning them, let us radically change our notions of matter" (Tyndall 1874/1902, 202). It was Darwin's developmental and selective hypotheses that convinced many naturalists that the choice was an either-or. This specific Darwinian opposition to theology finds its epitome in Leslie Stephen's essay on "Darwinism and Divinity." Stephen focused on the sheer incompatibility of Darwinism—for him the quintessential expression of science—and natural theology:

> For Darwinism is, in fact, the scientific embodiment of that attack upon final causes. . . . The eye and the ear are no longer to be regarded as illustrating the cunning workmanship of the Divine artificer, but as particular results of the uniform operation of what are called the laws of nature. . . . The man of science refuses to see anything beyond the operation of invariable laws, whilst the theologian still urges that the laws imply a lawgiver, though forced to abandon the anthropomorphic conception of the Supreme Being. (L. Stephen 1873, 100)

The rhetoric of the militant naturalists Lubbock, Clifford, and Galton, and the lay popularizers Stephen, Spencer, and Winwoode Reade, was redolent of a fervent new religious piety. Clifford spoke of the history of mankind as "a mystic progress under the guidance of divine Nature." The sacralizing of nature and the Reign of Law and Progress was apparent in the unselfconscious way that these words nature, law, and progress were regularly capitalized. It is not inappropriate, then, to use terms such as *scientific priesthood* and *church scientific* when referring to the efforts of Huxley, Lewes, and Galton to forward the new creed and the institutional program of scientific naturalism. Central to these efforts was, of course, the vision of science as serving what Beatrice Webb called its "self-sacrificing" and salvific purpose. Lewes's earnest warning that "science is a futile, frivolous pursuit unless it serves some grand religious aim" (Lewes 1853, 92), was not uncommon among the apologists for the new science.

The religious feeling that one encounters in the scientific naturalists of this period frequently includes a breathtaking eschatological utopianism such as to make many a parallel theistic vision appear rather bland. At the conclusion of his weighty *Pre-Historic Times* (1865), John Lubbock assured his readers of the self-evident fact that the ignorance under which they presently suffered would soon be diminished by the progress of science and that

science now could "boldly predict the future happiness of the race." While
the past had considered a utopia as "too good to be true," it now "turns out,
on the contrary, to be the necessary consequence of natural laws" (Lubbock
1865, 491–92). This utopian vision was most extravagantly predicted in
Winwoode Reade's popular *Martyrdom of Man* (1872). Reade's hymn to science, which in later years would provoke dismissive ridicule, was spoken
with the most passionate assurance and sincerity:

> When we have ascertained, by means of Science, the methods of
> Nature's operation . . . the laws which regulate the complex phenom-
> ena of life, we shall be able to predict the future as we are already
> able to predict comets and eclipses. . . . Not only will man subdue the
> forces of evil that are without; he will subdue those that are within;
> he will obey the laws written in his heart; he will worship the divinity
> that is within him. . . . The earth will become a Holy Land which will
> be visited by pilgrims from all the quarters of the universe. . . . Man
> will then be perfect; he will be a creator; he will therefore be what the
> vulgar worship as God. (Reade 1872)

What is of moment here in citing this florid rhetoric of the "church scientific" is not only to expose its faith in inevitable progress and a utopian future
but, more to our point, its belief that the discovery of the reign of natural law
had worked a momentous shift that entailed the eclipse of the older theology and the concept of a providential guidance and purpose in nature and
history. For growing numbers, nature and *traditional* theology were now
sundered. As John Durant has acutely observed, the new scientific naturalism did not merely oppose providentialism; it all too often surreptitiously
"relied upon a transference of the notion of Providence from the transcendent realm of orthodox theology to the immanent world in which scientific
methods were applicable" (Durant 1977, 32). God either was replaced by, or
identified with, the forces and laws of nature itself—knowable, harnessable,
and therefore directable.

The Unitary Vision of Providence and the Reign of Natural Law: Varieties of Mediation

It was only late in his career that Darwin publicly attacked natural theology, as
he does in *The Descent of Man* (1871). Yet even in the 1870s he remained
attracted to ideas of a "grander" teleology. Peter Bowler has shown that in both
British biology and philosophy after 1860 there also persisted an idealist

version of designed evolution that saw design in the overall unity and harmony of the system of nature (Bowler 1977, 29–43; see also 1983, ch. 3; and
1988, ch. 4). This was especially attractive to theologians and religious apologists who wished to maintain a unitary vision of truth and of the relation
between science and theology. This "grander" view of the reign of divine law
was, as we have seen, earlier championed by Richard Owen. In the latter
decades of the century various idealist or transcendentalist conceptions of
design were proposed by both professional scientists and theological apologists. Representative of this alliance were the scientists St. George Mivart, W.
B. Carpenter, and a group of Scottish thinkers who were well versed in the
science of their day.

St. George Jackson Mivart (1827–1900) was an eminent zoologist and an
early follower of Darwin who came to regard aspects of Darwin's theory of
evolution as highly suspect. Mivart's was a fiercely independent mind, one
that got him into trouble with both the "church scientific" and the Roman
Church. He converted to Catholicism at the age of sixteen—which barred
him from attending an English university. He read law at Lincoln's Inn but
never took up the profession. He studied zoology privately under Owen and
then became a student of Huxley's at the London School of Mines in 1861.
Huxley later supported Mivart's appointment in comparative anatomy at the
medical school of St. Mary's Hospital in London.

Through his friendship and devotion to Huxley, Mivart became a supporter of Darwin, although the hold of Owen on him was never broken, and
through his own studies of the primate order Mivart firmly embraced basic
Owenite conclusions. In the decade after 1859, he followed with great interest
the growing critical literature on *The Origin of Species*, noting Darwin's additions and deletions, particularly his mounting concessions. Mivart's increasing sense of the glaring weaknesses in Darwin's argument resulted in his own
On the Genesis of Species (1871). At the time, it proved to be the most thorough
and formidable scientific criticism of Darwin's great book and his theory of
natural selection. It also poisoned and embittered the relations between Mivart
and both Darwin and Huxley; the latter came to regard his former friend as
dishonest because of his metaphysical interests. Despite Huxley's criticism of
On the Genesis of Species, critics of Darwin long used Mivart's arguments, frequently without acknowledgment. Mivart neither could give up his scientific
belief in evolution nor his religious faith. As his biographer notes, "Since both
represented truth, neither could be rejected without danger to that harmonious world of truth whose ultimate description and understanding were the
goal of both scientist and theologian" (Gruber 1960, 49–50).

Mivart was convinced by the mounting negative evidence that Darwin's
theory could not fully explain the facts of evolution. He was also certain

that the facts did support belief in a directed purpose in nature, the sudden mutations occurring along predetermined paths. He focused on the many features in organisms that have no immediate adaptive function or survival value, and the presence of similar characteristics—for example, the eyes of vertebrates and the cephalopods—that existed independently in these distinct evolutionary groups. The latter, he thought, implied some developmental predisposition, and he argued that the idea of an *internal force* or tendency "as the main, determining agent" in the genesis of species was more congruent with the facts of development.

Mivart soon came to see his own position as an alternative to those of both Darwin and Owen. In Mivart's estimation, Darwin's natural selection perceived grandeur in the idea of several powers having been originally breathed by the Creator into a few forms or into one. Owen, on the other hand, saw in Darwin's view a narrow invocation of a special miracle and, therefore, unworthy limitation of creative power. Mivart believed that his own position allowed for "a greater and more important part of the share of external influences" but that these external factors, equally with certain internal tendencies, were "the result of one harmonious action underlying the whole of nature." Thus, according to Mivart, "an internal law presides over the actions of every part of every individual, and of every organism as a unit, and of the entire organic world as a whole. It is believed that this conception of an internal innate force will ever remain necessary, however much its subordinate processes and actions may become explicable" (Mivart 1871b, 239).

Among the "subordinate processes," Mivart recognized natural selection as playing a significant role in rigorously destroying monstrosities, in removing antecedent species rapidly when new ones evolved, in favoring useful variations, and so on. Yet the difficulties that he had laboriously enumerated against Darwin were telling, and thus he concluded that while "Natural Selection is accepted," it does not "fulfill the task assigned to it by Mr. Darwin" (241). He saw no reason to believe that the three conceptions of natural evolution—the typical (Owen), the transformationist (Darwin), and the teleological—were mutually exclusive. Good grounds could be advanced for requiring each conception if full justice were to be done to the facts. In any case, a reasonable examination would have to admit the fact of final causes if, on other grounds which Mivart had argued, "there are reasons for believing such final causes exist." Mivart was sure that it is not only possible but highly probable "that an internal power or tendency is an important if not the main agent in evoking the manifestations of new species" (242).

Mivart was certain that his conviction that nature evolved by ordinary natural laws, largely unknown, and was controlled by subordinate conditions, principally natural selection, in no way precluded the further judgment that those natural laws acted "with Divine concurrence and in obedience to a creative fiat originally imposed on the primeval Cosmos, 'in the beginning,' by its Creator" (288).

William Benjamin Carpenter (1813–1885) was, in the estimation of many, the leading English physiologist of his time. His *Principles of General and Comparative Physiology* (1839) was an influential book, the first English treatise to contain truly adequate conceptions of the science of biology. He had a deep influence on biologists but also on Herbert Spencer and William James. After medical education in Bristol and Edinburgh, Carpenter was appointed in 1844 as Fullerton Professor of Physiology in the Royal Institution and was elected a fellow of the Royal Society. He also served as lecturer in physiology at London Hospital and professor of forensic medicine at University College. Throughout his scientific career Carpenter remained a devout and active Unitarian. For seventeen of his busiest professional years he served as organist at the Unitarian Church, Rosslyn Hill, Hampstead. His science always posed wider questions for him, a fact evident in his many papers on philosophical and religious themes.

Carpenter heartily welcomed Darwin's *Origin of Species*, which he felt gave a distinct shape to ideas about which many scientists had been speculating. "It showed that the doctrine of Progressive Development might be put in the form of a definite scientific hypothesis" (W. B. Carpenter 1888, 103–4). Carpenter believed that the doctrine of continuous descent with modification was Darwin's fundamental idea and that it would remain the basis of all biological science in the future. He also believed, however, that Darwin attached far too great importance to natural selection or the survival of the fittest as the *vera causa*. Carpenter suggested, rather, that natural selection was capable of operation only "where a capacity for variation is inherent in the type." In his estimation, the effect of natural selection was "only to perpetuate, among varietal forms, that one which best suits the conditions of existence." Consequently, he insisted that "we must look to *forces* acting either within or *without* the organism, as the real agents of producing whatever developmental variations it may take on" (110), forces about which, at present, he felt very little was known.

What was certain for Carpenter was the fact that there is "a determinate capacity for a certain fixed kind of development in each [primordial] germ, in virtue of which one evolves into a zoophyte, and another (though not originally distinguished from it) into a man. Each primordial germ is thus endowed with its determinate capacity for a particular course of development." It is by virtue of this capacity that the germ "has evolved the whole succession of forms that has ultimately proceeded from it." Carpenter considered it inconceivable that such an orderly evolutionary succession could have been *produced* by the "accidents" of natural selection. "I cannot but believe," he professed, "that [the germ's] evolution was part of the original Creative Design; and that Natural Selection has been simply to limit the survivorship, among the entire range of forms that have successively come into existence, to those which were suited to maintain that existence at each period" (110). Natural selection was no *vera causa*.

Carpenter further argued that no physical agencies could adequately account for varietal modifications, "since, for those agencies to take effect, there must have been a concurrent capacity for variation, either in the organism itself, or in its germ" (438). In his essay "The Argument from Design in the Organic World" (1884), he had sought to show that natural selection could not effectively dispose of teleology. He was convinced that natural selection could not possibly account for the progressive modifications required in the structure of each individual organ to convert, for example, a reptile into a bird. Nothing short of "intentional prearrangement" was competent to bring about such a wonderful result. To prove his claim of prearrangement, Carpenter illustrated in great detail the orderly sequence of progressive variations in the organization of *Foraminifera*, a group of simple marine animals, especially the complex *Orbitolite*, which in aggregate formed limestone strata. He showed that in the sequence of variations, following definite lines of advance, there is no "struggle for existence" or "survival of the fittest." All variations follow a definite direction of ever increasing complexity, but the more complex varieties gain no advantage since they are fully as incapable of escaping from their enemies by movement. "In fact their chief destroyers would be likely to be most attracted by the larger disks of the 'complex' type" (458).

Carpenter felt justified in concluding that his illustrations—"merely samples of an immense aggregate"—proved that natural selection not only fails to account for the consistency of advance in evolutionary progress but that "it leaves untouched the evidence of Design in the original scheme of Organized Creation." What evolution has done, however, is to "transfer the idea of Design from the particular to the general, making all the special cases of adaptation the foreknown results of the adoption of that general Order which we call Law." In the laws of organic evolution Carpenter saw "nothing but the orderly and continuous working-out of the original intelligent design" (W. B. Carpenter, 1888, 463), as opposed to the doctrine of successive creations *de novo*.

Carpenter believed that much of the conflict between theology and science was traceable to a confusion of thought regarding "law." It was common in both camps to hear laws spoken of as "governing" or "regulating" phenomena and that phenomena were thought to be "accounted for" when they were shown to be "consequences" of a particular law. In an essay entitled "Nature and Law" (1880) aimed at clarifying the issues, Carpenter pointed out that "no law of pure science *can* be anything but an expression of the *fact* of its orderly uniformity." In itself that fact gives us no clue as to its *cause*, and it clearly does not exclude the idea of an intelligent first cause. The latter idea appeared to Carpenter (he argued the point on numerous occasions) to be implied in our own experience of volitional or purposive agency. The wonderful combination in nature of unity in variety and harmony in diversity was evidence of

> a Designing Mind as we recognize in any great human organization which approaches our notion of ideal perfection such as a well-conducted orchestra. . . . To see a great result brought about by the consentaneous but diversified action of a multitude of individuals each of whom does his own particular work in a manner that combines harmoniously with the different work of every other, suggests to me nothing but admiration for the Master-mind by which the order was devised, and by the influence of which it is constantly sustained. (1888, 382)

Mivart and Carpenter were among the most prominent post-Darwin professional scientists who sought to maintain a unitary vision of science and theology and who did so by appealing to a "wider teleology" that was consistent with aspects of Darwin's theory and the reign of natural law. It was left to the theological apologists to draw out the implications of this new teleology for a reconceived doctrine of Divine Providence. This was undertaken most thoroughly by a group of influential Scots.

Scottish Ideas of Providential Evolution and the Reign of Law

James McCosh (1811–1894) was educated at the universities of Glasgow and Edinburgh and served many years as a minister of the Church of Scotland. The high praise received for his first book, *The Method of the Divine Government, Physical and Moral* (1850), led to his appointment in 1851 to the chair of logic and metaphysics at Queens College, Belfast. He remained there until 1868 when he left Ireland to become president of the College of New Jersey, later Princeton University. In his many publications throughout a long career, McCosh insisted on the ultimate unity of nature and revelation. As different as they are in many respects, it is equally true, he wrote in an early work, "that they meet in a higher unity, and that, after all, they are two aspects . . . of one Great Truth" (McCosh and Dickie 1857, 5; see Livingstone 1987, 106–12).

Following Owen's idealist or transcendental morphology, McCosh repeatedly expounded on what he called the two great principles operative in the constitution and development of the cosmos: "the Principle of Order, or a General Plan, Pattern, or Type, to which every given object is made to conform" and "the Principle of Special Adaptation or Particular End, by which each object, while constructed after a general model, is, at the same time accommodated to the situation which it has to occupy, and a purpose which it is intended to serve" (McCosh and Dickie 1857, 1). While McCosh remained committed to the Paleyian teleology of utilitarian adaptation, he also recognized that the larger teleology of an interconnected, unitary plan was a firmer support for natural theology. He saw, as had Owen, that scientists such as Geoffrey Saint-Hilaire and Lorenz Oken attended to a class of phenomena to which Paley never had alluded in his *Natural Theology* (27).

What impressed McCosh in the work of these biologists was the emphasis on a class of adaptations exhibited by general laws ingeniously adjusted to each other. "The agents of nature are so arranged into a system, or rather a system of systems," so that a vast array of independent agents are made to conspire for the achievement of a great end (McCosh 1850, 121). The wisdom of God is especially revealed in those skillful arrangements by means of which no part of the cosmos is useless:

> We see before us what we reckon a useless plant; and we conclude that the species might be eradicated, and no evil follow. But the conclusion is rash. For the seed of that plant may be needful to the support of some kind of bird, or the root of it to some insect; that the bird or insect may serve an important purpose in the economy of the earth; and were we completely to root out that plant bearing seed after its kind, we might throw the whole of nature into inextricable confusion. (154)

McCosh was convinced that such order and unity argued in favor of a supreme intelligence. Omniscience, he contended, is necessary to the planning of such a vast system, omnipotence and omnipresence to its execution.

The principle of order or general laws in nature requires, then, the coincident principle of particular adaptation, that is, Providence. Every natural law might be good in itself, but if not curbed or restrained it can, in combination with others, produce disastrous results. It is little comfort to the man disabled for life to tell him that his calamity was the result of a beautiful mechanical law. Scientists who exult in the reign of law do not take sufficient account of their joint crossing and clashing and what McCosh called the "Fortuities of Nature." To our human view this complication must appear to result in chance accidents, their good not seen by even the greatest human sagacity, but to God they are the instruments of his government. What appears as accidental cannot, McCosh insisted, be so, for it is in the very constitution of things. It is, he wrote, "the grand means which the Governor of the world employs for the accomplishment of his specific purposes, and by which his providence is rendered a particular providence, reaching to the most minute incidents" (155).

The "Fortuities of Nature," seen in the light of a providential plan of nature's government, accomplish many purposes beyond the limiting of human foresight and the rendering of humanity absolutely dependent on its Maker. Such "fortuities" also require variety in the works of God. Providence thus produces effects that could not have followed from the operation of natural laws acting singly, and God makes general laws accomplish individual ends. The reign of laws would be intolerable if it were mere brute force under no control, but it is not so when perceived under the providential government of God. The nice adaptation of an immense number of laws, "like the innumerable rings in a coat-of-mail," gives to adaptation its flexibility, "whereby it fits in to the shape and posture of every individual man" (175).

McCosh's conception of Providence and the reign of law, as here described, was fully developed in his first book, *The Method of Divine Government* (1850), and he never felt the need to revise radically this widely admired, but distinctly pre-Darwinian, natural theology, even after the revolution inaugurated by *The Origin of Species*. In *Christianity and Positivism* (1871), McCosh courageously admitted that he was now "inclined to think" that Darwin's theory of evolution by natural selection contained "a large body of important truths which we see illustrated in every department of organic life," although, he insisted, it did not contain the whole truth about evolution (1871, 42). The proof of divine plan in the organic unity and development of the world that McCosh outlined in *Christianity and Positivism* was, in all essentials, that of 1850. Everyone trained in the great truths of advanced science, he remained convinced, would see "purpose in the ways in which the materials and forces and life of the universe are made to conspire, to secure a progress through indeterminate ages." Among those elements working to this end may be "the law of Natural Selection," but whatever the forces, "all and each work in the midst of a struggle for existence, in which the strong prevail and the weak disappear. But in all this," he assured his readers, "there is a starting point and a terminus, and rails along which the powers run, and an intelligence planning and guiding the whole, and bringing it to its destination freighted with blessings" (1871, 90).

George Douglas Campbell (1823–1900), the eighth duke of Argyll, was a statesman of the Liberal Party, an amateur naturalist, and a popular writer on science and religion between the 1860s and 1890s. He is representative of the providential evolutionists who sought a new alliance between science and theology. *The Reign of Law* (1867) was the first of his popular forays into the relations of science and religion. By the 1860s, the reign of law had, Argyll observed, passed into every domain of thought, including the theology of the Church, but, he estimated, with mischievous effects on the latter. The theologians now were seen "coming out to parley with the men of Science—a white flag in their hands, and saying, 'If you will leave us alone, we will do the same by you. . . . The Reign of Law which you proclaim, we admit—outside these walls, but not within them: let there be peace between us'" (Argyll 1867, 53–54). The theologians had reason, of course, to be wary of the pronouncements of the aggressive scientific positivists whose every profession pretended to represent scientific truth. But Argyll considered it a feeble reason for erecting a barrier that demanded that science and theology be kept entirely separate and that they belong to entirely different spheres of thought. Such a divorce offers a temptation to each side: "It is grateful to scientific men who are afraid of being thought hostile to Religion. It is grateful to religious men who are afraid of science" (55–56). Yet the fatal objection to such a notion of "double truth" is simply that it is not true. Our instinct "impels us to seek for harmony in the truths of science and the truths of Religion" (57).

Argyll placed great weight on humanity's preconceptual, instinctive, and intuitive insights. The unity of truth was one of these—"a necessity of the mind," he called it. Another intuition that remained self-evident to Argyll throughout his life was the apprehension of purpose in all of nature. He commented on how laboriously scientific writers try to expel what he called "the necessary and involuntary Anthropopsychism of human thought and speech." Scientists invent phrases like "reflex action" that attempt to avoid the fact of human reason, "but it is well worthy of observation that in exact proportion as these phrases do avoid it, they become incompetent to describe fully the facts of science" (1887, 298). So it is that eminent scientists inevitably turn to the metaphoric language of personification in order adequately to convey the facts before them. Darwin is the chief case in point. The "greatest observer" of nature, Argyll wrote, continually reverts to the mental attributes of Purpose in speaking of plants and animals—of the tip of a root "perceiving the air to be moister on one side than on the other." Or take Darwin's basic metaphor, natural selection:

In this phrase Nature is supposed to act as a pigeon-fancier acts in so breeding his favorite birds as to produce varieties with specially developed powers or aspects. The whole attractiveness of this phrase . . . and as accounting for a great variety of accomplished results, depends upon the analogy between the working of "Nature" as a personification and the personal working of a breeder of stocks. (1887, 289)

Darwin did not, of course, use this language for a theological purpose but quite naturally, because "he cannot help it." The great naturalist's language was "an instinctive recognition of that special kind of agency which is, indeed, familiarly known to us as existing within ourselves, but which is also universally recognized and identified as existing outside of us, and around us, on every side . . . not less pervading than it is mysterious" (Argyll 1896, 9). When Darwin and his followers used the language of mind and contrivance to describe adaptations, they did so simply because the language helps to understand the facts—a language eminently teleological and anthropopsychic.

Argyll contended that science is possible because our minds are part of nature and can know nature and thereby also transcend nature. He found a curious inconsistency in the position of the scientific positivists and the materialists. They recognized that humans alone possess a rational mind and stand alone outside of nature. But how does this "accord with the great conception whose truth and sweep become everyday more apparent—the Unity of Nature? How can it be true that Man is so outside of that Unity that the very notion of seeing anything like himself in it is the greatest of all philosophical heresies?" If a human being is the product of the evolutionary process, in every atom of body and mind a child of nature, "is it not in the highest degree illogical so to separate him from it as to condemn him from seeing in it some image of himself?" Is it not remarkable, Argyll pointed out, that

we find that the very men who tell us that we are not One with everything above us, are the same who insist that we are One with everything beneath us. Whatever there is in us or about us which is purely animal we see everywhere; but whatever there is in us purely intellectual and moral, we delude ourselves if we think we see it anywhere. . . . There is nothing in Nature or above it which corresponds to our Forethought, or Design, or Purpose. (1887, 278–80)

Following his mentor, Richard Owen, Argyll thought it incontrovertible that the growth of every organism—and nature taken as a whole—revealed a plan, a pattern. Although any immediate function may be absent, yet it will manifest itself in the future. When Owen referred to certain jointed bones in the whale, in the mole, in the bat, and in man as the same, he did not mean

LORETTE WILMOT LIBRARY
NAZARETH COLLEGE

that they are physically the same bones, or that they have the same uses. "He means that in a purely ideal or mental conception of the plan of all Vertebrate skeletons, these bones occupy the same relative place—relative, that is, not to origin or use, but to the Plan or conception of the skeleton as a whole" (1867, 33). Here mind or the "Supernatural" element is the one unquestionable fact. Whatever may be the physical means, they imply mental purpose. Biology, of all the sciences, is, according to Argyll, the most anthropopsychic because it inevitably uses the language and concepts of development that imply adaptive purpose:

> For in the course of this development, it is above all things remarkable, that always in the earliest stages every step in growth must go before the use which it is to serve when finished. No Organ can be used until it is fit for use, and the gradual adaptation to that use, through innumerable stages of growth and of development, is an adaptation which is always anticipatory and prophetic. (1887, 262)

For Argyll it was not surprising that structures often should run ahead of function, since every creature must have existed potentially in the earliest "germs" that have an innate tendency to develop along certain lines. Hence, "it is quite intelligible that some portions of the perfect structure should be traceable in creatures that are never destined to have them completed, or to need their services." This, Argyll believed, was a more intelligible explanation for the presence of vestigial organs, what Darwin called "silent members," than Darwin's explanation of descent from an animal for whom the organ served some use. It was here that Argyll could appeal to a "grander teleology" (1887, 263).

At first sight the presence of useless structures and organs may appear to count against the supremacy of mind and purpose in organic development, but our observations have been too circumscribed; they have not taken in a larger canvas. "Exceptions to one narrow rule, such as we might have laid down and followed for ourselves, are now seen to be in strict subordination to a larger rule which it would never have entered into our imagination to conceive. These useless members . . . which puzzle us so much, are parts of a universal Plan" (1867, 206–7).

Argyll not only saw order in such a larger purpose; he saw progress as well. The long, progressive developments

> bring purpose into view, because nothing is more striking in the history of organic life, than the growing adaptations between the new forms of life and the function which many of them do now actually

discharge with reference to man. We can hardly estimate how different this life of ours would have been, and would now be, if the beasts
and birds which are capable of domestication, were omitted from the
world. Without sheep and oxen, and without the horse, we could not
use or enjoy life as we do now. Yet we know that all of these were
introduced very recently, and in a special correlation, as to time, with
the introduction of our own species. (1896, 174–75)

In cases such as these, Argyll considered fortuity inconceivable. He saw the
horse, as Buckland had seen the coal deposits in the Midlands, as predestined for the use of man.

Scottish theologian James Iverach (1839–1922) took a bolder stand
on Darwin's doctrine than did either McCosh or the Duke of Argyll. He
acknowledged that the evidence for natural selection "seems irresistible"
and "a good working hypothesis" but, like all hypotheses, was not without
difficulties (Iverach 1894, 107). Iverach had taken honors in mathematics
and the physical sciences at the University of Edinburgh and then prepared
for the ministry at New College. He served Free Church parishes for almost
twenty years before his appointment to the chair of Christian apologetics at
the Free Church College, Aberdeen. He remained there for three decades,
occupying a variety of chairs and serving as principal of the college from
1905 to 1907. His greatest contribution lay in addressing the issues between
theology and natural science, the subject of his two most important books,
Christianity and Evolution (1894) and *Theism in the Light of Present Science
and Philosophy* (1899).

Iverach was convinced that the central question between modern science and theology was the same as that which engaged the ancient Greek
atomists against those Greeks who postulated mind as the true cause—with
the important difference, of course, that the modern antagonists were more
knowledgeable of the universal reign of law. This meant that theology was
"able to separate from the idea of God everything like caprice, arbitrariness,
whimsicality" (1894, 54). The question between the two parties, however,
remained: "What is implied in the thought of an orderly universe, moving
under law?" Some of the naturalists rejected the idea of a designed evolution, but Darwin's doctrine, Iverach was convinced, supported such a higher
teleology. Iverach sought to show that intelligence and purpose were not
only not opposed to a mechanical science but clearly strengthened it, for
"purpose excludes arbitrariness and irregularity." He opposed those theologies that "were constantly looking about for imperfections in a mechanical theory in order to find a chink through which a theistic argument may
enter" (26). On the contrary, each new law and convergence of laws was, for

Iverach, fresh testimony for theism, since intelligence is the source of order and the ground of law.

For Iverach the nub of the issue between the theist and all purely mechanistic doctrines of evolution, or the nebular hypothesis, was the latter's claim that causation advances from the simple to the complex. The nebular hypothesis exemplified the issue. The unity of the primitive nebulosity could not, Iverach contended, have been simple. It must have been complex, a unity of elements in relation to one another. "It is not undifferentiated stuff, but definite molecules existing in definite relations. It is not chaotic but orderly, and existing in relations that can be thought. Thus the unity of the primitive nebulosity is already rational and intelligible, and the outcome also will be rational" (17). Iverach argued that the unity of related elements cannot, as such, be only material; it must also be rational. And so it is with organic evolution. The evolutionist has to take into account a multitude of factors and cannot, like the mathematician or physicist, neglect numerous elements for the sake of simplicity. This Iverach saw as the great error in Spencer's notion that the effect is more complex than the cause. Surely, he argued, "in any view of a cause, we must take into account all the conditions necessary for the production of the effect. If we take these into account, we shall be constrained to say the cause is as complex as the effect" (32).

It follows, then, Iverach believed, that evolution is best explained by purpose and not by mechanism. While the chain of causes and effects is, of course, the same in both cases,

> in the one case we contemplate the bare result, in the other case we look at it as intended, and the ordered causes are grouped together with a view to accomplish the end. In the last event we have a cause sufficient to bring about the result; in the former case we have no account whatever of the order, adaptation, and method of the universe. We must go back to the fortuitous concourse of atoms, and trust to chance . . . chance looked at as a real cause.

Again, while it is quite appropriate to speak of chance in regard to the calculation of probabilities as a way of expressing our ignorance, it is not allowable, Iverach argued, "to speak of chance as a substitute for causation, and to this we are brought if we deny purpose to the universe" (66–67).

Iverach was convinced that Darwin's theory of selection implied evolution by design, despite the fact that other Darwinists, such as Huxley, saw evolution "as a fortuitous result." Huxley had contrasted evolutionary teleology and natural selection as the difference between a rifle bullet and grape shot. "According to teleology," Huxley wrote, "each organism is like a rifle bullet fired straight at a mark; according to Darwin, organisms are like grape shot, of which one hits something and the rest fall wide" (T. H. Huxley 1893–94a, 84). Iverach countered that, first, Huxley was wrong to suppose that teleology requires that "each organism is fired straight at a mark."

> What is necessary is that the organism hits the mark. If the hitting of the mark is accomplished by a persistent process prolonged through-out the centuries, implying completeness of arrangement and adjust-ment of means to ends in a complicated series, then the result is not against teleology; on the contrary, it simply heightens our view of the skill of the teleologist. (Iverach 1894, 105)

Second, Huxley's "grape shot view" of evolution implies fortuity or chance, yet it was he who was indignant at those who "charge Mr. Darwin with hav-ing attempted to reinstate the old pagan Goddess Chance." "Do they believe," Huxley had asked, "that anything in this universe happens without reason and without cause . . . or could not have been predicted by anyone who had sufficient insight into the order of nature?" But who, asked Iverach, "has done more than Professor Huxley to fasten the charge on Mr. Darwin of having reinstated the goddess of Chance? How does one reconcile Huxley's grape-shot illustration with 'the confession of the universality of order, and of the absolute validity in all times and under all circumstances of the law of causation'? Where is the causation in the organism which hits and the organ-isms which fall wide?" (1894, 106).

Huxley's apparent confusion about chance and causality aside, both the-ology and natural science must leave chance and accident out of account. When this is done, teleology, Iverach believed, gives the better explanation of the history of life on the earth. From the religious perspective, natural selection can be seen as expressing the sum of all the causes that have con-verged to the achievement of the ends that we observe in the world today. So observed, Iverach believed that natural selection actually strengthens belief in a designed evolution. In any case, the Christian creed does no more than "simply affirm that God is the Maker of the world and all that is in it, and does not say anything about the way and manner in which He made them" (107).

The writings of McCosh, Argyll, and Iverach were typical of the efforts to maintain a unitary vision of truth and of science and theology, a com-mitment to the reign of law in both spheres, and a rejection of particular divine interventions to account for the apparent discontinuities in the natu-ral world. Paradoxically, as God's agency now is seen as working immanently through natural laws and processes, the belief in a particular providence is turning out to be more ambiguous and problematic. God's immanence now appeared to many to accentuate his absence. R. H. Hutton's remark that the uniformity of nature had become the veil behind which God is hidden was, for some, all too plain. This "grander" teleology of the whole raised doubts for many persons about the infinite value of each *individual* soul as rooted and safe in God's care and solicitude.

The ambiguities of the new theistic cosmology are especially pronounced in the writings of Henry Drummond (1851–1897), the most popular and influential of the Scottish evangelical theologians. Drummond, the second son of a wealthy merchant, entered the University of Edinburgh in 1866 with little sense of direction. In 1870 he switched from the arts faculty to New College to study for the Free Church ministry. However, his interest in science had already been aroused by P. G. Tait, professor of natural philosophy in Edinburgh, and during his three years at New College he studied several of the sciences part-time at the university. During his third year of divinity, Drummond was attracted to the work of the evangelists Dwight L. Moody and Ira Sankey, the result of a mission they had held in Edinburgh. Postponing his final year of theological training, Drummond joined Moody in his evangelistic efforts. After some delay, Drummond completed his theological course and, on the recommendation of one of his science professors, was appointed lecturer in natural science in the Free Church College in Glasgow in 1877. Drummond was advanced to professor in 1883 and remained in this post until shortly before his death. However, for a quarter of a century he combined his academic responsibilities with an active ministry of evangelism, not only in Britain but on the Continent, in America, and the Far East. He also found time to carry out experiments as a field geologist in the western United States in 1879 and to conduct scientific work during a six-month expedition to Africa in 1883 and 1884, on which he reported in *Tropical Africa* (1888).

Drummond's effort to join natural science and theology in a new cosmological vision is most clearly and fully set out in his two best-selling volumes, *Natural Law in the Spiritual World* (1884) and *The Ascent of Man* (1894). *Natural Law in the Spiritual World*, the book of interest here, was enormously successful. It sold a thousand copies a month in Britain a year after its publication. In 1905 the hardback edition continued to sell a thousand copies a year, and it is estimated that during the first twenty-five years of its publication, roughly half a million copies of the various English editions of the book had been sold (J. R. Moore 1983, 383–417).

In the preface to *Natural Law in the Spiritual World*, Drummond declared that he had set himself the task of demonstrating that the "Laws of the Spiritual World" were *identical* to the "Laws of the Natural World" by attempting to specify those natural laws operative in the spiritual domain. He was confident that what was required to rescue religious belief from the present state of uncertainty was "a truly scientific theology," one that would involve "the introduction of Law among the Phenomena of the Spiritual World" (Drummond 1886, v–vi, ix). The key to Drummond's effort to draw science and theology together—and "to exhibit Nature in Religion"—was the "Law of Continuity," the popular articulation of which he had found in W. R. Grove's 1866 Presidential Address to the British Association, entitled "The Correlation of Physical Forces." The law had been advanced more recently by two Scottish physicists, Balfour Stewart (1828–1887) and Drummond's earlier mentor, P. G. Tait, in their anonymously published *The Unseen Universe* (1875).

Grove had found that the most convincing argument for the continuity of law throughout the entire universe was our genuine difficulty in conceiving a real *per saltum* act of nature. "Who," he asked, "would not be astonished at beholding an oak tree spring up in a day, and not from seed or shoot?" While our ignorance of the past may not allow us presently to explain why and how matter is impressed with certain structural tendencies, "we are satisfied that continuity is a law of nature, the true expression of the action of Almighty Power," rather than "to look for special interventions of creative power in changes that are difficult to understand" (Grove 1867, 343–44). Stewart and Tait built on Grove's doctrine of the correlation of forces or energy. The whole universe was, of course, subject to the law of conservation of energy. However, the second law of thermodynamics implied that this visible world would come to an end in time. Nevertheless, they insisted, the uniformity of nature denies such an outcome for the universe taken as a whole. Since the principle of continuity upon which all such arguments are based still demands a continuance of the universe, "we are forced to believe that there is something beyond that which is visible," an "unseen universe" that exists independently of, but in communication with, the visible universe (Stewart and Tait 1875, 64). The visible and invisible worlds are, according to Stewart and Tait, connected by the transference of energy from one sphere to another. Divine providence is, then, to be understood in terms of the transference of energy from the invisible to the visible sphere, according to the operation of natural laws. Events that may appear miraculous from our visible perspective need "no longer be regarded as absolute breaks of continuity . . . but only as the result of peculiar action of the invisible upon the visible universe" (189). If we could see the "Great Whole" we would recognize that miracles are not "the absolute interference of the Divine Governor," for God's actions are not to be viewed as "in defiance of law, but in fulfillment of it" (60ff.).

Building on the theological implications of the "Law of Continuity" as developed by Grove and by Stewart and Tait, Drummond carried the argument one step further by contending that the laws governing the spiritual world were *identical* to laws of the natural world:

> The Natural Laws, as the Law of Continuity might well warn us, do not stop with the visible and then give place to a new set of Laws bearing a strong similitude to them. The Laws of the invisible are the same laws, projections of the natural not supernatural. Analogous Phenomena are not the fruit of parallel Laws, but the same Laws—Laws which at one end, as it were, may be dealing with Matter, at the other end with Spirit. (Drummond 1886, 11)

If theology is to have any foundation and credence, if the spiritual world is a real world, then "in the nature of things they ought to come into the sphere of law" (20). The mark of the unity and perfection of the whole is the presence of an infinite variety of phenomena and a complexity of relations conjoined with the great simplicity of law. "Science will be complete when all known phenomena can be arranged in one vast circle in which a few well known Laws shall form the radii . . . uniting all to a common center" (22). To show that the most characteristic phenomena of the spiritual world are already to be found to be drawn within that circle by science was the object of Drummond's task.

Drummond was impatient with the idea that there were other laws in the spiritual world beyond those now known in our experience of the natural world. He insisted that the margin left for such additional laws is small (49). In any case, such new laws "cannot diminish by a hair's-breadth the size of territory where the old laws still prevail. . . . The region of the knowable in the spiritual world is at least as wide as these regions of the Natural World which by the help of these Laws have been explored" (50). The greatest of the theological laws simply "are the Laws of Nature in disguise." The task of theology is then "to take off the mask and disclose to a waning skepticism the naturalness of the supernatural" (52). Drummond was confident that when theology carried out this splendid task, humanity would see "that to be loyal to all of Nature, they must be loyal to the part defined as Spiritual" (xxii). Science and theology must work to their reciprocal benefit. In the nature of things we cannot be separated into two incoherent halves:

> Even as the contribution of Science to Religion is the vindication of the naturalness of the Supernatural, so the gift of Religion to Science is the demonstration of the supernaturalness of the Natural. Thus as the

Supernatural becomes slowly Natural, will also the Natural become slowly Supernatural, until in the impersonal authority of Law men everywhere recognize the Authority of God. (xxiii)

Drummond's refusal to divide theology and science into two irrelative spheres may be judged commendable, and his empirical approach to theology signaled the increasing attention that theologians would give to religious experience in the 1890s and beyond. But when one reflects on the ease with which Drummond suggested continuities between the laws of the natural and the spiritual worlds—for example, in his writings on such themes as death, mortification, and eternal life—one cannot help but wince at the forced and shallow comparisons that he drew. For example, on the awesome subject of death, Drummond called upon Herbert Spencer's "masterly elucidation." We are to understand, Spencer said, that "the root idea of Death" is "that breakdown in an organism which throws it out of correspondence with some necessary part of the environment" (Drummond 1886, 151). Drummond did not appear to recognize the abysmal difference between what the New Testament portrays as the personal attentiveness of a loving heavenly Father and his own insistence that men everywhere should recognize the authority of God in the impersonal authority of law.

Frederick Temple (1821–1902), the Anglican bishop of Exeter and later archbishop of Canterbury, had demonstrated his progressive attitude toward science in his contribution to *Essays and Reviews* in 1860 while serving as headmaster of Rugby School. In 1884, as bishop, he sought to reconcile theology and the new Darwinian naturalism in his Bampton Lectures on *The Relations between Religion and Science*. It is interesting to note that 1884 also was the year that Argyll's *Unity of Nature* and Drummond's *Natural Law in the Spiritual World* were published—the high-water mark in the effort to achieve a unitary vision of science and religion and a post-Paley, Darwinistic defense of divine immanence and teleology.

The crux of Temple's lectures is the argument that natural theology is strengthened by Darwinism. What is touched by Darwin's doctrine "is not the evidence of design but the mode in which design is executed" (Temple 1884, 114). In an often cited passage, Temple summed up his view that the Creator

impressed on certain particles of matter which, either at the beginning or at some point in the history of His creation He endowed with life, such inherent powers that in the ordinary course of time living creatures such as the present were developed. The creative power remains the same in either case; the design with which that creative power was exercized remains the same. *He did not make the things,*

we may say; no, but He made them make themselves. And surely this
rather adds than withdraws force from the great argument. (114–15;
italics added)

It is more befitting of the Deity, Temple proposed, to conceive him impressing his will once for all on his creation "than by special acts of creation to be
perpetually modifying what He had previously made" (115). The grandeur is
in the Creator's original plan that is thereafter carried out by natural means.
"There is more divine foresight, there is less divine interposition; and whatever has been taken from the latter has been added to the former" (123).

Temple believed that theology's foundations were secure, since scientific
materialism was incapable of explaining the two fundamental convictions of
religion: God's original creation and the reality of the human soul. Indeed,
for Temple, these two supernatural acts appeared to be the full compass of
God's direct commerce with the world: "However far back Science may be
able to push its beginning, there still must lie behind that beginning the original act of creation." Similarly, "Science cannot yet assert, and it is tolerably
certain will never assert that . . . the spiritual faculty, which is man's characteristic prerogative, was not given to man by a direct creative act as soon as
the body . . . had been sufficiently developed to receive it" (106, 186).

Charles Kingsley, too, hymned the praises of evolutionary naturalism
for its having banished the concept of God as "a master-magician," as he
called that deity. Kingsley believed that evolution now left only two choices:
"the absolute empire of accident, and a living immanent ever-working God"
(Mrs. Kingsley 1876, 253; see also C. Kingsley 1871, 369–73). Darwinistic
theologians such as Frederick Temple appeared, however, to offer a third and
more deistical alternative.

Christian Darwinism: Design and Teleology

As we have seen, the mid-1880s represented the pinnacle of post-Paleyian
teleology as represented by Argyll, Temple, and Drummond. The late 1880s
and the 1890s disclosed an even greater openness to Darwin's theory (as
distinct from the evolutionary theory of Spencer and the neo-Lamarckians)
by orthodox theologians such as Iverach and the English Anglo-Catholic
Aubrey Moore. Evolutionary theory, now reinforced by a renewed interest
in patristic thought and neo-Hegelian philosophy at Oxford and the Scottish
universities, gave impetus to new theologies of "divine immanence." Some
of these sought to repudiate the naïve optimism and progressivism of Argyll

and Drummond, but their own realism also entailed a rethinking of special providence and teleology.

We begin this account with Aubrey Moore (1843–1890). Moore entered Exeter College, Oxford, in 1867 and was elected a Fellow and tutor of St. John's College in 1873. After serving as a parish priest for four years, he returned to Oxford in 1880 to take up tutorships simultaneously at Keble College and Magdalen College, posts he held until his early death. He was extraordinarily talented and learned, shown by the fact that he was an examiner in both the School of *Literae Humaniores* and the Faculty of Theology. Moreover, he served as curator of the Botanic Gardens in Oxford.

Moore was thoroughly at home not only in the field of botany but also in biology and evolutionary theory, occasioned in part through his friendships with the able Darwinians E. B. Poulton and George Romanes. In his memoir of Moore, included in the latter's posthumous essays, Romanes wrote:

> If it were true that no one was more fully imbued with the faith spiritual, it was quite as true that no one was more fully imbued with the faith scientific, or the assured conviction that, lead where she may, it is the first intellectual duty of a man to follow the guidance of science, leaving all the "consequences" to take care of themselves. (A. L. Moore 1890a, xxviii)

Moore wrote a dozen or so trenchant papers on aspects of Darwinism, on August Weismann, on Romanes's work on mental evolution in humans, and on Argyll, Temple, and Drummond. We will focus attention here on his reflections on evolutionary theory and the new scientific naturalism as these relate to theological ideas concerning design, teleology, and providence.

Moore rejected as false the antithesis between natural evolution and supernatural creation of species, popularized by naturalists such as the German Ernst Haeckel. In an address before the Church Congress at Reading in 1883, Moore argued for a third alternative, what he was willing to call either "supernatural evolution or natural creation." The separation between evolution and creation is, he argued, simply false. Moore feared that Christian theologians had acquiesced to a form of dualism. "They are content to let the student of nature devote himself to the elucidation of natural processes" as long as the naturalist is not a dogmatic antitheist. The defender of science is, of course, more than willing to accept such a division of territory. "'Give me,' he will say, 'the region of the knowable, the intelligible, and your fancy or your faith may revel as it will in the region of the unknown.'" The naturalist will insist that nature is the sphere of intelligible law with no capricious divine irruptions or interferences, no lawless miraculous interventions. But "very soon those who have thus unwisely become the champions of the supernatural against the natural find that as knowledge grows they have to retire farther and farther back." Moore protested that it is impossible for the theologian even to imply that God's work is partly natural and partly super-natural. "The moment that we accept such a division as real, we practically recognize a power other than God," and nature becomes the sphere of order, law, and rational procedure, while God is represented as "a principle of inde-terminateness which it is hard to distinguish from caprice." There cannot be, Moore asserted, any divine interpositions in nature, since God's creative activity is everywhere. "*For the Christian theologian the facts of nature are the acts of God*" (1883, 48–49; cf. 1904, 43–44).

Moore welcomed Darwin as helping to save British theology from a crude deism that represented God "as an occasional Visitor":

> Science had pushed the deist's God farther and farther away, and at the moment when it seemed as if He would be thrust out altogether, Darwinism appeared, and, under the guise of a foe, did the work of a friend. It has conferred upon philosophy and religion an inestimable benefit, by shewing us that we must choose between two alternatives. Either God is everywhere present in nature, or he is nowhere. . . . He cannot delegate His power to demigods called "second causes." (1904, 73–74)

Darwinian science, Moore argued, had shown that there is nothing useless or meaningless in nature, nothing due to caprice, or without a cause, or outside the reign of law: "This belief in the universality of law and order is the scien-tific analogue of the Christian belief in Providence" (A. Moore 1889, 197).

Moore was deeply concerned about the deistic tendencies that he observed in the apologetics of much post-Paleyian natural theology. Commendable as were the efforts of, for example, Bishop Temple's Bampton Lectures in reha-bilitating a wider teleology and the argument from design, comments about God impressing his will "*once for all*" on his creation, or God providing for nature's variety by "His *one original impress*" were hardly Christian. "It is one thing," Moore pointed out, "to speak of God as 'declaring the end from the beginning,' it is another to use language which seems to imply . . . that God withdraws Himself from His Creation and leaves it evolve itself" (A. Moore 1889, 87). Moore's theological critique of the deistic tendencies in the writings of some Christian apologists, such as Frederick Temple, may be telling from a traditional Christian providentialism, but as J. H. Brooke sug-gests, Moore failed to recognize that Darwin's position is itself semi-deistic.

For Darwin, the details of the evolutionary process were left, of course, to a certain fortuity, thus leaving God or the divine laws free of the responsibility for the more devilish aspects of the creative process. (In chapter 3, we will see that Moore addressed this problem in a radical, if not wholly adequate, proposal.) Darwin's position points to the issue soon to be posed by the conception of a finite God (Brooke, in private correspondence).

Moore was confident that Darwinism had "done good service in overthrowing the dogma of separate creations" and the depiction of God as a kind of "absentee landlord." Darwinism "*as a theory* is infinitely more Christian than a theory of 'Special Creation,'" since Moore believed "it implies the immanence of God in nature, and the omnipresence of his creative power." The special creationists

> seem to have failed to notice that *a theory of occasional intervention implies as its correlative a theory of ordinary absence.* . . . Anything more opposed to the language of the Bible and the Fathers can hardly be imagined. . . . Cataclysmal geology and special creation are the scientific analogue of Deism. Order, development, law, are the analogue of the Christian view of God. (A. L. Moore 1889, 184–85)

Moore's critique of an implicit deism in some of the defenses of a wider teleology, as well as his insistence on a thoroughgoing divine immanence, appear sound from the perspective of a classical Christian theism. However, when he asserts that "the facts of nature are the acts of God" (1883, 48–49), Moore raises real questions about a personal providence, human freedom, theodicy, and hidden panentheist tendencies that he either did not appear to see or did not have the opportunity to explore.

Biologist George Romanes (1848–94) was a friend of Moore and of Darwin whom many thought would be the great man's successor. A brilliant young scientist, Romanes was elected to the Royal Society in 1879 at the age of thirty-one, and was, for more than a decade after 1874, the most resolute of the supporters of Darwin's theory. Romanes's Darwinism gives little indication, however, of his stormy intellectual career—from youthful faith, then to skepticism and scientific naturalism, then on to a "pure" agnosticism and back to faith, to what can be called a Jamesian "right to believe." Here we will examine only his mature thought on natural theology, on design and teleology.

During the 1880s and early 1890s, while he pursued his work on evolutionary psychology, Romanes resumed his earlier reflections on evolution and theology. In a lecture on "The Scientific Evidence of Organic Evolution" (1881) he returned, once again, to the argument from design. While he acknowledged that Darwinism was unquestionably contrary to the Paleyian understanding of teleology, he unexpectedly announced that Darwin's theory had no logical point of contact with a theory of design in the larger sense, that is, "that behind all secondary causes of a physical kind there is a primary cause of a mental kind" (Romanes 1881). Having admitted as much in principle, Romanes nevertheless remained agnostic about intelligent design. He persisted in this frame of mind as long as a decade later, although it is clear that his sentiments were moving back to a theistic hypothesis. His thoughts on the moral issue raised by theodicy were darker, as we will see later.

In a paper delivered before the Aristotelian Society in 1889, Romanes argued that even if the world were explainable in terms of natural causes, it would not rule out the possibility that God used natural causation instrumentally. The philosopher Samuel Alexander (1859–1938) had argued that intelligent design was negated by the fact that "the fair order of nature" is achieved only "by a wholesale waste and sacrifice," in short, by the "failures" of the less fit. Romanes answered that this presumes that what Alexander called "failures" are really such. But "so soon as we extend the area of our vision, so as to take cognizance of ["the failures'"] relations to the system of Nature as a whole, we see that even within the sphere of human observation they can no longer be designated failures," since they are so "only if it be supposed that their *telos* is that of maintaining themselves: not that of ceasing to do so, if it need be, in order to secure the higher or more general *telos* of advancing their type"—which Romanes considered a matter of observable fact (1889–1890, 72–73; 1896b, 56ff., 92–94). Such a modus operandi is no failure, assuming design in nature, if it achieves the higher purposes of design. This is so despite the fact that such a development involves the continual elimination of less efficient types. What may be called "random trial" or "blind blundering" is only valid against what Alexander called "a 'Carpenter-God,' i.e., that if there be Design in Nature at all, it must everywhere be *special* Design." Romanes conceded that design in this latter sense had been "totally destroyed by the proof of natural selection" (1889–1890, 73).

We have seen that Romanes's theological ruminations in his last years of illness reveal a spiritual struggle that found resolution in a right to believe, in a religious sensibility that also is a marked characteristic of the writings of Arthur Balfour and William James. Romanes acknowledged that all the deductions of a divine existence and purpose in nature presume a preformed theistic supposition or belief, analogous to the natural scientist's belief in the unity of nature, which our reason is capable of interpreting. What the theistic prepossession amounts to is only "the argument that there is nothing in the constitution of Nature inimical to the hypothesis of Design"; it does not offer independent verification of that hypothesis. "Innumerable, indeed, are the evidences of Design in Nature if once a Designer be supposed." The reason, simply, is that we have no means of ascertaining what is itself the cause of the uniformity of nature. There are, Romanes concluded, two, and only two, viable alternatives: divine immanence or mechanical necessity. "In short, is it original or derived—final, and therefore inexplicable because self-existing; or is it the effect of a higher cause in the existence of a disposing Mind?" (1889–1890, 74–75).

From a purely scientific point of view, Romanes was at one with his mentor Darwin: The question of design must rest in a "pure agnosticism." But Romanes now was convinced that the issue need not rest with science; the ultimate, *metaphysical* question of causation is a legitimate one, and the answer to that question cannot be determined by natural science, nor by abstract philosophy, nor by any inquiry concerning the truth of a supposed revelation. "It can only be determined by those mysterious depths of human personality which lie beyond the reach of human investigation" and which finally decide for "the presence or the absence of an indissoluble persuasion that 'God is.'" Romanes confessed that his own "antecedent belief" was "extremely vague" and that he therefore did not perceive evidence of design in nature. However, he recognized that for others there may be, indeed must be, an immense body of evidence for design. The cogency of the evidence, Romanes now was certain, "is properly or rationally influenced for each individual mind by the character and degree of the antecedent belief in question." As long as the grounds for holding one's antecedent theistic belief are sound, that person is as logically justified in seeing the evidence for design in nature as the other person is justified in not seeing it (1889–1890, 75–76).

Romanes represented a newly emerging religious sensibility, more skeptical of the pretensions both of science and the new natural theology. Personally, he was not persuaded by the "wider teleology" of Argyll or Mivart, and, through his friend Aubrey Moore, he recognized the limitations of Frederick Temple's "deism." Romanes's contemporaneity is also reflected in his break with the idea of the unity of truth and the effort to achieve a higher reconciliation of science and theology, the view that characterized the thought of most of the thinkers examined in this chapter. Romanes was convinced that the assumption of a personal Providence, which he insisted was essential to a Christian theism, was incompatible with scientific causal explanation. "In their purest forms," he wrote, "Science and Religion really have no point of logical contact." If science could transcend the limits of phenomenal relativity and human limitation, then it could perhaps speak on matters theological, that is, the supernatural. "But obviously, if Science could do this, she would cease to be Science." On the other hand, theology is "incompetent to affect Science," since "her theory of ontology cannot have any reference to the How of phenomenal causation." The two spheres move in entirely different planes. Theology does not explain *any* phenomenon in nature; "it is itself an ultimate and universal explanation of all possible phenomena taken collectively." When these two departments of thought are allowed to overlap, only confusion and conflict can result (1896b, 43–46). Such a radical separation of science and theology had already become the dominant view in Germany, largely through the revival of neo-Kantian philosophy and the growing influence of the Ritschlian school of theology, particularly in the writings of Wilhelm Herrmann (Gregory 1992, ch. 6). It never commanded such a position in British thought in the nineteenth century. Some would consider that to be a gain, for while the radical separation was able to claim an autonomy for theological belief, the cost of such a dissociation may have been too high a price to pay because it may have restricted theology's scope to purely existential questions of value.

We have seen that British theology in the immediate post-Darwin decades was required to reconceive the ideas of providential design and teleology. This resulted in a shift in natural theology to notions of a wider teleology and new, more thoroughgoing reconceptions of divine immanence. While these doctrines were more congruent with the now dominant evolutionary worldview, they also required a rethinking about God's providential agency in a law-abiding world that, for some, also entailed the revising of anthropocentric views as they recognized a more modest role of individual human lives in the divine purpose. This, in turn, sparked new questioning on such matters as theodicy, miracle, and prayer, and initial explorations of panentheistic doctrines of God's interdependence with the world.

CHAPTER 3

God and the World—
The Reign of Law

Providence, Evil, and Theodicy

I have long ago found out how little I can discover about God's absolute love or absolute righteousness, from a universe in which everything is eternally *eating* everything else. . . . The study of nature can teach no *moral theology*. It may unteach it, if the roots of moral theology be not already healthy and deep in the mind.

Charles Kingsley, to F. D. Maurice

Darwin's solution had also to be the theologian's solution. . . . Precisely because waste, pain, and suffering were endemic to the creative process they could be given a new rationale.

John Hedley Brooke

[God] is on the side of the cat and the mouse. . . . He does not will but He cannot help, the conflict and the agony. His will is plainly to minimize and abolish it if possible. . . . It is, therefore, a libel to say He is careless of individuals. He cares for them and for nothing else. He does not sacrifice them as means to some far-off, universal and impersonal end.

George Tyrrell

The Reign of Law and Theodicy before Darwin

We have observed that the early nineteenth-century British discussion of providential design and purpose was marked by a considerable variety of proposals.

However, there was a rather broad consensus on the question of teleology. This is also true on the issue of theodicy. Not only the theodicy of William Paley and those of the Bridgewater Treatises but also the theodicy of writers attracted to a "wider" teleology all concurred in their appeal either to a more immediate or to some ultimate harmony or utility in nature's fecundity. It is only in the last years of the century, however, that less sanguine theological voices were heard on the subject—and they raised profound questions.

The last chapters of Paley's *Natural Theology* (1802) were specifically directed to a discussion and defense of the goodness of God. Evil was not to be denied, but neither could it be seen as simply opposed to God's design and nature's contrivance. While Paley did not hesitate to point out the "superfecundity" of nature and the struggle and apparent waste which that fecundity exhibits, he nonetheless believed that "in a vast plurality of instances the design of the contrivance is *beneficial*," especially if we take the longer view. Evil is not, then, without design and compensation. Physical pain, for example, "may be violent and frequent; but it is seldom both violent and long continued: and its pauses and intermissions become positive pleasures. It has the power of shedding a satisfaction over intervals of ease, which . . . few enjoyments exceed" (Paley 1802, 345). As the author of an appreciative study of Paley remarks, the words of this sanguine author of *Natural Theology* "must have been cold comfort to the less hearty souls who could not appreciate the 'wonderful manner' in which mortal illness reconciles men to the idea of death" (Mahieu 1976, 346).

If Paley's appeals to the compensations derived from struggle, pain, disease, and death itself are astonishing, more provoking, certainly, are his arguments for the inequalities of civil life. For Paley, the disparity in social status must be seen as divinely contrived, and the poverty of the mass of society, he suggests, is a prod to enterprise, diligence, and improvement:

> Providence, which foresaw, which appointed, indeed, the necessity to which human affairs are subjected (and against which it were impious to complain), hath contrived, that, whilst fortunes are only for the few, the rest of mankind may be happy without them. . . .
>
> The labour of the world is carried on by *service*, that is, by one man working under another man's direction. I take it for granted that this is the best way of conducting business, because all nations and ages have adopted it. (Paley 1825, 320, 324)

The natural theodicies of the Bridgewater Treatises generally replicated the theodicy of Paley. However, as Frank Turner demonstrates, these writers also prepared the way for the secularization of theodicy in the post-Darwinian decades—or for what, in some cases, might be called the transformation of theodicy to *anthropodicy* (Turner 1993, 101–27). The Bridgewater authors rationalized suffering by appealing to those larger utilitarian goals that justify the competition and struggle in both animal and human societies. Peter Mark Roget's mode of argument in *Animal and Vegetable Physiology Considered with Reference to Natural Theology* (1839) is characteristic. For Roget the superfecundity of nature reveals "the inexhaustible fund from which she has so prodigally drawn forth the means requisite for the maintenance" of her diversified life, for the repetition of this diversity in endless perpetuity, "and for their subordination to one harmonious scheme of general good." Even the apparently distressing fact of beings living off the destruction of one another can be shown to contribute to a greater good:

> We must take into account the vast accession that accrues to the mass of animal enjoyment from the exercize of those powers and faculties which are called forth by this state of constant activity; and when this consideration is combined, as it ought to be, with that of the immense multiplication of life which is admissible upon this system alone, we shall find ample reason for acknowledging the wisdom and the benevolent intentions of the Creator, who, for the sake of a vastly superior good, has permitted the existence of a minor evil. (Roget 1839, 25)

The Paleyian theodicy was, in its essentials, carried forward by other pre-Darwinian thinkers who adapted it to a "grander teleology." Scottish philosopher James McCosh exemplifies the argument. What impressed McCosh was the extraordinary way in which the array of singular organisms and processes in nature skillfully conspire to achieve wonderful ends. No organism is useless; each plays its part. Apparent accidents are only so, since they are the mysterious means by which God accomplishes his wise purposes. McCosh's theodicy was Leibnitzian. The German philosopher had written that "God has provided everything. He has remedied everything beforehand. There is in his works a harmony, a beauty already pre-established," which does not at all exclude belief in Providence. That is, God does not have to interpose his will to meet special occasions, as Leibnitz's English critic Samuel Clarke (1675–1729) had supposed, since, for Leibnitz (1646–1716), God is "a workman too perfect to make a work which needs to be repaired" (McCosh 1850, 183–84).

In McCosh's Calvinist formulation of the divine, preestablished harmony, one detects, however, the chill stoicism of an Epictetus, hardly the warm assurance of a fatherly solicitude. McCosh likens the working of Providence to a postman delivering the varied contents of his mailbag:

What a crowd of events huddled together, and apparently confused . . .
are the objects bound up in that bundle and very varied are the emotions which they will incite when opened up, and yet how coolly and
systematically does the vehicle proceed on its way. . . . Each has a name
inscribed upon it. . . . Each, too, has a message to carry, and a purpose
to fulfil. Some inspire hope and joy, others raise only fear and sorrow.
(1850, 200–201)

McCosh's considerable influence is an indication of the staying power of
natural theology and its attendant theodicy at mid-century and even beyond.
But it was difficult for some to see how McCosh's reign of law and stoical
theodicy enhanced belief in a *personal* Providence. Paley's and McCosh's
rationalization of pain and loss on the grounds of a wider utility and teleology left the poet Alfred, Lord Tennyson, grave and depressed. His poem *In
Memoriam* appeared in 1850 and was extraordinarily popular. For many it
summed up their own rising doubt and anxiety concerning the compatibility
of theology and the new science and, with this, their mounting melancholic
belief that nature no longer could lead them to God. The new sciences of
geology and paleontology left Tennyson and others with the haunted vision
of the transience, the "perpetual perishing" of all forms of life, from the seemingly impregnable, majestic hills to humankind itself. The superfecundity of
nature now implied a carelessness on the part of the divine governance.

The ambiguities inherent in the apologetics of this "grander teleology"
would further distress sensitive souls with the arrival of the new Darwinian
science. The "rigorous mood" so evident in the Paleyian and Malthusian
theodicies would provide, as we now know, the critical element in the development of Darwin's own explanation of nature's workings, as well as the
social theodicy that was to emerge from it.

The Paleyian Theodicy and Darwin

The relationship between Charles Darwin and British natural theology of the
early nineteenth century is critically important to the theme of this chapter,
for it illuminates perfectly the issues and the ambiguities, and the ultimate
parting of ways, in the late Victorian debate on nature, evil, and Providence.
Young Darwin did not believe that the laws of nature ruled out a harmonious
design. His transmutation notebooks register his confidence in perfect adaptation as assured by a wise God. Even as late as 1842, in the first sketch of his
theory, Darwin spoke of the divine laws that led to "death, famine, rapine,
and the concealed war of nature" as justified because they eventuate in "the

highest good, which we can conceive, the creation of higher animals" (De Beer 1952, 87). But uncertainties had, in fact, been seeping in for years.

The question of when and what caused Darwin to cast off his religious belief and its theodicy is a complex and disputed issue, and one that we cannot pursue here. Recent scholarship does appear to agree that it was not his science alone, that is, natural selection, that brought about his loss of faith. While not underestimating the intellectual factors, James Moore has shown how aspects of Darwin's personal life, especially his bereavement over the death of his young daughter Annie, were crucial in the eclipse of his faith (J. R. Moore 1979, 195–229; Desmond and Moore 1991; see also Brooke 1985; Brown 1986). Darwin's unusual sensitivity, his personal experiences on the *Beagle* and within the family circle, and his science all collaborated in his abandonment of Christian belief by 1851.

Shortly after the publication of *The Origin of Species*, Darwin exchanged a number of letters with the American botanist Asa Gray on the subject of design in nature. Gray repeatedly insisted that variation had been directed along certain beneficial lines. Always tactful, Darwin repeatedly confessed to Gray that he could not think that the world was the result of chance; he was, he replied, in a "hopeless muddle." In fact, each time Gray reverted to his belief in providential design, Darwin respectfully but firmly countered with a telling objection. "I own," he replied in May 1860, that

> I cannot see as plainly as others do, and as I should wish to do, evidence of design and beneficence on all sides of us. There seems to me too much misery in the world. I cannot persuade myself that a beneficent and omnipotent God would have designedly created the *Ichneumonidae* with the express intention of their feeding within the living bodies of Caterpillars.

On another occasion, he told Gray that he could not believe that "God designedly killed" an innocent and good man who, standing under a tree, was struck by lightning, or "that when a swallow snaps up a gnat that God designed that that particular swallow should snap up that particular gnat at that particular instant." "I believe," he added, "that the man and the gnat are in the same predicament. If the death of neither man nor gnat are designed, I see no reason to believe that their first birth or production should be necessarily designed" (F. Darwin 1887, letters of April 1860; May 22, 1860; November 26, 1860; September 17, 1861; December 11, 1861).

It is important to note what Darwin opposed. He frequently reiterated that he could "look at everything as resulting from designed laws, with the details, whether good or bad, left to the working out of what we may call chance." That is, at least through the early 1860s Darwin believed in a form of deism. What he now could not abide was the Christian belief in a *particular* Providence. As J. H. Brooke has suggested (Brooke 1985), Darwin's loss of Christian belief was to a large extent due to two related elements in the orthodox position that, for him, cried out for explanation: the fact of a superfluity of pain, waste, and loss *and* the offense of a particular Providence.

In the last years of his life, between 1876 and 1881, Darwin wrote an *Autobiography* that was not intended for publication. (It was published in an expurgated version in 1887 and in 1958 with the omissions restored.) It contains a section on his "Religious Belief," wherein he enumerates his reasons for giving up Christianity. These include doubts about the reliability of the Bible, his rejection of miracles, his abhorrence of the doctrine of eternal damnation ("a damnable doctrine"), but most prominently mentioned is the excess and inutility of suffering and waste in a world overseen by a personal Providence:

> There is much suffering in the world no one disputes. Some have attempted to explain this in reference to man by *imagining* that it serves for his moral improvement. [One may well suppose that here he had "innocent," "angelic" little Annie, his daughter, in mind.] But the number of men in the world is nothing compared with that of all other sentient beings, and these often suffer greatly without any moral improvement. A being so powerful and so full of knowledge as a God who could create the universe, is to our finite minds omnipotent and omniscient, and it revolts our understanding to suppose that his benevolence is not unbounded, for what advantage can there be in the sufferings of millions of the lower animals throughout almost endless time? This very old argument from the existence of suffering against the existence of an intelligent first cause seems to me a strong one; whereas . . . the presence of much suffering agrees well with the view that all organic beings have been developed through variation and natural selection. (C. Darwin 1969, 90)

How could the theologians and theistic apologists in Britain after 1860 accommodate Darwinism to their providential theodicy? One answer is ignorance of his real position. Darwin was a private man, so few outside a small circle had any idea of his real estrangement from Christian orthodoxy. But the truer answer is that many theists were able to *rationalize* natural selection and its suffering and waste in terms of the nobler ends of a wider teleology, albeit a purpose that must remain a mystery to faith (Christian Darwinism), or they could *transform* Darwin by injecting into evolution both a benevolence and an inevitable progress (Christian Darwinisticism) (J. R. Moore 1979, chs. 10–12). In either case, as James Moore observes, "the seeming waste of life and matter becomes part of the general 'economy of nature'; and the imperfections and failures of life are explained in the Darwinian scheme as the necessary result of competition, struggle, and natural selection, without which there would be none of the diversifications that lead up to 'higher and nobler forms'" (1979, 273).

Darwin himself, however, felt the awful pain and senseless loss in nature as deeply as did Tennyson and many others. Something, they sensed, was terribly wrong when this scheme was joined to the traditional Christian belief in a particular Providence. The theologians who sought an easy accommodation with what they interpreted as Darwin's doctrine did not appear to plumb the depths of the issue that he posed—at least not until late in the century.

There is another aspect of Darwin's theory that also is critical here, namely, his so-called social Darwinism. It had a profound influence on the secular theodicies—or rather, the *anthropodicies*—of the latter decades of the century. The debate over whether Darwin was himself a "social Darwinist" is ongoing (Greene 1981, 95–127), although the evidence shows that he at least embraced elements of this ideology. Darwin struggled to reconcile two convictions. One was his belief that natural selection also was operative in the development of societies and that competition, not only between individuals but between tribes and nations, was essential to social progress. He was also convinced of "the obligations of enlightened humanity" toward peoples "lower in the scale" of human life, and felt that a restraining of our highest humanitarian impulses would injure "the noblest part of our nature." Yet at the same time that he would single out the role that virtuous habits, education, and religion play in improving society, he also insisted on the necessity of "severe struggle" if society is to advance and not degenerate: "Our natural rate of increase, though leading to many and obvious evils, must not be greatly diminished by any means," he insisted. "There should be open competition for all men; and the most able should not be prevented by laws or customs from succeeding best and rearing the largest number of offspring" (C. Darwin 1886, 618).

Darwin was overconfident that virtuous behavior, continued over several generations, would give those individuals and groups demonstrating it the advantage in the struggle for life. Furthermore, he believed that those social virtues would become more widely diffused: "Looking to future generations, there is not cause to fear that the social instincts will grow weaker, and we may expect that virtuous habits will grow stronger, becoming perhaps fixed by inheritance. In this case the struggle between our higher and lower impulses will be less severe, and virtue will be triumphant" (1886, 124).

Recent studies of Darwin have shown how very much he was a man of his own time and national ethos. He shared in and was influenced by the ideas of contemporary British writers on social evolution—men such as Francis Galton, W. R. Greg, and Walter Bagehot—who believed in the heritability of intellectual and moral capacities, as well as the deleterious role of "negative selection" or survival of the "unfit" in civilized societies, but who also held optimistic views of social progress through competition and conflict. John Greene is convincing in his judgment that Darwin shared these ebullient beliefs in the upward progress of humankind "through the competition of individuals, tribes, nations, and races . . . and in the gradual triumph of superior races over those 'lower in the scale'" (Greene 1981, 121–22).

It is not surprising that Darwin held views that were similar to those of his contemporaries and that we identify them, fairly or not, by the term "social Darwinism." What is significant, however, is the undoubted fact that Darwin's *Origin of Species* gave enormous impetus to this kind of social theorizing. Furthermore, he provided *the* naturalistic interpretation of the development of mental and moral instincts in *The Descent of Man*. Scores of writers were then able to apply Darwin's theories, or what they considered consistent with them, to their own views of the progressive evolution of society through competitive struggle. Thus, Darwin played a crucial role in advancing a new, secular theodicy or anthropodicy between the 1860s and 1890s, exactly at the time when older conceptions of Providence were under attack by an aggressive scientific naturalism.

The Christian Darwinistic Theodicy

In examining the post-1860 theodicies we turn first to a group of Christian writers who, in James Moore's nomenclature, we may refer to as Christian Darwinists (J. R. Moore 1979, ch. 10). These thinkers adopted a variety of forms of the post-Paleyian "wider teleology," and they offered distinctive reconceptions of traditional Christian teaching. It has been said that the theologian's problem, that is, theodicy, had become Darwin's solution. But the Darwinistic theologians also demonstrated that there is, arguably, "a sense in which Darwin's solution had also to be the theologian's solution. . . . Precisely because waste, pain, and suffering were endemic to the creative process they could be given a new rationale" (Brooke 1991, 316–17). This "solution" is especially conspicuous in the theodicies of the two Scotsmen, the Duke of Argyll and Henry Drummond.

In chapter 2 we saw how resolutely the Duke of Argyll presented his anthropocentric view of the evolutionary process. This is not unusual in a theistic context deeply informed by biblical ideas. What is striking, however, about Argyll's theistic evolutionism—indeed, about so much of the post-Darwinian religious apologetic—is its conception of Providence and, more specifically, the theodicy that is implied by it. While the Darwinian view of nature had superseded the older Paleyian teleology, it was not at all clear what purpose any given development served, since that purpose was identified with the *telos* of the process taken as a whole. Therefore, as we have seen, the reign of law struck many as veiling, not revealing, the providence of God.

The Duke of Argyll regarded such feelings as unwarranted. He saw Tennyson as the example of a distinguished writer who had mistakenly associated human doubts about particular "purposes" in nature as grounds for a lack of confidence in Providence, in divine purpose as such. Tennyson had wrongly assumed that because the primary purpose of all seeds is that they "bear" fruit, that that purpose necessarily fails when they are otherwise disposed of. What, Argyll asks, "would become of the bread—the staff of life—if, for example, the cereals did not produce even more than 'fifty seeds' for consumption to every one seed required for reproduction?" It is a mere confusion of thought that "regards various, opposite, and even apparently contradictory purposes" as inconsistent with assurance that the several elements cohere in a work of art, or in nature, to achieve their ends (Argyll 1896, 178).

Argyll did concede, nevertheless, that the facts of immense variety and complexity do suggest "that the mind which we see exhibited in *Nature* is one so vast and so far-reaching, that its working, its aims, and its methods, can only be imperfectly understood" (1896, 179). There, of course, was the rub, since for many nature had become an opaque and uncertain witness to God's personal providence. Easy resort to "imperfectly understood" did not suffice.

Was not Argyll—so persistent in his appeal to analogies between the organic and the human spheres—able to apply imaginatively the inference from Tennyson's "fifty seeds" to its human bearing? Does God require "millions of souls" to bring his kingdom to "bear"? George Henry Lewes, champion of the positivist creed, asked just this question in his review of Argyll's *The Reign of Law*:

It must strike every reflective mind, as humanly speaking, strangely at variance with a wise vision of ends, that structures so marvelously complex and capable of so complete an existence as those of man and animals, should be formed by millions under conditions which prevent their development; not only are ova sacrificed by millions, but even where the ova have been fertilized this "end" is frustrated—the embryo perishes, the child perishes, the youth perishes, and the organization we are called upon to marvel at as a work of "exquisite contrivance," attains its "end" as an exception to the general failure. . . . Obviously we can only escape from the terrible conclusions such facts force upon us, by ceasing altogether to apply the human standard to creation. Design, contrivance, skill, are phrases to denote human, not Divine agencies. (Lewes 1867, 100–101)

Lewes represents the paradigm shift in the 1860s—initiated but not unambiguously avowed by Darwin himself—from a creationist episteme entailing providential design to a positivist episteme that excluded teleological concepts of mind and purpose from nature (Gillespie 1979). Lewes drove home this shift in his review of Argyll, revealing the irreconcilable gulf that, for him, now marked the two "streams that cannot mingle." He pointed out that when a scientist observes how each part, say, of an embryo, is related to the whole, he will "form an abstract conception of that whole by a process of mental shorthand." While it may be highly useful to call this abstract scheme "a Plan of the phenomena," the mind "by an unfortunate infirmity" tends to reify the abstract conception into an objective existence. "Thus the Plan—which is the abstract expression of the results—is converted into a Purpose which existed *before* the relations were established, and which arranged the results . . . according to an ideal scheme." What had been a law of causation is transformed into a divine purpose. Lewes did not deny that a law may also be a purpose; he only wished to confess to "an absolute ignorance respecting the Creator's intentions" (Lewes 1867, 108–9).

Argyll found the idea of purpose in nature an unquestionable intuition, and he could never really appreciate the scientific issue at stake. What is noteworthy, however, is an observation made by Lewes in his review. He pointed out the extraordinary similarities between Robert Chambers's *Vestiges of the Natural History of Creation* (1844) and Argyll's *Reign of Law* and the fact that Chambers's book "excited bitter wrath" while Argyll's work had left "the public unagitated." This is surprising, since the very idea that had alarmed the public in 1844—that all of nature, both physical and moral, is subordinated to unchangeable law ascertainable by science—was the theme that runs through the Duke of Argyll's book (Lewes 1867, 97). Was the public now prepared to accept the implications of this view of nature for a radically reconceived doctrine of Providence and theodicy or, unlike Argyll, were they prepared to accept with Baden Powell that nature and theology are now to be understood as two incommensurate sources of truth?

The former option, a radically reconceived theodicy, is apparent in Frederick Temple's accommodation to Darwinism. We saw earlier that Temple understood the beauty and the attraction of the new evolutionary teleology to rest in its unity of plan, in its binding of all things into one. "Every mineral, every plant, every animal," he wrote, "has such properties that it benefits other things beside itself and derives benefit in turn. The insect develops the plant, and the plant the insect, the brute aids in the evolution of man, and the man in that of the brute [Temple is thinking of animal domestication]. . . . All things are embraced in one great design." And this "grander teleology" of variety revealing a higher unity makes for a more intelligible theodicy (Temple 1884, 122).

Temple saw all history as "gathered as it were into one original creative act." But what of the needless pain and waste? The answer that theologians often proposed is that we cannot see the whole picture, that our knowledge is partial. This had seldom persuaded. "But what force and clearness is given to this answer" now, Temple replied, for "the doctrine of Evolution tells us that we are looking at a work which is not yet finished, and that the imperfections are a necessary part of a large design the general outlines of which we may already trace, but the ultimate issue of which . . . is still beyond our perception!" (117).

Temple conceded that there is no waste like that seen in nature. But "the inevitable operation of this waste, as Darwin's investigation showed, has been to destroy all those varieties which were not well fitted to their surroundings, and to keep those that were" (165). The justification for all the pain and waste is, then, in the promise that evolution displays not mere continuance of species but a perpetual progress. "Things are so arranged that animals are perpetually better adapted to the life they have to live." Temple proceeds to propose, as a law of nature, that the survival of the fittest "implies a perpetual diminution of pain and increase of enjoyment for all creatures." Temple's conclusion of the matter takes away one's breath: "And, as if to mark still more plainly the beneficence of the whole work, the less developed creatures . . . are less sensible to pain and pleasure; so that enjoyment appears to grow with the capacity for enjoyment and suffering diminishes as sensitivity to suffering increases" (117–18).

This appropriation of Darwin by religious writers such as Argyll, Temple, and Drummond involved a more optimistic and progressive use of Darwin's evolutionary doctrine than most Darwin scholars consider consistent with Darwin's own positivism. James Moore (1979, chs. 10 and 11) has adopted the word "Darwinisticism" in contrast to "Darwinism" to distinguish this progressive reading of Darwin (often through the prism of Herbert Spencer) from orthodox Darwinian doctrine that did not entail a progressive teleology.

The high noon of "Darwinistic" theodicy, with its built-in idea of progress, is best exposed to view in Henry Drummond's last popular work, *The Ascent of Man* (1894). Drummond granted that, viewed *simpliciter*, the struggle for life appears irreconcilable with moral ends. He insisted, however, that evolution displays a second factor, which he called "the Struggle for the Life of Others." All living things exhibit two functions. The first is "Nutrition," the basis of the "Struggle for Life"; the second is "Reproduction," which he associated with the "Struggle for the Life of Others." When these two struggles are taken together, the struggle for life no longer can be viewed as the villain, for like the villain in the drama, "its chief function is to re-act upon the other players for higher ends." It has, after all, proven to be the efficient instrument of progress (Drummond 1894, 16).

Drummond acknowledged that through the centuries the struggle for existence has required repeated justification, since this instrument of evolution has brought pain and loss as well as victory and progress. The usual response has been that a verdict must wait until the record is closed and a balance of gains and losses can be struck. But Drummond insisted that, on the contrary, modern evolutionary studies have shown that such a far-off eschatological verification is unnecessary, since the results of the evolutionary process are largely known. "And it would be affectation to deny that on the whole these results are good, and appear the worthier the more we penetrate into their inner meaning" (258–59).

Furthermore, Drummond argued, the apparent unfavorable implications of the struggle for existence operating at the lower ranges of nature have, doubtless, been exaggerated, projecting onto it "accompaniments of emotion borrowed from our own sensations." At the lower levels of creation these so-called adverse affects are less than they appear. Certainly in the lower animals "it can never approach in terror what it means to us." Moreover, Drummond found that at the subhuman level "the fight is a fair fight. As a rule there is no hate in it, but only Hunger. It is seldom prolonged, and seldom wanton. As to the manner of death, it is generally sudden. As to the fact of death, all animals must die. As to the meaning of an existence prematurely closed, it is better to be eaten than not to be at all" (259–60).

Warming to his defense of the struggle for life and the "vigorous mood," Drummond reminded his readers that science did not invent the struggle for life; it is a natural fact. What science has recently done "is to show not only its meaning but its great moral purpose." And while it is true that a price, a terrible price, has been paid, "the Struggle for Life has been a victorious struggle; it has succeeded in its stupendous task. . . . Without the rigorous weeding out of the imperfect the progress of the world had not been possible" (263–64). And so it is recognized that

> only when one considers the working of the Struggle for Life on a large scale . . . that one can even begin to discuss its ethical and teleological meanings. . . . The result may sometimes involve the dethroning of a

species, or its entire extinction; it may lead in the case of others to degeneration; but in the end it must result in the gradual perfecting of organisms upon the whole, and the steady advance of the final type. (266)

Drummond further wanted to insist that the guarantor of spiritual as well as material progress is the continuous interaction of the struggle for life *with* the struggle for the life of others. He maintained that the latter was not a latecomer to the evolutionary process; rather, it is deeply ingrained in the life process, for "without the Struggle for the Life of Others, obviously there would have been no Others" (38). In the mere fact of its multiplying lives one sees the final condition of progress. And its ethical reality waxes as the struggle for life alone wanes. Drummond called upon Herbert Spencer's *Principles of Ethics* for confirmation: "By care of offspring, which has become greater with advancing organization, and by survival of the fittest in the competition among adults, which has become more habitual with advancing organization, superiority has been perpetually fostered and further advances caused" (Drummond 1894, 43).

Struggle, of course, can never cease. "What ceases," Drummond was certain, "is its so-called anti-ethical character." Nothing, he believed, is more evident in nature's rising in the scale and in the complexity of life "than the gradual tempering of the Struggle for Life" itself. While its amelioration has been the work of ages, "the animal qualities in the social life of Man are being surely left behind; and though the mark of the savage and the brute still mar its handiwork, these harsher qualities must pass away" (45).

Drummond believed that the refashioning of the "Struggle for Life" and the "Coming of the Kingdom of Love" is a certain prophecy of science. There are, he perceived, whole regions of human life "where every animal feature is discredited, discouraged, or driven away" (270). While civilization cannot wholly improve the human moral condition at once, it will in the future "be the Struggle with its fangs drawn" (272). In language anticipating Pierre Teilhard de Chardin (1881–1955) a half century later, Drummond wrote, "The path of progress and the path of Altruism are one. Evolution is nothing but the Involution of Love, the revelation of Infinite Spirit, the Eternal Life returning to Itself" (46). In less than twenty years, the horrific events of the twentieth century would, for many, expose such prophecies as unreal.

The Christian Darwinian Theodicy

By the late 1880s and early 1890s the optimistic progressivism of the scientific naturalists and the disciples of Herbert Spencer was under ever increasing attack, even ridicule. Drummond's "Spencerian" theodicy in *The Ascent of Man*, while initially receiving mixed reviews, was to suffer a similar fate. In an address to the Church Congress in October 1888, Arthur Balfour already had sounded what was to be an escalating refrain, namely, that historical experience does not support faith in a progressive millenarianism. Balfour confessed that he could not discover those so-called laws of nature that aroused the "flattering anticipations" of Spencer and Drummond. Experience simply does not give us "any confident expectation that if perfection be attainable we are in the right way to attain it." Do we humans have reason for confidence that we have truly increased in intellectual grasp or moral wisdom? Balfour thought not. "Many people," he observed, "have degenerated, many have become stationary, and I am wholly at a loss to know why we—the group of Western nations—and we alone may hope to escape the common destiny of man" (Balfour 1905, 301–4).

The severest blow to the Spencerian theodicy came, however, from within the scientific camp itself. On May 18, 1892, T. H. Huxley delivered his provocative lecture on "Evolution and Ethics," a devastating attack on the Spencer-Drummond contention that the progress of natural "fitness" could be identified with improvement in moral "goodness." With his usual rhetorical vigor and bite, Huxley drove home the point that a species normally is fit to survive simply by virtue of its violence and brutality. The realism of Balfour and Huxley was shared by the Christian Darwinists, although, as we will see, they continued to place their faith in the ultimate vindication of a divine justice and goodness. Writers such as Aubrey Moore and George Romanes did not attempt to transform the Darwinian worldview by interpreting the evolutionary process itself as a vindication of beneficent progress. Theirs was a far sterner doctrine. It too appealed to a wider teleology, but it was dismissive of Drummond's sanguine view of nature and history.

Aubrey Moore was certain that the old, easy move from nature to a beneficent Author was given its death knell by Kant long before Darwin administered its deathblow. "The old *couleur de rose* view of nature is no longer possible," he wrote. "'Destruction is the rule; life is the exception.' The waste is enormous; the suffering terrible. . . . The law of God's work is indeed progress, but progress at a tremendous and as it seems to us, reckless cost" (A. L. Moore 1889, 193, 195). These are facts, Moore insisted, that any theology must take seriously—and they are fatal to the older Christian teleology. How then is theology to respond to Darwin's "deeper and wider view of purpose"? It must begin, Moore affirmed, by discarding the long-held assumption that everything exists solely for the good of humanity. The new scientific teleology seeks, rather, "to give a reason for the existence of each species, by fitting it into its place in the genealogical tree, and relating all the species to one another in the unity of the whole" (196). And so the theologian now must fearlessly ask: What is the use of each part? If the history of the individual gives us no answer, then we must look at the history of the race. In any case, what science has taught us is that "there is nothing useless[,] . . . nothing irrational, nothing outside the reign of law." Such a belief is the "scientific analogue of the Christian's belief in Providence" (197).

Moore believed that what human reason resents is not "facts which *we* cannot explain, but facts which *have no* explanation." Similarly, our moral natures rebel not at pain and suffering themselves but at *meaningless* pain that might have been avoided. It is here that Darwin's doctrine gives us a hint, if no more. As Darwin insisted, natural selection works solely by and for the good of each being. In this sense the world tends to progress, to the perfecting of the natural world. What Darwin and Moore meant by "the good of each being" is not, of course, the individual person but the species. Or, more precisely, each species has its rationale and, for Moore, its theological explanation in its past or in the future, for neither individuals nor species are ends in themselves, but all, taken as a whole, contribute to the highest good or perfection of being itself, whose good is known only to God.

Moore concluded that the Christian is bound to believe that creation is God's rational and beneficent work from end to end. "But he is not bound to know, or to say what that purpose is, or to show that marks of beneficence are everywhere apparent." Just as the theory of evolution starts with an "act of faith" that everything is rational and has a meaning despite the fact that much at present remains unexplained, so the theist starts with an "act of faith" that "God is good and cannot be the cause of meaningless and unnecessary pain. And our faith is not staggered by much which seems, as yet, like useless suffering" (198–99).

Moore's reflection on theodicy is stern in its call for a radical faith in the face of the "terrible suffering" and "reckless cost" of nature's "progress." Some, surely, would judge that Moore had cast too dark a veil over the divine workings in the world. But the zeitgeist would soon prove to be more in accord with Moore than with Drummond or Argyll. It remains true, however, that in the essays left behind at his early death, Moore did not explore adequately the theological implications of God's being in relation to the world of rational, free creatures—especially the question of God's limitation, self-willed or otherwise. After Darwin, both God's relation to the world and the reality of pain and waste would require a deeper analysis and rethinking than Moore provides.

George Romanes's position as a Darwinist is rather similar to Moore's in his defense of the possibility of a divine design in nature as long, that is, as the suffering and waste of countless creatures and species are seen as securing some higher *telos* for other beings or for nature as a whole. But does such a defense of design save the moral character of God? Romanes did not think this possible, at least until he reconsidered the entire matter during his last illness in the winter of 1893–1894.

Romanes reflected at length on the question of theodicy in articles written for the *Nineteenth Century* some time before 1889. He acknowledged that the apparent waste and seeming purposelessness of nature may be met by the claim that what to humans may appear wasteful and purposeless may not be so when reviewed in relation to the completed cosmos. Yet he clearly saw that any such argument for a divine intelligence and purpose "scarcely becomes less incompatible with any inference to the morality of that Cause." Nature "red in tooth and claw with ravin" is an irrefutable fact; indeed, as Moore had recognized, it is among "the principia of the Darwinian" (Romanes 1896a, 76–77). No teleology can dismiss it. The rational defenses of the theologians, for example those offered in the book *Theism* by the Scotsman Robert Flint, horrified Romanes:

> Let us pause for a moment to think of what suffering in nature means. Some hundreds of millions of years ago some millions of millions of animals must be supposed to have become sentient. Since that time till the present, there must have been millions and millions of generations of millions and millions of individuals. And throughout all this period of incalculable duration, this inconceivable host of sentient organisms have been in a state of unceasing battle, dread, ravin, pain. . . . [We] find teeth and talons whetted for slaughter, hooks and suckers moulded for torment—everywhere a reign of terror, hunger and sickness, with oozing blood and quivering limbs, with grasping breath and eyes of innocence that dimly close in deaths of cruel torture! (77–78)

The theologian is wont to reply that Romanes is not competent to judge the purposes of the Almighty. Romanes addressed this matter in a letter to Flint:

> If there are *purposes*, I *am* able to judge them so far as I can see; and if I am expected to judge of His purposes when they appear to be beneficent, I am in consistency obliged also to judge of them when they appear malevolent. And it can be no possible extenuation of the latter to point to the "final result" as "order and beauty," so long as the means adopted by the "*Omnipotent Designer*" are known to have been so terrible. (78)

All that one can legitimately claim in such a case is that God "cares for animal perfection *to the exclusion of* animal enjoyment, and even to the total disregard of animal suffering" (78–79). Romanes concluded with David Hume that without being either supramoral or immoral, God may simply be amoral. For on any theory of *beneficent* design, it is impossible to explain why the mechanisms in the same species are correlated for the benefit only of that species. Why should there never be such correlations between mechanisms in different species?

How magnificent a display of Divine beneficence would organic nature have afforded if all, or even some species had been so interrelated as to minister to each other's necessities. . . . But, as it is, we see no vestige of such coordination; every species is for itself . . . an outcome of the always and everywhere fiercely raging struggle for life. (84–85)

Without question, Darwinism had proclaimed a hard new law: Blessed are the fit, for they shall inherit the earth. When Romanes reflected on this fact, it pained him deeply. Yet in the last two years of his life this experience of pain and loss took on a new aspect. As he dwelt more on the contemplation of the life of the human spirit in his broodings over nature, he began to see a positive role for suffering in the economy of human life. He was deeply struck by the paradox that Christianity has always been "a religion of blood and tears, and yet of profoundest happiness to its votaries." The apparent paradox was due, he felt, "to the union of these seemingly diverse roots in Love." No longer suspicious of instinct and feeling in regions where reason failed him, Romanes now suggested that "probably it is only those whose characters have been deepened by experiences gained in [Christianity] who are so much as capable of intelligently resolving this paradox" (164). In any case, that a larger good might evolve from the moral winnowing process that we see played out in the human drama is, he believed, for the poet to tell us, not the scientist. "The whole creation groaneth in pain and travail," St. Paul tells us. But science ought to leave the question of pain in nature "to be answered by the general voice of humanity . . . which is able to acknowledge that at least its own allotment of suffering is not an unmitigated evil" (1897, 55). Romanes's last reflections on evil were expressed in verse:

> . . . clouds of sorrow deepness lend
>   To change joy's early rays,
> And manhood's eyes alone can send
>   A grief-ennobled gaze. (1896b, 27–28)

The Theodicies of James Martineau and J. R. Illingworth

The prevailing Christian theodicy in the last two decades of the nineteenth century is represented neither by Drummond nor by the Christian Darwinists Moore, Romanes, and James Iverach. It is a rather more orthodox theodicy, one that availed itself of more traditional arguments—for example, the free will defense and the claim that suffering is necessary in the building of moral character—although these arguments were joined with efforts to take account of current science and specifically of Darwinism. J. R. Illingworth's contribution to *Lux Mundi*, entitled "The Problem of Pain" (1904), is characteristic, although a more rigorous attempt to canvass the scientific facts is present in the work of the great Unitarian philosopher-theologian James Martineau (1805–1900), especially in his classic *A Study of Religion* (1888). Both Illingworth and Martineau wrote from Idealist suppositions that prevailed in Britain in the 1880s.

Martineau thought deeply about the reality of animal pain, especially where any marks of human intention are absent—for example, in matters of want, physical decline, encounters with the elements, and the law of prey. These realities are present to all sentient life *in spite of* the purposes of the organism that these afflictions profoundly disturb and obstruct. Martineau was forced to conclude that these must be regarded as "undesigned imperfections," however they may be conceived within some grander scheme in whose larger good their partial evil may seem to vanish. But the question remained: Has not an Infinite Being the power to bar such imperfections? Martineau's reply led him to reflections on the Creator's own self-limitation.

It is, of course, possible, Martineau asserted, for God to bar imperfections "if he lives out of his boundless freedom and, from moment to moment, acts unpledged, conducting all things by the miscellany of incalculable miracles." Then "there is nothing to hinder his Will from entering 'where it listeth,' and all things will be 'possible to him.'" However, once God commits his Will to Creation by any determinate method, "and for the realization of his ends selects and institutes a scheme of instrumental rules, he thereby shuts the door on a thousand things that might have been before" (Martineau 1888 27–28). That is, a system of laws, by providing for the operation of one set of phenomena, clearly relinquishes the conditions for another. It is simply vain, then, to call upon the ancient conception of the omnipotence of God and to maintain at the same time his relation to an *established* universe. In creating this cosmos God has given up his almightiness, and this means that there is a limit to what one may demand of God's power within *this* world. If there were to be "any determinate action at all, *some* limits had to be assigned" (28).

The sufferings of animals arise, then, from some relation between the organism and its determinate physical environment: desolating cold, floods, and disease, for instance. Yet these "are the occasional results of that scheme of physical laws which, while preparing the theatre of animal existence and favoring its development yet goes beyond it and steps from world to world negotiating for other interests also and contemplating more enduring good" (81). In launching power to a million ends whose confluence is instrumental in working out these ends, "it is surely conceivable," Martineau proposed, "that the Creator's Will, while subjecting his means to steady rules, may realize some elements of his design less absolutely than if they had stood alone." To create is, therefore, to enter into the realm of the finite, and it is this recognized limit of possibility, of unequal approximation to the ideal, that is the root of natural evil. The value of such a doctrine is, Martineau argued, that it, mercifully, dispenses "with the necessity of seeking for some end in view to justify each type of suffering" (81). The only question, then, is whether such suffering be allowed or whether it be better that sentient life itself not exist.

Martineau thus urged that we give up the effort to find in the sphere of the finite, in the physical order of storms, floods, and volcanoes, a *moral* meaning, that we forego searching for some end for which they were ordained. The things of the physical order "occur in conformity with atmospheric and meteorological laws which alone render life possible . . . so that the same laws that are death-dealing for an hour or a day are life-giving forever" (85).

With the admission of human willing and sin, the matter is, of course, altogether different. Assuming sin, it would be monstrous if there were no suffering. However, there remain those who would find fault with the extent of human freedom and the radical contingency that it entails. If the protest against natural evil is against too much *necessity*, the complaint against moral evil is directed at its dreadful *possibility*. Both objections, Martineau noted, "assume that there is nothing which we may not ask from the omnipotence of God, and that no petition can be unreasonable, addressed to such a Being." But we have already seen that this is no longer true when God gives up unconditioned infinitude and undertakes a finite determinate creation that thereby excludes some possible options. And so, by the same reasoning, Martineau insisted that "every *contingent* system, having its own range of alternatives, must admit such ineligible options: if there is to be liberty for the worse, there cannot be necessity for the better" (100–101). God is then the source of moral evil's *possibility*, but God is not to be charged as the *author* of specific evil actions on the grounds that he has not rendered them impossible. To do so, God would have had to substitute mechanism for free agency. By abstaining from the imposition of necessity, God allows for the genuine exercise of character. In virtue then of this abstinence, God "is at once the *cause of the existence of Character*, and *not the cause of what that character should be*" (101).

In striking contrast to Martineau, the Anglican priest and philosopher J. R. Illingworth (1848–1915) made rather short shrift of the question of animal pain, a fact that deeply troubled naturalists such as Darwin and Romanes, as it did Martineau. The degree and intensity of animal suffering, Illingworth judged to be "entirely a matter of conjecture." Furthermore, he believed that animals "would seem, like children, to give strong indication of slight pain" and that much animal pain is "prophylactic and directly contribute[s] to the avoidance of danger and the maintenance of life" (Illingworth 1904, 83).

What can be said about human pain is quite another matter, since we experience the process not only from the outside but deeply from within. Illingworth insisted that human pain is an ultimate fact, one not to be explained away. But neither can it be wholly explained; it is a mystery, but a mystery that is full of meaning. Illingworth found that meaning in the fact that the development of moral character is a primary end of human life, the proof being that ordinary persons never have denied that human life is better for the presence of penal, corrective, and preventive uses of pain. Neither social progress nor individual nobility would be conceivable without them. In its simplest aspect, pain is punishment—since shame, guilt, and justice are essential not only to the building of character but to social development and civilization (84).

Of course, pain and suffering also fall on the innocent. But it is here, Illingworth believed, that the more profound corrective and purgatorial uses of pain play their role, since unmerited suffering refines and elevates the character. Illingworth here reveals a deep insensitivity to the very real travail, the grinding, senseless pain experienced especially by many of the less fortunate. He points to the vicarious suffering of Christ as the "complete expression of the process to which we owe the entire evolution of our race." But he continues with the following remarkable observation:

> The pleasures of each generation evaporate in air; it is their pains that increase the spiritual momentum of the world. We enter into life through the travail of another. We live upon the death of the animals beneath us. The necessities, the comforts, the luxuries of our existence are provided by the labour and sorrow of countless fellow-men. Our freedom, our laws, our literature, our spiritual sustenance have been won for us at the cost of broken hearts, and wearied brains, and noble lives laid down. And this is only the human analogue of that transference of energy by which all life and movement is forever carried on. (91)

Finally, Illingworth suggests, human pain is to be understood as preventive. It "sounds the alarm bell of disease in time for its removal. Mental and moral pain arrest the issues of ignorant or evil courses before it is too late." In all of these ways, human suffering is, he concludes, "eminently useful, and therefore consistent with providential and beneficent design" (89–90). To this point in his essay, Illingworth's comments on animal and human suffering strike one as failing terribly to plumb some obvious realities of animal and human life. The essay proceeds, however, to sound a more profound theological note on the personal dimension of suffering.

Illingworth proposes that a study of the history of the world's religions demonstrates the instinctive tendency of human beings to view pain, whether in ascetic practice or sacrifice, as inseparably connected with self-surrender to a divine reality, no matter how crudely it may be imagined or expressed. This too he finds is the heart of the matter in Christianity and its inner secret of sorrow that never can be explained from without, only personally from within the terms of its practical moral power. If finally pressed to explain the secret of suffering, the Christian can only answer, "Come and see" (89–90). But the one thing that the vicarious suffering of the cross does reveal is that suffering is severed from sin once and for all. Rather than conflicting with the Christian's sense of justice, the cross is, Illingworth observes, the very emblem of the divine life itself. It is true, of course, that if a person shrinks from taking up a share of self-sacrifice, that person will easily be convinced that the system of the world is wrong and unjust. "But if we accept it, and resolve that we too in our turn will spend and be spent for others, we find beneath all the superficial [sic] suffering the deep truth of the benediction, 'It is more blessed to give than to receive'" (91). In self-sacrifice, then, one may at least glimpse the mysterious meaning of humanity's pain and sorrow.

Illingworth insists that our human effort is not only to work for others, but in so doing to be thereby deeply united with them. And, surprisingly, it is the sacrifice and sorrow that bring about this bond in a way joy does not. "It is . . . the soldiers who have faced the shock of battle side by side . . . the husband and wife who have known common suffering that are most intimately, indissolubly one." A person also can find that the paradoxical human experience of pain and blessed communion has its antitype in the Divine. "For we are told that God is Love; and love, as we know it, must be shewn in sacrifice" (92).

We have seen that George Romanes, very likely through his association with members of the Oxford *Lux Mundi* group, came to understand, in a deeply personal way, that pain and loss could enrich his own life. He remained, nevertheless, troubled by the obvious cost, in suffering and waste, of such a divine educative process. Wisely, both Moore and Romanes refused to trivialize the suffering of all sentient creatures through the millennia. In the end, they simply acknowledged their ignorance and trusted the larger hope in a divine goodness and justice. Neither the *Lux Mundi* theologians nor the theistic Darwinists could abide the Absolute Idealist's monistic denial of evil or their merging of the individual personality in the universal. Yet if one were to grant, with Martineau, a relative metaphysical pluralism, that is, affirm the real independence and freedom of individual souls, could not Christian theism, the philosopher James Ward asked, "let contingency into the very heart of things?" Was it possible to recognize very real limits to the ancient claim of divine omniscience and omnipotence?

Martineau had argued persuasively for a transcendent God who, in creating free creatures, had shut the door on certain possibilities and thereby had given up his unconditional infinitude and omnipotence. Pursuing a different path, the *Lux Mundi* theologians, and others who were to follow, restored the ancient christological theory of *kenosis* (from the Greek *kenoun*, "to empty"), in Philippians 2:7, to account for the real limitations in Christ's human knowledge, a point newly driven home by recent historical criticism. But this divine self-limitation in the incarnation pointed also to a deeper insight into the divine nature, one that could illuminate the problem of theodicy. If Christ's self-limitation reveals the very being of God, has not God laid aside, emptied himself, of the divine attributes of omniscience and omnipotence as well? Furthermore, in taking on human existence, is not God capable of suffering, of giving up his impassibility and, in fact, taking the world's sufferings into his own experience? The *Lux Mundi* theologians discovered in kenotic Christology the key to the mystery of suffering, as well as the means of refuting a docetic conception of the historical Jesus, Docetism being a conception that their contemporaries increasingly found to be incredible.

It was Charles Gore, respected as a patristic scholar and as an Anglo-Catholic, who more than any other gave credence to the kenotic theory. He did so initially in "The Holy Spirit and Inspiration," his, at the time, provocative contribution to *Lux Mundi*. He further elaborated on the theme in his Bampton Lectures of 1891, *The Incarnation of the Son of God*, and in *Dissertations on Subjects Connected with the Incarnation* (1898). In *Lux Mundi*, Gore spoke of the Incarnation as a "self-emptying of God to reveal Himself under conditions of human nature and from the human point of view," thus *using* human nature, its genuine conditionedness, and its growth and limitation in knowledge. Gore wished to make it clear that Christ's human limitation was "not to be confused with fallibility or liability to human delusion," since it was protected "by the Divine purpose which led Jesus Christ to take it upon Himself" (Gore 1904, 264–65). Nonetheless, Gore insisted that Jesus' personhood entailed a real human self-determination; it was no longer possible to speak credibly in the traditional language of Jesus' "impersonal" manhood.

Gore proposed that the Incarnation pointed to the divine *voluntary* abandonment of omniscience in taking on human flesh. In the *Dissertations* he wrote that the Son did "—doubtless by *a voluntary action of his own self-limiting* and self-restraining love—cease from the exercize of those functions and powers, including the divine omniscience, which would have been incompatible with a truly human experience" (Gore 1895, 95; italics added). Yet it was a genuine act of divine self-sacrifice. While Gore focused on the giving up of divine omniscience, others in the *Lux Mundi* group stressed God's self-relinquishing of his omnipotence and what that entailed for theodicy. Suffering, as Illingworth affirmed in his *Lux Mundi* essay, is at the very heart of God's being as love.

The Theodicy of the Personal Idealists

A characteristic of the discussions of theodicy in this period—from Martineau through *Lux Mundi* and on to such figures as the Scottish theologian P. T. Forsyth—is the attention given to God's self-limitation, the divine renunciation of omnipotence (Rashdall 1902a, 1–58; Fairbairn 1893; Forsyth, 1909; Tennant 1902). That is, the British discussion of God's relation to the world and, by extension, the question of theodicy, remained largely within the bounds of a classical theism. The period from 1890 to 1910 did not, however, only attend to the question of divine passibility; it witnessed a deeper exploration of the question of a finite God.

During these two decades, Idealistic monism came under heavy attack. Many theologians and theistic philosophers who did not wholly repudiate Idealism—and many did not—championed one or another form of Personal Idealism. The latter entailed a genuine pluralism of selves interdependent with, at least in some aspects, other selves, including God. Martineau, we saw, gave credence to such a position. But metaphysics now demanded an even more thoroughgoing rethinking of the God-world relationship and what was implied, for example, in the fact of genuinely independent, self-determining persons, at the same time being attentive to the stark reality of suffering and loss. Various positions emerged that attempted to come to grips with the growing conviction regarding divine passibility. Some thinkers remained within the bounds of orthodoxy; others moved into the unchartered regions of panentheism and similar heterodox ideas.

In a paper read before the Synthetic Society in 1903, Oliver Lodge (1851–1940), physicist and psychical researcher, noted the ambiguity that increasingly had attached to the use of the term *God*. This, he found, was present even in the discourse of traditional theists, but also among Idealists of various stripes and the new breed of metaphysical pluralists. The latter, Lodge remarked, conceive of God as a kind of manager of the evolutionary process, "a being infinite in comparison with ourselves, but still a being with potentialities ahead, and with the possibility of advance: conditioned therefore to some extent by what we are conscious of as 'time'" (Lodge 1903, 385–86).

The idea of a limited God was not an entirely new hypothesis to British theology in the latter years of the nineteenth century. In his *Dialogue Concerning Natural Religion* (1779), David Hume had pointed out the theistic dilemma. If we abandon human analogy in our talk of God, he observed, "we retain no conception of the great object of our adoration." Yet if we preserve human analogy, "we must for ever find it impossible to reconcile any mixture of evil in the universe with infinite attributes." There was, Hume suggested, a third supposition, namely, "the Author of Nature to be finitely perfect, though far exceeding mankind. . . . In a word, benevolence, regulated by wisdom, and limited by necessity, may produce just such a world as the present" (Hume 1947, 203).

Hume's proposal was familiar to the late Victorians, most conspicuously in its more recent guise in J. S. Mill's posthumous *Three Essays on Religion* (1874). In his essay "Theism," Mill had written:

> It is not too much to say that every indication of Design in the Kosmos is so much evidence against the Omnipotence of the Designer. For what is meant by Design? Contrivance: the adaptation of means to an end. But the necessity for contrivance—the need of employing means—is a consequence of the limitation of power. Who would have recourse to means if to attain his end his mere word was sufficient? The very idea of means implies that the means have an efficacy which the direct action of the being who employs them has not. . . . The evidences, therefore, of Natural theology distinctly imply that the author of the Kosmos worked under limitations; that he was obliged to adapt himself to conditions independent of his will, and to attain his ends by such arrangements as those conditions admitted of. (Mill 1969, 451)

The new interest in Hume's notion of a limited God was due to the convergence of two contemporaneous movements: the embrace of kenotic theology by a widening circle of orthodox thinkers and the growing attraction of the metaphysics of Personal Idealism. The most sustained discussions of the question of a "limited" or "finite" God occurred in the meetings of the Synthetic Society in London during 1902–1903. The issue had been joined concurrently by Hastings Rashdall in his contribution to *Contentio Veritatis* (1902), "The Ultimate Basis of Theism," and by F. R. Tennant in his discussion of "Theodicy" in *The Origin and Propagation of Sin* (1902).

In February 1902, Rashdall read to the Synthetic Society an abbreviated version of a long paper on "personality," inquiring how the term might be applied both to individual human beings and to God. Rashdall's remarks launched a wide-ranging discussion on the implications of belief in God as personal in a world peopled by genuinely independent, spiritual beings. Rashdall sought to uphold the metaphysical interdependence between the person of God and finite spiritual persons while rejecting all forms of pantheistic idealism, and to avoid what he considered to be the extreme metaphysical pluralism currently popularized by American philosophers William James (1842-1910), G. M. Howison (1834–1916), and others. In Rashdall's estimation, the pluralist hypothesis of many independent, coeternal, and uncreated intelligences failed to answer a number of crucial questions, such as accounting for the unity of the world. According to Rashdall, if a personal God includes the idea of will and creative activity, there cannot possibly be a pantheistic identification between God and the world. Finite persons and minds are derived from one supreme mind and will.

While Rashdall rejected the tendency of some pluralists to make other souls wholly independent of God, he nonetheless was insistent on positing the distinctness and separateness of individual self-conscious agents against all neo-Hegelian monistic tendencies. "To talk of one self-conscious being including or containing in himself or being identical with other selves is to use language which is wholly meaningless and self-contradictory, for the essence of being a self is to distinguish oneself from other selves" (Rashdall 1902b, 359). God must know every self as a distinct consciousness, as possessing a will that is its own—that is, as a being that is not identical with the knowledge that God has of it.

Rashdall conceded that for many persons such a communion of distinct centers of consciousness and will carries with it the implication that God is limited or finite. But so be it, he replied, for "everything that is real is in that sense finite. God is certainly limited by all other beings in the Universe." God, nonetheless, is not limited by anything that does not ultimately proceed from his own nature or will. "The limitation is therefore, what theologians have called a self-limitation: only that this self-limitation must not be regarded as an arbitrary self-limitation, but as arising from the presence of that idea of the best that is eternally present to a will whose potentialities are limited" (1902b, 360).

Rashdall thought that it may only be a semantic quibble as to whether or not it is a "limitation" that God should not be able to evolve highly developed beings without, for example, a struggle for existence. For God is limited by nothing outside his own nature, except what he has himself caused. Rashdall admitted, nevertheless, to the difficulty that such a self-limitation may imply, namely, that God's purposes may be defeated. And in a later essay he granted that God needs human help:

> We are engaged not in a sham warfare with an evil that is really good, but in a real warfare with a real evil, a struggle in which we have the ultimate power in the Universe on our side, but one in which the victory cannot be won without our help, a real struggle in which we are called upon to be literally fellow-workers with God. (1910, 85–86)

Cambridge metaphysician John Ellis McTaggart (1866–1925) was a persistent and sharp critic of the belief in a God both good and omnipotent, and he detected a serious flaw in Rashdall's defense of God's self-limitation of power when conjoined with his goodness. This he exposed in a trenchant response delivered before the Synthetic Society in March 1903. Let us grant, he argued, that God's power is limited, self-limited "by a simple cessation at a certain point." But this limitation is a limitation that also *thwarts* God's self. "For it compels him to create, as the best possible world, a world which is not as good as the one he would have wished to create," since he had to create a world full of suffering and sin (McTaggart 1903, 395). The limitation of his power, therefore, thwarts what Rashdall considered to be the essential attribute of God's nature—his will toward the good.

McTaggart's difficulty was that Rashdall's theory required the joining of two notions that together are incompatible: the idea of self-limitation and the idea of self-thwarting limitation. We all have experienced self-limitation in taking the best possible alternative among others. While limited, in no way is our nature thwarted; rather, it is realized. And so it can be with God. We can also conceive of a self-thwarting limitation. Our desire to save a drowning friend may be thwarted by our being paralyzed—but it is not a self-limitation. McTaggart could not see how a limitation that thwarts the self can proceed from the self, since that which proceeds from the self must be an expression of its nature. The metaphysical and ethical strength of Rashdall's God, McTaggart conceded, is in Rashdall's insistence on God as a person, one who not only thinks and wills but also feels pleasure and pain. But Rashdall appeared to take God's will and God's power as separate realities. It is in respect to his goodness that God is thwarted, not in respect to his self-limited power. But God's unity must be insisted upon. McTaggart asked:

How can that which is produced *solely* by God's nature thwart God's nature? . . . In choosing the best possibility rather than any inferior possibility God must be conceived as acting freely and gladly. But in choosing the best possibility, which still contains much evil, rather than an impossible greater good, God must be conceived as acting reluctantly and sorrowfully. How, then, can the determining grounds of his action be attributed exclusively to his own nature? (1903, 398)

McTaggart contended that Rashdall had not gone far enough to really save the goodness of God. One solution would be to follow the metaphysical pluralists and conceive of God as one being—albeit the most powerful, wise, and good member—within a community of not wholly perfect beings: William James's "one helper, *primus inter pares*, in the midst of all the shapers of the great world's fate." In any case, McTaggart found the serious discussion of the doctrine of a finite God of the highest importance for the future of religious devotion. While logically "it does not prove the existence of a good God, at least it does not leave his existence *a priori* impossible." Most important, it does have a great advantage over the doctrine of God's infinity, which, he insisted, does "make his goodness *a priori* impossible, since it leaves him responsible for all the evil in the universe" (403).

Having commended Rashdall for his forthright personalism, it is odd that McTaggart could not appreciate that the existence of pain, or its analogue in God, need not prevent God's happiness, since suffering in humans often leads not to a diminution but to a deeper sense of joy, as Illingworth and others had pointed out. Orthodox critics in the Society also posed questions similar to those raised later by opponents of Alfred North Whitehead's (1861–1947) panentheism, particularly questions regarding "the religious availability" of a finite God. McTaggart had suggested that an "enormously superior" person, such as a finite God, is morally a fit object of worship. But the Jesuit theologian George Tyrrell, replying to McTaggart in a characteristically lively response, confessed that he could not in all "humility and modesty" be constrained "to kow-tow to all those who are morally my betters—else I should have to worship the saints." McTaggart, it appeared to Tyrrell, did not recognize that "it is the infinitely, not the enormously, better, that I must adore." As an inferior member of McTaggart's divine syndicate, Tyrrell could not worship God; he could only respect him, "as a Catholic bishop respects the Pope" (Tyrrell 1903, 404–05). Tyrrell insisted that God cannot simply be a superior member of the same order of being as himself. That is what theology's insistence on God's infinity is all about.

Tyrrell also believed that the concessions of a McTaggart, or even of a Rashdall, were a retrograde response to Mill's dilemma. What McTaggart had, in fact, shown is "how slightly, if at all, the good of God can be saved by limiting his power" and "how the admission of his finitude opens the way back to polytheism, nay, to atheism" (406). We will see later, however, that Tyrrell's protest against the concept of a finite God, as proposed in the metaphysical pluralism of McTaggart and William James, veiled the radical character of his own reflections on the God-world question and his own emerging heterodox theodicy.

The Theodicy of F. R. Tennant and James Ward

At the beginning of the twentieth century, certain convictions regarding God's providence and theodicy were widely shared by British theologians and philosophical theists. The "wider teleology" that evolved after about 1840 in reaction to the Paleyian teleology was by now, in turn, repudiated in its more extreme deistical forms. In their attempts to take account of scientific developments, many exponents of the new teleology had sought essentially to confine the divine action to the setting in motion of the entire stream of secondary causes. God's purpose and design were not to be seen in the details of nature and history but, rather, in the general order and progress toward the divine goal, whether that could be clearly or dimly perceived, or not perceived at all. God does not contrive the details by his direct action. God's handiwork must be seen in the beginning and in the end of the process. According to this "wider teleology," many developments in the natural world may be inherent in the finite process as a whole but not essential to its purpose, that is, not intended by God as ends in themselves. We have seen that the deistical features of this cosmology, and its failure to deal adequately with the immanence of God's ongoing creative presence in the world, were exposed both by the theistic Darwinians and by the *Lux Mundi* theologians and, in a different manner, by the neo-Hegelian Idealists.

There was, however, a second conviction widely shared at the turn of the century by most post-Darwinians, one not obviously consistent with belief in divine immanence. It was the acute awareness of the stark moral and physical pain, loss, and waste in the world and the theological costs of ascribing these evils to the immediate will and intention of God. Darwinian science had exposed the seemingly diabolical nature of physical evil in the world and yet, paradoxically, showed how essential it was to the emergent process. This obviously required a deeper theological analysis, one that was related to a third, almost irresistible fact, namely, that such a system of nature required, for any credible doctrine of God, some idea of divine self-limitation and passibility. And this required a more adequate conception of the metaphysical interdependence of God and the world. All of these convictions converged in the work of the Cambridge philosophical theologian F. R. Tennant (1866–1957). They are conspicuous in his 1909 article "The Influence of Darwinism upon Theology."

The *Lux Mundi* theologians had proposed one way of understanding the passibility and self-limitation of God, which found favor not only with Anglo-Catholics but with Scottish thinkers such as the theologians A. M. Fairbairn and P. T. Forsyth and later with the philosopher A. Seth Pringle-Pattison (see Fairbairn 1893; Forsyth 1909; Pringle-Pattison 1917). Others, however, were compelled to push the question of divine limitation further, along the lines laid out by Martineau and Rashdall. Among the latter was Tennant, first in an essay on "Theodicy" included in his influential book *The Origin and Propagation of Sin* (1902). Tennant was constrained to take his stand on the problems of providence and theodicy as a result of his commitment to an ontology that would find room for a pluralistic conception of reality. This entailed giving all finite spirits real power capable of thwarting the divine purpose in the world (Tennant 1902, 125). A credible notion of the relations between God and finite spirits must, then, be sufficiently loose "to find room for an utter discord and opposition in the world of time between . . . the many and the all-embracing One" (124). God must allow entire new streams of causation into the world that may lead a creature to "grieve the Love which called it into being" and that may delay the achievement of God's purpose. God "reveals the ideas, supplies the inspiration, prepares the heart: but the activity which responds . . . is ours" (124, 125, 128).

Tennant's pluralism insisted on a radical contingency as an essential feature of his theism. "Any other world," he argued, "would be meaningless." It could not, for example, assume a moral order. Tennant's position was similar to Martineau's before him and to that of Pringle-Pattison somewhat later. All three understood the limits of divine omnipotence to be a willed self-limitation by God, not a divine necessity. Paradoxically, such a limitation discloses the highest power as one of self-limiting love. This, Tennant believed, in no way detracts from God's infinitude. Since God is pledged to a definite finite plan for creation as a means of achieving his purposes, it follows "that many of the details accompanying the execution of the plan are not essential parts of it but only necessarily incidental." Examples are physical catastrophes, earthquakes and floods, and the contingent distribution of the ills of life that "bear no relation whatever to individual circumstances" (132–33).

Tennant was critical of much of the writing on teleology and theodicy in the post-Paleyian era. He thought that Argyll, Temple, and Illingworth were too quick to urge that human and animal suffering was prophylactic, or a warning against danger, or that human suffering was either punitive or

purgatorial "and thus subservient to certain benign ends." It was not necessary, Tennant urged, to suggest that every form of suffering "is antecedently
willed by God as a means to some particular end," indeed, to do so is "to
attribute devilishness to the Deity" (1930, 312, 316).

Tennant was confident that individuals would not regard suffering as too
high a price to pay for their freedom and ethical dignity once they recognized
that physical evil is inevitable in a genuinely moral world. Physical affliction
arising from our relations with the natural world is not to be understood as
"willed" by God at all. Nor should the self ever regard itself as a means. "My
ills," Tennant wrote, "can only be justified to me if the remoter advantage of
there being ills at all be *mine*: not humanity's or even God's alone." Nor can
a tenable theodicy any longer abide the idea of a compensation stored up for
individuals in some future world. A God who can be worshiped by moral
beings "must be a respecter of the persons whom He has moulded into His
own image. Hence theists generally regard the Supreme Being as a God, not
of the dead, but of the living" (1930, 204).

Tennant's pluralistic ontology and theism were influenced by James Ward,
his teacher at Trinity College, Cambridge. Late in his own life Ward, too,
directed his thought to the problem of God and evil, which found expression
in his Gifford Lectures on *The Realm of Ends or Pluralism and Theism*, published in 1911. Ward's lectures illustrated the new sense of an open, strenu-
ous, "unfinished universe," as William James was then describing it. In the
Jamesian world, the notion of evil was more ambiguous, for, as Ward pointed
out, a world congruent with moral striving and growth *must* be full of hindrances in which there will be real gains and real losses. A world of becoming that is also perfect, in the sense of complete, is a contradiction in terms.
Evolution, as now understood, is not the unfolding of what was implicitly
present at the beginning; it is, on the contrary, epigenetic, the emergence
of ever new possibilities. It is only consistent with such an ontology, Ward
insisted, that the world be the joint work of both God and finite intelligences.
Where finite agents have real initiative, "contingency and conflict, fallibility
and peccability seem inevitable" (J. Ward 1911, 353). And no one can doubt
that these conditions entail suffering. However, they must be understood as
relative evils, not absolute, since they do not represent unlimited obstacles
that allow for *no* amelioration or progress.

No one can pretend, Ward argued, that there is no unnecessary suffering in this world. But neither is one compelled to show that certain specific
physical evils—plagues or tumors—have their place in the world's economy.
At the same time, no one is competent to judge that the physical causes of
suffering are really superfluous. Ward turned back the objection that if one
maintains that certain evils are unavoidable, it follows that one must assume a

non-omnipotent, finite God. The claim fails to recognize that creation entails a certain restriction by the presence of determinate possibilities; furthermore, it assumes that "omnipotence absolutely excludes impassibility" (354).

Ward admitted that if there is a God he cannot have made the world *what it is to be*. Rather, God has created intelligences who, coworking with God, may work out their own perfection by trial and error. "This working out is what we call experience, and experience can never pre-suppose the knowledge or the skill that is only gained by means of it." Trials will naturally involve errors, and such errors we rightly call evils. And yet we cannot straightaway call them superfluous, "still less an absolute evil if it is an inevitable incident of experience as such." Ward regarded it as futile to ask whether our human experience is, in general, worth what it costs, for who can say that it is not? He reminded his critics that *he* was "not arranging the constitution of the world"; it is for those who claim to be doing so "to make their indictment good" (356).

The contingency of the world, which, of course, includes physical pain and evil, cannot be interpreted as a sign of the imperfection of the world's moral constitution. Contingency is inseparable from any creation that is genuinely evolutionary, that is, that allows for real epigenesis, in which finite intelligences have real initiative in interaction with their environment. Yet one may well ask: If God does not intervene in the form of special providential interferences in the world of moral agents, is not the only moral government there is in the world the work of his creatures alone? What sort of a God is it "that only conserves the world on its physical side[,] . . . sends the rain on the just and the unjust[,] . . . but leaves it morally to itself, to sink or swim as it may?" (379). Could such a moral government be the best possible? Again, Ward regarded this objection to his conception of providence as colored by a "crude anthropomorphism," as was the older doctrine of creation that conceived of God's creative activity in the same "piece-meal fashion of a human artificer." Ward declared that such a conception of "special providences" and special creations belongs to an outworn creed. The theological doctrines of creation and providence, nevertheless, remain valid. "But from the standpoint of pluralism they will be conceived as one continuous process of evolution, not as two distinct series of acts, one of which is an interference with another" (380).

Ward admitted that if theism were to remain a defensible doctrine this must be the best possible world. Of course, a world in which moral evil, though possible, was not actual would be a better world than this one. The two positions may appear inconsistent, but they are not. The reason, Ward argued, is that evil obtains in this world not because of "any necessitation on God's part but because of the free acts of us, who are joint-workers with

[God] in the world's evolution." So far as *God's agency* in the world is concerned, the present world and any future better world that we might suppose are equal. Any inferiority in this world is due, therefore, to human agency. We cannot conceive of an evolving world "without its peccability passing over into sin just as its fallibility passes over into error" (382–83).

Providence and Theodicy at the Turn of the Century

James Ward and the other philosophical pluralists represent a shift in thinking about the problem of theodicy. The change is especially noticeable in the discussions of the Synthetic Society. The new frame of mind took several forms. The first was a transformation of perspective from a human-centered world to a much wider vision of humanity's place in the divine creation. The second was the appearance of varied efforts to articulate a credible understanding of God's radical interdependence with the world, preliminary to later panentheist doctrines, such as those of Alfred North Whitehead. A third discernible change was the displacement of theodicy with what, more recently, has been called an "anthropodicy," a shift from the question about evil and the justice of God to an indictment of human folly and sinfulness itself: "How can human beings act in this way?" replaces the question "Why does God permit this?"

One can observe this latter change in attitude in the British response to two catastrophes that shocked the world in late 1908 and in early 1912. The first disaster was the earthquake in southern Calabria and eastern Sicily on December 28, 1908. It is estimated that 200,000 people were killed within minutes, and the towns of Messina and Reggio were laid waste. An editorial in the Manchester *Guardian* conveyed a sense of this new state of mind. There was no talk of the judgment or the purposes of God, no theodicy whatsoever:

> We do not suppose that the twentieth century will find as much food for thought in the destruction of Messina as the eighteenth century found in the destruction of Lisbon. It may help to make a system of seismology, but it will not help to overthrow a system of theology. . . . There are no doubt many reasons why one generation should be affected differently from another. We have no need of cataclysms to overthrow a philosophical system which once saw in every portion of nature's mechanism a contrivance especially designated for the convenience of man. That kind of optimism is dead. ("Earthquake in Sicily" 1908, 4)

Likewise, the accounts of the earthquake that appeared in the Roman Catholic *Tablet* throughout the weeks following the earthquake did not moralize or theodicize at all. The tone was straightforward, factual, and practical, offering gratitude for world assistance and raising questions of how the destitute survivors could best be assisted.

Catholic priest George Tyrrell kept abreast of the accounts of the earthquake as they appeared in the Italian Catholic press. The responses in *Unita Cattolica* were, theologically, representative and traditional. They pronounced that earthquakes and tidal waves were sufficient assurances "that God exists and makes Himself felt," and that "if He punishes the innocent with the guilty, He does not on that account cease to be a most loving Father" (Tyrrell 1914, 245). Tyrrell found the Italian responses "very hard sayings," and they prompted him to offer his own reflections on the human devastation at Messina and its demand for a theodicy. This he did in a lecture on "Divine Fecundity," delivered in Kensington Town Hall on March 25, 1909, just a few months before his death. Tyrrell's words would prove to be rather too astringent and unconventional for many and more threatening, certainly, than the traditional theological sops offered by the Italian Catholic press. Despite its chastening message, Tyrrell's meditation on providence and suffering was closer to the sentiments and the intellectual temper of the British intelligentsia in 1909.

Tyrrell began by throwing cold water on all collective hopes for a future, more perfect destiny for the human race. He foresaw that the extinction of humankind in the midst of its career was as inevitable as that of any other extinct species. He scoffed at humanity's crude anthropocentrism that had created its God in its own likeness, the embodiment and guarantor of our own highest aspirations. No, he wrote,

> there is no guarantee that man, in obeying the innate law of his being, in struggling upward and onward out of bestiality to savagery, to barbarism to grade after grade of civilization, is a favoured child of nature, or is destined to prosperity, or that it may not fall prey of some new microbe, or some wild upheaval of the earth's crust. (1914, 252)

God's universe has not been planned with a view to human progress. "Can we say," Tyrrell asked, "that our past has been co-operant to this end?" Manifestly not, "for only a miniscule trickle of the past is traceable in the present. The rest has sunk into the earth or evaporated into the clouds, and affects us as little as the history of Mars or Jupiter" (255). Each species goes its way independently, indifferent, even hostile, to the rest of nature. It is only in the individual manifestations of life that we find anything resembling what "looks like plan or finality in Nature . . . each a little world apart, adjusting itself to its surroundings . . . as best it may." Does this mean then that the world is aimless and meaningless? No, Tyrrell replied, for the alternative is not a "blind materialism."

> Rather [the universe] teems with aims and meanings, although it has no *one* aim or meaning. It is like a great tree, that pushes out its branches, however and wherever it can, seeking to realize its whole nature . . . in every one of them, but aiming at no collective effort. This is its play, this is its life, this is, if you will, its end. (259)

Tyrrell insisted that the providence of God must be reconceived and that it can no longer be thought of in terms of the image of the artisan who carries his or her work through from a beginning to a definite end. Rather, God's providence must be conceived after the image of an artist. "'What is He going to make of it all?' Perhaps nothing; perhaps the universe is His eternal keyboard; His eternal canvas. Perhaps each melody, each picture, may have a worth in itself apart from all the rest" (260–61). The theodicy of an Argyll or a Drummond was a deceptively attractive solution, for while the individual was often brutally sacrificed it claimed to serve a higher, more universal end, about which God was not careless. That glorious end was simply pushed forward into the unknown future.

Tyrrell's vision of God's work, he conceded, only intensified the problem of theodicy, for it required that we give up the idea that the universe must have a meaning, a telos, *as a whole*. The garden that we envision turns out to be a protean wilderness with no pattern. But even more difficult by far, Tyrrell confessed, is that God appears to be bound by a twofold metaphysical necessity. First, his creativity is radically impartial and disinterested. "To each microbe He says: 'Increase, multiply, replenish the earth and subdue it'; to every force and energy: 'Be thou the ruler over thy brethren.'" The second, related necessity is the fact that all individual beings interfere with and impede one another (264–65). Here Tyrrell allowed himself to reflect, prospectively, on a nascent sort of Whiteheadian panentheism:

> [God] is on the side of the cat and the mouse. . . . He does not will, but He cannot help, the conflict and the agony. His will is plainly to minimize and abolish it if it were possible. Here it is that His freedom is exercised—i.e., in dealing with the problem produced, and ever renewed, by His necessary fecundity. Such progress as we see is the work of immanent wisdom and intelligence, striving to make

room for the swarming children of life. It is, therefore, a libel to say He is careless of individuals. He cares for them and for nothing else. He does not sacrifice them as means to some far-off, universal and impersonal end. (266)

Orthodox Christianity had traditionally perceived evil and suffering as inseparable from human finitude and freedom. The heterodoxy of Tyrrell's cosmological vision lay, however, in the necessity of universal fecundity that it imposed on God. Its merit is that it explains the reality of evil as attendant to the overcrowding of good. The theological objection is, of course, that it makes God dependent on something other, namely, a world not under divine control. Tyrrell recognized that many would object, but he judged the conception both more religious and more ethical than the traditional alternatives. First, God is exonerated of all burdens of evil and suffering that, in one alternative, "He is supposed, if not to will, at least to permit deliberately, in the interests of some final scheme, compared with which the individual interest is of no importance in His eyes" (269). On the contrary, God is on the side of life, and his whole effort is to minimize the inevitable evil that attends nature's creative fecundity. Furthermore, God bears our griefs and carries our sorrows. He also inspires our highest ideals, the highest being the love and care of individuals. But such a divine inspiration is no guarantee of either present or eventual triumph, for all of God's works perish, from the least to the greatest. God alone abides and strives eternally.

Tyrrell's second point was that we humans must learn to give up our anthropocentric eschatology, "our confident assurance that the whole creation centres around a chance page of human history, that has escaped the moth and mildew of Time." Why should we, he asked, expect to have a special privilege that allows us to fare better than the anthill "built up by toiling generations to be annihilated by the ox's hoof or the peasant's dog"? (270–71). We, like the ants and all other living things, must go on striving and building and must not sit down with a *vanitas vanitatum* on our lips, despite the pathos of knowing, unlike the ants, that we as individuals, and the race as a whole, shall come to an end. The grandeur of our human pilgrimage is that we can divine Kant's great intuition that the only true end, the only absolute good, is a good will and that a good will is the Will of God. "To be at one with that will, to enter into and cooperate with God's struggle in the battle of life, that alone is the inspiring motive, the justifying end of all our endeavors" (272).

Tyrrell concluded that the Christian eschaton is neither an otherworldly reward in Heaven—"an eternal Sabbath of inaction"—nor the progressive achievement of an earthly kingdom of God or utopian millennium. The true kingdom of God is life in union with God's will, the only real eternal life. And such a life, he wrote, "is exercised, strengthened and deepened by our co-operation with the Divine cause . . . that bids us take our part in the eternal problem of the universe." There is, then, no final solution; what there is and can be "is the multiplication of the sons of God, of wills reconciled and atoned with the Divine Will in its endless joys and sorrows" (273).

We have seen that the changing ethos with regard to providence and theodicy introduced new themes represented in Tyrrell's response to the Italian tragedies, especially his repudiation of all anthropocentric assumptions regarding humankind's place in nature. Another notable shift, both in thought and sensibility, was Tyrrell's move from theodicy to "anthropodicy." This is particularly conspicuous in the responses to the great catastrophe of 1912: the sinking of the British ocean liner *Titanic* on the night of April 14 after it had hit an iceberg south of Newfoundland while on its maiden voyage to New York. It was the largest ship afloat and it sank in less than three hours. Approximately 1,500 of the 2,200 persons aboard perished in the North Atlantic. An insistent response in the press was one of judgment—but a judgment not of God but of man. "When," asked the bishop of Winchester, "has such a mighty lesson against our confidence and trust in power, machinery, and money" confronted the nation? "The *Titanic*, name and thing, will stand as a monument and warning to human presumption" (Manchester *Guardian*, April 22, 1912, 9). Writers in the *Church Times*, a High-Church paper, dwelt on two moral lessons. The first was the nemesis that inevitably wreaks its havoc on human pride and folly, for example on "the breathless haste which dictated the [*Titanic's*] course"; and the second was "the barbaric luxury with which the last of the titans was furnished forth." Is it not, wrote the editorialist, "megalomania at its worst?" The surpassing of all other ships in size and speed and luxury, wrote another correspondent, represents "the very climax of that most poisonous of all industrial diseases: the law of unrestricted competition." The *Titanic* was a condemnation "of reckless lust, of self-advertisement and of self-indulgence" (*Church Times*, April 19 and 26, 1912, 529, 560).

Most commentators on the wholesale death wrought by the *Titanic* took the occasion to point not only to human pride and presumption but to the utter weakness and helplessness of humanity in the face of nature's blind forces. The extraordinary scope of individual self-determination, coupled with the power of random circumstance and fate, brought home to many clergy, as it did to Tyrrell, the deep pathos of the human condition. Hensley Henson, Anglican canon of Westminster and later bishop of Durham, asked his congregation to think of the sad spectacle of humanity's efforts to resist the laws that circumscribe its mortal condition: "They cheat themselves," he told those assembled, "by a hundred devices into the notion that they can circumvent their fate" (H. Henson, *Times*, April 22, 1912, 13). Tyrrell and Henson both proposed a chastened and demanding Christian anthropodicy. Rather than reproving God, or offering casuistic defenses of God's actions, Christians were bid to be one with the will of God that is exercised in the sacrificial love and care of other individuals.

CHAPTER 4

God and the World

The Reign of Law and Miracle

Doubtless the founder of Mohametanism could have contrived false miracles had he chosen, but the fact that he did not consider miraculous evidence at all wanted to attest a supernatural dispensation, but that his word was enough shews an utterly barbarous idea of evidence . . . which unfits his religion for the acceptance of an enlightened age and people.

J. B. Mozley

Mankind did not originally accept miracles because it had formed proof of them, but because its imperfect experience inclined them to them. Nor will mankind now drop miracles because it has formal proof against them, but because its more complete experience detaches it from them. The final result was inevitable, as soon as miracles began to be relegated . . . to a certain limited period long ago past and over.

Matthew Arnold

A miracle is what is characteristically called in the New Testament a "sign." . . . It is wrong to speak of miracles as being in a primary sense proofs of a revelation or of Christianity in particular. . . . They are fitted to awaken, to arouse, to arrest the faith which is latent. They bring men who already believe in God into his presence.

B. F. Westcott

The Early Victorian Setting

In the early decades of the nineteenth century many theologians continued to view scriptural miracles as vital evidence of Christianity, the authorization of God's revelation. Few hesitated to speak of miracles as special divine acts that were, by their very nature, outside or beyond the laws of nature, known or unknown. It was considered reasonable to suppose that God would authenticate his message by the performance of supernatural, miraculous acts. However, by the 1830s the confidence in God's law-abiding creativity and governance raised serious questions in the minds of clerical naturalists about the conception of miracle as a violation of natural law. On the whole, they did not doubt the reality of the scriptural miracles, and they often opposed the allegorization of, for example, the miraculous events recorded in Genesis. There were, nevertheless, significant differences between the more conservative and the progressive thinkers, and they often centered on the issue of the origin of living species, which touched on the question of miracles. For example, writers such as W. D. Conybeare (1787–1857) saw the emergence of the inorganic and organic world as the work of mixed agencies, in part by the laws of nature expressing God's *observed* method of working, and in part by the immediate exercise of God's power in the creation (W. D. Conybeare 1834). The difficult question was how the emergence of new species involved the miraculous intervention of God. Here the clerical naturalists were divided, although they agreed that God works according to law.

Men such as the geologists William Buckland and Adam Sedgwick (1785–1873) wished to steer a middle way between those who saw miracles as a violation of law and those who interpreted miracles—or explained them away—as divine superintendence carried on by the force of laws originally impressed on matter. For Buckland, geology had demonstrated that there was a time when no organic beings existed. They must have had a beginning subsequently, and that beginning was to be found in the miraculous "will and *fiat* of an intelligent and all-wise Creator." But these miraculous origins were not supernatural in the traditional sense of violations. They were, rather, produced by secondary causes that were, at least in principle, open to scientific investigation. "When therefore we perceive that the secondary causes producing these convulsions have operated at successive periods . . . we see at once the proofs of an overruling Intelligence continuing to superintend, direct, modify, and control the operations of agents, which he originally ordained" (Buckland 1820, 21, 18–19).

It was critical to Buckland, as it was to Sedgwick and William Whewell, that the source or agency of these secondary instruments may never be known by human induction. Sedgwick insisted that the great changes in the condition of organic life evidenced "creative introduction" of new organic structures, which afforded proof of a continuous, miraculous providence—but one that is "altogether different from what we commonly understand by the laws of nature" (Sedgwick 1834, 305). Such miracles, while presently inexplicable, were unquestionably part of the laws of nature, though not presently known.

The scientific case for ignorance concerning the mechanism of organic change in past ages—and hence for miracles as beyond our investigation—was argued by William Whewell:

> In the sciences which trace the progress of natural occurrences, we can in no case go back to an origin, but in every instance appear to find ourselves separated from it by a state of things, and an order of events, of a kind altogether different from those which come under our experience. The thread of induction respecting the natural course of the world snaps in our fingers, when we try to ascertain where its beginning is. (Whewell 1840, 145)

For this reason science can neither confirm nor contradict what is taught by Scripture. Whewell's appeal to miracle was not, however, grounded in scriptural evidence. Belief in miracles is based, rather, on scientific requirements:

> It may be found [that natural occurrences] are quite inexplicable by the aid of any natural causes with which we are acquainted; and thus the result of our investigations, conducted with strict regard to scientific principles, may be, that *we must either contemplate supernatural influences as part of the past series of events, or declare ourselves altogether unable to form this series into a connected chain.* (116; italics added)

The conception of miracle as involving no arbitrary action but rather as a law-abiding sequence of intelligible events outside the purview of natural laws *as we know them* is perhaps best represented by Sedgwick in his 1860 reply to Charles Darwin. He spoke of the miracles of creation as a hypothesis that "does not suspend or interrupt an established law of Nature" but, rather, one that "appeals to a power above established laws, and yet acting in harmony and conformity with them" (Sedgwick 1860, 285). Both Whewell and Sedgwick opposed what they considered to be the *a priori* assumption that miracles work wholly within those natural laws known to us or as may be inferred from our present experience. This appeared, in effect, to explain away ongoing providential miraculous intervention and to move toward a dangerous naturalism, certainly to an implicit form of deism. A thoroughly deistic view was typified at the time by John Herschel (1792–1871), eminent Victorian astronomer and physicist. According to Herschel, one is led by all analogy to suppose that God operates through a series of intermediate causes and that in con-sequence, *the organization of fresh species, could it ever come under our cognizance, would be found to be a natural in contradistinction to a miraculous process*—although we perceive no indications of any process actually in progress which is likely to issue in such a result. (Herschel 1836)

In 1837 Charles Babbage (1792–1871), Lucasian Professor of Mathematics at Cambridge and inventor of the calculating machine, published his unof-ficial *Ninth Bridgewater Treatise*. Part of his purpose was to offer an inge-nious argument, based on the calculation of probability, to further Herschel's point, that is, that the origins of species do not involve miraculous inter-ventions at frequent or even distant intervals. Rather, miracle—if it be so called—is really the working of higher law and therefore is consistent with the working of natural law *as we know it* (Babbage 1837, 127). We will see how the appearance in 1843 of J. S. Mill's *System of Logic* strengthened the move toward a naturalistic conception of the reign of law and the invariable uniformity of nature.

The Legacy of J. S. Mill: Baden Powell on Miracles

The appearance of Mill's *System of Logic* greatly strengthened the belief in the reign of law and the inductive proof of the invariable uniformity of nature. Because Mill's canons of inductive science were so widely adopted in the mid-Victorian decades, his empiricism ushered in a new debate on miracles that proceeded with surprising vitality through the 1870s, the late summer of Victorian rationalism. The essence of Mill's argument was, simply, that whatever contradicts a complete induction must be perceived as incredible. And a complete induction is achieved, Mill was certain, when observations or experiments have been undertaken so often by so many observers that they are found to stand the test of time. In cases such as these, Mill wrote, "we cannot admit a proposition as a law of nature, and yet believe a fact in real contradiction to it. We must disbelieve the alleged fact, or believe that we are mistaken in admitting the supposed law" (Mill 1865b, 167). David Hume was correct, then, about the alleged credibility of miracles, for no evi-dence can prove a miracle to anyone who has not previously believed in the existence of a supernatural being or cause. "The miracle itself," Mill asserted, "considered merely as an extraordinary fact, may be satisfactorily certified by our senses or by testimony; but nothing can ever prove that it is a miracle:

there is still another possible hypothesis, that of its being the result of some unknown natural cause" (168).

For Mill and his disciples, the knowledge that we now possess regarding the uniformity of nature requires that religion, following the lead of science,

> acknowledge the government of the universe as being on the whole carried on by general laws, and not by special interpositions. To whoever holds this belief, there is a general presupposition against any supposition of divine agency not operating through general laws, or in other words, there is an antecedent improbability in every miracle. (169)

A reign of law, it appeared, was rigorously established, not on mere rationalist suppositions, but on inductive, scientific grounds.

Baden Powell, Anglican cleric, Savilian Professor of Geometry at Oxford, and contributor to the celebrated *Essays and Reviews* (1860), emerged as theology's chief advocate of Mill's inductive philosophy, especially as it touched on the question of miracles. It was he who engaged in the fullest, most sustained effort to discredit the evidential value of miracles and to interpret "miraculous" occurrences as being, while inexplicable and unexpected, nonetheless law-abiding phenomena. Struggling during his lifetime to defend Christianity in light of the advances of science, Powell finally eliminated miracles from his religious apologetic as being contrary to scientific knowledge and without evidential value. For him, the only sure evidence of God was the order of nature and the fixed reign of law. However, earlier he was impressed by Charles Babbage's *Treatise* that attempted to justify miracles as consistent with natural law as we know it. And in his early apologetic work, *The Connexion of Natural and Divine Truth* (1838), Powell had appealed to the evidential value of miracles. He insisted, nonetheless, that their evidence was antecedently founded on belief in the divinely ordained order of nature and the rule of law (Powell 1838, 162–64). This odd, qualified support for miracles was to fall away after the 1830s. His final and most provocative treatment of miracles appeared in his contribution to *Essays and Reviews*, entitled "On the Study of the Evidences of Christianity." It ignited a firestorm of protest and rebuttal, but he was denied the opportunity to explain and defend his position, having died of a stroke in June 1860, within weeks of the publication of the essay.

Powell's 1860 critique of miracles was many-faceted. His position on the antecedent improbability of a miracle is essentially that of Hume. The question is not merely one of human testimony but has also to do with "those *antecedent* considerations which must govern our entire view of the subject, and which, being dependent on higher laws of belief, must be paramount to all *attestation*, or rather belong to a province distinct from it" (Powell 1860,

107). If one claims that an event is so intrinsically incredible as to set aside even a high degree of testimony, such a claim in no way impugns the honesty of the witnesses or the reality of their impressions about sensible fact. "It merely means this: that from the nature of our antecedent convictions, the probability of *some* kind of mistake or deception *somewhere*, though we know not *where*, is greater than the probability of the event really happening in *the way* and from the *causes* assigned" (106–7). Powell pointed out that, while it is true that certain parties continue firmly to believe in certain miracles, it is also true that such persons "utterly discredit all such wonders alleged as occurring within the pale of any other religion except their own" (108).

There will remain, of course, those who contend that it is idle to reject miracles as violations of natural laws, since we do not, nor ever shall, comprehend the extent of nature's law. Inexplicable phenomena, or mysteries, these persons will argue, always will baffle the human mind in its attempt at explanation, therefore antecedent rejection of miracles is mere prejudice. Powell protested, however, that this kind of argument simply fails to grasp the meaning of the *order of nature*:

> The boundaries of nature exist only where our *present* knowledge places them, the discoveries of tomorrow will alter and enlarge them . . . and what is at present least understood will become as familiarly known to the science of the future, as those points which a few centuries ago were involved in equal obscurity, but are now thoroughly understood. (109)

The argument from inexplicable phenomena to miracles is, therefore, a futile one. First, it trusts that the mystery will not find a natural explanation. But, second, it confuses the concept of mystery with miracle. A miracle is said to be something at variance with nature and law. But there is not the slightest analogy between an unknown or inexplicable phenomenon and a supposed suspension of a known law. If there were an exceptional case of a known law, it would be included in some larger law.

On the evidential value of miracles, Powell made two additional, and crucial, points beyond the high probability of the error or deception of witnesses. First, there is the "confusion between the force of *testimony* in regard to *human* affairs and events in *history* in regard to *physical* facts." The former can properly be accepted, even in cases of surprising occurrences, on slight testimony. Miracles, however, involve claims of "violations of the laws of *matter*, or interruptions of the course of *physical* causes" (132). Second, Powell pointed to a growing consensus that no doctrine or moral truth should be received merely in obedience to an alleged miracle present to our sensory experience. Rather, it is the other way around:

> Even in the estimation of external evidence, everything depends on our *preliminary* moral convictions, and upon deciding in the first instance whether, on the one hand, we are "to abandon moral conviction at the bidding of a miracle," or, on the other, to make conformity with moral principles the sole test both of the evidences and the doctrines of revelation. (123)

Here, at least, Powell's comments on miracles were to gain wide endorsement.

Powell further proposed that the miracle narratives of the Bible be viewed not in the positive light of science but in their parabolic and mythic character, which are the sensible means by which the doctrine or the moral teaching are best conveyed and taught. Science itself acknowledges that beyond the domain of physical causation "there lies open the boundless region of spiritual things, which is the sole dominion of *faith.*" In the present day, said Powell, "the most earnest advocates of evangelical faith [Coleridge and Thomas Arnold, for example] admit that outward marvels are needless to spiritual conviction and triumph in the greater moral miracle of a converted and regenerate soul" (127). He thus prophesied that the more that knowledge advances the more it will be "acknowledged that Christianity . . . must be viewed apart from connexion with physical things" (128). While in a former age miracles were among the chief supports of Christianity, declared Powell, in our present day they are "among the main *difficulties* and hindrances to its acceptance" (140).

Powell concluded his essay with the assertion that alleged miracles can only be regarded in one of two ways:

> either (1) abstractly as a physical event, and therefore to be investigated by reason and physical evidence, and referred to physical causes, possibly to *known* causes, but at all events to some higher cause or law, if at present unknown; it then ceases to be supernatural, yet still might be appealed to in support of religious truth . . . or (2) as connected with religious doctrine, regarded in a sacred light, asserted on the authority of inspiration. In this case it ceases to be capable of investigation by reason. . . . It is accepted on religious grounds, and can appeal only to the principle and influence of faith. (142)

In the eyes of many, Powell had fallen into skepticism in severing reason and faith. Few churchmen came to his defense. The remark that "no testimony can reach the supernatural" was fixed upon as especially dangerous. Many of the pamphlet attacks and attempts to refute Powell were, however, crude and conventional in their argument. There was also a good deal of semantic confusion as to the meaning of *miracle*, so that the antagonists often failed to engage Powell's real position (see, e.g., Forbes 1861, 21).

A more substantial critique was offered by H. L. Mansel, who was prominent in the agnostic controversy. In *The Limits of Religious Thought* (1859), he had proposed two defenses of miracles that, three years later, he essentially repeated as a refutation of Powell's critique of miracles. The latter appeared in a volume entitled *Aids to Faith* (1861). His first argument was that a person such as Powell cannot help conceiving of God's existence as manifested under the conditions of duration and succession, that is, under time. If the condition of time is inseparable from all our conceptions of the Divine, "what advantage do we gain," Mansel asked, "by substituting the supposition of immutable order in time for that of special interposition in time?" For "both of these representations are doubtless *speculatively* imperfect: both depict the Infinite God under finite symbols" (Mansel 1859, 122–23). In relation to our regulative purposes in life, both have proven necessary.

Second, if analogy is to be used, our experience of the world is of two kinds: that of the world of matter and that of the world of mind. In the physical world it is true that science establishes a system of fixed and orderly recurrence. In the mental world we are continuously confronted with the reality of contingency and free will, of a self as an acting and originating cause. Indeed, the very conception of immutability of cause and effect is compelling because of the negative evidence derived from our experience of mind. "Nothing but mind can be conceived as interfering with the succession of matter," said Mansel, "and where mind is excluded, we are unable to imagine contingence." Experience imperatively forces us then to take account of the relations of mind to matter, to "that mysterious, yet unquestionable presence of *Will*" (124). In the will of persons we have the instance of an efficient cause "acting among and along with the physical causes of the material world, and producing results which would not have been brought about by any invariable sequence of physical causes left to their own action." Here we encounter the *elasticity*, so to speak, of nature, "which permits the influence of human power on the phenomenon of the world to be exercized or suspended at will, without affecting the stability of the whole" (1861, 28). Here then we have a precedent for considering the possibility of the interference of a higher, divine will. Reduced to its simplest terms, the question is whether matter or mind is the truer image of God. For Mansel, nature conceals God—only humanity reveals God. If this be anthropomorphism, so be it.

While Powell saw the orderly reign of physical law as the rational foundation of moral law—and Mansel the other way around—Mansel, again, did not take proper account of Powell's distinction between physical causation, the action of *matter* on *matter* and moral causation, or the action of *mind* on *matter*. It is not clear that they really differed on this point. One has to ask whether Powell's separation of science and religious faith or Mansel's agnosticism coupled with biblical positivism is the more problematic when considering the question of miracles. But even when the real limitations of his essay are recognized, Powell's position would, as A. P. Stanley judged, represent "the common view of the religious world much more nearly than [his critics] like to admit" (Prothero 1893, 34).

J. B. Mozley's Bampton Lectures *On Miracles* as a Turning Point

In April 1864, J. B. Mozley (1813–1878), soon to become Regius Professor of Divinity at Oxford, wrote to his friend R. W. Church to report on the subject of his forthcoming Bampton Lectures. The topic, Mozley confessed, is "a subject on which there is not much new to say—Miracles." Furthermore, he lamented, "what there is new is not, unfortunately, particularly good or correct." He and Church were depressed by the fact that influential men like A. P. Stanley, Broad Church divine and professor of ecclesiastical history at Oxford, were so insensible "to the immeasurable difference that miracle or no miracle makes in our idea of religion" (Mozley 1885, 260). Little, of course, did Mozley realize that his Bampton Lectures *On Miracles* (1865)— whose arguments, though vigorous and thorough, were very traditional— would have the paradoxical effect of: (1) igniting a lively new debate on the nature, evidence, and value of miracles, a discussion that would last for over a decade; and (2) prove to be the nadir of apologetic attempts to appeal to miracles for the proof of theism and Christianity.

Mozley was perfectly candid about the new historical context and how minds had changed decisively on the subject of miracles, despite the fact that arguments respecting their evidential value persisted in orthodox circles. This new context had, of course, struck Baden Powell, and later Matthew Arnold and the Broad Churchmen, as sociologically decisive. Mozley acknowledged that miracles now appeared "plainly contradictory to our experience," as "much to everybody as to the deepest philosopher" (1865, 2). He defined miracle as the "visible suspension of the order of nature for a providential purpose" (6) and insisted that miracles served an absolutely necessary purpose. His argument was as simple as it was old-fashioned. Christianity is based on a revelation. A revelation is given to tell us something we could not know without it. Since our reason cannot prove the truth of the message, there must be some supernatural sign to certify the revelation and to distinguish it as a true message from God. Such a sign is a miracle.

It might be argued that religious doctrines communicated in a revelation could as well be conveyed to a person without a visible miracle. True enough. "But, then, when the extraordinary idea was there, what evidence would there be that it was true?" To have an idea conveyed to one's mind is not to say that it is true. After all, Christianity asserts some extraordinary things. If a person came into a country and made claims about himself—for example, "that he had existed before his natural birth from all eternity," or "that he was the only-begotten Son of God," or "that he should descend again at the end of the world to judge the whole human race," what "would be the inevitable conclusion of sober reason respecting that person?" Would not, Mozley asked, our answer be that the person was deranged? No integrity of character, no benevolence of life would be accepted as proof of such claims. Miracles alone, Mozley insisted, "are necessary to the justification of such announcements, which indeed, unless they are supernatural truths, are the wildest of delusions" (13–14). Christianity and miracles thus stand or fall together. Here was a type of Kierkegaardian argument divested of all its dialectical dexterity and subtlety.

The boldness and oddity of Mozley's argument are evident in his comparison of the claims of Christianity and those of Islam. The latter, Mozley pointed out, established itself without any pretense on the part of Muhammad to miraculous powers. But this is just its weakness and irrationality, since Muslims "accept Mahamet's supernatural account of himself, as the conductor of a new dispensation, upon Mahamet's own assertion simply, joined to his success" (30). In Mozley's judgment, the absence of miraculous certification condemns the Muslim faith to ultimate dissolution. Doubtless Islam's founder could have contrived false miracles had he chosen, but the fact is he did not consider miraculous evidence as necessary to attest to his message, assuming that his word was enough. To Mozley, this shows Muhammad's "utterly barbarous idea of evidence and a total miscalculation of the claims of reason which unfits his religion for the acceptance of an enlightened age and people" (31–32). This side of Mozley's argument would sound fantastic to a later generation, but it was not at all convincing to many of his contemporaries. That said, his argument in lectures two and three of *Miracles*—on the principles of inductive philosophy and on the uniformity of nature—were another matter. They raised questions that can be appreciated by philosophers of science even today.

Mozley focused his critique of writers such as J. S. Mill and Baden Powell on their conceptions of the order of nature and their understanding of inductive science. As we have seen, the received notion of the "order of nature" involved the connection of that part of nature about which we are ignorant with that part of nature which we know. The former, it is assumed, is such and such *because* the latter is so. But how do we account for the belief? The answer is that we see the future "by ever suspending before our eyes, as it were in a mirror, a reflexion of the past. . . . The mind, full of the scene behind, sees it again in front" (37; see also Mill 1865b, 159). Here Mozley called to his defense Hume's appeal to experience: "Experience can be allowed to give direct and certain information of those precise objects only, and that precise period of time which fell under its cognizance; but why should this experience be extended to future times and objects?" (Mozley 1865, 40). Inductive inference, of course, merely *supposes* as its foundation that the future will resemble the past, or the past the present. Our human experimental reason is, in fact, merely customary, "nothing but a species of instinct . . . that acts in us unknown to ourselves" (45). So, Mozley argued, has philosophy loosened the assumed connection of the order of nature as recurrence with its foundation in reason—and so has left a place for the principle of miracles.

The same line of argument applies to the principle of induction. The inference that converts scientific observation into law is the same instinct that converts common experience into law, namely, the habit by which we extend existing recurrent facts into the future. As William Whewell rightly argued, it is from the human mind, not from outward experience, that we derive the "law" that similar causes will produce similar effects. By whatever penetrating faculties scientists may discover *facts*, we cannot attribute to them any peculiar perception of *law*. This is the great failure in the reasoning of men like Powell. "Language has been used as if science generated a perception of mathematical or necessary sequence in the order of nature," explained Mozley. "But science has herself proclaimed the truth that there *is no* necessary connexion in nature." Science has only to do with discovery. What it discerns is arrangement and adjustment among different things, by which it can speak of the "order of nature." But science does not rightly prophesy nature's *inevitable* repetition (54).

Powell had spoken carelessly of the "universal immutable natural order" and of "the one grand principle of law pervading nature, or rather constituting the very idea of nature," a language which, Mozley suggested, violates the very caution prescribed by the logic of induction. Since the scientific part of induction has only to do with the pursuit of particular fact, Mozley argued, "miracles cannot in the nature of the case receive any blow from the scientific part of induction. It is only the inductive *hypothesis* that resists the idea of miracle" (302). Mozley therefore contended that Mill's confidence in the uniformity of nature as "proved" and "absolute" was not well founded. And he saw Mill's confusion as especially evident in the philosopher's own comments on miracles. On the improbability of a miracle happening, Mill had written the following:

A miracle is no contradiction to the law of cause and effect, it is a new effect supposed to be produced by the introduction of a new cause. Of the adequacy of that cause, if present, there can be no doubt; and the only antecedent improbability which can be ascribed to the miracle, is the improbability that such a cause existed. (Mozley 1865, 302)

Here, it appeared to Mozley, Mill had acknowledged that a miracle is possible if there is an adequate, that is, probable, cause to account for it. But elsewhere he had asserted that a miracle contradicts a "completed induction," for example, that men do not after death return to life. Mill's test of impossibility and his notion of what constitutes a "completed induction" were not, in Mozley's estimation, coherent. Mozley did not deny that the inductive *principle*, the order of nature, must operate as the practical basis for the carrying out of our everyday affairs. But such a principle should not lay down absolutely what can and cannot take place in this world. Mozley warned against the working of the passive imagination, by which he meant the mind's adding to a fact something the fact does not supply itself. Such a work of the imagination is evident in our translation of our practical expectation of the uniformity of nature into a scientific necessity. Again, repetition tends to make itself believed.

Mozley further offered some interesting comments on the much discussed apologetic use of the ideas of "unknown law" and "higher law," now introduced to accommodate the acceptance or the explanation of miracles in a world ordered by "the reign of law." The expression "unknown law" often was intended to mean "unknown connexion with known law." In this regard, the criterion to be applied to the gospel miracles "is whether they admit or not of a physical hypothesis being constructed about them . . . *upon* which this connexion would follow" (147; see also Tulloch 1862, 35–37). It is evident, for example, that an entire class of gospel miracles are such that the physical result itself is capable of taking place by the laws of nature. This is true of most of the gospel miracles that involve cures, for example. If one were to disregard the connection with a personal agent, "there is nothing in the event itself to exclude the supposition that it was the result of some unknown cause." "But," Mozley cautioned, "to say that the material fact which takes place *in* a miracle admits of being referred to an unknown natural cause, is not to say that the miracle itself does." For by definition "a miracle is the material fact *as* coinciding with an expressed announcement or with express supernatural pretentions in the agent" (148). It is the correspondence of the exceptional fact with such notification that distinguishes a miracle from a mere natural marvel. Mozley contended that apologists such as Powell did not take this connection sufficiently into account. To give a natural explanation without due consideration of the purposes of the agent is to confuse a miracle with a marvel and to miss the entire point of the former.

The second way of looking at the question of "unknown laws" is to ask whether miracles may not be instances of laws that are as yet unknown. This is the question of "higher law." Here Mozley turned his critique against Charles Babbage and the argument that any "exception" to the order of nature (a miracle) may be included under a higher original law. Known law involves known facts. For science any new law must, then, imply a new class of facts. "But such being the case," Mozley asked, "what does this whole supposition of the discovery of such an unknown law of miracles amount to, but the supposition of a future new order of nature?" (155). However, a law of nature, in the scientific sense, has reference to our experience alone. A miracle, being beyond our experience, is thus understood as a violation of nature. "A miracle, could we suppose it becoming the ordinary fact [Babbage's example] of another different order of nature, would not be the less a violation of the present one; or therefore the less a violation of the laws of nature in the scientific sense" (156).

It matters not a whit whether the Deity operates in nature by immediate single interventions or by secondary causes as regards the question of miracles. As for "higher laws" that embrace unexpected new facts, "the date of [their] causation would be put back, but the miracle itself would remain exactly what it was before" (161). The ultimate question of "unknown" or "higher" law is, then, whether the suspension or counteraction of physical laws by a spiritual being is inconceivable. Mozley believed that the fact of human free will gives us, by analogy, reason to believe it credible. If nature is moved by a supreme free agent, then a miracle would be "a natural production." Here Mozley's argument followed that of his Oxford contemporary H. L. Mansel. It matters not whether we speak of miracle as a "violation" or "suspension" of law, or a "counteraction" to law:

> What is of importance is that, if a miracle *be* a violation or suspension of *particular* laws, there are higher laws of which it is an *instance*, at the very time that it is a violation or suspension of the lower ones: and that a miracle is thus not against law upon the scale of the *whole* of the universe; the giving way of lower to higher being itself an instance of law. (362)

Mozley's arguments regarding "higher law," and the analogy from human free will acting on matter were taken up by the popular press and the religious magazines and were the staple of the apologies for miracles for some time (see Ellegard 1958, ch. 7). Also, Mozley's critique of Mill's apparent question-begging *a priori* claim that nature's laws were "invariable" was considered by many to be telling. Where Mozley clearly failed was in his appeal to the testimony of witnesses and his defense of the necessary evidential role of miracles. Here, as F. R. Tennant later was to remark, Mozley "nailed his colours to a mast which has since disappeared beneath the waves of critical research" (Tennant 1925, 17).

Mozley's Bampton Lectures were generally praised and little criticized by the orthodox. R. W. Church's influential review in the *Times* was typically generous in its assessment. However, what is also of interest in these otherwise sympathetic reviews is how little attention was given to Mozley's discussion of the *necessary* evidential function of miracles, premised as it is on the claim that revelation, by its very nature, is arational. This line of Mozley's argument was rarely pursued in subsequent orthodox apologies. What became the prevailing orthodox response to Mozley's defense of the evidential role of miracles was represented in the Bampton Lectures of 1877, delivered by C. A. Row, prebendary of St. Paul's Cathedral. While a conventional work in most respects, it parted company with Mozley.

Row insisted that Jesus never performed miracles to prove the truth of his teaching—nor did the apostles. What troubled Row and others was Mozley's assumption that revelation had essentially to do with conveying doctrine and that revelation did not consist of truths that possess for the conscience and the understanding a self-evidencing power. To Mozley's question, "How do we know that the revelatory communication is true?" Row replied, "By beholding it." For such "revelations require no note or sign to certify that they are true communications from God, other than themselves, when contemplated by the eye of reason" (Row 1879, 121). Furthermore, "surely the presence of the divine is as clearly recognized in superhuman holiness and loveliness as in acts of power in nature." It therefore follows that the believer's acceptance of Christ's testimony respecting himself "is founded on His entire divine working, manifested during His life on earth, and not on His miracles pure and simple" (122).

This line of criticism was, of course, not new. It echoed the view of Coleridge and his followers over the previous thirty years. For the Coleridgeans, spiritual truth is spiritually discerned—by conscience, the will, and the affections. This was the teaching of the great preacher Frederick W. Robertson (1816–1853) and preeminently the theme of F. D. Maurice's (1805–1872) theology. As early as 1842, Maurice had discarded the very idea of miraculous evidence as later proposed by Mozley. Maurice abhorred the conception of a miracle as a prodigy that certified the divine commission of the miracle worker. It was, he felt, contrary to the very teaching of Christ himself, who warned against a sinful and adulterous generation seeking after and being deceived by wonders (Maurice 1842).

The moral criticism of the external proof of Christianity from miracles was shared by the Coleridgeans, the liberals, and the rationalists alike. It is a theme found in the writings of Benjamin Jowett, in the rationalist W. R. Greg's influential *The Creed of Christendom* (1851), and in the freethinker Francis Newman's *Phases of Faith* (1850). It is an especially marked feature of the natural philosopher John Tyndall's rationalist critique of Mozley's Bampton Lectures. Tyndall was shocked that Mozley required a miracle as certification of Christ's moral goodness. "There is at least moral congruity between the outward goodness and the inner life," he wrote, "but there is no such congruity between the miracle and the life within." Jesus' test, he reminded Mozley, is: "By their fruits ye shall know them." It was quite another who demanded: "If thou be the Son of God, command that these stones be made of bread" (Tyndall 1892, 386).

Despite growing recognition of the limitations of the arguments for miracles offered by H. L. Mansel and J. B. Mozley in the 1860s, two lines of argument continued to characterize much of the theological apologetic for some years. Both are prominent in the Duke of Argyll's popular *The Reign of Law* (1867). The first line of defense contended that miracles do not necessarily imply a violation of natural law, an idea that had so long been associated with the very concept of miracle. The apologists argued that miracles are performed by God through presently unknown natural means, guided by supernatural knowledge. The second line of argument was that proposed by Mansel and Mozley: A superhuman interference in the uniformity of nature can present no difficulty for anyone who acknowledges the reality of human freedom. This assumes that a person can of his own free will produce effects in nature that would not have been produced without his personal intervention. The greater one's knowledge of the laws of nature, the more is one's power enhanced for adapting them to one's purpose. Belief that a personal supernatural agency is capable of producing effects transcending our knowledge is, by analogy, entirely reasonable (see Lecky 1870, 159–80).

The first line of argument was problematic, but it persisted. The one thing Baden Powell and J. B. Mozley had agreed on was the fragility of the argument that miracles were performed by means of presently unknown laws or causes and therefore were not violations of the reign of natural law. They both recognized that "unknown laws" could just as easily imply natural explanations. This was the reason why Powell had contrasted miracles and marvels. The "marvelous" character of an event does not require that it be ascribed to a supernatural, perhaps not even to a superhuman, agency. It simply can be the effect of a presently unknown cause. It was the biologist A. R. Wallace's reconception of the idea of miracle, in his *Miracles and Modern Spiritualism* (1875), that confirmed Mozley's fear about the direction of the discussion about miracles as a threat to orthodox theism.

Wallace was provoked by what he saw as the rather common fallacy in the arguments of his scientific colleagues against the credibility of any fact that was deemed marvelous, on the grounds that it violated or subverted the laws of nature. Wallace pointed out that this really assumed "the very point to be decided, for if the disputed fact did happen, it could only be in accordance with the laws of nature" (Wallace 1891, 43) that regulate all phenomena. The word "supernatural," when applied to matters of fact, is "an absurdity" in Wallace's estimation. On the other hand, to refuse to admit what in other instances would be considered conclusive evidence of a purported fact, simply because explanations are not forthcoming within the bounds of the laws of nature as now known, "is really to maintain that we have a complete knowledge of those laws, and can determine beforehand what is or is not possible." The history of scientific progress has, of course, demonstrated that "the disputed protege of one era becomes the accepted natural phenomenon of the next, and that many apparent miracles have been due to the laws of nature subsequently discovered" (44).

Wallace's imagination certainly was livelier and more commodious than that of most of his naturalist and positivist colleagues. He had no difficulty conceiving the possibility of many unknown forms of matter and of ethereal modes of activity that our present earthbound, human senses could not recognize or acknowledge. He envisioned beings that might, for example, "have a power of vision as acute as that of our most powerful telescope and microscopes," or be capable of perceiving instantaneously "the intimate constitution of matter under every form." Such beings, with such powers, would be inconceivable to us, of course, but that would not imply that they were *supernatural*. And if those powers were perchance "exerted in a manner to be perceived by us, the result would not be a *miracle*, in the sense in which the term is used by Hume or Tyndall," since there would be no violation of nature (52).

Miracles in the Debates of the Metaphysical Society

The middle years of the 1870s represent the high-water mark of the debate on miracles, but it is also true that by the end of the decade there was a distinct shift in the discussion to more historical questions concerning particular miracles, their nature, and their role and significance in the Bible. Nevertheless, in the early 1870s the disciples of Mill were out in full force. Their larger targets were the grounds and the ethical warrants of theistic belief, but a special object of criticism was the evidential value of miracles.

Huxley, W. K. Clifford, Leslie and Fitzjames Stephen, J. A. Froude, Walter Bagehot, Shadsworth Hodgson, and W. B. Carpenter all examined the credibility of the miraculous from philosophic, scientific, historical, legal, and psychological perspectives. But the new attack on miracles that received the widest publicity was the centerpiece of an anonymously published book (in two, later three, volumes) entitled *Supernatural Religion* (1874). The author was W. R. Cassels, a retired English businessman who had until 1865 been a merchant in Bombay. False rumors had it, however, that the author was either Bishop Thirlwall of St. David's or Sir John Seeley (1834–1895), author of the anonymous *Ecce Homo* (1865), a popular life of Jesus. He later was professor of history at Cambridge.

The entire first volume of Cassels's work focused on the philosophical criticism of miracles, relying heavily on the weapons of Hume and Mill against the arguments of Mansel and Mozley. Cassels shrewdly turned the theistic apologists against one another. For example, by employing Mansel's and Powell's argument that God as a personal miracle worker cannot be inferred from nature but only from scriptural revelation, he showed that Mozley's argument, that miracles attest to a genuine revelation, is merely circular. He further used Mozley's trenchant critique of the appeal to "unknown laws" against apologists such as the Duke of Argyll. Cassels's volumes were received by the freethinking intellectuals with great applause. Even H. I. D. Ryder, superior of the Roman Catholic Birmingham Oratory, felt obliged to report that Cassels was "saluted as a choice compound of colossal learning, accurate scholarship, and invincible logic" (Ryder 1875, 271). Whatever the merits of Cassels's philosophical argument (his historical scholarship in the second volume was devastated by the learned New Testament scholar J. B. Lightfoot in the pages of the *Contemporary Review* in 1874–1875), his attack was widely reviewed and ignited a whole new discussion of the question. This enormous response to *Supernatural Religion* helped to sustain the extended debate on miracles in the meetings of the Metaphysical Society in the years immediately following 1874.

James Fitzjames Stephen initiated the discussion with "Remarks on the Proof of Miracle." Taking the point of view of a lawyer examining evidence, he sought to show the limitations inherent in two forms of argument that were current in the writings of the religious apologists. One argument generally took the following form: If a person is not considered deceitful, and if that person had opportunities to observe an event and affirms that he saw it occur, therefore it did occur. The argument is, of course, specious. Without thorough corroboration, no jury, Stephen argues, would possibly charge Mr. A with murder on the testimony of Mr. B who claimed that he saw A push Miss C into the river above Niagara Falls—no matter what B's reputation for veracity. Experience teaches us that far too many possible reasons might lead a person such as Mr. B to make a false statement, whether willfully or innocently. Stephen's point is that the evidence for miracles is not distinct from the evidence that we require for the proof of any other purported fact (J. F. Stephen 1875; see also T. H. Huxley 1879, 130–39).

A paper offered the following month by the distinguished physiologist W. B. Carpenter examined miracles from the perspective of both the physiologist and the psychologist. While his conclusion regarding the testimony to miraculous interventions reflected his Unitarian rationalism, he did not hold any *a priori* preconceptions against divine miraculous intervention itself. Carpenter insisted on the crucial point, made earlier by Thomas Carlyle (1795–1881), that our eyes see what they bring the power to see, and not only in matters miraculous but in the most common of our experiences. Carpenter's long scientific career had forced upon him the belief that in matters concerning supernatural agency—for example, in cases of mesmerism and spiritualism—due allowance must always be given to what he called the "subjective" elements and that, in most cases, such attention practically destroys the evidential value of any human testimony that is not submitted to the most severe scientific scrutiny.

Carpenter proposed that the issue of miracles no longer is what it was in an earlier period, whether the authors intended to speak the truth or were fabricating stories. The honesty of those who claim to have witnessed miraculous happenings need not be in question. Yet, psychologically, the eye and ear in fact see and hear what is expected, and we must, therefore, take into account and allow for prepossession as it modifies both the witnesses' interpretation of the event at the time of its occurrence and their subsequent remembrance of it. Also, in the case of narrative redactions, allowance must be given to possible untrustworthy elaboration. Prepossessions are both ideational and deeply emotional, and Carpenter's extensive experiments with human psychology led him to conclude that we are "affected by our prepossessions at every stage of our mental activity, from our primary reception of impressions from without, to the highest exercize of our reasoning powers." And because the instances of both visual and interpretive self-deception in cases of supernatural agency are so great, Carpenter found that the value of such witnesses demanded the greatest skepticism and scrutiny. If we grant that the witnesses believed they had good evidence for what they had seen or recorded, we must ask: Is *their* belief a sufficient justification for *ours*? (W. B. Carpenter 1876, 95).

The discussions of miracles in the meetings of the Society often were carried on at a fairly abstract level, focused as they were on the general question of the evidential value of testimony. W. G. Ward made much of this fact, and chided his fellow disputants in the Society for failing to grapple with the testimony and professed evidence for *particular* scriptural miracles. Not being a zealot who would "botanise upon his mother's grave," and assured that such a specific investigation would not be seen as "an offensive attack" on the beliefs of his pious auditors, Huxley rose to Ward's challenge with a paper on "The Evidence of the Miracle of the Resurrection."

In many respects his argument was unexceptional. It echoed the earlier criticisms of the German rationalists, and yet on the restricted question of evidence alone—to which Huxley carefully limited his case—it possessed force and moral passion characteristic of Huxley's writing. He began by reminding his fellows that the question "whether an organism said to be dead has been revived or not is a question of evidence." Moreover, the question of evidence here is not one for the jurist or the psychologist but for the biologist to determine—which was within Huxley's special competence. He followed the narratives of the resurrection as they are recorded in all three Synoptic Gospels, assuming their general accuracy. Indeed, he found it quite possible to accept the final conclusion of the Palestinian Jewish friends of Jesus that God raised him from the dead, that is, he said, "if we are careful to attach to their words the significance which they attached to them [that God had intervened] and if we avoid the modern connotations of which they certainly had little conception" (T. H. Huxley 1876).

If, however, the matter were put in terms physiological—namely, that Jesus died in the strict sense of a *molecular death* and that this dead organism was miraculously reendowed with healthy life—in such a case, Huxley concluded that there is not even a shred of evidence to substantiate the occurrence of molecular death in what is told by the gospel witnesses. Huxley's point was that the ancient Jews—and the Oriental mind generally—made no distinction, as do we, between somatic and molecular death. The former involves the cessation of certain functions of the living body that allow for restoration under particularly favorable conditions. The restoration of Indian fakirs after long periods of burial is a well-known case in point. Molecular death, involving *rigor mortis* and general putrefaction is, however, quite another matter, for according to the present state of knowledge, no person has or can in such a state be restored to life; the dissolution of the living organism is irreversible. Now the fundamental scientific point in the testimony to the resurrection is "whether molecular death did or did not occur." But, as Huxley points out, from the gospel narratives themselves no evidence exists or could exist for a strictly miraculous restoration of Jesus. "It would be at once foolish and revolting to suggest that Joseph of Arimathaia, or any of the sorrowing friends who bore the body of their beloved Master to his resting-place, looked upon it with the eye of a physiologist." But if no such investigation took place, or could have taken place, the question whether Jesus died or not—in our present sense of that word—"not only never can be answered, but never should be answered." Therefore, the further question as to whether it was a *miraculous* resurrection is a "mere futility" (Huxley 1876).

This stream of criticism directed at the evidence for the biblical miracles by an array of illustrious scientific and philosophical empiricists resulted in a mixed outcome. The claims for a "complete induction" earlier defended by Mill were maintained, in the teeth of criticism, by disciples such as George Henry Lewes (1817–1878). Nevertheless, concessions were now made under the acute counterattack of philosophers such as W. G. Ward and Henry Sidgwick. Many thought that Mill himself had dangerously compromised his position on evidence in the posthumous *Essays on Religion* (1874). Whether or not that is the case, Huxley, the Stephens, W. B. Carpenter, and their colleagues had, many agreed, made telling points against the *evidential* status of the ancient miracle accounts.

By 1880, however, the grounds of the debate clearly had shifted. By then the theologians and their empiricist critics had reached agreement on several points. First, the issue clearly was no longer the possibility of miracles. Not only Huxley but Mill had put that to rest—apparently for good. Second, it was generally agreed that the discussion had been conducted at too general and abstract a level. It was important to be specific and to look at the evidence for the scriptural miracles in particular cases. This point was, in fact, finally agreed upon by almost all of the parties represented in the Metaphysical Society. Each case of an alleged miracle should be subject to literary-historical inquiry. If found to be a myth or to be mixed with the alloy of legend, then it should be acknowledged as such. If found to be historical, then it should be so understood. This perhaps surprising agreement was based, nonetheless, on a further and widely agreed-upon point—one that marked a general acceptance of miracles as consistent with the reign of natural law. Most parties agreed that a historically confirmed "miraculous" event, while legitimately interpreted as the effect of a divine action, should be understood, as in physical science, as a new and surprising fact, but one that challenges us to reorder our preconceptions about the scope of nature's laws. A rather typical view was proposed by G. Curteis in his Boyle Lectures on *The Scientific Obstacles to Christian Belief* in 1885. A miracle is not to be understood as contradicting nature. It is to be perceived, rather, "as a point of intersection between some vast outer circle of God's ways and the smaller inner circle to which we ourselves are better accustomed" (Curteis 1885, 76)—a law not known to us but known to God.

Earlier, liberal theologians such as Thomas Arnold and F. D. Maurice had argued that whatever one's belief about the reality of miracles, its apologetic value was nil. By 1880 highly orthodox theologians too recognized that the scriptural miracles could not prove the gospel message. The faith was and now had to be built again on firmer foundations. The now prevailing apologetic said in effect: Look for the evidence of Christianity not in external proofs but in the recognition by the individual conscience of its stamp of moral truth.

The Broad Church View: Miracle and the Zeitgeist

Many members of the Anglican Broad Church party had long considered miracles as "signs" that conveyed a moral or spiritual lesson. They also regarded *all* forms of external evidence as incompatible with the gospel's moral message and its internal, evidential power. For these reasons they were often indifferent toward or prepared to dismiss miracles as such. A. P. Stanley, Benjamin Jowett, and Matthew Arnold looked favorably on the spirit of the time; they saw it as slowly but inevitably diminishing the appeal to miracles. It was, Stanley declared, the zeitgeist itself that was spiritually at work.

Benjamin Jowett never had considered miracles as playing a vital role in Christianity. While he did not explicitly deny their possibility, in later life he was willing to say that he considered miracles "the most improbable of all things." He clearly regarded them as an impediment to Christian belief since, to his mind, they were not reconcilable with the findings of science (E. Abbott and L. Campbell 1897, 2:87). In 1870, while proposing to Edward Caird that a second volume of *Essays and Reviews* be prepared, Jowett mentioned that his own intention was to write an essay for the volume on the reign of law that would show "the impossibility of basing religion on miracles" (1:441). For Jowett the groundwork of Christianity is found in its moral witness in the heart of the individual. Over the years this had been the insistent theme of his sermons in Balliol College chapel: "Belief," he preached, "must radiate from life. . . . And the degree of our belief must in great measure depend upon the inward evidence we have ourselves obtained of the truth of the Gospel—no ingenious arguments, no historical evidence, can supply the lack of this" (Jowett 1895, 22).

Among the modernist Anglicans, it was the poet and critic Matthew Arnold's treatment of miracles in *Literature and Dogma* (1873) that proved to be the most notorious. It provoked scores of indignant replies. Arnold rather foolishly spiced his argument with some irresistible but provocative references to the theological zeal of the bishops of Winchester and Gloucester. Otherwise, his treatment of miracles was similar in many respects to that of other Broad Church liberals. Arnold too believed that the zeitgeist signaled a movement of mind that made impossible the old forms of belief and apologetic. In this he followed his father, Thomas Arnold, who earlier had argued that as men grow in intellectual and moral stature, the need for miracles as evidence and sanction recedes.

Arnold made his point about the zeitgeist in his essay on "Dr. Stanley's Lectures on the Jewish Church" (1863): "Intellectual ideas are not the essence of the religious life; still the religious life connects itself . . . with certain intellectual ideas, and all intellectual ideas follow a development independent of the religious life" (Arnold 1968, 76–77). For example, the Articles of the Church of England are intellectual ideas to which the Church at the time of the Reformation connected itself. But being the ideas of the English Reformers they are, in their particular formulation, the ideas *of their time*. The zeitgeist, Arnold was certain, now makes the inadequacy of many of these sixteenth-century ideas plain—and believers find themselves in a false position. Such ideas cannot be restored any more than can the Ptolemaic system or belief in magic.

Arnold's approach to miracles was characteristically dialectical, an attempt to show the weakness of the opposing extremes. The High Church *Guardian* had chided Arnold for not producing a solid treatise against Mozley's Bampton Lectures, for he offered only scant six pages on miracles in *Literature and Dogma*. But Arnold reminded the *Guardian* that Walter Cassels, the author of *Supernatural Religion*, had occupied half a thick volume in refuting Mozley but, for all that, had not begun to convince the editors of that illustrious paper. To write a refutation of Mozley on miracles would be, Arnold suggested, "to do what [David Friedrich] Strauss has well called 'going out of one's way to assail the paper fortifications which theologians choose to set up.'" To engage in an *a priori* argument to prove that miracles are impossible against a person who argues *a priori* for their reality, "is the vainest labour in the world." On the other hand, it is easy to exaggerate the demonstrative force of the case against miracles. *Supernatural Religion* is the best case in point. Cassels had asserted that miracles contradict a complete induction but, as Arnold pointed out, no such law of nature as Mill had described it has been or ever can be established against the Christian miracles. "Nor does the evidence of their reporters fail because the evidence of no men can make miracles credible." This all being so, Arnold had "no inclination either to dwell at excessive length on the subject of miracles, or to make a grand show of victoriously demonstrating their impossibility" (Arnold 1970, 164–65).

What Arnold found so unsatisfactory about a work such as *Supernatural Religion* is that when the author had proven the untrustworthiness of miracles in two volumes, his work was done. The essential question, "What becomes of religion, so precious, as we believe, to the human race, if miracles cannot be relied on?" was left entirely in the shade. But as soon as we satisfy ourselves that we cannot build on miracles, said Arnold, we should be done with questions about them and begin to build on something surer.

Arnold believed that the time was now past for using miracles as a buttress for the Christian faith. His reason for thinking so was one that some orthodox religious apologists also found increasingly compelling, namely, that as our historical experience widens we are more acquainted with the natural history of miracles in antiquity and in the non-Christian religions. The time has come, thought Arnold, "when the minds of men no longer put as a matter of course the Bible-miracles in a class by themselves; and from the moment this time commences . . . the conclusion is certain, the reign of the Bible-miracles is doomed" (1970, 164, 166). The old grounds are no longer safe, nor are they useful. Arnold's fundamental argument against miracles was that they no longer are a part of that set of concepts that modern persons find necessary in explaining or understanding nature, human life, or God. Miracles had gone the way of seventeenth-century magic.

Arnold acknowledged that the rule for the reporters of Jesus' works and teaching undoubtedly was that those who believed in Jesus did so when they saw the miracles he performed. But the crucial point is that this was not the evidence appealed to by Jesus himself. That evidence was the central theme of *Literature and Dogma*. The following is a fair summary of Arnold's conception of that evidence:

> These same reporters [who saw miracles as the evidence of Christianity] indicate another and totally different evidence offered for the Christian religion by Jesus himself. *Every one that heareth and learneth from the Father, cometh unto me. As the Father hath taught me, so I speak.* . . . This is inward evidence, direct evidence. . . . To walk on the sea cannot really prove a man to proceed from the Eternal that loveth righteousness. (1968, 263–64)

Arnold's moral and experiential restatement of the grounds of Christianity had a wider favor among his contemporaries than one gathers from some accounts of the religious history of the period. And this regard was due in part to the fact that his attitude toward miracles was shared by an increasing number of progressive clergy and laity. Indeed, views rather similar to Arnold's were voiced by highly reputable liberal churchmen in the years following without eliciting any notable grievance. Two respected liberal churchmen, J. Llewelyn Davies (1826–1916) and J. M. Wilson (1836–1931), represent this advanced view.

Earlier in his career Davies was associated with the F. D. Maurice circle. He was a liberal in politics, a staunch supporter of trade unions and of higher education for women. He was much sought after and an influential voice of the Church in London while serving as rector of Christ Church, Marylebone, from 1856 to 1889. His theological position was close to the moderate liberalism associated with the distinguished biblical scholars B. F. Westcott, F. J. A. Hort, and J. B. Lightfoot in Cambridge. Davies was regarded as a wise and a sensible theological apologist. Yet his views on miracles were similar to Arnold's. He denied that either Jesus or the apostles had sought to produce faith by means of miraculous prodigies. The gospel, Davies was insistent, "glories in being above [miracles] and independent of them." It is, rather, "the offer of peace with God, appealing to the sense of sin, to the desire of righteousness, to the instinct of gratitude, [that] leaves miracles on another and lower level." He proposed that any purported miraculous wonders associated with Jesus, in which no spiritual or moral truth could be discerned, allowed any believer "the right in being sceptical about them." Furthermore, if a skeptic were to challenge a believer to produce historical demonstration of miracles that could overpower hostile incredulity, Davies proposed that the believer simply "surrender them to his scepticism," since they were not given to force unbelievers into faith. Furthermore, if one were to yield as a penitent sinner to God's gift of grace, such a person may feel quite "free to accept or reject the miraculous element in the Gospels" (Davies 1879, 636–37). The stumbling block of miracles therefore called for tolerance and diffidence on the issue.

J. M. Wilson was a graduate of St. John's College, Cambridge, where he distinguished himself in mathematics and classics. He proved to be an inspiring teacher of science at Rugby School for a period of twenty years after 1859. There he came under the influence of its headmaster, Frederick Temple. He then served successfully as headmaster of Clifton College from 1879 to 1890 before accepting Bishop James Moorhouse's offer of the living parish at Rochdale and the archdeaconry at Manchester. Wilson never saw himself as a member of a church party, but he felt it his mission "to widen Orthodoxy," and to interpret Christianity to the scientists and secularists and to interpret science to those Christians who were troubled by the difficulties science posed. He often was identified as a Modernist, but he saw Modernism not as a school or system but as a commitment to those spiritual beliefs that were, as he saw them, the ultimate basis of union among Christians.

Wilson was invited to give a paper before the annual Church Congress held at Rhyl in 1891. The subject was "Criticism of Holy Scripture," but the paper actually devoted major attention to the subject of miracles. What is significant is the connection that Wilson, like Arnold, drew between the discussion of miracles and the recent interest in the comparative study of religion. Wilson had developed a warm friendship with the Oxford Sanskrit scholar and comparativist Friedrich Max Müller, who had encouraged him in his writings and deeply influenced his thinking. Among all of the scientific achievements of the Victorian era none, Wilson thought, would bear as lasting fruit for religion as the fifty volumes of the *Sacred Books of the East*, which Müller edited. In his Church Congress address, Wilson presented what, for him, was a "practically unanimous" conclusion of modern criticism, namely, the conviction that the miraculous framework of the New Testament narratives constitute a mix of history and nonhistorical legend and myth, and that in this respect "the sacred books of Christianity are like those of Mosaism, or Buddhism, or Islam, or other religions." Furthermore, he stated, modern criticism "is practically unanimous in saying that an atmosphere of the miraculous in a certain stage of the human mind is an inseparable accompaniment of the profound reverence with which a great teacher, and prophet, and saint is regarded by his followers." Miracle is, then, the natural literary form in which such reverence would tend to express itself. "It is impossible, therefore, that such an atmosphere should not have gathered round the memory of Christ." Wilson did not doubt in the least that Christ exercised extraordinary powers as, indeed, did St. Paul. But he held that the zeitgeist has made the appeal to the miraculous unnecessary, even impossible: "Criticism suggests that the belief in miracles has done its work" (Wilson 1891, 152, 155; see also 1903, 88–93).

By the 1870s Broad Churchmen were used to distinguishing between "miracles" and "mighty works," often associating the former with the Old Testament and the latter with the New Testament. "Mighty works" were seen as works superior to those of ordinary persons but not as particular suspensions of the laws of nature. While "mighty," they were explicable in terms of natural law. Furthermore, in the New Testament Jesus' marvels were conditioned necessarily by the faith of those touched by Jesus' words and actions.

A number of Broad Church liberals also wished to retain a *supernatural but nonmiraculous* view of Christ's incarnation and resurrection. Their insistence on divine immanence precluded any sharp separation of the natural and the supernatural. This characterized the position of Edwin Abbott (1838–1926), Anglican priest and distinguished educator and headmaster of the City of London School, and a prolific writer. In his fictional *Silanus the Christian* (1906), Abbot defended a natural yet supernatural interpretation of Christ's "mighty works." He endeavored to show, on historical and psychological grounds, "how the rejection of the claim made by most Christians that their Lord is miraculous, may be compatible with a frank and full acceptance of the conclusion that he is, in the highest sense, divine" (Abbott 1906, 9).

A Way between J. B. Mozley and Matthew Arnold: B. F. Westcott

The zeitgeist was not entirely on the side of the Arnolds and the Jowetts. In the 1880s and 1890s, a defense of the miraculous came from a rather unexpected quarter. The emerging reaction against scientific naturalism and positivism, from writers such as Henry Sidgwick, A. R. Wallace, F. W. H. Myers, and James Ward, coincided with an interest in the study of psychic experiences and paranormal phenomena by respected members of the intellectual community, such as those just mentioned. The consequence was a serious discussion of the supernatural and the miraculous in circles outside the usual ecclesiastical and theological contexts.

The formation of the Society for Psychical Research in 1882 was symptomatic of this new interest (see Gauld 1968; T. C. Williams 1990). Among its early supporters and members were two prime ministers, William Gladstone and A. J. Balfour, eight fellows of the Royal Society, including the scientists A. R. Wallace, Oliver Lodge, Balfour Stewart, and J. J. Thomson, as well as literary figures such as Alfred Tennyson and John Ruskin. Led by Sidgwick and Myers, the Society's output was prodigious: some 11,000 pages in its *Proceedings* and *Journal* between 1882 and 1900. Speaking to the purpose of the Society in his presidential address, Sidgwick told his associates that they "were not prepared to bow with docility to the mere prejudices of scientific men." The Society was confident, he continued, "that there was an important body of evidence—tending *prima facie* to establish the independence of soul and spirit—which modern science has simply left on one side with ignorant contempt, and thus has not been true to her own professed method" (Sidgwick 1888, 35). It was difficult to dismiss the explorations of a society presided over by Henry Sidgwick as the work of superstitious knaves.

A number of the leading British exponents of the new "science of religion"—E. B. Tylor, John Lubbock, James Fraser—were rationalists who did regard belief in the supernatural as a vestige of a prescientific past. Yet this new work in comparative religion also had a contrary effect. The rich diversity of belief in an "unseen" world that now was brought to light awakened not only appreciation but striking new defenses of the supernormal and the miraculous by some comparativists. The change in the intellectual climate in the 1880s was palpable, and it proved influential in challenging earlier positivist certainties regarding the reign of law. The older doctrine's assumptions about "uniformity" were now under acute analysis, especially the concept of law as the immutable connection characteristic of a closed mechanical system.

Religious apologists, nevertheless, remained eager to associate miracles and the workings of the Divine with "law-abidingness," that is, by appeal to "higher" yet unknown laws. While this continued to be considered a gain, even a victory, for theology, it introduced a crucial limitation, as J. B. Mozley and others had recognized earlier. It remained clear to many that there was no criterion by which any extraordinary event could be recognized as a genuine miracle, that is, as evidence of divine agency. The resolution of natural abnormalities into higher normalities was beside the issue with regard to any claim to divine action, as the philosophical theologian F. R. Tennant was soon to make clear. Take the scriptural case of Christ's healings. What had been a miracle for early Christianity was no longer so considered in light of the new knowledge of the psychology of faith healing. Science's hope, of course, was to increasingly close the gap. But theistic apologists were now heard to say that it was not absurd for the scientific imagination to entertain the possibility of restoring life in a body from which life had only recently withdrawn. The appeal to "higher laws" might, then, allow that earlier "marvels" were caused by supernatural means. But logically it removed the grounds of certainty of such a cause, since it did not negate naturalism. It took a long time for this fact to have any effect on theological apologetic.

The critical point that came to be made was that law per se cannot furnish the criterion for differentiating a miracle from a natural marvel. Thus, it became apparent that the entire discussion was required to shift to the *mode* of causation as the only distinguishing mark between a natural and a supernatural event. While a supernatural event cannot be ruled out *a priori* by science, neither can it be proven that the purported miracle is not causally the effect of natural means. All that can be done is to define miracle ontologically as supernatural—that is, as not wholly reducible to natural agencies—and to affirm its possibility. But its evidential value had vanished. It was now becoming clear to all concerned that any belief in miracles presupposes belief in God. Tennant remarked that by the 1880s the most that could be claimed for miracle, in respect to its extraordinariness, "is that it is an event which *suggests* divine activity," and "this brings into emphasis the aspect of miracle expressed by the word 'sign'" (Tennant 1925, 66).

Here we are brought to B. F. Westcott and his important contribution to the discussion—something of a middle ground between the older orthodoxy and the Broad Church liberals. For Westcott the miraculous "signs" in the Gospels were essential to the content of the spiritual revelation, but they were not the external proof of the revelation's truth and authority. Though committed to the most advanced results of historical and scientific work, there were scholars who, now, were not convinced that these results entailed the radical conclusions assumed, for example, by Benjamin Jowett, or that they were contrary to orthodox doctrine. And many of these scholars discovered this mediating position articulated in the doctrinal writings of the Cambridge biblical scholar and theologian, and later bishop of Durham, Brooke Foss Westcott (1825–1901), especially in *The Gospel of the Resurrection* (1884), and *The Gospel of Life* (1892).

Westcott was a progressive, but he belonged to no party. He was a meticulous scholar, learned in the fields of textual and historical criticism and yet orthodox in his conclusions. His treatment of miracles in his two doctrinal books conceded much to recent liberal criticism, but he profoundly disagreed on one point: He was certain that miracle was crucial to Christianity. He opposed the wholesale rationalization or naturalization of the scriptural miracles, for example, the recent efforts to call them "mighty works," since this could imply a thoroughly natural explanation of their nature and cause. Using the word in its strictest sense, Westcott defined miracle as "a phenomenon which either in itself or from the circumstances under which it is presented, suggests the immediate working of a personal power producing results not explicable by what we observe in the ordinary course of nature" (Westcott 1884, 35). He did not deny that many scriptural facts may be regarded as either exceptional or as miraculous, for instance, the healing narratives. We may "look at them as resulting from powers already existing in man and evoked by special circumstances, or as immediate acts of divine blessing" (35–36). The "special circumstances," while natural, are not thereby to be understood as denying that they are the immediate work of a divine personal power. To say that miracles are unnatural is, Westcott contended, to translate the general laws of nature "into a fate superior to God, or to deny his personal action." To do so in the physical world also involves "denial of His action on the hearts of men," for there is no reason to suppose that God is more likely to act on one part of his creation than on another (38).

For Westcott to maintain that miracles are "natural," it was necessary to guard against two explanations that had gained currency among liberal apologists. Some had said that a miracle is, in fact, the "compression" of a result that is obtained slowly in the general course of nature. Westcott cited the biblical story of the wedding in Cana. "The water, it is argued, which was made wine by a word at Cana once, is made wine by vintage every year" (39). Yet from the religious perspective the two processes have nothing in common. "Even if the parallel were perfect it would be equally nugatory, for in that case it would tend in proportion to its completeness, to exclude the idea of personal action which is the essence of miracle" (39–40). The second type of explanation, first suggested by Charles Babbage in his 1837 Bridgewater Treatise and later by others, is based on the comparison of natural law to a mathematical series in which the action of the same law may have one result for a million times in succession and then produce a different result the next time. Miracles can, in such a circumstance, be declared "exceptional." But if so, their significance as miracle is, again, negated. "Their moral and spiritual value vanishes at once when they are derived from the constant action of the same forces as commonly work around us" (40).

Westcott laid down preconditions that are essential to any consideration of the scriptural miracles, without which the entire discussion, he believed, reduces itself to a consideration of particular theories of natural causality. First, a miracle, in its strict usage, assumes the existence of a spiritual power, and in the Christian context, God. Second, the moral element in the biblical miracles is predominant and is essential. No judgment can be made on the reality of a purported miracle until its moral circumstances are understood. "A miracle, in other words, is what is characteristically called in the New Testament, a 'sign.' Its essence lies not so much in what it is in itself as in what it is calculated to indicate" (1892, 207–8). Third, and in view of the previous points, "it is wrong to speak of miracles as being in a primary sense proofs of a revelation or of Christianity in particular" (1892, 222). Westcott believed that no such claim is made for them in the New Testament. The presence of faith is always assumed and required. The most that any particular effect can require of an observer "is that he shall admit the existence of a power sufficient to produce it," but that in no way justifies the logical conclusion of the workings of an agent with infinitely greater power or wisdom. In short, Westcott insisted that "the idea of the spiritual Being must precede the idea of the miracle which is referred to His agency . . . before the phenomenon is recognized as a miracle" (208–10).

While miracles do not serve as proofs, their role in the divine working is indispensable. "They are," Westcott insisted, crucial "signs" that are "designed to cast light upon mysteries, to be sacraments, as it were, of divine working." Therefore, they serve an indispensable function in the divine economy: "They are fitted to awaken, to arouse, to arrest the faith which is latent. They bring men who already believe in God into His Presence" (226).

The miracle of the resurrection is, for Westcott, the "sovereign sign," the key to the whole mystery of Christianity. Again, the resurrection is not the proof of the Christian message but is itself the message, not as an overwhelming wonder, "but so far as it was recognized as the beginning of a new life" (224). While other scriptural "miracles" may, when scrupulously examined, prove to be misapprehended as such—for example, cases of healing—the resurrection is for Westcott unequivocally a miracle. It is either a miracle or it is an illusion. "There is no alternative: no ambiguity, for the Resurrection is not an accessory of the Apostolic message, but is the sum of the message itself"—the very ground of religious hope (1884, 52).

Westcott spoke of the resurrection as a "fact of history," an objective, external event of the same order as Christ's death and burial. Yet, he argued, "like all historical facts it differs from the facts of physics as being incapable of direct and present verification." It also differs from other facts of history "because it is necessarily unique" (1884, 77). It is at this point that some of his colleagues found Westcott drifting into obscurity. Since all historical events are, in an important sense, unique, Westcott's language here is unclear. He proceeded to argue that while the resurrection is "absolutely unparalleled" in itself, nevertheless "its verification lies in its abiding harmony with all the progressive developments of man and with each discovery which casts light on his destiny" (17). This latter expansive yet shadowy claim remains unexplained. Despite such lapses into obscurity, Westcott's general principles regarding the miraculous in their scriptural context and in their essential theological import as "signs" are clear enough. He recognized that the moral truths claimed for Christianity in the New Testament—the ethics of the kingdom of God—are rooted in a belief in a spiritual world and power. He had sought to shift the debate on miracles away from the Victorian obsession with the reign of law and the discussion of "higher laws" consistent with the uniformity of nature. He focused attention on the distinctive role of miracle as a supernatural "sign," as it evoked faith in the Divine, rather than on its extraordinary character as a breach of nature's uniformity. Assuming the possibility of miracle, he thought that the issue was now essentially delimited to the question of the credibility of the historical sources. Here he proved to be too sanguine. The work of the historical critics in the 1890s and beyond was to raise deeper questions about the New Testament and history. In the first decade of the new century these issues set off a final, acrimonious chapter in this long debate.

Miracle and the *Lux Mundi* Theologians

Westcott believed that the effort to establish the original text of the New Testament, as the indisputable historical witness of what happened, was the scholar's essential task. But it was exactly this interpretive supposition regarding the gospel sources that many of the younger generation of New Testament scholars found impossible to accept. And this response highlights the more guarded position of liberal Anglo-Catholics such as J. R. Illingworth and Charles Gore, who, well into the second decade of the twentieth century, resolutely defended the historicity of the gospel miracles.

Illingworth had offered a thorough defense of miracles in *Divine Immanence* (1898), and he pursued the argument in a book-length study, *The Gospel Miracles* (1915). In 1915 Illingworth expanded the earlier philosophical defense, centered on the analogy of human freedom, but what is noteworthy is the considerable attention that he gave to the gospel evidence. Here Illingworth followed Westcott in insisting that the gospel testimony is of a unique kind. He also saw Jesus' appeal to miracles as a means of enhancing the effect of his message by arresting the attention of the people, although he insisted that they were not meant as proofs. Christ came, as Westcott had earlier emphasized, to found a kingdom of God, and the miracles were a "sign," an earnest of that kingdom. Illingworth granted that these wonder works were "relative to their time, and that they would possibly not have fulfilled the same function, if enacted at the present day." Yet they do possess "an essential value as permanent factors in the presentation of Christianity to the world" (Illingworth 1915, 48–49). Therefore he was reluctant to follow the lead of the distinguished contemporary New Testament scholar William Sanday, who now bid his colleagues go back behind the New Testament narratives and "apply to them the standards of our own age, which in the treatment of evidence are more exacting" (172). Rather, Illingworth proposed what, late in the twentieth century, was spoken of as a postcritical, or "realistic" reading of the biblical narratives, free of the encumbrances of historical-critical interpretation:

> Now it is in the form in which we possess them, and as traditionally interpreted by the Church, that these books have really lived and done their work. And when we withdraw them from . . . the throbbing centre of human interest, into a library remote from the world, and there analyze them apart from all thought of what they have actually been, and actually done . . . we can only arrive at very partial results. . . . The experience of those two thousand years alone is amply sufficient to create an overwhelming presumption that the message of the Christian Church has after all been true, that the Incarnation is a fact. (174–75)

It is apparent that here the concept of historical evidence for the New Testament miracles shifted for Illingworth. And his argument appears circular. He first argued from results: the witness of two thousand years of history, the *consensus gentium* that is sufficient to create an "overwhelming presumption" that the supreme miracles of the incarnation and resurrection are historical facts in the sense that William Sanday used the term. But then he argued, in turn, that all the grandeur of Christian history—its martyrs and saints, its philosophy and art, its myriad social and practical institutions, its worship and spiritual experience—required something to account for such a moral revolution in human consciousness, "some adequate cause for this stupendous effect; some power to originate this Christian Church that was to revolutionize the world." That cause, Illingworth argued, is the resurrection, "the only cause that could conceivably be adequate thus completely to reverse the situation" (29, 30).

Illingworth's comments on the gospel miracles help to place his "critical orthodoxy"—and that of Charles Gore—in their relation to developments in New Testament studies at the end of the century. First, the *Lux Mundi* theologians came to associate the reality of such central doctrines as the resurrection and the virgin birth with their literal, historical mode of representation in the New Testament narratives, while scholars such as Hastings Rashdall, William Sanday, and even the radical J. M. Thompson believed in the reality of the resurrection but questioned its literal, historical representation in the Gospels. Related to this is the equivocal use of the words *miraculous* and *supernatural*. Orthodox theologians, such as Illingworth and Gore, insisted on the miraculous, while the liberals often sought to distinguish between the miraculous, which they largely disparaged, and the reality of the supernatural, in which they believed. For example, the latter saw the resurrection as a supernatural reality but did not consider it necessarily miraculous. These verbal distinctions may appear to be little more than semantic quibbles, but, while the source of much confusion, they were hermeneutically significant. Finally, and most importantly, there proved to be a very real impasse over the use of the New Testament testimony as evidence for miracles in view of the actual historical status of the miracle stories in the New Testament. This latter issue appeared in a paper Rashdall read before the Synthetic Society in 1905.

Rashdall was at pains to show that his negative criticism of the empty tomb narratives and the "materialized" bodily appearances of Christ in no way discredited belief in "any sort of Resurrection" (Rashdall 1905, 514). He judged that the evidence was strong for the apostles, who believed they had seen the risen Christ, and he interpreted those appearances as "real, though supernormal, psychological events," involving "nothing which can properly be spoken of as a suspension of natural law" (516). What concerned Rashdall was the claim of some orthodox theologians to have proven the occurrence of the resurrection by historical evidence. Here the meaning of *historical* evidence, he felt, needed to be made clear. To talk of the evidence of the resurrection "as being as good as the evidence for any historical event whatever" struck Rashdall as an extravagant misuse of the accepted meaning of the words *historical* and *evidence*. It failed to "realize how completely the usual canons of historical evidence presuppose what we call the laws of Nature." The historian's craft has necessarily depended for its judgment of "facts" on interpretations that accord with previous experience. That may, of course, be a limitation, but "once admit that the best ascertained laws may be violated, and the possibility of proof by historical testimony disappears" (515).

Theologians may say, for example, that Jesus' body must have been gone because the apostles saw that it was not in the tomb. But these theologians are simply making assumptions that their own hypothesis regarding natural law denies. For example, explained Rashdall, "in ordinary life, we say that a man has proved his *alibi* because he was seen a hundred miles from the scene of the murder. But if the laws of Nature are to have real exceptions, the inference is invalid; he might have been in two places at once" (515).

For such reasons Rashdall considered it obvious "that completely isolated exceptions to laws of Nature (though not *a priori* inconceivable) could not be adequately established *by the kind of historical evidence to which the believers in such suspensions appeal,* even if that evidence were far stronger than it is" (516; italics added). Appeal to "higher laws" simply begged appeal to a wider naturalism. Rashdall wanted to insist, however, that his appeal to the idea of natural law was not to be confounded with the idea of a mechanical uniformity of succession. There are different kinds of causality in, say, physics, biology, and psychology. Thus, "in the present state of our knowledge of the kind of causality which is discoverable in the relations between mind and mind, or between mind and body, there is nothing to be said against the possibility of an appearance of Christ to his disciples." They would be real psychological and supernormal occasions, but they would involve nothing that could properly be spoken of as a suspension of known natural law (516).

Rashdall believed that his psychological interpretation of the resurrection possessed all the spiritual meaning and value that is claimed for the conventional materialized view and that anyone who accepts such an interpretation "has as good a right as the traditionalist to say 'The third day He arose from the dead'" (515). Since the universal church had not defined the manner of the resurrection, and since orthodox persons were now prone to interpret the concept of the resurrected "body" in ways quite other than the literal and obvious meaning of the Second Article of the Thirty-Nine Articles of the Church of England, Rashdall concluded that few churchmen presently would be anxious to institute a policy of anathematizing those for interpreting the central miracle narratives in other than a literal-historical sense.

J. M. Thompson's *Miracles in the New Testament* and Bishop Gore's Challenge to Criticism

In 1891 Arthur T. Lyttleton, bishop of Southampton, delivered the Hulsean Lectures on "The Place of Miracles in Religion," which were published in 1899. Lyttleton's views on the subject were representative of the *Lux Mundi* group that presently dominated orthodox apologetics in the Church of England. In what can serve as a summary of his position, Lyttleton wrote:

> We do not assert that miracles are necessary to revelation because a supernatural doctrine can only be proved by a supernatural fact, or because revelation is undiscernible by reason, and therefore needs the proof of miracles. We do not, indeed, take upon ourselves to assert that miracles are necessary at all to the accomplishment of God's purposes. We dare not set bounds to His Almighty wisdom, and declare either that miracles cannot have happened, or they must have happened. All that we can venture to say is that, *having happened*, they have revealed to us something of the character and purposes of God. (Lyttleton 1899, 135; italics added)

This passage is instructive on several counts. It rejects the traditional apologetic, represented by Mozley, that had placed undue emphasis on the preternatural character of Christ's wonder works as the evidential basis of his message. Furthermore, and consistent with the emphasis on divine immanence, Lyttleton distances himself from the idea that miracles are God's normal means of accomplishing his purposes. The idea of "higher laws" does not require the ontological disjunction of the natural and the supernatural. The gospel miracles, nevertheless, served a special purpose in their time. "Having happened," they must be seen as revelatory of God's character and purpose.

It was Lyttleton's third point that especially struck J. M. Thompson, the young New Testament scholar and dean of divinity at Magdalen College, Oxford. Thompson was convinced that the new orthodoxy's apologetic for miracle was based on a foundation as vulnerable as that offered by Mozley. Lyttleton insisted that, "*having happened*," the gospel miracles "revealed to us something of the character and purposes of God." Here, Thompson perceived, was the fatal difficulty. "It has always been assumed, and we are still asked to assume, that the events really happened as they are related, i.e., as miracles" (Thompson 1912, 18).

What the current orthodox apologist was defending, Thompson suggested, was not miracles but an outmoded, literal reading of the biblical sources, rendered possible only because this school of apologetics had resisted recent biblical scholarship. But the question of historical evidence must, Thompson contended, precede every other *a priori* consideration of the discussion. Lyttleton did not say that the miracles are to be believed because they are helpful, but that we must believe in them because they happened. Thompson replied that if "criticism can give good grounds for thinking that they never happened, the main reason for wishing to keep them is abolished" (18). The fundamental question for Thompson was: Did the miracles really happen? And scholarship alone could determine the issue, for if the miracles did not happen *as* the tradition records them, every other philosophical consideration of the matter was inconsequential.

Thompson had published *Miracles in the New Testament* the previous year (1911) in an attempt to refute the orthodox claim regarding the *historicity* of the New Testament accounts of the virgin birth and the physical resurrection of Christ and their place in the creeds. The book caused an uproar and launched a new chapter in the ethics of belief debate. E. S. Talbot, bishop of Winchester, who as Visitor had episcopal jurisdiction in Magdalen College, withdrew Thompson's license to exercise his ministry. Bishop Charles Gore of Birmingham drafted a resolution for convocation in an effort to have Thompson condemned. Only through the intervention of other bishops did Gore agree to content himself with a private discussion of the Thompson matter, rather than initiating a public debate. However, in 1911 Gore succeeded Francis Paget as bishop of Oxford. Then, in 1912, two new books appeared, each by a noted churchman, and these Gore recognized as giving support to Thompson's handling of the New Testament miracles. One of the volumes was *Foundations*, edited by the Oxford New Testament scholar B. H. Streeter (1874–1937), which included a contribution by him on "The Historic Christ." Streeter's essay advanced a radical conclusion regarding Christ's resurrection appearances. Gore felt compelled to cancel Streeter's license, but again he was dissuaded. Streeter considered the efforts of both Bishop Talbot and Bishop Gore to be dangerous attempts to establish their own measure of orthodoxy in the Church of England. Streeter's essay was intended as a defense of Thompson's freedom as a theological scholar but, more broadly, as a deliberate challenge to the Anglo-Catholic party in the Church, of which Gore was the theological leader. As Paul Avis comments, "It was vital that freedom of discussion and opinion should be recognized as allowable to the clergy" (Avis 1988, 79).

The second book that disturbed Gore was Hensley Henson's *The Creed in the Pulpit*. In the preface, Henson (1863–1947) had criticized the action of both Talbot and Gore with regard to Thompson. He touched specifically on the historical-critical question that Gore had raised, for Henson saw that the root of the present problem lay in the discrepancy between the most recent methods and results of scriptural criticism and a theological apologetic that was based on outmoded critical methods—hence the confusion and turmoil. For Henson, as for Thompson, the alternatives were plain: whether the clerical scholar was to use all the resources of modern knowledge and the exact methods of modern critical science, or whether he would ignore both and limit himself "to illustrating the dogmatic decisions of the Church by the cunning craft of the allegorists or the adroit dovetailing of harmonists" (Henson 1912, xvi).

Thompson's book focused on the working assumptions of the historian's craft, the issue earlier attended to by Rashdall. As a historian, Thompson was dismissive of the popular appeal to unknown "higher laws." It allowed, of course, for an ambiguity regarding what was natural, though not common, and what was miraculous; Thompson saw no difference between saying "Every event is a miracle" and "Miracles do not happen." Furthermore, recent work in the history of religions had shown that the direct actions of supernatural agents were evil as well as good. Thompson concluded that it is "a special hypothesis of religious faith, not a general postulate of experience, that miracles are a sign of *divine* agency," rather than the work of devils or Satan. But the question of "higher laws" and the moral judgment regarding miracle must remain subordinate to the more basic evidential question, "Did the events happen as recorded, or did they not?" (Thompson 1911, 4).

Thompson was forthright in admitting that there is no method of estimating evidence that does not involve appeal to certain preconceptions. Here he argued, with Rashdall, that the guiding principle of historical investigation, the only one appropriate to *its* subject, is that any purported *historical* matter of fact occurring within the limits of human experience must be explained in terms of the laws of nature *as at present conceived*. Otherwise, a Pandora's box of explanations is let loose to justify any marvelous claim. Thompson believed that the question of miracles, in particular, was open to such a danger. "Thus," he writes,

> no general argument as to the probability of miracles can be admitted as direct evidence for this or that miracle. No theological presupposition—as, for instance, that miracles are or are not a corollary of the Incarnation [Illingworth and Gore]—has any place as such in the historical inquiry whether miracles have or have not occurred. (1911, 7)

The question of evidence takes us back to the New Testament documents. But for Thompson this could not mean merely wanting to know whether the biblical writers themselves thought that miracles occurred. The question was "whether they were right in so thinking." Neither was it enough to get back to the earliest tradition: "We must reconstruct the facts that lie behind it." For Thompson the earliest traditions simply challenged further inquiry:

> When, as in the case of the story of the Empty Tomb, we are able to trace the development of a comparatively simple and natural story

into one that is miraculous and elaborately evidential, we cannot be sure that the earliest extant tradition is really the starting-point of the whole process: we must raise the question whether it may not itself be a development of something simpler still. (8)

The critic's task is, then, to follow out the several stages of a growing tradition in an effort to reconstruct the facts. Pursuing this task, Thompson arrived at not unexpected conclusions. He interpreted the virgin birth, the empty tomb, and the physical appearances of the resurrected Jesus as later developments of the tradition *about* Jesus, but not as historical events. He concluded: "As we may believe with St. Mark that Jesus was born of human parents, and yet call Him divine; so we may believe with St. Paul that His body remained in the grave, and yet worship him as risen and alive" (211).

In the conclusion to his book, Thompson sought to anticipate certain objections that he knew would be urged against his views and to offer a more theologically constructive position. First, he argued that "to reject miracles is not to reject the supernatural." Science and supernaturalism can survive side by side *only* if miracles are rejected as essential to belief. God must be looked for in the normal events and processes of life, not in the abnormal. "Natural laws are the normal rule of God's working and natural events the ordinary form of His acts." Second, Thompson argued that the new orthodoxy tended toward a docetic view of Christ, and that implicit in the older orthodox Christology was "the hypothesis of the *non-miraculousness* [but supernatural character] of Christ as an extension of the belief in His humanity*" (211). Thompson proposed that a person miraculously born, with a mind that does not share natural limitations, and with the power to perform miracles not subject to natural laws, cannot possess a wholly human body or mind.

While the *Lux Mundi* theologians offered some cogent responses to Thompson's objections, Thompson's more significant point—one that was to become central to much christological thinking in the twentieth century—was the fallacy of thinking that the divinity of Christ was to be found elsewhere than in and through his full humanity. "Jesus Christ, as living in space and time, and as studied by historical science, is at once human and divine. But the divine in Him is entirely mediated by the human." As studied by faith, Christ remains both human and divine, "but now it is the human which is mediated by the divine. The pure in heart see that he is God" (216). And so, Thompson concluded, "no miracles accompanied His entry into, or presence in, or departure from this world. . . . He yields nothing to historical analysis but human elements; yet in Jesus Christ God is Incarnate—discovered and worshipped as God can be, by the insight of faith" (217).

For a number of reasons, Gore was deeply troubled by the New Testament criticism represented by Thompson and supported, if not wholly accepted, by men such as William Sanday, Hensley Henson, and William Inge. First, Gore and his colleagues believed that the crucial distinction between the supernatural and the natural was eroded by the immanentism of the modernists' criticism—and the distinction was, to Gore's mind, connected with belief in miracles. Second, Gore had reached certain critical principles with regard to the historical study of the New Testament miracles that remained essentially unchanged during the last forty years of his productive life as scholar and apologist. As early as his *Lux Mundi* essay—published at the age of thirty-six—Gore had made a sharp differentiation, as we have seen, between the status of the narratives of the Old and New Testaments. Thus, while he could recognize the mythical, legendary, and idealized character of the Old Testament narratives, he maintained that a similar position was unacceptable in the case of the New Testament, that is, without results disastrous to Christian belief. Gore insisted that in certain crucial New Testament narratives there be an absolute coincidence of theological or spiritual idea and historical fact, and he accepted as "trustworthy" the apostles' witness as to what had been seen and heard. He therefore believed that the virgin birth, God's incarnation in Jesus, and the empty tomb and bodily resurrection all were grounded in solid *historical* evidence—and that any skepticism regarding them was based on *a priori* secular preconceptions. Moreover, Gore did not think it possible, as a matter of historical inquiry, to go behind the apostolic witness as preserved in the New Testament documents in an effort to determine "what really happened." This was crucial for him and *the* point of contention with the new generation of biblical scholars.

Gore's views on miracles are briefly summarized in a sermon on "Christianity and Miracles," preached before the Church Congress at Middlesbrough in 1912 in the full flush of the debate initiated by the celebrated books just published. For Gore, to belittle or dismiss miracles was to attack the very nature of the Christian idea of God based on a false modern conception of nature that was incompatible with the biblical idea of God. The latter sees God the Creator as "presenting Himself as from outside in an action which the system of observed nature could never account for." While the biblical writers recognized that God worked according to the law of his being, and that nothing, not even God's most miraculous action, could be called arbitrary, God nonetheless could not be confined within the observed order of nature, since "an exceptional situation allows of an exceptional action" (Gore 1912, 19–22).

Gore's view of the New Testament miracles highlights a number of key issues that were at stake between his own "critical orthodoxy" and ideas that were shaping British theology in the early years of the twentieth century. One crucial issue had to do with the interpretive assumptions regarding the work of historical criticism. Both Gore and his critics charged one another with insinuating "arbitrary" *praejudicia* into their biblical interpretation— the one naturalistic, the other dogmatic and ecclesiastical. It can be said that, measured by present-day scholarship, both parties were naïve on the issue of hermeneutics. The evidence can, however, also be read somewhat differently, since both Gore and Illingworth used the term *historical* equivocally.

At times they linked the evidential force of history to the remarkable results produced by the historic Christian community. At other times they connected historical evidence to the trustworthiness of the "apostolic tradition," as that term was commonly understood as representing the evolving catholic tradition in the first century and a half of Christianity. It is this that possesses the *historical* authority. But for Gore, in particular, the historical evidence also meant the "bare facts" recorded by the apostolic witnesses. He implied that it was the apostles' explicit intent "to record things as they happened." Today few critics would suggest that such a "recording" was the intention of the apostolic witness. They were, rather, interpreting the spiritual meaning of certain events and, more significantly, preaching the "good news," the primitive Christian *kerygma*. Biblical scholars such as Thompson, Streeter, and Sanday were more aware than was Gore of the literary character and redactions of the "apostolic" witnesses, and they were more sensitive to the quite different meanings and uses of the word *historical*. They were alert, that is, to the confusion involved in Gore's apologetic conflation of the uses of the word *historical*.

There remained at the heart of the hermeneutical dispute a tacit but crucial matter. Both Rashdall and Thompson were mindful of a moral and intellectual principle that is essential to any professional vocation (see Harvey 1985). It involves the role-specific commitment to those methods, proper procedures, and rules of evidence that must commonly be assumed in the carrying out of a particular professional craft, for example, that of the historian. There is a repertoire of procedures that are agreed upon by historians—just as there are by doctors, journalists, or scientists—that carry both an intellectual and moral imperative. If the theologian makes *historical* claims, that is, claims about past events and their interpretation, does this not logically entail the use of *historical* norms and procedures, or can these be circumvented or ignored? This was the often unspoken issue at stake, and it continues to haunt theological discussion to the present day.

Finally, the dispute between Gore and his critics was often obscured by the use of other deceptive words such as *normal, abnormal, miraculous,* and *supernatural*. Gore equated the supernatural with the miraculous. His critics thought that the two concepts were distinguishable. Gore insisted that the rejection of the miraculous entailed a fateful perversion of the Christian doctrine of God. Thompson, Sanday, Streeter, and a host of others denied any such consequence. They sought to show that rejection of the literal-historical and miraculous character of narratives, such as the accounts of the virgin birth and the empty tomb, did not involve disbelief in supernaturalism, or the incarnation, or the spiritual meaning and truth of either the virgin birth or the resurrection.

Professor Sanday and the Winds of Change

The response to Gore's defense of miracles, and to his call for action against those clergy who denied the miracles enshrined in the creeds, was wide ranging. The liberal and modernist clergy were the most emphatic in their protest, but they were joined by some liberal Evangelicals and liberal Catholics. The editors of the *Modern Churchmen* cited Gore's admission that the new scientific cosmology was compatible with a view of God as the spiritual ground of the world's order and law, with a personal and moral conception of deity, with the incarnation, and with the influence of spirit over matter. Yet Gore continued to insist that a nonmiraculous Christianity would be devoid of moral and religious power and could not continue to maintain itself in the world.

The various counterattacks made it clear that the issue of miracles now was centered on the question of the sources. This is prominent in B. H. Streeter's response to Gore. He urged that, with regard to the miracles of the virgin birth and physical resurrection, "it is precisely the nature of the evidence that gives men pause today" (Streeter 1914, xi–xii; see also Inge 1919, 122–23). It was the respected New Testament scholar William Sanday (1843–1920), however, who proved to play the decisive role in the controversy provoked by Thompson and Gore. From the early 1890s on, Sanday was absorbed with the issue of miracles as he understood their bearing on a range of technical New Testament questions and their broader theological significance for Christian apologetics. Sanday always considered the evidence of the sources to be the essential question regarding miracles, and it was the progression of his own thought on this question that signaled a broader change in attitude toward miracles among other leading biblical scholars and theologians.

Sanday was a well-regarded scholar, noted for his caution. He was also a liberal Evangelical, though not strictly identified with any theological party. His early writings gave no clue to the conclusions that he would embrace as an elder scholar. In his first book, on St. John, he expressed no doubts about the factual basis of the numerous miracles recounted in that gospel (Stephenson 1965–1966, 269–71). He believed in the literal account of the changing of water into wine, the feeding of the five thousand, and the raising of Lazarus.

In 1899 Sanday wrote a long article on Jesus Christ for Hastings's *Dictionary of the Bible*, which later was published as *Outlines of the Life of Christ* in 1905. It is evident in this essay that his position on miracles was close to that of the *Lux Mundi* group. However, in the *Outlines*, Sanday allowed for an ambiguity that he later was to take special efforts to avoid. He asserted that there had to be something extraordinary about the life of Jesus that his contemporaries "*could recognize* as supernatural and divine—not that we can recognize, but that they could recognize with the ideas of the time." This was written in the immediate context of his rejection of efforts "to eliminate miracles from the career of Jesus" (Sanday 1905, 114). It does appear, however, that here Sanday also wanted to distinguish supernatural occurrences from the miraculous *mode* in which they were originally apprehended. That is, he already was concerned with making the distinction for which he became famous, namely, that miracles are not *contra naturam* but rather *supra naturam*. From this point on he often referred to the statement of St. Augustine that "a miracle is not against nature but against what is yet known about nature" (*De Civitate Dei* 21.8). This, of course, was the now familiar appeal to "higher laws." Over the next decade, Sanday gradually moved on to embrace more controversial principles.

In 1911 he preached a sermon on "The Meaning of Miracle" before a congregation in the University of Cambridge. It was included in a book that same year entitled *Miracles*, edited by Henry Scott Holland. The sermon was preached only a few days after the appearance of Thompson's *Miracles in the New Testament*, but Sanday was able to incorporate into Holland's volume some of his initial responses to Thompson's essay. Sanday's treatment of miracles in the sermon repeated much of what he had said earlier on the subject. But the striking new feature was his bold defense of those younger scholars who, believing in the supernatural and denying miracles, now called for a "non-miraculous Christianity." Sanday was not disturbed by this development, for he now believed that these younger men had "the essence of the idea of miracle" even though they denied the word. He regarded the matter as largely one of definition and that the effort to translate miracle into the supernatural—"to lay stress upon the Divine cause rather than upon the exceptional mode"—was "entirely wholesome and to be welcomed" (Sanday 1911, 3, 4, 9).

Sanday's next "weather report"—as the Catholic writer Ronald Knox amusingly dubbed them (Knox 1914, 35)—appeared within the year in a paper on "The Historical Evidence for Miracles," delivered at the same Church Congress (Middlesbrough) in 1912 where Bishop Gore had opened the assembly with his sermon on the same subject. Sanday called upon his large audience of churchmen to consider the difference between a snapshot of a passing event as a reproduction of what really happened and the evidence of witnesses to an event testifying in a court of law. He pointed out how much more complex and varied is the latter and, in a manner similar to W. B. Carpenter's earlier remarks, that the work of the mind on perception increases in proportion to the complexity of the event and the length of the interval of time between the event and its telling. "And if the witness was interested in the event, the mental contribution would be determined very much by dominant interests and habits" (1912, 182).

Sanday then told his colleagues that a similar process was at work in the New Testament, and proceeded into deeper waters. He submitted that we moderns now are called upon to *recover* what had happened after the original, extraordinary event occurred. No photograph was taken; an interval of fifteen to thirty years had passed, "long enough for the record to be colored more or less by the ideas that were in the people's minds." It is here, Sanday urged, that the process of symbolic expression is at work upon the presentation of the original events. The writers and redactors followed their own ideas, and could not do otherwise. "But," he insisted, "we also cannot help following our ideas. And the whole problem of miracles seems to me to reduce itself to this: to find the exact point at which the supernatural ends and the really abnormal begins." In some important cases this will be difficult if not impossible to do. There, he suggested, we "leave the ancient narrative as it stands, and say to ourselves that, if we knew more, it would probably turn out to be less abnormal than it seems" (1912, 184).

Here Sanday advanced, unconsciously it would appear, to a rather different hermeneutical principle, one more consistent with the positions of the New Testament scholars Streeter, Kirsopp Lake, or J. M. Thompson. This is further reflected in Sanday's response to his colleague A. C. Headlam's insinuation that, in his Church Congress paper, Sanday had been too quick to embrace the spirit of his time in refusing to accept the abnormal. Sanday's reply was that he wished to lay stress "on the *really* abnormal" and that only our collectively historical experience can give us a clue as to what that might be. As Sanday later was to admit, after the Congress at Middlesbrough the progress of his thought was rapid.

By the time that Sanday wrote his pamphlet entitled *Bishop Gore's Challenge to Criticism* (1914), his fundamental ideas regarding the New Testament miracles, history, and criticism were fixed, and he never looked back. He acknowledged that it had become "quite impossible to dismiss from

[his] mind the *praejudicium* which had been gradually forming against the permanent validity of the conception of miracles *contra naturam*" (Sanday 1914, 27). It continued to be urged against him that this preconception was simply "reading back modern ideas into the distant past." But Sanday would not waver or be cowed. He replied that what was said about his prepossessions was undoubtedly true, "but that we do so in regard to other departments of history" and that "the process is in fact unavoidable." He once again asserted that it is imperative that we go back behind the received narratives that have come down to us "and to apply to them the standards of our own age, which in the treatment of evidence is more exacting" (23-24).

When this critical task is undertaken, Sanday was convinced that, on the balance of the evidence, "the group of miracles that are really *contra naturam* is found to be exceedingly small" (24). He thought that this left the narratives associated with the miraculous to the beginning and ending of Christ's earthly career. In regard to Christ's birth, Sanday most emphatically believed in Christ's supernatural birth, but he could not bring himself "to think that His Birth was unnatural." For Sanday, whatever the virgin birth could spiritually mean was guaranteed by his belief that the birth points to a "higher" supernatural cause at work in the world.

The same holds for the resurrection. The only real question for Sanday was the detail associated with the resuscitation of Jesus' dead body from the tomb. Yet the accounts that have come down to us are too conflicting and confused to be conclusive. What they do seem to show is that the detail is of less importance than is supposed. "Because, whatever it was, the body that the disciples saw was not the natural human body that was laid in the grave." Since various ideas were current at the time as to the manner of Jesus' resurrected life, "Is it not enough for us," he asked, "that the first disciples were convinced by signs . . . appropriate to the world of ideas in which they moved? And is it not proved beyond question that the Risen Lord as Spirit still governs and inspires His Church?" (1914, 20).

Sanday's fullest mature statement of his understanding of miracle in Christianity is contained in a collection of long letters between himself and N. P. Williams, the chaplain and Fellow of Exeter College, published as a discussion entitled *Form and Content in the Christian Tradition* (1916). Sanday here reviewed in detail his basic principles and his conclusions on the matter. What is arresting is the emphasis that Sanday now placed on what he called "the modernists' ideal," which amounted to a statement of the historian's commitment to the canons of his profession. If the modernist churchman's "proper province is history, he will not," Sanday wrote, "have one measure for sacred history and another for profane. There will be no closed compartments" (1916, 104). He was confident that it was not necessary for the believing historian to subordinate himself either to the catholic tradition or to modern science, as N. P. Williams had implied. Sanday firmly asserted "that a presentation of Christianity is possible which shall be at once in strict and full continuity with the past and shall yet be in complete harmony with the most assured results of progressive science" (105).

In the context of our theme of miracles and the reign of law, Sanday's concluding remarks are of special note. As we saw earlier, A. C. Headlam had chided Sanday for his adherence to the methods and presuppositions of Victorian physics. Sanday was not intimidated, although he assured Headlam that he was not ignorant of the changes that had occurred in that science at the turn of the century. So far as he was concerned, they only reinforced his theological convictions. He adverted again to the often cited analogy of the causal agency of personal spirit or will: "The action of spirit or mind constantly overrides, controls and deflects, the lower laws of matter. But while it does this, it never 'contradicts' them." The interaction of spirit and matter has laws of its own. Nature is regulated by spirit, but this regulation is subject to laws and limitation. "Mind is superior to matter, but its superiority is exercized constitutionally, and not despotically. Laws of the lower order are overruled, but they are never violated." As far as our experience goes, what is true of the human will is, for Sanday, true of the divine will. It too works through laws it has established. "But if it does so in the present, the presumption is that it has done so equally in the past" (1916, viii). Sanday was certain that the long process that had seen the elimination of miracles as *contra naturam* could not be arrested, nor, he thought, ought we to wish that it could be stopped. For him, miracle, so understood, was the last great difficulty in the way of reconciling Christianity and the modern, scientific world. In this expectation one can say that he was wrong, but his position regarding miracles and the New Testament sources now remains crucial in theological discussions of this question.

CHAPTER 5

Humanity's Place in Nature— The Challenge to Christian Anthropology

Human Origins, the Fall, and Sin

For my own part I would as soon be descended from that heroic little monkey, who braved his dreaded enemy in order to save the life of his keeper . . . as from a savage who delights to torture his enemies, offers up bloody sacrifices, practices infanticide without remorse.

Charles Darwin

Language is our Rubicon, and no brute will dare to cross it.

Friedrich Max Müller

Adam was harder to defeat than Noah.

John Burrow

The Background to 1860

In the period between the late eighteenth and the mid-nineteenth centuries the sciences of geology, paleontology, and zoology opened up a vast and unfamiliar history of the earth, of the animal kingdom, and of the human race itself. With the coming of the Darwinian revolution the cumulative force of all these sciences transformed the vision of man's[1] place in natural history, both in relation to the immeasurable sweep of time and the relation of humans to the nonhuman world.

---

1. I have chosen to retain the word *man* in references such as "man's place in nature," since that was the language used in all the influential books, essays, and reviews in nineteenth-century Britain. The use of gender-neutral language in telling the story of this earlier historical context appears artificial and anachronistic.

As heirs to two hundred years of these developmental and progressionist ideas, we may find it difficult now to conceive of a largely static and *perfect* order of things. However, such a stable worldview largely dominated thinking in the West well into the eighteenth century. The common view was expressed by Joseph Clarke: "Not only *Angels* and *Men*, but *every other species of creatures*, every *Planet* with *all its Inhabitants*, are eternal." What is more, "God *cannot* hereafter create any new Species of Being; because, whatever it is good for him to create in time, it was equally good from all Eternity" (Clarke 1734, 166).

In the early years of the nineteenth century a significant change took place in the conception of natural history, namely, its temporal progression. This shift was marked by the dominant role that biblical history and anthropology played in the thought-world of the British "philosophical naturalists" in the first three or four decades of the century, for example, in the writings of the authors of the Bridgewater Treatises—men such as William Buckland and William Whewell (see Bynum 1974).

As clergymen, these English scientists and theorists of science were obliged by their religious profession to relate their science to the teachings of sacred Scripture. By reconciling Genesis and geology or astronomy they were able to assimilate a science—which otherwise was looked upon as profane and dangerous—to received religious views. They accepted the continuity of organic life without accepting evolution. They believed in special divine creations and agreed with the French naturalist Georges Cuvier (1769–1832) that the animal kingdom is divided into discrete groups. While there is a natural continuity *within* these groups, they denied any continuity or transmutation between them.

George Stocking describes the powerful convergence of ideas in British science represented by this biblical perspective, one that prevailed through the first half of the century:

> The pre-Darwinian period in Britain is one in which . . . the biblical tradition reassumed a kind of paradigmatic status. Within this framework, all men were presumed to be descended from one original pair, who had been formed by God as the final act of Creation. . . . Implicit in this view were more specifically "anthropological" assumptions: the unity of man, the recency of his appearance on earth, the degeneration of the non-Christian savage peoples, and a sharp distinction between man and other animal forms. These assumptions were in fact interlocking. The qualitative distinction between man and animal reinforced the rejection of a plurality of human origins, which would tend to fill the gap between ape and man with a hierarchy of

biologically differentiated forms. Correspondingly, degeneration . . .
provided an alternative explanation for the manifest human diversity
that increasingly forced itself on anthropological observers in this
period. (Stocking 1987, 44)

In 1820 William Buckland was with confidence able to conclude that "the
evidence of all facts that have yet been established in Geology coincide with
the records of Sacred History and Profane Tradition to confirm the conclusion, that *the existence of mankind* can on no account be supposed to have
taken its beginning before that time which is assigned it in the Mosaic writings" (Buckland 1820, 23–24). He argued that geology has to do with those
great lapses of time before the creation of man, while biblical history covers
only the story of man. "The disappointment of those who look for a detailed
account of geological phenomena in the Bible, rests on a gratuitous expectation of finding therein historical information, respecting all the operations of
the Creator in times and places with which the human race has no concern"
(1836, 14–15). Devising an ingenious exegesis of Genesis 1:1–2, Buckland
was able to read verse 1 ("In the beginning God created heaven and earth") as
referring to a primeval creation. The second verse ("And the earth was without form and void"), he argued, takes up natural history after a prolonged
period at the time of the destruction of the last geological age and just prior
to the creation of the human world. Thus, according to Buckland, "millions
and millions of years may have occupied the indefinite interval, between the
beginning in which God created the heaven and earth, and the evening or
commencement of the first day of the Mosaic narrative" (21–22).

The scriptural naturalists found scientific support for a biblical anthropology not only in Cuverian geology ("L'homme fossile n'existe pas") and
in Buckland's conclusion regarding the fossil record but also in the work of
the German Johann Friedrich Blumenbach (1752–1840), one of the founders of scientific anthropology. In his *De generis humani varietate nativa liber*,
Blumenbach had offered the first reliable survey of the characteristics and
distribution of the human races. More significant for our subject is his classification of *mammalia*, which established a gap between *Homo sapiens* and
Simia or *(Homo) troglodytes*. Buckland and the geologist Adam Sedgwick
fully agreed with Blumenbach's conclusion regarding breaks in the historical progression and his rejection of transmutation, especially as they concerned the distinctive place of *Homo sapiens*. They considered the empirical
evidence to be conclusive against the idea of species change; the geological
evidence pointed, rather, to successive creations (see Rupke 1983, ch. 14).

For a time, the arguments of the scriptural naturalists concerning "the
recent appearance of man" appeared to carry the day for special creations.

There were, however, several concurrent factors that were challenging the assumptions about humanity's late appearance, as well as belief in the discontinuity between humanity and the lower animals. First, there were some clerical naturalists and theologians in the period before Darwin who were not troubled to contemplate a continuity between humans and the animals, especially as regards the use of reason. Indeed, these writers assisted Darwin in reaching what was considered by many, but by no means by all, as a most damaging conclusion (see Richards 1987, esp. ch. 3).

Among them was John Fleming (1785–1857), a clergyman and Scotland's premier zoologist. He dismissed the Paleyian view that animal instinct was wholly fixed and lacking the human reasoning faculty. He saw reason working with instinct throughout the animal world. Fleming, nevertheless, remained an opponent of Lamarck and transformism: "The effect of circumstances on the appearance of living things, is circumscribed within certain limits, so that no transmutation of species was ever ascertained to have taken place" (Fleming 1822, 27).

Henry Lord Brougham (1778–1868), a statesman and amateur theologian-scientist, was another who distinguished, but did not sever, instinct from reason in the animal world. Like Fleming, Brougham argued that animals could rationally adapt their instinctive behavior to meet altered circumstances (Brougham 1839, 203–5). He even ventured that no wider gulf separated a dull or idiotic human from a "sagacious retriever or a clever ape than from a Pascal or a Newton" (175). The clergyman William Kirby (1759–1850), a respected entomologist and author of the seventh Bridgewater Treatise, also supported the continuity between animal instinct and human reason. He based his claim, as did Fleming, Brougham, *and* Darwin, on the ability of small creatures, even insects, to adopt means to achieve ends, to gain knowledge from experience, to mutually communicate and receive information, and to use memory (Kirby and Spence 1823, 517–29).

On the HMS *Beagle*, Darwin read Kirby's Bridgewater treatise, *On the Power, Wisdom, and Goodness of God as Manifested in the Creation of Animals and in Their History, Habitats, and Instincts* (1835), in which Kirby carried forward his views on the "mixed actions" of instinct and reason in animals (Kirby 1835, 204, 278–79). Kirby's and William Spence's *Introduction to Entomology* especially influenced Darwin and confirmed some of his own basic ideas. It also proved, however, to be one of the more significant challenges to Darwin's evolutionary hypothesis (see Richards 1987, ch. 3).

Clerics like Fleming and Kirby could rest easily in acknowledging a continuity between animal instinct and human reason because they thought the evidence for the fixity of species was solid and the ascertaining of any links or transitions highly unlikely. Others, such as William Lawrence (1783–1867), professor of anatomy and surgery at the Royal College of Surgeons, were now more confident that a naturalistic explanation of progressionism and continuity was available or forthcoming.

A second factor was the popular phrenology movement (see Cooter 1984; De Guistino 1975), which focused the discussion of man's place in nature specifically on the relation of the mind to the physiology of the brain. George Combe (1788–1858), a Scotsman and a leader of the movement, summarized its basic principles as three: 1) that the brain is the organ of the mind; 2) that the brain is an aggregate of several parts, each subserving a distinct mental faculty; 3) and that the size of the cerebral organ is, an index of power or energy of function.

The phrenologists identified numerous distinct mental faculties, some unique to humans. While it affirmed the unity of the race, phrenology also recognized that some human groups (races) have more highly developed (larger) mental faculties than do others. It also taught that the sexes have different developed faculties.

Because the differences between races and cultures were thought to be based on brain size and function, social change was assumed to be a slow process. Culture was a matter of brain size, human psychology essentially a matter of anatomy. What is significant in the present context is that while phrenology was resisted by the scientific establishment, it gave popular support to a naturalistic, biologically based science of man. Though inherently anti-evolutionary, phrenology, ironically, did influence the views of evolutionists such as Robert Chambers, Herbert Spencer, and A. R. Wallace. During this same period, work on anatomy and taxonomy, especially in relation to the brain, played a crucial role in the shift in thinking about man in the debates over psychology that were to reach a climax in the late 1850s. A third crucial development was associated with the discoveries in human prehistory.

By 1860, increasing numbers of persons were receptive to the idea of human evolution. This was conditioned in part by an acceptance of humanity's early antiquity and the recognition that humans had lived for immense periods of time in a primitive state. For anthropology this was as significant as Darwin's discovery of evolution's mechanism. Moreover, it was independent of Darwin's influence.

In 1830 a Belgian doctor, P. C. Schmerling, made important discoveries of human remains in caves near Liege. During the 1830s a Frenchman, Jacques Boucher de Perthes (1788–1868), discovered flint tools in an antediluvian geological stratum in the Somme valley. He published his findings in 1847, but they were dismissed by the experts as amateurish speculation. However, discoveries in England and elsewhere were accumulating rapidly by the 1850s, the most significant breakthrough being in 1858 at Brixham cave near Torquay on the Devon coast.

The Brixham cave excavation was carried out by geologists William Pengelly and Hugh Falconer, and the Geological Society of London appointed a committee of eminent scientists, including Joseph Prestwick (1812–1896), Richard Owen, and Charles Lyell, to investigate (see Gruber 1965). Impressed by the Brixham cave findings, Prestwick and Lyell went to Abbeville in France to reevaluate the claims of Boucher de Perthes. They were convinced by what they found. Prestwick reported his findings to the Royal Society in May 1859. A week later, at the meeting of the Society of Antiquaries, John Evans confirmed Prestwick's findings. He concluded his address by underlining the significance of these recent discoveries: "This much seems to be established beyond a doubt; that in a period of antiquity, remote beyond any of which we have hitherto found traces, this portion of the globe was peopled by man" (Evans 1859).

While the eminent anatomist Richard Owen remained unconvinced ("No discoveries had been made up to this time calculated to show that man is of higher antiquity than has commonly been supposed"; Gruber 1965, 390), by 1859 he represented the diminishing authority of the scriptural naturalists. This change is seen in the transformation of Charles Lyell, the preeminent scientist of his day, on the question of the early antiquity of man. Lyell announced his conversion in 1859 in his presidential address to the Geological Section of the British Association for the Advancement of Science (C. Lyell 1859, 93). As late as 1851, however, this staunch advocate of uniformitarianism, the man who was committed to showing that all natural phenomena could be explained naturalistically, had held back in the case of man (Bartholomew 1973, 261–303). As William Bynum points out, Lyell's position in 1851 was a sort of Cartesian compromise, separating man's rational faculties from his physical aspects, leaving his philosophy of nature in a kind of limbo (Bynum 1974, 302). This allowed Lyell to minimize the physical difference between humans and animals, since human uniqueness was of another order.

The geological and ethnological discoveries of the 1850s increased Lyell's unease and forced him to recognize that facts now were being brought to light that "may shake our confidence in some of our articles of faith in which our estimate of the dignity of man is founded" (C. Lyell 1970, 331). A few days after reading the proofs of Darwin's *Origin of Species*, Lyell reflected on the ironic course that continued to be taken by the scriptural naturalists and the progressionists. He wrote in his species journal that they

> approach what they desire to avoid, but this may show that the current of facts is too strong and that the wind which fills their sails, the

gale of their wishes and preconceived desires to isolate man, is too
feeble to enable them to keep clear of the rocks on which their old
theology will be wrecked, tho' doubtless to create a new and improved
one. (1970, 292–93)

Lyell's belief in the uniqueness of the human species remained for him,
nonetheless, an article of faith, whatever science may find. In 1863 he published his popular *Geological Evidence of the Antiquity of Man*, in which he
discussed not only human antiquity but also the origin of species through
natural descent. He unequivocally affirmed the former but rejected Darwin's
theory of evolution by natural selection, much to Darwin's disappointment. In defending humanity's uniqueness, Lyell adopted Archbishop J. B.
Sumner's point regarding the human "power of progressive and improvable
reason" (Sumner 1816, 19), using the same language. While acknowledging
that human beings are physiologically similar to primates, Lyell persisted in
his conviction that "Man must form a kingdom by himself if once we permit
his moral and intellectual endowments to have their due weight in classification" (C. Lyell 1863, 495). In the margin of his copy of the book, Darwin
penciled "No."

The vast majority of scientists in 1860 accepted the very great antiquity
of man, but they also rejected transmutation. Most scientists believed in
the uniqueness of the human species, allowing for a "leap" or special creation in the progression to *Homo sapiens*, a development not wholly explicable by scientific evidence. They generally agreed with a reviewer in the
Anthropological Review that the great antiquity of man "does not give any
support to the theory of progressive transmutation" (Anon. 1863, 136).
This was the case in 1860, but after the impact of Darwin's *Origin of Species*
it became more difficult to separate the question of antiquity from that of
transmutation.

Darwin on the Descent and Future of Mankind

The role that Charles Darwin played in the late Victorian discussions about
humanity's place in nature was, of course, crucial. Yet it is important to place
Darwin in historical perspective. The emerging naturalistic, evolutionary
worldview of the midcentury had many sources. It was, as R. M. Young has
shown, a river "fed by many streams" (Young 1985, 68). These included uni-
formitarian geology, paleontology, embryology, prehistoric archaeology, and
comparative philology. Evolutionary theory was dependent on all of these
burgeoning sciences in the years before Darwin published *The Origin of*

Species. And evolutionary anthropology was relatively well ensconced by 1860. But what Darwin did was profound. He offered a compelling theory that established humanity's kinship with the animals—that is, its place *in* nature—and that held that human behavior, therefore, was amenable to scientific analysis, prediction, even control. Darwin, along with Huxley, raised new issues about the human species and its history, but their views were also countered in highly plausible ways. The religious responses frequently were anti-Darwinian, but they also were neo-Darwinian in one or another sense. The variety of replies frequently was due to Darwin's own ambiguity, or to his change of position over time, but also to clear misreadings of his meaning. Before we turn to the religious critics of Darwin's naturalistic anthropology, it is well that we turn, first, to Darwin's own writings on the descent of man and its implications.

The significance of Darwin's scientific journey—from the HMS *Beagle* voyage to the publication of *The Origin of Species* in 1859—for his reflections on anthropology has often been told (see, e.g., Greene 1959; Gruber and Barrett 1974; Durant 1985). We know that before the publication of *The Descent of Man* (1871), Darwin long had been convinced of the human race's animal origin. As early as 1838 he had jotted down in a private notebook, "I will never allow that because there is a chasm between man . . . and animals that man has different origin" (De Beer 1960, 109). Yet he kept this conviction a public secret for more than thirty years for social and political reasons, in part because of fear of persecution and, more importantly, because he had not worked out a convincing theory of transmutation. The scope of *The Origin of Species* had been limited intentionally to the question of "the origin of species by means of natural selection." The specific subject of the human species was dealt with obliquely rather than directly. However, in the closing paragraphs of the book, Darwin prophesied that he could see in the future "open fields for far more important researches," works in which "Light will be thrown on the origin of man and his history" (C. Darwin 1859, 488).

Between 1859 and 1871 much light, of course, was thrown on a range of questions about the beginnings of human life and culture. In the 1860s the question of the origin and antiquity of man was thoroughly discussed by T. H. Huxley in *Evidence as to Man's Place in Nature* (1863), in Lyell's *Antiquity of Man* (1863), and in A. R. Wallace's "The Origin of Human Races and the Antiquity of Man Deduced from the Theory of 'Natural Selection'" (1864)—as well as in the scores of responses to these works. Huxley's book requires special mention because of its popularity and influence. It was also a much bolder work than Lyell's *Antiquity of Man*; it clearly and forcefully set out the view that humans were, indeed, animals. Historically, it became *the* classic statement of the anthropoid nature of the human species (Peterson 1932, 145).

Evidence as to Man's Place in Nature was intended to refute Richard Owen's effort to establish a distinct biological classification of humans through analysis of brain anatomy. "I have endeavoured to show," Huxley announced, "that no absolute structural line of demarcation, wider than that between the animals which immediately succeed us in the scale, can be drawn between the animal world and ourselves" (T. H. Huxley 1893–1894a, 152). Huxley allowed that his treatise would produce "a certain shock" in even the least reflective person (80–81). Nonetheless, he rather cheerfully called upon his readers to adopt a stance of disinterestedness and to imagine themselves "Saturnians," investigating the relations between other earthly animals and this new "erect and featherless biped," brought to Saturn "well preserved in a cask of rum" (95).

Evidence as to Man's Place in Nature consists of three essays that explore the question of the physical relation of man and the brutes from different perspectives. The first essay, "On the Natural History of the Man-like Apes," offers a series of reports of the encounters of explorers and naturalists with African and Asian primates—from semi-mythical accounts to those of the likes of Alfred Wallace. What emerged is a vivid portrayal of the humanlike behavior of the great brutes, juxtaposed to descriptions of African cannibalism—a not too subtle and graphic reminder of that human appetite for engaging in the most brutal activity. The second essay, "On the Relations of Man to the Lower Animals," traces the unities in animal embryological development, pointing out that it is only late in the embryo's growth that the human embryo becomes differentiated from that of a dog and that the ape embryo departs as much from that of a dog as does the human. Further, Huxley demonstrated that anatomically the ape differs less from humans than from the other animals.

In his final essay, "On Some Fossil Remains of Man," Huxley marshaled the findings of German paleontologists as evidence for very primitive protohuman skulls: the Engis, named after the Belgian cave where they were discovered, and the famous Neanderthal skull, uncovered near Düsseldorf in 1856. While rejecting claims that the Neanderthal bones were the remains of a "missing link" between apes and man, Huxley nevertheless suggested that the Neanderthals were a variant of modern human beings. He left little doubt in his readers' minds of humanity's animal descent and of man's existence on the earth for eons of time in some brutal, prehistoric form.

Evidence as to Man's Place in Nature was persuasive regarding both the antiquity of man and his animal origins in the lower orders of nature. The book did not, however, touch on the unique character of human consciousness and mind. In fact, Huxley concluded the treatise by declaring his conviction of the vast "gulf between civilized man and the brutes," while at the same time insisting that any true study "of man's nature reveals, at its foundations, all the selfish passions, and fierce appetites of the merest quadruped" (153–4).

In the 1870s an intense and wide-ranging debate on humanity's unique place in nature came to focus on the relations of brain, mind, and volition. Huxley was a major player in this debate, siding, albeit ambiguously, with the scientific materialists and necessitarians. It was only late in life that Huxley finally was able to develop a consistent position regarding humanity's dual material and moral being—a position, it turns out, that was looked upon with chagrin by the scientific materialists and supporters of evolutionary ethics.

When Darwin's *The Descent of Man* appeared in 1871, it served as a catalyst in forcing again to center stage those questions raised by Huxley concerning human origins and man's place in the natural order. Darwin had persisted through the 1860s in his reluctance to write on the origins of human life and importuned upon A. R. Wallace to pursue further the subject of his 1864 essay. He even offered Wallace his own extensive notes. Pressures, however, prevailed. In 1869 Darwin wrote to Fritz Müller (author of *Für Darwin*) that he was "thinking of writing a little essay on the Origin of Mankind, as I have been taunted with concealing my opinions" (F. Darwin 1887, 112). *The Descent of Man* was his long-delayed response.

Darwin's purpose was to consider "whether man, like every other species, is descended from some pre-existing form" (C. Darwin 1871, 1:2). In the first chapter he drew heavily on the work of Huxley and others in marshaling the proof of our animal descent from the evidence of the structure of the human body—homologous structures, embryologic resemblance, and the presence of rudimentary organs. The heart of Darwin's argument rested, however, on the evidence of human continuity with the animals in the spheres of intelligence, morality, and even religion. It was his goal to show that "the difference in mind between man and the higher animals, great as it is, is certainly one of degree and not of kind" (1:105). It was here where some of his strongest supporters, such as Lyell and Wallace, could not follow him. Darwin amassed anecdotal evidence from a wide range of sources to show that man and

the higher animals, especially the Primates, have some few instincts in common. All have the same senses, intuitions and sensations—similar passions, affections, and emotions, even the more complex ones; they feel wonder and curiosity; they possess the same faculties of imitation, attention, memory, imagination, and reason, though in very different degrees. (1:48–49)

In his *Prehistoric Times* (1865), the Duke of Argyll had claimed that the fashioning of tools and implements for a special purpose was unique to man, but Darwin drew attention to the way in which the apes manipulate sticks and stones as instruments, how they build temporary platforms against volcanic lava, how an orangutan covers himself at night with leaves, and how a baboon covers his head with a mat against the heat of the day. In these activities Darwin saw "the first step towards some of the simple arts," for example, architecture and dress (1:52–53).

Other scholars had argued that human beings alone possess an aesthetic and religious sense. Darwin rebutted them by calling attention to the way male birds elaborately display their plumes and feathers before the females, a practice which, he was certain, made "it impossible to doubt that females admire the beauty of their male partners" (1:63). As to theology, Darwin pointed out that not even humans in their aboriginal state possessed belief in God, a fact that he had observed among the Fuegians and the Australians while on the *Beagle* voyage. However, if by religion one means "belief in unseen or spiritual agencies, the case is wholly different." As E. B. Tylor (1832–1917) had recently shown, primitive peoples tend to imagine "that natural objects and agencies are animated by spiritual or living essences." Darwin proposed that animals also reveal this sense of the mysterious unseen, and gave as evidence the behavior of his own dog. Lying on the lawn during a hot and still day, the creature observed an open parasol as it was moved by an occasional breeze. Each movement was followed by the dog's fierce growl and bark. "He must," Darwin concluded, "have reasoned to himself . . . that movement without any apparent cause indicated the presence of some strange living agent" (1:67).

Darwin perceived in the sentiment of religious devotion a complex of feelings that included love, submission to a superior, a strong sense of dependence, fear, reverence, and so on. While such a complex religious sense is present only in a being advanced in intellectual and moral faculties, Darwin nevertheless saw "some distant approach to this state of mind in a deep love of a dog for his master" (1:70). As Robert Richards has only half-facetiously noted, "Darwin's comparison surely struck a resonant chord in the heart of every English huntsman" (Richards 1987, 200).

The great Oxford philologist and comparativist Friedrich Max Müller had declared that "language is our Rubicon, and no brute will dare to cross it" (Müller 1864, 367). He was widely supported by professionals in the field. Darwin, however, pointed out that birds, monkeys, and dogs emit a variety of sounds to express different emotions, or in the presence of certain objects. A young bird's first attempt to sing can be compared to the imperfect effort of a child to babble. Darwin could not doubt that human language, like the inarticulate language of animals, "owes its origin to the imitation and modification, aided by signs and gestures, of various natural sounds, the voices of other animals, and man's instinctive cries" (1:56).

Darwin acknowledged that conscience and the moral sense were what marked the highest distinction between humans and the other animals. Yet even here Darwin saw a difference only of degree, and he sought to show how the moral sense can be accounted for "exclusively from the side of natural history." In his investigations of many animal species, Darwin found evidence of social instincts that had been acquired over time by natural selection. "For with those animals which were benefited by living in close association, the individuals which took the greatest pleasure in society would best escape various dangers; whilst those that cared least for their comrades and lived solitary would perish in greater numbers" (1:80). Darwin conceded that these social instincts alone were not sufficient to pass for conscience, as we humans understand autonomous moral acts, but with growth of intelligence the threshold to genuine morality is crossed: "Any animal whatever," Darwin proposed, "endowed with well-marked social instincts would inevitably acquire a moral sense or conscience, as soon as its intellectual powers had become well developed, or nearly as well developed, as in man" (1:71–72; see also Cronin 1991, 225–53).

In the case of humans, as their moral sentiments are extended beyond their own kind and to all species, so, Darwin prophesied, would human morality rise higher and higher until it attained the heights of the Golden Rule. Darwin's discussion of conscience and human morality was one of the subjects that both challenged and provoked his critics. They pointed to Darwin's apparent failure to see the moral problematic in, for example, altruism. As one recent critic comments, "The Darwinian problem of altruism has to do with the costs to the altruist. . . . He cares less about whether behavior is costly than whether it is caring" (Cronin 1991, 347). Darwin's views on both conscience and altruism were related to his 1832 encounter with the natives of Tierra del Fuego. The experience, which is reflected in *The Descent of Man*, left an indelible impression on Darwin that remained for the rest of his life. In the book's conclusion, he reverts to the experience:

The astonishment which I felt on first seeing a party of Fuegians on a wild and broken shore will never be forgotten by me, for the reflection at once rushed into my mind—such were our ancestors. These men were absolutely naked and bedaubed with paint, their long hair was tangled, their mouths frothed with excitement, and the expression was wild, startled, and distrustful. They possessed hardly any arts, and like wild animals lived on what they could catch; they had no government, and were merciless to every one not of their own small tribe. . . . For my own part I would as soon be descended from that heroic little monkey, who braved his dreaded enemy in order to save the life of his keeper . . . as from a savage who delights to torture his enemies, offers up bloody sacrifices, practices infanticide without remorse. (1874, 404–5).

Darwin's observations of the Fuegians impressed on him two features of primitive life that are apparent in his argument in *The Descent of Man* and that were vulnerable to criticism. The first was the enormous gulf that he perceived as existing between primitive savagery and contemporary European civilization. The second was the similarity he saw between the lowest humans and the higher animals such as the monkeys and apes. What these perceptions did was to dispose Darwin both to lower his estimate of early man and to resort to an exaggerated anthropomorphism in his depiction of animal behavior. As John Durant has remarked, Darwin's

> use of anthropomorphic imagery was closely related to the rejection of anthropocentrism. Darwin's commitment to the principle of continuity led him to treat man as a "traveling instance" in nature, and this in turn allowed him to project into nature as immanent properties and powers many of the complex human attributes whose origins he sought. (Durant 1985, 302–3)

This anthropomorphic projection was used against Darwin by many critics, especially by those who wished to defend man's unique place in nature. It was Darwin's treatment of moral instincts in animals that was, and is today, considered especially precarious.

The great distance that Darwin perceived between the Fuegian and the Victorian Englishman, reinforced by the anthropological studies of John Lubbock (1834–1913) and E. B. Tylor, also convinced him that human history followed a path of evolutionary progress from savagery to civility. This too could be appropriated by his critics and used against him. Darwin rejected the theory of a racial degeneration as earlier proposed by Richard Whately (1787–1863), the Anglican archbishop of London, and later by the Duke of Argyll and others. But his utter disdain of the idea that man was aboriginally civilized and then suffered degradation may have been due to dislike of such "a pitiably low view of human nature" and his sanguine supposition that it is a "truer and more cheerful view . . . that progress has been much more general than retrogression; that man has risen, though by slow and interrupted steps, from a lowly condition to the highest standard as yet attained by him in knowledge, morals and religion" (C. Darwin 1886, 145).

Darwin was required, of course, to explain the forces at work in social progress, and he saw natural selection as the principal cause. The competitive struggle for existence should not, therefore, be stayed:

> Man, like every other animal, has no doubt advanced to his present high condition through a struggle for existence consequent on his rapid multiplication; and if he is to advance still higher, it is to be feared that he must remain subject to a severe struggle. Otherwise, he would sink into indolence, and the more gifted men would not be more successful in the battle of life than the less gifted. . . . There should be open competition for all men; and the most able should not be prevented by laws or customs from succeeding best and rearing the largest number of offspring. (1886, 618)

Darwin was certain that the social instincts had naturally evolved to a "higher morality," one where the Golden Rule had become morally normative. Sounding the optimistic note of future Darwinistic theologians regarding continuous moral progress, Darwin predicted that "there is no cause to fear that the social instincts will grow weaker, and we may expect that virtuous habits will grow stronger, becoming perhaps fixed by inheritance. In this case the struggle between our higher and lower impulses will be less severe, and virtue will be triumphant" (1886, 125).

It was evident to Darwin's opponents that his conception of evolutionary progress rested on unresolved issues having to do with the importance of the mechanism of natural selection. According to the theory, the "ablest" are those who succeed in producing the largest number of offspring—a purely biological criterion. However, for Darwin, "ablest" also involved moral qualities that were more dependent on the workings of habit and use—inheritance, sexual selection, and other factors. But the latter were essentially Lamarckian, with the potential of undermining the biologically "ablest." Notions of an inevitable cultural and moral progress appeared to them to be antithetical to the contingency and openness required by the operation of natural selection. Most social evolutionists in the late nineteenth century either rejected or downplayed natural selection in theorizing about human evolution; they followed Lamarck and Herbert Spencer (see Bowler 1983). It was Darwin's own hedging on the role of natural selection in his discussion of social evolution that gave an opening to his critics. Consequently, the appearance of *The Descent of Man* set off another intense discussion. The reviewers pounced on

the objections to natural selection and on the weaknesses in Darwin's anecdotal, anthropomorphic evidence in defense of his claims for animal language and a moral and religious sense in animals. They also made good use
of A. R. Wallace's recent defection from the Darwinian camp on the question
of human evolution.

Darwin and the Theistic "Darwinians"

In the years following 1859, no scientist defended natural selection more con-
sistently—except in the case of man—than did the naturalist A. R. Wallace
(1823–1913). He admitted to being "more Darwinian than Darwin" (Wallace
1905, 22; see Raby 2001; Shermer 2002). After 1865, however, Wallace became
increasingly attracted to spiritualism, and in 1874 he published an article in
the *Fortnightly Review* entitled "A Defense of Modern Spiritualism." The next
year "A Defense" appeared in a book, *On Miracles and Modern Spiritualism*,
that included two papers defending miracles and psychical phenomena. "My
position," he wrote, "is that the phenomena of Spiritualism in their entirety
do *not* require future confirmation. They are proved, quite as well as any facts
are proved in the other sciences" (Wallace 1875, 204–5).

Wallace's deepening involvement in spiritualism had coincided with his
publication of two papers, in 1864 and 1869, that marked his changing views
on the role of natural selection and human evolution. From his correspondence it is clear that his new convictions about spiritualism had a profound
influence on his views about human origins and natural selection. However,
the resistance of his scientific colleagues to spiritualism caused him initially
to avoid metaphysical argument and to rely solely on scientific evidence and
logic. By March 1869 Wallace felt compelled, however, to write to Darwin in
order to prepare him for the shock that was to come, mentioning vaguely the
source of his radical change of view:

> In my forthcoming article in the "Quarterly" [1869] I venture for the
> *first time* on some limitations to the power of natural selection. I am
> afraid that Huxley and perhaps yourself will think them weak and
> unphilosophical . . . but [they] are the expression of a deep conviction
> founded on evidence which I have not alluded to in the article but
> which is to me absolutely unassailable. (Marchant 1916, 240)

Darwin wrote back expressing his curiosity and his hope that Wallace had
"not murdered too completely your own and my child" (Marchant 1916, 241).

On learning that Wallace had done just that, Darwin expressed his surprise and disbelief, to which Wallace replied:

> I can quite comprehend your feelings with regard to my "unscientific" opinions as to Man, because a few years back I should myself have looked at them as equally wild and uncalled for. . . . My opinions on the subject have been modified solely by the consideration of a series of remarkable phenomena, physical and mental, which I have now had every opportunity of fully testing, and which demonstrate the existence of forces and influences not yet recognized by science. (242–44)

Before 1869 no one would have known the significant role that spiritualism played in Wallace's developing view of man's place in nature, for it was not until then that he drew attention, in his published scientific papers, to these recent discoveries. Wallace had first expressed these new ideas about human origins in an 1864 paper entitled "The Origin of Human Races and the Antiquity of Man Deduced from the Theory of Natural Selection," presented to the Anthropological Society of London. The crux of the paper was the contention that the human mind had "shielded" the body from the action of natural selection and in so doing had put an end to human structural change. Wallace thus proposed that human evolution occurred in two stages. The first involved a series of physical changes that ended in man's bipedal posture and the freeing of the hands to carry out a variety of tasks. This occurred at an early period of geological history. The second stage of human evolution involved the emergence of mental attributes that brought to an end the human body's need to change physically in order to survive. The emergence of mind represented a radical change in evolutionary history:

> From the moment when the first skin was used as a covering, when the first rude spear was formed to assist in the chase, when fire was first used to cook his food . . . a grand revolution was effected in nature—a revolution which in all previous ages of the earth's history had no parallel, for a being had arisen who was no longer necessarily subject to change with the changing universe—a being who was in some degree superior to nature, inasmuch as he knew how to control and regulate her action. (Wallace 1864, 182)

In 1869, at the close of his *Quarterly* review of new editions of two books by Charles Lyell, Wallace publicly expressed his conviction that natural selection was not capable of explaining certain facts about prehistoric and primitive races. Darwin's theory of selection was based on the principle of utility, but Wallace pointed out a variety of human features that appeared to reflect inutility. This led him to suggest that "we must therefore admit the possibility that in the development of the human race, a Higher Intelligence has guided the same laws for nobler ends" (1869, 394).

A year later Wallace expanded on his "heresy" in an essay entitled "The Limits of Natural Selection as Applied to Man." Here he simply drove home Darwin's principle of utility, again pointing out the several human characters that exhibited inutility, thus casting doubt on natural selection as the sole principle or cause of human evolution (1870; see also 1891, 187–88). Among the most important new pieces of evidence marshaled by Wallace were the discrepancy between the brain size of primitive man and his actual requirements, and the several mental faculties possessed by early man that clearly served no practical purpose. The savage, Wallace argued, "possesses an organ [the brain] quite disproportionate to his actual requirements—an organ that seems prepared in advance, only to be fully utilized as he progresses in civilization" (1870, 199).

Wallace saw the same problem in the case of certain mental faculties that could not be accounted for by natural selection. These included the ability to form abstract ideas about form and number in geometry and arithmetic, about space and time, eternity and infinity, as well as the capacity for intense artistic interest in form, color, and composition. None of these were of use to man in his earliest stages. Nor could natural selection explain "the higher feelings of pure morality," for instance "the constancy of the martyr, the unselfishness of the philanthropist, the devotion of the patriot" (1875, vii).

Wallace moved from his evidence of the insufficiency of natural selection to the conclusion that spiritual powers therefore were required in an otherwise inexplicable evolution of man. He conceded that his theory did have the disadvantage of necessitating the intervention of a distinct individual intelligence "to aid in the production of . . . ever-advancing spiritual man." But the fact remained that the laws governing the material world "were insufficient for [humanity's] production." The emergence of humanity required the action of a higher intelligence augmenting the material laws (1891, 204–5).

We have seen that St. George Jackson Mivart was an early Darwinian. Later, however, his persistent and telling criticisms of Darwin led to his excommunication by the Darwinians following his review of *The Descent of Man* in 1871 (see Gruber 1960; Vorzimmer 1970; Richards 1987). As early as 1863 he had recognized that his mentor Huxley, in *Evidence as to Man's Place in Nature*, had left no doubt about his conviction that humans had evolved from lower forms—and that Darwinism entailed, implicitly if not explicitly, a mechanistic materialism. Furthermore, it became obvious to Mivart that in *The Descent of Man* Darwin was required to look to factors that had until then explained variations but not species change. Darwin now found it necessary to emphasize, to a greater degree than before, Lamarckian factors in modification.

In his review of *The Descent of Man* in the *Quarterly Review*, Mivart sought to show that by assigning the law of natural selection to a subordinate position Darwin virtually had abandoned his theory (Mivart 1871a, 67). More importantly, Darwin's chief mechanism of evolution, while possibly explaining the development of the human body, was not able to account for the human psyche. Undermining a theory inherently mechanistic and materialistic—"the besetting sin of our day . . . 'sensationalism'"—was then only half of Mivart's task. The second part of his review focused on what he regarded as the unique character of human intellectual and moral faculties, features that marked the qualitative difference between human and animal. Unlike W. B. Carpenter and others, who sought to counter the (at least implicit) mechanistic sensationalism of Darwinism on scientific grounds, Mivart saw no comparison, no continuity between the physiological aspects of humans and animals and the human intellect and conscience. The profound human psychological realities—self-consciousness, moral virtue, rationality—transcended biological explanation. "Sensation," Mivart insisted in his review, "is not thought and no amount of the former would constitute the most rudimentary condition of the latter, though sensations supply the conditions for the existence of thought" (68).

Mivart distinguished at least six kinds of action to which the nervous system ministers. The first four in no way imply reflection; they simply "minister to and form *Instinct*." There are, however, two other kinds of mental activity:

> V. That in which sensations and sensible perceptions are reflected on by thought and recognized as our own and we ourselves recognized by ourselves as affected and perceiving—Self-Consciousness.
> VI. That in which we reflect upon our sensations or perceptions and ask what they are and why they are—Reason. (68)

Mivart believed that possession of the first four "preventative" kinds of action by no means implies the possession of the last two faculties that "are distinct, not in degree but in *kind*." Animals, of course, have "mental images of sensible objects combined in all degrees of complexity," and these are "governed by the laws of association." But these powers are a world apart from "knowing themselves as knowing," that is, from reason or "the power of asking the reflective question . . . as to 'what' and 'why'" (73).

Mivart's review proceeded to examine, and to dismiss as fallacious, the legion of anecdotal illustrations Darwin offered of the reflective powers of animals. Darwin had offered the illustration of his dog. The pet "was savage and averse to all strangers," and yet after Darwin's five years' absence he obeyed his master's command. "A train of associations," Darwin argued, dormant during five years, had thus been instantaneously awakened in [the dog's] mind," illustrating the brute's rationality. But Mivart saw Darwin's example as "no better instance of the mere action of associated sensible impressions." "What," he asked, "is there here which implies more than memory, impressions of sensible objects and their association?" (78–79).

Before moving to the question of human conscience, Mivart proposed two additional considerations that tended to prove the difference between the mental powers of humans and animals. The first had to do with the mental equality of animals of different grades of structure and their nonprogressiveness. Oddly, Mivart pointed out, ants and bees display phenomena that at least simulate those of human intelligence to a far greater degree than any phenomena exhibited by the higher brutes. The second matter had to do with articulate speech. Mivart charged Darwin with confusing articulate signs and gestures, in response to sense impressions, with rational speech. "It is not," Mivart urged, "emotional expressions or manifestations of sensible impressions, in whatever way exhibited, which have to be accounted for, but the enunciation of deliberate judgments as to 'the what,' 'the how,' 'the why,' by definite articulate signs. . . . For these Mr. Darwin . . . does not adduce anything even tending to account for them" (79–80). A parrot, for example, can be taught to speak certain words and phrases, which he associates with some gratification or response, but this differs vastly from rational speech. Mivart called upon the expert research of E. B. Tylor and John Lubbock to verify the universality of the *verbum mentale* in humans, even among the very lowest races. The discussion of language led Mivart to the question of the "moral sense."

As we have seen, Darwin argued that the moral sense had resulted from the development of animal social instincts through natural selection. According to Mivart, however, human beings "have a consciousness of an absolute and immutable rule *legitimately* claiming obedience with an authority necessarily supreme and absolute—in other words, intellectual judgments are formed which imply the existence of an ethical ideal in the judging mind." For Mivart, "no amount of benevolent habits tend even in the remotest degree to account for the intellectual perceptions of 'right' and 'duty'" (79–80).

In the second edition of *The Descent of Man* Darwin responded to this criticism by amending his earlier words. The original version read, "Thus at last man comes to feel, through acquired and perhaps inherited habit, that it is best for him to obey his more persistent instincts. The imperious word *ought* seems merely to imply the consciousness of the existence of a persistent instinct, either innate or partly acquired, serving as a guide, though liable to be disobeyed." In the second edition, the first sentence closes with the words "persistent impulses" and the second sentence speaks of "a rule of conduct, however it may have originated" (C. Darwin 1871, 1:79; 1874, 1:486).

Mivart was not placated by such vague emendations. The fact is that no amount of benevolent habit could account for the perception of "right" and "duty." "Liking to do acts which happen to be good is one thing; seeing that actions are good, whether we or others like them or not, is quite another" (Mivart 1871, 80). Darwin always seemed to confuse a benevolent or benefi-cial action with a moral one. A dog may act well but is not thereby a moral agent. Darwin had defined conscience as that act which "looks backwards and judges past actions, inducing that kind of dissatisfaction which if weak we call regret, and if severe remorse." To this Mivart replied:

> Conscience certainly "looks back and judges" but not all that "looks back and judges" is conscience. A judgment of conscience is one of a particular kind, namely a judgment according to the standard of moral worth. But for this a *gourmand*, looking back and judging that a particular sauce had occasioned him dyspepsia, would, in the dis-satisfaction arising from his having eaten the wrong dish at dinner, exercise his conscience! (83)

For Mivart morality is an intellectual judgment of "right," excluding all ref-erence to either pleasure or utility. Yet the Darwinians claimed that human moral action is rooted in and evolved from utility and pleasurable sensation.

In his *Lessons from Nature*, Mivart also charged Darwin, Huxley, and other scientific naturalists with failure to distinguish *material* moral acts from acts that are *formally* moral. The former are good apart from any inten-tion on the part of the agent. Formally moral actions are not only good in themselves but also in the *intention* of the agent who recognizes the act as being "right" and a "duty." An act "may be *materially* moral or immoral in a very high degree, without being in the least formally so" (1876, 106).

Huxley, in turn, charged Mivart with maintaining that no act is "good" unless it is done with deliberation. What, in fact, Mivart was asserting was that "for an act to be good it must be really directed by the doer to a good end, either actually or virtually." The merit of that virtue, Mivart continued, which shows itself even in the spontaneous, indeliberate actions of a good man, "results from the fact of previous acts having been consciously directed to goodness, by which a habit has been formed" (1872, 193). It is in this habit of mind that the beauty of moral virtue consists. If Huxley "utterly rejects" the distinction between material and formal morality, as he claims to do, then, Mivart argued, he denies freedom to the human will, either making the word *virtue* meaningless or oddly equating it with instinctive action or feeling.

For Mivart even the highest brutes lack the human capacity to form rational judgments; nor do they have even the dimmest consciousness of moral "oughtness." Furthermore, they lack the potential of achieving these mental actions through their sensible experience. Humans, however, not only are conscious but are conscious of their own consciousness and are capable of analyzing the process of inference itself. Humans not only are capable of selfish and benevolent acts but understand the meaning of moral duty, hence of freedom of choice and responsibility (1876, 188). Mivart sought to show, in forty tightly argued pages, that it could be demonstrated scientifically that human beings are unique and are set apart from the rest of the animals and that it is impossible to explain humans by the mechanism of natural selection.

What set Mivart apart from his fellow scientists was, as Jacob Gruber observes, "his erection of the human mind as an entity distinct, and absolutely distinct from the body it inspired. Consequently, no relationship between the corporeal aspects of man and other animals had significance for psychological relations or origins" (Gruber 1960, 134). Mivart's defense of humanity's unique place in the creation thus required a sharp dualism of mind and body, of man and animal—rational language, morality, and religion being original and divinely gifted to humankind from the beginning. For Mivart an unbridgeable gulf separated human beings from the brutes.

W. B. Carpenter, England's great physiologist, took a very different tack. In chapter 2 we saw how Carpenter argued on scientific grounds for a theistic conception of evolution. He did so through a critique of the explanatory adequacy of natural selection and by reinterpreting the argument from design. As a student of physiological psychology Carpenter also directed his major efforts at refuting the Darwinian doctrine of human automatism and to establishing on a scientific basis the reality of the human will and humanity's distinctive conscience and sense of morality. He defended these doctrines in such a way as to do justice to what he perceived to be the truths of both the materialist and the spiritualist hypotheses. The mind and brain, Carpenter argued, "are so intimately blended in their *actions* that more valuable information is to be gained by seeking for it at the point of contact" (Carpenter 1888, 473) than by giving over the mind for study by metaphysicians and leaving the brain to the anatomists and chemists. It was critical to Carpenter that he refute the materialist doctrine of human automatism which, he believed, was inherent in strict Darwinism. He wished, at the same time, to repudiate the dualism inherent in the position of Mivart and other theists.

Carpenter believed that the same progressive development that one observes in the animal and vegetable world applies to *Homo sapiens*. He was certain that the higher animals possessed rational and moral attributes that, while below the human in degree, were of the same kind. He believed, furthermore, that there was nothing in the idea of humanity's rational and moral development from the lower animals that would present a problem for theology. Mivart was wrong and Darwin perfectly justified in finding the rudiments of human moral and spiritual life in the animal world, the human conscience being the higher development of that sense of obligation that is observable, for example, in Darwin's well-trained dog. "It has long been a tenet of mine," Carpenter wrote,

> that a careful study of the Intellectual and Moral Development of a child, by a competent observer, would enable him to detect a series of stages comparable to the different grades of the like development which are presented to us in the ascent of the Zoological scale. And I cannot see that the truths of Morality and Religion which apply to Man's Moral and Religious nature *as it is*, are more imperilled by carrying back the development of that nature into the Dog or the Horse stage, than they are by deriving it from the *brute* stage of the savage . . . or from the *child* stage of the civilized Christian. (1888, 473)

What distinguishes humans from the higher animals is the high achievement of "a self-directing power," of "distinct purposive intervention" of the self-conscious will, and the "capacity for unlimited progress."

Carpenter felt deeply that it was wrong for theologians to insist, in the case of humanity, on a *special* creative act of divine power "when everything points to *a continuity of the same original plan of action*, that has previously manifested itself in the progressive evolution of the highest mammal from the primordial jelly-speck." Indeed, for Carpenter, the conception of a continuity of action requiring no special creative acts "because the plan was all-perfect in the beginning, is a far higher and nobler one than that of a succession of interruptions" (1888, 407). What was dangerous in Darwinism and, to Carpenter's mind, where it failed on scientific grounds, was to deny the reality of will, both divine and human, as a purposive and self-determining power. These realities granted, Carpenter saw no threat of Darwinism to theology.

George Romanes, one of Darwin's most zealous disciples, vastly extended his master's work in the field of comparative psychology. But it was that labor that ultimately drew Romanes back into metaphysical speculation and led him to support a doctrine of monism that was meant to be a bulwark against evolutionary materialism and mechanism. His mature conceptions of mind and will were not essentially different from those of Carpenter, and they were similarly directed toward the reconciliation of Darwinian evolution and a spiritual anthropology.

During the 1880s Romanes produced a series of books—*Animal Intelligence* (1881), *Mental Evolution in Animals* (1883), and *Mental Evolution in Man* (1888)—in which he sought to carry Darwin's work in *The Descent of Man* further and to trace human psychology to its animal origins by means of a comprehensive empirical and naturalistic evolutionary account. His purpose was to demonstrate "that there is no difference *in kind* between the act of reason performed by the crab and any act of reason performed by man" (Romanes 1883, 337). But, characteristically, Romanes's intellectual convictions would not remain settled for long.

In his 1885 Rede Lecture at Cambridge on "Mind and Motion," Romanes made public his private doubts about the claims of a materialist naturalism. To the surprise of many, he denounced the "barbarisms" introduced from the side of an aggressive scientific positivism—typified by W. K. Clifford— and called for a "pure agnosticism." The lecture concluded with an appeal for a union of spiritualism and materialism in which, he suggested, "we obtain a product which satisfies every fact of feeling on the one hand, and of observation on the other" (1895, 27). As R. J. Richards suggests, the evolutionary analysis of mind, which occupied Romanes throughout the decade of the 1880s, "seems to have revealed depths unfathomable, seems to have required a metaphysical hypothesis that it could not tame" (Richards 1987, 346).

The metaphysical hypothesis that did satisfy Romanes was monism. He believed that it alone gives room for free will, for faith, and for a theism that "if it be more vague, may also be more worthy than that of earlier days." Romanes worked out his monistic theory and its implications in a series of articles, some left in manuscript, that were published after his death in 1894 by his friend C. Lloyd Morgan as *Mind and Motion and Monism* (1895). Monism construes the antithesis between mind and motion as only apparent and not real. As Romanes concluded, "Any change taking place in the mind, and any corresponding change taking place in the brain, are really not two changes but one change" (1895, 28). In other words, there is "only one stream of causation," just as we may suppose "that nerve strings and a process of thought are really one and the same event," though they may appear diverse in our modes of perceiving them (136). Monism not only gives a rational explanation of the place of mind in the natural world; for Romanes it also made intelligible human free will and morality. Both materialism and traditional spiritualism, to Romanes's thinking, denied human freedom and moral responsibility, since both were dualistic and thereby entailed a concept of the will as an agent bound to act in accord with conditions dictated by some external necessity.

According to Romanes's theory of monism, all physical and mental processes are consubstantial; therefore, causation can be regarded as essentially psychical and not determined by anything from without. If that be true, wrote Romanes, then any "portion of it which belongs to, or is manifested by, my own personality is not laid upon me by anything from without; it is merely the expression of my own psychical activity" (136).

Determinism presupposes that the principle of causality is prior to that of mind, but once we see that the principle of causality is coextensive with that of mind, the entire conflict between freedom and necessity collapses. In Romanes's estimation, the only restraints on the human will are those of reason and conscience.

> But neither of these restraints can properly be said to constitute bondage in the sense required by Necessitarianism, because neither of them requires that the man's Will must will as it does will; they require merely that his Will should act in certain ways if it is to accomplish certain results; and to this extent only is it subject to law, or to the incidence of those external influences which help to shape our motives. (148)

Since, according to monism, moral responsibility has to do with a causation not external but inherent in the mind itself, it follows that "the moral sense no longer appears as a gigantic illusion: conscience is justified at the bar of reason" (149).

Romanes acknowledged that monism was not empirically provable; rather, it was a logical and reasonable doctrine once one reflected deeply on the role of mind in nature. Romanes remained a true Darwinian in his study of mental activity in animals and humans, but he came to believe that *science itself* pointed to the role of intelligent action, veiled perhaps, but working with the material processes of selection. Romanes's appeal to metaphysical principles clearly distinguished him from Darwin; in this he was much closer to Wallace, Carpenter, and even Mivart. The fact that Wallace and Romanes, and many others who claimed to be Darwinians, differed from the master in important ways raises an interesting question about the very definition and boundaries of Darwinism. Indeed, was the Darwin of *The Descent of Man* a true Darwinian?

Whether true to Darwin or not, Romanes was increasingly convinced of the "unquestionable evidence of some one integrating principle [namely, psychism] whereby all its many and complex parts are correlated with one another in such wise that the result is universal order" (108). This "integrating principle" or "Superconscious" he later was to call "God." In a letter to the American botanist Asa Gray, Romanes, the Darwinian, concluded:

> The doctrine of the human mind having been proximately evolved from lower minds is not incompatible with the doctrine of its having been due to a higher and supreme mind. Indeed, I do not think that the theory of evolution, even if fully proved, would seriously affect the previous standing of this more important question. (1896a, 154–55)

As we will see in chapter 6, Romanes's preoccupation reflects the fact that the British debate over man's place in nature increasingly focused its attention on the mind-brain question. But before exploring that issue we will turn to the response of theologians to the challenge put by evolution to the Christian doctrines of humanity's beginnings—to the fall, original sin, and redemption.

The Premature Death of Adam:
Evolution and the Reconceiving of the Doctrines of the Fall and Sin

At the conclusion of *The Descent of Man*, Darwin spoke of having "given to man a pedigree of prodigious length, but not, it may be said, of noble quality." He went on to remark that "if any single link in this chain had never existed, man would not have been exactly what he is now" (C. Darwin 1874, 405). The idea that earliest man, like the infant child, was not the noble Adam—not even fully a person as we unwittingly assume but rather, at best, impulsive, unrestrained, unmoralized—profoundly challenged earlier interpretations of the biblical account of man's fall from a paradisical perfection. Furthermore, Darwinian evolution implied a radical contingency and anti-anthropocentrismism that belied the providential drama of humanity's unique creation, fall, and redemption. Evolution, whether it was Darwinian, Spencerian, or Tylorian, saw humanity as having risen from a species of dumb animal, not fallen from a state of perfection. Was it not, then, contrary to the empirical facts to impute a sinful fall and an indelible taint of sin to a creature so superior to its brutish ancestors in both intellect and morals? And if humans are the chance product of natural variation, does it make sense to speak of man as the predestined crown of God's plan or the foreordained image of the Creator?

Even late in his career, when he had declared his newfound commitment to the theistic hypothesis, George Romanes remained convinced that the biblical depiction of Adam, the fall, and the origin of evil were incompatible with an evolutionary worldview. These were, he wrote, "hard hit by the scientific proof of evolution," and as the basis of Christian doctrine they did at least appear "to involve the destruction of the entire Christian superstructure" (Romanes 1896b, 176). Evolutionary development, in almost any of its forms, did appear to entail ideas that ran counter to the Christian doctrine of humanity's origin, the fall, original sin, and the need for redemption. The questions were insistent: Is not the human story one of a rise from savagery rather than a fall from perfection? Does it not follow that sin is basically a "survival" of our savage past? Can we humans be held responsible for these vestiges of natural impulse, of egoism and aggression? And doesn't the doctrine of original sin involve the monstrous notion that children inherit the guilt and responsibility for the actions of their parents, which also presumes the questionable theory of the inheritance of acquired characters? The fast-growing recognition of polygenism, or hominoid descent from different ancestors, also raised doubt about the Genesis account of a human origin from a single pair. These were some of the questions that evolution now raised for a Christian anthropology.

While evolutionists such as Romanes may have found their conception of human development to be incompatible with the Genesis account of humanity's origin, fall, and sin, it is nevertheless the case that by the 1880s this was not the view of many respected theologians. There were, to be sure, some influential British theologians who persisted in the rejection of Darwinian theory on the grounds that it was contrary to the biblical account of human origins. Genesis, they argued, protects the doctrines of the original gift of the imago Dei, hence the radical gulf between the appearance of human life and the creation of the lower animals, as well as humanity's common ancestry in Adam and the fall. Methodist theologian William Burt Pope (1822–1903) is representative of this resolute defense of the older theology (Pope 1879, 402ff.). He is also typical of a position in British theology whose influence was fast ebbing.

The great antiquity of man, especially when seen in terms of the eons of human savagery, was increasingly troubling, and not only to the conservative theologians. While Pope did not think that this antiquity challenged the unity of the race, he nonetheless acknowledged that "it deepens the mystery of His (God's) long delay" (433). The Anglican J. R. Illingworth, too, admitted that if human savagery is not a "mere fringe of failure round human progress" but is recognized as our primordial common human condition during the greater part of our existence, then "the result is a stupendous shock to all our preconceived ideas." And Illingworth believed that the further question is forced upon us with insistence: "Can a race that has been left for such limitless ages to itself really have been the object of divine solicitude the while?" (Illingworth 1895, 144–45).

Illingworth met the challenge by appealing to a particular version of the degeneration theory—one that attracted other apologists, including the Scots the Duke of Argyll and James Orr. Illingworth argued—against both Darwin and the anthropologist E. B. Tylor—that it was an error to compare prehistoric man with modern savages. "There is," he insisted, "all the difference between them of first and second childhood. The latter represents the remnant of humanity that has failed to progress; the other must have contained in himself the germ of all the progressive peoples." The similarity of their external condition is no proper indication of "a similarity of capacity or character." Illingworth considered it a justified presumption, on the evidence available, that prehistoric man "was within the reach of religious influence," and that those scattered modern savage tribes that seem to have no God can be "accounted for by gradual moral degeneration" (1895, 146, 144; see also Griffith-Jones 1899, chs. 3 and 4). In Illingworth's estimation, human savagery was in fact, and contrary to Tylor, "a mere fringe of failure" among our progenitors and not their normal condition.

The idea of an actual Adamic "higher," prefall state of man, before the threat of moral degradation intruded, was difficult to give up, even among those theologians who were trained in and sophisticated about science. They were faced with either taking recourse to an increasingly suspect theory of degeneration or, in Hegelian fashion, in positing a primeval state of "dreaming innocence," a condition that, lacking rational and moral discrimination, was nevertheless called "higher" or "perfect," but only in the most equivocal way.

Aubrey Moore chose the former path. He believed that the doctrine of the fall was, perhaps, the one Christian belief that remained for evolutionists wholly unwarranted. "While science seems to teach a continuous evolution," Christianity, with its doctrine of the fall, "is committed to a theory of degradation." And the fall, according to Moore, "means that the first man was what his descendants are not, and that, in spite of all that we know . . . was a higher creature than an Aristotle or a Raphael or a Darwin" (A. L. Moore 1890b, 61).

By "higher creature," Moore meant that Adam's greatness lay not only in being a free, self-conscious personality but also "a being who, by the grace of God, was living in happy communion with God." What distinguished primordial man from the amoral animals "was that while both alike obeyed God's Will, he did it consciously, knowing what he did, and rejoicing in the knowledge" (62). The change brought about by the fall "was a change in the moral region," which had its effect elsewhere, for example, in the misuse of scientific knowledge. Hence, there was a "retarded development" of the species. So it was that "man before the Fall was in right relation to God, though he knew nothing of modern science and modern civilization" (63).

Moore spoke of the fall as "happening at a definite time, and yet affecting the whole human race," and wrote that "we are here on ground where natural science can help us little." The reason why science cannot help is not only because "moral facts cannot be put under the microscope" but because science "cannot compare man, as he is, with man as he came forth from his Creator's Hand" (64). At the same time, both moral science and theology bear testimony to a moral disorder and struggle in human life. Moore may have been right that "no theory of evolution is complete which ignores the fact of sin in man" (65). Yet his claim for a primal, self-conscious, human obedience and communion with God, followed by a fall "happening at a definite time," would prove difficult to sustain in the light of increasing knowledge about human origins and life. So would his assertion that science can shed no light on the question.

This aspect of Moore's writing on Christian anthropology was challenged by theological colleagues. His defense of Darwinism was, however, in almost every respect unqualified. In this he was among the most advanced theological writers of the period. He insisted that humanity was not to be thought of as an independent creation but, rather, a creation in the manner of other species by evolution from lower forms. Contrary to claiming that Darwinism was degrading, a "gospel of dirt," Moore was persistent in reminding Christians that Darwinism was consistent with a religion that believed that "the Lord formed man of the dust of the ground." Darwin had "done something to give man his true place in the physical universe" (A. L. Moore 1892, 204–5).

What, however, of the soul? Was that also created by evolution, or was it "a special creation?" (207). Moore insisted that the soul cannot be a "special" creation, whether in Adam or his children, the reason being that there is no "species" of soul. "We may call it, if we will, an 'individual' creation, but is not all creation an individual creation from the religious point of view? And if so, it is a phrase that does not help us."

Moore pointed out that Christianity has instinctively been against traducianism, or the physical derivation of the soul. Despite the fact that creationism may separate the soul from the body in a way that neither orthodox theology nor science will accept, it nevertheless guards an important truth. Moore insisted that Christian theology is not bound to any theory of the origin of the soul so long as it guards the fact "that by God's creative act, man's relation to Himself is unique among created beings . . . [and is] a free, self-conscious personality, made 'in the image of God'" (210–11). Science cannot deny the soul of man any more than it can reject an original creation, for both lie outside the province of scientific knowledge. Science *may* deny both, of course, with the assertion of a major premise: What science cannot know cannot be known. "From this, no doubt," Moore responded, "the conclusion follows with logical necessity. But we answer with *negatur major*" (208). Moore was willing to leave to science full reign so long as it did not trespass into metaphysical dogmatism:

> The original creation of the world by God, as against any theory of emanation, is a matter of faith. The existence of the soul—i.e., the conscious relation of man with God—lies at the root of all religion. Guard those two points, and they are both strictly beyond the range of inductive science, and for the rest, we are bound to concede to those who are spending their lives in reading for us God's revelation of Himself in nature, absolute freedom in the search, knowing that truth is mighty and must in the end prevail. (1883, 51–52)

A number of theologians, from the 1880s on, rejected the view, held by Moore and others, that the Christian account of the fall and sin required belief in a prefall state of human perfection or a "higher" state of conscious relation to God. They also denied the corollary idea of degeneration. They reinterpreted the fall and sin in developmental terms. This was the tack taken by the Scottish divine George Matheson (1842–1906) in *Evolution and Revelation* (1885). He denied the older theology's claim that humanity was originally sinless and that there was a beginning period when the race was mostly free from sin and sorrow. Rather, the picture of primeval humanity that we find in the book of Genesis is not, as is often thought, "the picture of a perfect being, but of a perfectly innocent being. It is the picture of one who is potentially virtuous and actually harmless." For Matheson the theological implications of this picture are twofold. First, Genesis establishes that the birth and progress of science and the arts proceed not from an unfallen but from fallen humanity. Second, and more importantly, the Bible testifies that the first Adam is not the climax of humanity, "for St. Paul himself has sharply distinguished between the perfection of a mere negative innocence, and the perfection of a life that has triumphed through suffering" (Matheson 1885, 202–3). The life of morality begins, then, only with the loss of innocence, with the rise of a double consciousness and the struggle of motives. For Matheson this explains theology's congruity with evolutionary development:

> The primitive innocence of man was broken by the mere fact of this choice, but we cannot agree with Augustine that in the view of the

writer of Genesis the choice was the beginning of his fall. In itself it was a rise, and might have resulted in the transition from innocence into conscious virtue. It is quite certain, at all events, that conscious virtue could not have been attained by any other method than a presentation of the alternatives of good and evil. The power to choose was in itself a step in the direction of evolutionary progress; it brought the highest product of creation nearer to the ideal of the second Adam, to the measure of the stature of the perfect man. (204–5)

Matheson did not deny that the result of human choice was a fall that was and continues to be fatally adverse to the fortunes of the individual and the race. But progress and degeneration are concomitant features in the world of human evolution. Matheson saw evolution as "a progress over the whole mass, but . . . a progress which is reached not by successive advances, but by movements of alternate advance and regress" (205).

J. M. Wilson, the Anglican vicar of Rochdale and archdeacon of Manchester, was an astute apologist for a conciliation between evolution and Christian anthropology. He strongly opposed the popular conception of a definite temporal fall of an Adamic head of the race. Further, he disapproved of the belief in a prefall state of human perfection. Wilson held aloof from all speculations of origins and of a historical fall. "We are what we are, whatever our origin may have been," he insisted. The fall and sin must then be understood individually and existentially—which is the way, he believed, that science understands the way humans "fell," that is, the way in which we "first became conscious of the conflict of freedom and conscience" (Wilson 1896, 132). Each individual person falls as his ancestors fell.

If we see these doctrines in personal-existential terms, we must recognize that the child is born with all the human faculties undeveloped and absolutely without conscience. This is hardly a condition of perfection. The child has not yet sinned, "for its mind has acknowledged no law, no standard of right and wrong. The knowledge of sin, as St. Paul tells us, comes by law" (Wilson 1903, 69–70). The time comes, however, when the child hears the awful voice of conscience, conjoined with a clear sense of freedom—the power of saying "I will." Wilson does not intend to say, however, "that there is a particular moment" at which time each child or each person falls. It is, rather, "a continuous struggle of good and evil," and the Genesis narrative "is the way in which it pleased God that the minds of our early forefathers should conceive and impress upon the world this all-important fact." So read, there is no conflict between science and the Genesis narrative understood as "a temporary and figurative mode of expression" pointing to "an all-important and verifiable" spiritual truth (70). The ever present personal struggle of freedom and conscience is what Genesis relates as the fall *sub specie historiae*.

Wilson, like Matheson, also wished to insist that the fall must be seen as a rise "to a higher grade of being," one which "gives a deeper meaning to the truth that sin is lawlessness." It is here that Wilson, in the eyes of his critics, conceded too much to the evolutionist. Verging on Pelagian tendencies, Wilson approved of the evolutionists' claim that sin is not to be seen as an innovation but as the survival, or misuse, of habits and tendencies that were incidental to an earlier stage of development, whether of the individual or the race. These tendencies were not originally sinful but actually useful. "Their sinfulness," he continued, "lies in their anachronism: in their resistance to the evolutionary and divine force which makes for moral development and righteousness." Society, as the collective conscience, is, in Wilson's estimation, advancing under the laws of evolution toward righteousness. And as society evolves it condemns as sin actions it once not only tolerated but approved. "The survival of these actions is sin" (1896, 133).

On several occasions in the 1890s, the Anglo-Catholic Charles Gore addressed the question of the Christian doctrines of the fall and sin in their relation to science (Gore 1890; 1900, 219–37). During this period he served, consecutively, as Bishop of Worcester and of Birmingham. His views were attended to and influential. Gore argued, as had Moore and Wilson, that there is no difficulty in reconciling science and theology on the fall and sin so long as science rejected determinism and admitted "the idea of free, responsible action, with its correlative, the possibility of wrong action that may have been avoided" (1900, 223). Gore also agreed with the position taken by more liberal thinkers that the Bible does not suggest man was created perfect and then subsequently fell into sin and misery. Gore pointed out that from the time of St. Augustine onward some theologians had, it is true, either claimed or implied that Adam, created perfect, was not in need of development—that, in the words of one, "an Aristotle was but the rubbish of an Adam" (1900, 221–22). Milton had indelibly implanted this idea in the minds of Englishmen. However, Gore protested that this view is not biblical; moreover, it is expressly repudiated by church fathers such as Clement and Irenaeus.

The Bible, Gore contended, is a book of development. But having said this, it is also true that the Bible represents this development as having turned out to be "a second-best thing," for sin or rebellion against God has darkened the human prospect. Development is not synonymous with progress, for it is broken and partial, and "distinct deterioration is not uncommon." Gore believed that current anthropological science held a similar view of the human story, and that humanity's actual development, while tainted and thwarted, had not been the only possible development—it could have been better. Only social determinists will insist that our actual human evolution has been the only possible development, but this is not the view of most scientists. Moreover, Gore observed, social determinism is a theory that cannot be put into practice, since the holders of the theory themselves admit that it must be unrecalled or kept out of sight when action beckons.

Gore did not believe that either of the contrasting theories of monogenism or polygenism really challenged Christian doctrine, so long, that is, as neither "denies the unity of the race in such sense that the same postulates may be made with regard to all men" (1900, 228–29). Polygenism is not, as such, inconsistent with either the reality of human freedom or the fact and universality of sin. At the time in which he wrote, Gore believed that science backed monogenism because it then was widely held that the *hominidae* evolved through a single pliocene prototype from a single anthropoid precursor. In any case, the unity of the race, as understood theologically, was not tied to monogenism.

Gore proposed that the Christian belief in death as being "the consequence of human sin" was another doctrine misunderstood by science, which, of course, saw physical death as inextricably woven into the natural life of all organisms. Gore cited St. Augustine and St. Athanasius as examples of numerous Christian teachers who taught that death is the law of physical nature and that "man was by nature mortal." The sting of death for the human person is nevertheless tied to our spiritual nature, which we sense as corrupted, as having "fallen short." According to Gore, Christianity teaches that death, "with its horror and its misery," represents "not God's intentions for man, but the curse of sin." What Christ teaches when he says, "Whosoever believeth in me shall never die," is that "He has robbed [death] of its terror, its sting, its misery." Apart from sin, we humans would not know the fear and dread of what we call death, since "there would have been only some transition full of glorious hope from one [the mortal] state of being to another" (1900, 233).

To Gore, there remained one final difficulty in reconciling the Christian doctrine of the fall and sin with the doctrines of modern science. Christianity teaches "original sin," and traditionally that meant that a person's moral fault is the result of actual transgressions perpetrated by remote ancestors. But we know that science denies that acquired characteristics are inherited. If human nature is "corrupt," then it must be a natural predisposition derived from our prehuman ancestry. The biblical suggestion that the ancestral fathers have eaten sour grapes and their children's teeth are set on edge will not pass muster in a scientific age. Had not August Weismann's germ plasm theory proved that it was impossible?

Gore, however, lived during the time of the neo-Lamarckian revival, and he staked his argument for original sin on the Lamarckian hypothesis. Weismann's doctrine, he argued, "does not appear yet to have assumed a fixed form," and he cited George Romanes to the effect that no one is "thus far entitled to conclude against the possible transmission of acquired characters" (1900, 226). While in retrospect we can recognize Gore's appeal to the neo-Lamarckians as risky apologetic, at the time it was considered reasonable. And he concluded his discussion of original sin on firmer empirical ground. "There *may* be an inheritance of sinful tendencies," he wrote, "derived from sinful acts in the region of the spiritual personality, even if no physical transmission is possible" (227). That is, we cannot wholly escape our social solidarity, including our sense of culpability in society's failings and evils.

Furthermore, Gore noted "that 'original sin' is not a fixed quantity derived from one lapse of the original man." It suggests, rather, a moral weakness whose effects are not calculable or easily circumscribed or subdued. It is a condition "continually reinforced by every actual transgression." Gore also pointed out that original sin does not deny that "individuals start at very different levels of depravity" (228). It is a doctrine that attempts to speak realistically of the fact that, while there clearly is an inequality of human guilt, there is an equality of sin. That is, no one can say that he or she is morally pure and without the taint of destructive egoism. Original sin does not require a belief in the biological inheritance of Adam's fault. Here Gore's ideas are a forerunner to some of the themes in Reinhold Niebuhr's powerful *Nature and Destiny of Man* (1941).

Gore concluded his essay by underlining the fact that belief in the doctrines of the fall and sin—scientists' glib ridicule of an actual garden of Eden notwithstanding—is not and need not be based on the supposition that the third chapter of Genesis is literal history. In a manner typical of then current apologetics, Gore insisted that these beliefs "rest upon the broad basis of human experience." The Genesis story is then "a generalized account of what is continually happening" and points to a "vital spiritual truth" (231–32).

By the 1890s Gore's symbolic and experiential interpretation of the Genesis narrative of the fall had been widely adopted by British theologians and biblical scholars. For example, in their influential *Critical and Exegetical Commentary on the Epistle to the Romans* (1897), William Sanday and A. C. Headlam approved the position recently taken by scholars in the comparative study of religion, namely, that the story of the fall of Adam is not a literal record of historical fact but "the Hebrew form of a story common to a number of Oriental peoples." The Genesis narrative is, in the comparativist view, the representative account of an archetypal theme that portrays a deep human reality, "a series of facts which no discovery of flint implements and half-calcined bones can ever reproduce for us." These ancient accounts of the mysterious and ubiquitous tendency to sin are "naturally and inevitably summed up as a group of single incidents." It would be absurd, of course, to expect the Hebrew poet to speak in the language of modern science. In writing of the fall and sin, both the poet, and later St. Paul, used the only language available to them and their contemporaries. They expressed these profound truths "through symbols, and in the days when men can dispense with symbols [their] teaching may be obsolete, but not before" (Sanday and Headlam 1897, 146–47).

The symbolic interpretation of the Genesis story of Adam was given tacit official sanction with the publication of Samuel R. Driver's (1846–1914) distinguished and authoritative *The Book of Genesis* (1905). Driver was Regius Professor of Hebrew in Oxford and the most eminent Hebraist in the English-speaking world of his day. Moderate in his judgments, Driver was widely trusted and therefore was able to play a valuable mediating role. It was said of him that he taught the faithful criticism and the critics faith. In his book on Genesis, Driver concurred that the theological truths about human nature enclosed within the Genesis narrative are couched "in a figurative or allegorical dress, the details not being true in a literal sense, but being profoundly true in a *symbolic* sense." What these narratives do is seize upon and express, under powerful concrete images, certain moral and religious truths about human life, including humanity's natural mortality yet unique status in the creation, the possession of free will and a moral nature, and the awakening of conscience and the temptation that brings out the cunning and deceitfulness of sin and evil. The wide acceptance of Driver's measured and judicious judgments on the Old Testament literature was an indication of the remarkable change that had occurred in biblical studies and theology and of their public acceptance since *Essays and Reviews* (1860).

Frederick R. Tennant (1866–1957) was the theologian at the turn of the century who explored most deeply the Christian doctrines of the fall and sin. His historical and constructive analysis was directed toward refuting the traditional doctrines, which he felt were oppressive to thoughtful believers because they were both morally repulsive and scientifically unsound. Tennant wanted to rehabilitate these doctrines in order to save the vital truths enshrined in what he saw as their outmoded forms—and to do so on scientific grounds. His constructive, and at many points radical, reinterpretation supported the views of some of his progressive colleagues, but he also found fault with some of the positions taken by Aubrey Moore, J. R. Illingworth, and J. M. Wilson.

Tennant believed that Darwinism had had a salutary effect on rethinking the doctrines of the fall and original sin by undermining both the traditional view of humanity's original state and the cause of moral evil. "The Church owes a debt to science and to Darwinism in particular," he wrote, "for aid in getting rid of an antiquated doctrine long felt by many Christians to be an intellectual burden" (Tennant 1909, 424). It is here, ironically, that Tennant saw the weakness in Aubrey Moore's otherwise wise apologetic. To speak, as Moore had done, of "a moral change for the worse, happening at a definite time" that "has left its mark on human nature in the disorder and harmony of its parts" is to expose oneself to the full force of objections that have been made against the Augustinian position in the modern period. Moore had also said that sin could not be explained because it was "irrational." But this is to confuse the issue. Sin, Tennant pointed out, may be irrational in the sense of being foolish but not in the sense of being inexplicable (1902, 182–83). Rather than "resort to a hypothetical previous existence," or explain the human heart's corruption by appeal "to a timeless and almost inconceivable act of self-decision," the theory of human evolution gives sufficient grounds for the occurrence of sinfulness "in our natural constitution" and as "the normal result of the process of development through which our race has passed before acquiring morality" (1909, 426–27).

Tennant pinned down the fundamental problem that had exposed what he regarded as the implausibility of the traditional Augustinian idea of original sin. Sin, we assume, is coextensive with guilt, which implies accountability. But "'original sin' necessarily implies 'original guilt,' which is a contradiction in terms; for guilt is only predicable of the person's volitional act" (1909, 425). On this point, Tennant contended, Pelagius was wiser than St. Augustine in making guilt entirely a matter of personal responsibility. From the evolutionary perspective, the appearance of sin is not "a catastrophic plunge." Rather, it is found in the satisfaction of certain natural impulses that were innocent *until* recognized as traversing a moral law and after which were seen as precluded by ethical sanctions. It was by the discovery of moral law that humans came to know sin, as St. Paul had taught.

Tennant held that our natural propensities are not, as such, sinful. "They are simply the conditions which render virtue and vice equally a possibility when will and conscience have been acquired." The morality of both the race and the individual are gradually acquired. And so it is, according to Tennant, that "the sinfulness of sin would gradually increase from zero; and the first sin, if the words have any meaning, instead of being the most heinous and the most momentous in the race's history, would rather be the least significant of all" (1902, 114).

Tennant rejected the idea that anthropology can tell us nothing about our primitive ancestors because various theologians—for example, Illingworth and the Scottish theologian James Orr—claimed that it is not licit to draw conclusions about primitive man from a study of extant savage tribes. While the human sciences may not give us a full account of humanity's moral growth, Tennant was certain that they had shown us that our moral life was developed from extremely rude beginnings and along certain lines that are now widely recognized. It is legitimate, then, to infer from what we know about the dawn of human history to an estimate of prehistoric mental and moral life. What we find is that moral life in the primitive state "is largely still in germ" and that "the further back we trace man, the less we find him the person, or even the individual." What we do find is a "tribal self," a fact, Tennant urged, of great bearing on the question at issue. For "it enables us to see that the idea of moral personality, in terms of which Theology has been wont exclusively to formulate its doctrine of the origin of sin, emerged extremely late in human thought" (1902, 88–89).

If science teaches us that the origin of sin in the race is gradual and is connected with social heredity in the acquisition of the moral faculty, so it is with the individual. The infant's moral development recapitulates, to some extent, the history of the race. Here, however, we are on more solid, empirical ground. Drawing heavily on the research of James Mark Baldwin's *Mental Development in the Child and the Race* (1895), Tennant argued that the infant's natural impulses are in full sway, and necessarily so, long before the moral judgment appears, which is made and not born. Even the germs of "will" and "moral sense" are not apparent in the infant at first. "Social, rather than physical heredity, molds the child," imitation being essential for both mental and moral growth. But before the imitative period the child is utterly natural and impulsive. In the infant, the "ape" and the "tiger" are natural and necessary. Besides being amoral, "these animal propensities are *neutral . . .* indifferent material waiting to be moralized" (1902, 99). It is not possible, therefore, to speak of a "bias" to evil before the child has attained a moral conscience and accountability. Only later is the child capable of separating the abstract idea of good and evil from that of the will of a parent figure. As the ethical sense expands, the child becomes aware of new occasions for failure, and the experience of evil grows (107).

Sin is, then, the will's failure to moralize the raw material of impulse. And habit plays a crucial role in the growth of evil through a progressive weakening of the will. Tennant saw the role of habit, and the inability, despite freedom, to do that which we would, as one of the great truths seized upon by both St. Paul and St. Augustine. Life represents a constant struggle between the "old" self and the "new," and there is no resting point in the life of virtue, since moral advance makes one ever more sensitive to the need to "die to" and surmount the old. Conscience thus makes the reality of sin a universal human fact. "The absence of a solitary case of sinless life would seem . . . to be no marvel that needs to be violently accounted for" by a catastrophic historic fall or by the hereditary transmission of original sin (109).

Tennant further insisted that his natural account of the origin and universality of sin "neither excuses evil nor explains it away." For "if this account of sin sees in it something empirically inevitable for every man—which of course accords with all experience,—it by no means implies that sin is theoretically, or on *a priori* grounds, an absolute necessity" (110). In his reinterpretation of original sin, Tennant suggested the later view, popularized by the theologian Reinhold Niebuhr, that sin is existentially inevitable though not ontologically necessary. Tennant concluded that the scientific view not only accords with a symbolic reading of the Genesis account; it also provides a sounder basis for the idea of human solidarity in evil, which is an essential and permanent element in the problem of sin. Again, the social and unitary nature of the race was one of St. Augustine's great insights. But now "solidarity *and* guilt each finds its recognition in the theory of sin involved in the account of human nature which Science has supplied to Theology as a basis for its doctrine of man" (117).

Tennant finally urged that, "in an age which is inclined to take sin lightly," it is important to distinguish sin from "imperfection." In an evolutionary view of development, "imperfection" obviously characterizes every stage of human moral development until some final goal is reached. But sin is not imperfection, nor is it a theoretical necessity for any individual. Neither does evolutionary doctrine explain sin away. As for the Tylorians, anthropologists who often spoke of sin as a mere "survival," Tennant answered that if evolutionary doctrine

> calls sin "an anachronism," or declares it to be the survival of acts and dispositions once innocent because they knew no law imposing restraint upon them, it has nothing to object to the theologian's condemnation of precisely similar acts and dispositions as sinful or guilty when they occur *after* their agent has become aware that they contravene a moral sanction. (1909, 429)

They are, then, sins in the strictest sense of the word.

Tennant was wary, nonetheless, of exaggerated language concerning sin, for example, seeing all sin as *deliberate* enmity toward God. Neither is the universality of sin incompatible with recognizing the fact of degrees of sin. And when we observe the lives of many saintly souls, we may "look with equanimity upon the fact . . . that no man's manhood has been absolutely without flaw" (1912, 271).

Later critics saw Tennant's view of sin as too detached and composed to make sense, for example, of the events of World War I. Tennant's apparent equanimity had given way to a more somber, "realistic" view. The fact is, Tennant was genuinely troubled by the loss of the sense of sin and by current sanguine expectations. Any serious theologian must, he believed, oppose the easy optimism associated with the still popular theories of evolutionary advance. Tennant, like Gore, pointed out that evolution exhibits degeneration as well as progress and that "there is no reason for supposing sin to be a transient phase of human conduct" (1912, 287).

Philip N. Waggett (1862–1939) was an Anglican priest and member of the Oxford mission Society of Saint John the Evangelist, as well as a theologian also trained in science and conversant in the intricacies of evolutionary theory. Like Tennant, he was wary of theologians who made much of the "gaps" in scientific knowledge, which, they trusted, would leave room for the mysteries of the faith. He distrusted any theology that might be shaken by, for example, the discovery of some bridge between inorganic and organic life. He remained secure in the belief that the reign of natural law left untouched our wonder and our reverence for divine creative power.

Waggett insisted that theology allow science to pursue its course without any tethers or inhibitions. But he seriously disagreed with Tennant on the need for theology to square its belief in sin with scientific method and results. Waggett held that science qua science has nothing to say about human freedom and sin. Science must offer an account of the world considered "wholly and only as determined," that is, under the postulates of necessity and uniformity. It is just because this relative determinism is of the essence of science that the reflective scientist recognizes "that his discipline never can claim a universal or absolute character, except on pain of ceasing to be science at all." The man of science will not dispute "the claim that moral free actions have changed the world. He will only say they lie outside his science" (Waggett 1900). Waggett freely admitted that moral freedom and sin remained complex facts of experience and yet are incontrovertible realities that must be faced without too much impatience for a solution.

Waggett also found Charles Gore's language about sin unsatisfactory. The bishop had spoken of humanity as slowly developing toward its Creator's ideal but had also said that this evolution "has been much less rapid and constant than it might have been, owing to the fact of sin from which [it] might have been free." Waggett perceived in this language echoes of the failed "acceleration and retardation theory" that was espoused by certain contemporary evolutionists. They sought to account for significant variations in the human race by an appeal to mere differences of developmental *speed*. "If we try to explain sin as a matter of pace," Waggett asked, "shall we not approach the language in which 'the Pelagians do vainly talk'?" Waggett insisted that human sin is a new and unique moral line of evolutionary development. And what this new condition requires is not "a more rapid or a more constant advance along the line of fallen nature, but a complete standstill and a translation for which nature has no forces" (Waggett 1900).

New efforts at reconciliation between the Christian doctrine of human sin and evolutionary theory—by the Anglicans Moore, Wilson, Gore, Tennant, and Waggett—were often compelling. They either showed the congruence of evolutionary science with the theological belief in the reality and the solidarity or universality of sin, or that this moral question was beyond the scope of science. These same theologians were, however, not infrequently charged by their conservative colleagues with having Pelagian tendencies.

James Orr (1844–1913), professor of systematic theology in the United Free Church of Scotland College in Glasgow, is the best British representative of this line of criticism, expounded in his *God's Image in Man* (1906). While Orr believed that his liberal colleagues wrote "in fullest loyalty to what they regard as the settled teachings of science," their efforts inevitably, it seemed to him, "minimized the awful evil of sin"; sin had lost "the tragic and catastrophic character it possesses in the Biblical view." The reason, Orr suggested—and he was not quite fair to some whom he criticized—is that sin "becomes a necessity of man's development, a stage it was inevitable man should pass through in the course of his moral ascent" (Orr 1906, 204). Even when the word "necessity" is not used, sin still is viewed as an unavoidable result of man's nature and environment. The theistic evolutionist's depiction of primitive humanity's departures from the most basic notions of right are, in fact, so natural and inevitable "that nothing like *serious* responsibility" can attach to their actions; "the idea of guilt is weakened almost to the vanishing point." Evolutionary theory, in Orr's judgment, simply leaves much that traditional theology considered sin—cruelty, bloodshed, even cannibalism—as sinless, on the grounds "that the conscience of primitive man was not yet sufficiently developed to regard these things as wrong" (209). The evolutionists considered humanity's rudimentary ideas of right and wrong so childish as to make any transgression simply venial and excusable.

Orr exposed a vulnerable side of some of the evolutionary reconceptions of the doctrine of sin. However, his criticism was too often wide of the mark and undeserved. Neither Tennant nor Moore nor Gore held that sin was "an unavoidable result of man's nature and environment." And this was a signal point of Orr's indictment, the one on which he built his case about the loss of personal responsibility and the weakening of guilt. Orr's own interpretation of the Genesis account also was suspect on several counts. First, he maintained that the claims made for a comparison between primitive humans and modern savages, and for humanity's slow ascent from a low state, rested on unproved assumptions and therefore did not need to be taken seriously. Yet in view of the serious objections advanced by Tennant and others, Orr rather too confidently defended the belief in a historical primal perfection, that is, that humanity's earliest progenitor was "capable of knowing, understanding, conversing with, and worshipping and obeying his Creator" (157).

Orr's claims about the high capabilities of primal man further compelled him to declare for a catastrophic historic fall and for the theory of degenerationism. He spoke of a "*first act* of sin in the progenitors of the race" that brought about a "rupture of the original bond between the soul and God." It is this "hereditary sin," he insisted, that has left "a deep, dark stain in the history of our race" (243). Orr justified belief in a primal fall and the racial transmission of this original sin by recourse to current neo-Lamarckian claims about the transmission of acquired characters—a position that Tennant had taken care to squash. Tennant had, for example, pointed out that "it is almost impossible to conceive the nature of the mechanism whereby a specific effect produced upon any organism could so modify its reproductive organs as to cause a *corresponding* modification in the offspring" (37).

James Orr was not dissuaded, however. Like Charles Gore, he had found support—which proved to be tenuous—in the fact that Lamarckianism was currently an open question. While he acknowledged that physical changes ordinarily are not inherited, he continued to insist that it was a different matter when one moves from the physical to the region of the voluntary moral life. Here Orr found support in W. B. Carpenter's studies of alcoholism, the deleterious effects of which are, according to Carpenter, passed on to offspring. What is striking, however, is that Orr never raised what, for Tennant and others, was the crucial problem with original sin in *any* of its Augustinian forms: the issue of *personal* culpability and moral guilt.

Orr had built his scientific defense of a traditional Augustinian doctrine of the fall and sin on, what proved to be, the sands of anthropological and Lamarckian conjectures that were soon rejected. But writing at the turn of the century, Orr's stress on the intractable character of sin, rather than inevitable progress in history, accorded well with a new and rising "realistic" temper. Huxley had just broken with evolutionary optimism. He now saw "progression" as comparable to the trajectory of a mortar shell with its eventual turn downward, reminding his considerable readership that "the sinking half of that course is as much a part of the general process of evolution as the rising" (T. H. Huxley 1894, 9, 199).

Max Nordau's *Degeneration*, a dark prediction of the decline of the West, was published in English in 1895. This was the same year as the appearance of H. G. Wells's *The Time Machine*, perhaps the most powerful of the British imaginative portrayals of a degenerated human future. A year earlier Henry Drummond had published his grand, optimistic vision of the operation of natural laws in the spiritual world, *The Ascent of Man* (1894). But Drummond's "naturalization of the supernatural" was, within a short time, as passé as was the doctrine of his teacher, Herbert Spencer, whose ideas Drummond had essentially Christianized (see J. R. Moore 1983, 383–417). The temper of the times was by now antiutopian, and this was reflected in the work of the most acute theological minds. They knew well that the gospel of progress was not the doctrine of evolutionary science. There was, they protested, no essential connection between the survival of the fittest and the survival of the best; survival may well prove to be the victory of the morally degraded. Science, Charles Gore wrote, "indulges in no prophecies and would have no reason at all . . . to be disappointed when an epoch of change passes into an epoch of deterioration." Indeed, an imaginative tour of human history would reveal a "vast area of stagnation . . . [,] retrogression and decay." Gore assured his readers, as had A. J. Balfour, that if they observed the most "progressive nations," they would "find even more ambiguous the relation of civilization to moral progress" (Gore 1905, 36–37).

On the issue of the significance of evolutionary science for the Christian doctrines of the fall and sin, no theologian better represented the religious spirit of the years prior to World War I than the Scottish Congregationalist theologian P. T. Forsyth (1848–1921). While he was entirely open to the assured results of science, he also saw its limits when it came to exploring the realm of morality and the human spirit. Like Gore, he posed the question of human moral progress and underscored the counterevidence. He pointed out that the question of moral evil was now seriously discussed by men who would not even think of raising the same question about other aspects of social development. This only demonstrated for Forsyth that "they recognize the vast difference between the two worlds of morals and of civilization in their principles of progress." Such theological doctrines as the fall and sin would be discarded at great cost, since, as Forsyth suggested, these doctrines are efforts to explain things that only sanguine dreamers can ignore. They are grounded on "the existence of highly intractable facts" (Forsyth 1909, 226).

Forsyth was especially sensitive to the discontinuous and paradoxical character of historical development. If there is such a thing as human progress, it is "progress by crisis, by catastrophes," he wrote. "Seasons of calm and beauty discharge themselves in thunderstorms . . . which open space for new energies and new periods." Sanctity is, paradoxically, simultaneously a revelation of sin, for "the growth of the one accentuates the antagonism of the other." Forsyth further observed that the biblical idea of history is entirely at odds with that proposed by the believers in progress; it "is not a stream of evolution but a series of judgements." "It is," he continued, "an idea more revolutionary in its nature than evolutionary . . . a series of conversions rather than educations." For Forsyth the world is redeemed rather than perfected. The key to history in the biblical drama is a moral one, "and the principle of a saving judgement is deeper than that of a guiding providence" (1909, 226). In British religion P. T. Forsyth represents, perhaps better than any other, the conjoining of a modern critical mind with a thorough realism about human nature and history. This concurrence was a feature of much British and Continental theology in the decades immediately following 1914.

CHAPTER 6

Humanity's Place in Nature—
The Challenge to Christian Anthropology

Mind, Free Will, and the Foundation of Morals

Nature is made better by no means
But nature makes that means: so, o'er that art
Which you say adds to nature, is an art
That nature makes.

William Shakespeare

Man must begin, know this, where nature ends;
Nature and Man can never be fast friends.
Fool, if thou canst not pass her, rest her slave!

Matthew Arnold

The issue was not so much the specific results of science but the question whether the pursuit of science, whatever science, deprives man of his freedom and moral dignity.

John Passmore

The Science of Mind:
Controversy over the Brain, Mind, and Free Will

Chapter 2 briefly described the early Victorian shift in the perception of man's place in nature. We also saw how some of the implications of this change were resisted not only by the clerical naturalists associated with the Bridgewater Treatises but also by lay scientists such as Charles Lyell. While acknowledging the reality of a deep human antiquity, these scientists denied transmutation of

humans from lower animals. They steadfastly held to a belief in the uniqueness of the human species. Darwin's theory profoundly challenged this belief,
of course, but we also know that there were Darwinians (A. R. Wallace, St. G.
J. Mivart, W. B. Carpenter) who argued, on scientific grounds, for humanity's
unique status in the evolutionary process. Furthermore, there were a number of theologians, some well-trained in science, who were able to reconcile
biblical themes such as the fall and human sin with the latest findings in
natural history, anthropology, and developmental psychology. Furthermore,
their "biblical realism" regarding the human condition and doubts about
humanity's historical "progress" found powerful corroboration in the events
that shook Europe after 1914.

A perhaps deeper mid- and late Victorian challenge to a Christian anthropology was posed by those exponents of scientific positivism whose often
covert metaphysics entailed a mental materialism and determinism. The latter threatened a spiritual conception of freedom, of moral responsibility, and
the theological foundations of morals. The controversy, as it heated up in
the 1860s, centered on questions regarding the relations between the brain,
the mind, and human free will. Much of the work in the new physiological psychology, begun as early as the 1830s, was carried out in the medical
schools (see Desmond 1989). Initially, it had nothing to do with the question
of human origins. Its proponents viewed the mind as a product of the material conditions from which it originated, that is, the physical organism and
its neural system, in relation to its environment. They rejected concepts of
the mind that considered it to be derived from, or to be the essence of, some
distinctive spiritual reality. Furthermore, the new physiological psychology
insisted on the continuity between the mental life of the lower organisms
and that of the human race. To date, human mental life constitutes only the
highest stratum of natural history (see R. Smith 1977, 216–30; Jacyna 1981,
109–32; Young 1970). On the other hand, the theologians and theistic scientists argued that physiological psychology did not entail a materialist metaphysics or a naturalistic monism.

It was natural that the development of the study of experimental physiology in the schools at midcentury would lead to expectations of a greater
understanding of human psychology. The latter, in turn, increasingly was
discussed in physiological, rather than in philosophical, terms. In 1856 J. D.
Morell expressed the view that was to prevail:

The truth of the co-ordination of the sciences, which has been for
some time tacitly gaining ground amongst the fixed convictions of
philosophic minds, has naturally thrown psychological research back
upon physiological principles; proving to us beyond doubt, that we

need the data which the lower science can supply before we can give a proper foundation to the higher. (Morell 1856, 351)

The case for the new biology of mind was being made in Britain in the 1850s and 1860s by Alexander Bain in *The Senses and the Intellect* (1855) and *The Emotions and the Will* (1859), by Herbert Spencer in *The Principles of Psychology* (1855), and by G. H. Lewes in *The Physiology of Common Life* (1859–1860), among others. What Bain, Spencer, and Lewes shared was an empiricist physiological sensationalism, which became the premise of the new physiological and evolutionary psychology. Mind is the product of its material conditions, the object of biological and sociological study.

A number of scientists who drew very different philosophical conclusions than did writers such as Lewes nevertheless supported the new physiological basis of psychology. W. B. Carpenter is a case in point. He proposed a theory of correlation between vital and physical forces:

And thus we are led to perceive that, as the power of the Will can develop Nervous activity, and as Nerve-force can develop Mental activity, there must be a *Correlation* between these two modes of dynamical agency, which is not less intimate and complete than that which exists between Nerve-force on the one hand, and Electricity and Heat on the other. (W. B. Carpenter 1852, 513–14)

Despite his support of the new physiological psychology, Carpenter opposed the implicit, if not explicit, materialism and determinism that he found, for example, in Huxley's writings on human automatism.

The issues that inevitably were to emerge from the new evolutionary psychology burst into controversy in the 1870s with the appearance early in the decade of several provocative essays by W. K. Clifford, John Tyndall, and T. H. Huxley. A number of these essays, and the attacks on them by W. G. Ward, Henry Calderwood, Henry E. Manning (1808–1892), James Martineau, and others, were originally presented as papers at meetings of the Metaphysical Society. They were then made available to a wider audience in periodicals such as the *Contemporary Review*. The essays of Clifford, Tyndall, and Huxley sought to draw out the implications of an evolutionary naturalism for a conception of the human mind and behavior. They presupposed a scientific sensationalism and proposed to establish the physiological basis of human psychology.

This new psychology of mind became polarized over the question of volition, or the freedom of the will. Many defenders of the new physio-psychology considered neural events to be primary and mental events as secondary, that is, as epiphenomenal and reducible to the former. However, to counter the charge of a crude materialism, G. H. Lewes (1817–1878) and others adopted a "double-aspect theory," or the notion that both feeling and thought are functions of the same sentient organ under different aspects. Any claims about a *unique* human volition were regarded as a threat to scientific views of causation. This physio-psychological antivoluntarism is epitomized in Henry Maudsley's *Body and Will* (1883). He assimilated free will to chance: "The right and proper opposite of *necessary* is not *free*, but *fortuitous* or contingent; the contingency or chance lying not in the absence of determination but in the presence of unknown determinants" (Maudsley 1883, 36).

Materialism, or what turned out to be, in effect, its equivalent in psycho-physical parallelism, was appealing on the grounds of its explanatory parsimony. The real underlying issues, however, were metaphysical and even professional, as L. J. Dasten explains:

What psycho-physiologists, associationists, and evolutionists all shared was chiefly a belief that the expanding empire of deterministic scientific explanation was synonymous with intellectual progress, and that the category of mind, conceived as self-determining ego, posed the most formidable obstacle to that advance. (L. J. Daston 1982, 96)

Some Irresolute "Materialists"

One of the more fervent of the new scientific naturalists was W. K. Clifford, whose essay "The Ethics of Belief" had sparked the lively debate on the morality of believing. In his essay "Body and Mind" (1874) Clifford argued that "there is no reason to suppose anything but the universal laws of mechanics in order to account for the motion of organic bodies," including the brain (Clifford 1874, 727). He scoffed at the notion that the mind is a creative force. Mental facts are simply the product of physical energy operative in the nervous system and brain. If mind were directed by a will we should be able to perceive it, for matter, the brain, can be influenced only by the position and motion of matter itself: "If anybody says that the will influences matter, the statement is not untrue, but it is nonsense. The will is not a material thing, it is not a mode of material motion. . . . Now the only thing which influences matter is the position of surrounding matter or the motion of surrounding matter" (728).

If, in fact, we are merely conscious automata, what becomes of free will? Freedom, Clifford argued, is the capacity to originate activity independent of outside determining causes. The difference between an automaton and a puppet is that one goes by itself when properly fueled, while the other requires to be manipulated by another agent. Clifford proposed that the objection to the idea of human automatism is derived from the fallacious notion that a human being is a construction of an outside agent in a certain definite way. In fact, we make ourselves, or, rather, "the human race as a whole has made itself during the process of ages," and the "action of the whole race at any given time determines what the character of the race shall be in the future" (729). By the process of natural selection, the material inheritance and actions of our forebears are built into us and shape our character. Our conceptions of right and wrong, of good and evil, evolve "in the broad light of day out of natural causes wherever men live together"; they are products of "the social instincts which have been bred into mankind by hundreds of generations of social life" (729).

The writings of Tyndall and Huxley were, by contrast, curiously ambivalent. While they were, with Clifford, committed to a thoroughly naturalistic materialist cosmology and psychology, they were also anxious to deny that they were so foolish as to embrace a philosophical materialism. Even Clifford had taken refuge in a form of Berkeleian idealism, with sensory impressions being modifications of consciousness presented to us in the form of simple atoms, what he called "mind-stuff." His metaphysical reflections thus reposed in what his critics perceived as an unstable psychophysical parallelism, one in which physical facts and mental facts proceed on different planes, with no interference of one with the other. As his critics observed, Clifford, like Huxley, finally gave methodological priority to neural, physical facts. While Tyndall and Huxley took refuge in a Humean agnosticism, rather than in Berkeley, and denied any ultimate knowledge of either matter or spirit, they at the same time asserted that all knowledge and explanation were explicable solely in material and mechanistic terms.

In a lecture on "Matter and Force" given before a group of working men in Dundee in 1867, Tyndall outlined the bases of his "materialism":

> It is the sun that separates the carbon from the oxygen of the carbonic acid, and thus enables them to recombine. Whether they recombine in the furnace of the steam engine or in the animal body, the origin of the power they reproduce is the same. In this sense we are all "souls of fire and children of the sun" . . . and must be content to share our celestial pedigree with the meanest of living things. (Tyndall 1899, 71–72)

The scientist is by definition a "materialist," since his enquiries deal only with matter and force, whether in a plant or in the human brain. The scientific materialist thus forgoes speculation into final causes.

A year later, in his address to the British Association on "Scientific Materialism" (1868), Tyndall asked his auditors to imagine an analogy between the deposit of salt particles by solidification into crystalline, pyramidal forms and the construction of the pyramids of Egypt. The latter forms were laid down, of course, by human slaves, by powers external to the building blocks. By contrast, the salt molecules act upon each other without external intervention; their pyramidal forms being the result of the play of physical attraction and repulsion. But science too, Tyndall asserted, views the animal body as that of a being produced wholly by molecular forces. The human body creates nothing, neither matter nor force.

What of human consciousness, of thought and feeling? Tyndall reminded his colleagues that no scientist would deny that for every fact of consciousness there is a definite molecular movement and structure in the brain. Thought and its corresponding molecular action in the brain occur simultaneously. But the puzzle, he admitted, is that while they occur together, "we do not know why."

> Let the consciousness of love, for example, be associated with a right-handed spiral motion of the molecules of the brain, and the consciousness of hate with a left-handed spiral motion. We should then know, when we love, that the motion is in one direction, and when we hate, that the motion is in the other; but the "WHY?" would remain as unanswerable as before. (1899, 87; see also 168)

Tyndall conceded that here rests the materialist's position at the time. A scientist only can affirm, with Clifford, the association of the two classes of phenomena, of whose real bond of union he is in absolute ignorance. The critics of scientific materialism must not, however, take pleasure in such an acknowledged nescience, for "if the materialist is confounded and science rendered dumb . . . to whom has the arm of the Lord been revealed?" (1899, 88). Certainly not to the theologian and his recourse to invisible psychic forces or divine fiat. In the choice between the theological and materialist hypothesis, Tyndall was confident that there would, in due time, be no question. Not only the wonderful mechanism of the human body but "the human mind itself—emotion, intellect, will, and all their phenomena"—will be seen as "once latent in a fiery cloud." All our philosophy, art, poetry, and science—Plato, Raphael, Shakespeare, and Newton "are potential in the fires of the sun" (1899, 131).

In his 1874 Belfast Address, Tyndall appealed to Herbert Spencer's *Synthetic Philosophy* for an explanation of the development of human thought and feeling in the inherited experience of the race. He spoke, using Lucretian imagery, of "the myriad blows" by which "the image and superscription of the external world are stamped as states of consciousness" on the mind, "the depth of the impression depending upon the number of blows" (1899, 186). Quoting Spencer, he spoke of the human brain as the "organized register of infinitely numerous experiences received during . . . that series of organisms through which the human organism has been reached," slowly mounting "to that high intelligence which lies latent in the brain of the infant" (187–88).

Tyndall thus perceived only two possible courses: either acceptance of spontaneity and creative acts, events that elude or defy the laws of nature, or a refurbished materialism. For Tyndall the former was impossible.

> Believing as I do in the continuity of Nature, I cannot stop abruptly where our microscopes cease to be of use. Here the vision of the mind authoritatively supplements the vision of the eye. By an intellectual necessity I cross the boundary of the experimental evidence, and discern in that Matter which we, *in our ignorance of its latent powers*, and notwithstanding our professed reverence for its Creator, have hitherto covered with opprobrium, the promise and potency of all terrestrial Life. (191)

T. H. Huxley's materialism reflected the same ambivalence as Tyndall's. He alternated between definite materialist pronouncements and disclaimers regarding philosophical materialism. With his compatriots Clifford and Tyndall, he ended either in an inexplicable parallelism or a form of dualism. In 1869 Huxley delivered one of his more provocative lay sermons to an audience in Edinburgh. It was entitled "On the Physical Basis of Life," with emphasis on the word *the*. Huxley proposed that if it be granted that the properties of water are the result of the disposition of its component molecules there is no reasonable ground for refusing to say the same regarding the properties of protoplasm, and hence those of any animal. He then moved directly to his controversial point. He warned his auditors that the inference that necessarily followed may lead "to the antipodes of heaven" but that he could discover no logical halting place between the admission that what he had just said was the case

> and the further concession that all initial action may, with equal propriety, be said to be the result of molecular forces of the protoplasm which displays it. And if so, it must be true, in the same sense and to the same extent, that the thoughts to which I am now giving utterance, and your thoughts regarding them, are the expression of molecular

changes in that matter of life which is the source of our other initial phenomena. (T. H. Huxley 1869, 140)

Huxley confessed that he did not see an escape from utter materialism and necessitarianism. The progress of science simply means "the extension of the province of what we call matter and causation, and the concomitant gradual banishment from all regions of human thought of what we call spirit and spontaneity." He acknowledged that such a vision of the progress of materialism "weighs like a nightmare" on some of the best minds of the day, since it appeared to deny human freedom and to debase our moral nature. But to believe so, he thought, is to confuse the rise of materialistic language with a materialist ontology. The latter, he conceded, involves a "grave philosophical error." Once again, however, Huxley extricated himself from such dogmatism by recourse to a Humean agnosticism. What, after all, do we really know of matter or of spirit? "[They] are but names for the imaginary substrata of groups of natural phenomena. . . . The fundamental doctrines of materialism, like those of spiritualism, lie outside 'the limits of philosophical inquiry'" (1869, 142–44; 1893b, 158–62). Nonetheless, if a choice must be made, a materialistic language is to be preferred, for it alone suggests methods of inquiry and thought, a knowledge of which is accessible to us, and these can "help us to exercise the same kind of control over the world of thought as we already possess in respect of the material world." The alternative recourse to spiritualistic language simply "leads to nothing but obscurity and confusion of ideas" (1869, 145; 1893b, 164).

Huxley's rejection of a philosophical materialism was closely tied to the perplexities he personally felt regarding the problematic nature of the mind and human volition. He assured his auditors that we can be confident of two beliefs, despite all the evil that we experience and all that we do not and cannot know. One certainty is that the *order of nature* is ascertainable to our faculties to an almost unlimited extent. The other is that "our volition counts for something as a condition for the course of events" (1869, 163; 1893b, 163). To the attentive listener, "counts for something" appeared rather an afterthought, too perfunctory in view of what had been said of "the advancing tide" of materialism. Huxley failed to address the obvious metaphysical dilemma. As William Irvine remarks, "If man's will 'counts for something,' then he must only in a restricted sense be brother of the molecule." Agnosticism was, once again, "the fluid of uncertainty in which Huxley cushioned the shock of logical contraries" (Irvine 1959, 249).

Huxley, in fact, never did adequately explain how molecular activity issued in human thought and volition. He argued, in "Descartes' Discourse on Method" (1870), that the connection of consciousness and matter remained "an insoluble mystery" (T. H. Huxley 1893b, 194). However, in his essay "On the Hypothesis That Animals Are Automata" (1874), which was an enlargement of his Metaphysical Society paper "Has a Frog a Soul?" he proceeded a long way toward reducing consciousness to mechanism. "It may be assumed," he inferred from his analysis of animal automatism, "that molecular changes in the brain are the causes of all the states of consciousness of brutes." Furthermore, he saw no evidence "that these states of consciousness may, conversely, cause those molecular changes which give rise to muscular motion." He gave an example: "The frog walks, hops, swims . . . quite well without consciousness, and consequently without volition, as with it." It would appear then that the volition of brutes "if they have any, is an emotion indicative of physical changes, not a cause of such changes" (1893b, 239–40). Brute consciousness is a mere collateral product of the body's mechanical working.

The relation of consciousness to molecular changes in the brain did not, to Huxley's thinking, prevent us from ascribing a form of free will to brutes. "For the agent is free when there is nothing to prevent him from doing that which he desires to do. And if a greyhound chooses a hare, he is a free agent, because his action is in accordance with his strong desire to catch the hare." Such a notion of freedom, Huxley insisted, "is by no means inconsistent with the other aspect of the facts of the case—that he is a machine impelled to the chase" (1893b, 240–41). What applies to brutes holds equally true of humans. No state of consciousness is the cause of change of matter in the human organism:

> Our mental conditions are simply *the symbols of consciousness* of the changes which take place automatically in the organism; and to take an extreme illustration, the feeling we call volition is not the cause of the voluntary act, but the symbol of that state of the brain which is the immediate cause of that act. We are conscious automata, endowed with free will in the only intelligible sense of that much-abused term—inasmuch as in many respects we are able to do as we like—but none the less parts of the great series of causes and effects which, in unbroken continuity, composes that which is, and has been, and shall be—the sum of existence. (244)

If mental states are "symbols" of brain states, it is clear that causation occurred from one direction, namely, the antecedent brain state. Volition may be a feeling, but it has no causal efficacy. Huxley saw himself in the company of Jonathan Edwards and John Calvin, theologians who assumed a similar logical necessity in the divine order. He was not able to resolve adequately the "insolvable mystery" of matter and human moral action, as James Ward soon would effectively demonstrate. Humans remained an anomaly. Despite his scientific materialism, Huxley remained unsatisfied with deriving ethics from nature's mechanism. He was not, however, to reach a satisfactory solution for himself—in "Evolution and Ethics"—for another twenty years.

Taken as a group, the new leaders of scientific materialism—in spite of the formidable authority and the rhetorical skills with which they presented their views—were not successful in reconciling many of their confident claims simply with their agnosticism regarding an ontological materialism. As M. H. Carré writes, "They spoke for the most part as materialists and when the materialism became too obvious they fell upon Berkeleianism or upon the skepticism of the empirical philosophy" (Carré 1949, 354). The philosophical intuitionists, the realists, and the idealists were to make much of this maneuver of the scientific naturalists—and to mark its consequences.

The Response of Idealists and Realists

In the 1870s a stream of articles and books subjected the assumptions and claims of the materialists to a searching analysis and critique. They asked questions about human consciousness, the experience of self-transcendence, and valuation and moral choice. Were not Huxley, Tyndall, and Clifford endowing matter with some extramechanical power? Henry Calderwood (1830–1897), professor of moral philosophy at Edinburgh, was rather typical of the counter offensive, putting in high relief the contradictions and damning admissions of both Huxley and Tyndall.

In "The Present Relationship of Physical Science and Philosophy," Calderwood suggested that the struggle to arrive at a unitary materialist theory of life reveals the hopelessness of the effort when confronted with the facts of human self-consciousness. He quoted Tyndall's admission that "the chasm" between the physics of the brain and the facts of consciousness "remains intellectually impassable" (Calderwood 1871, 231). He boldly displayed Huxley's uncertainties, especially his waffling on the question of the brain and human consciousness. As Calderwood revealed, at one moment Huxley banished "spirit and spontaneity" and in the next used Descartes in support of his conviction that our knowledge of anything—either the self or the external world—is nothing "more or less than a knowledge of states of consciousness." Having rejected spiritualist terminology "as leading only to obscurity and confusion," Huxley proceeded to adopt the same in his

Descartes lecture, declaring that it is "an indisputable truth, that what we call the materialistic world is only known to us under the forms of the ideal world" (Calderwood 1871, 235). But in his more aggressive and "prophetic" pronouncements, Huxley reverted once again to his confident assertion of the attainment of a mechanical equivalent for the facts of consciousness.

During the last fifteen years of his life, Calderwood undertook an extensive exploration of Darwinian evolution, particularly the issues raised by studies in physiological psychology. The result was *The Relations of Mind and Brain* (1879) and *Evolution and Man's Place in Nature* (1893). These studies attempted to show that the higher forms of human mental life are not explainable by the laws of natural evolution alone. For Calderwood, the difference between mechanism and the higher reaches of mind is the same as that between muscle and tool, that is, the difference not in the grip but in the purpose that directs the hand's grasp. Calderwood insisted on the unity of mind and brain but also on their distinction. Rational insight, he argued, does not have its physical counterpart. A well-developed brain, after all, is no assurance of high intellectual attainment. While certainly "there is some natural correlation between physical and mental life—for example, the fact that poor food is a hindrance to intellectual advance—nevertheless, strict attention to nutrition and health is no guarantee of high intellectual effort (Calderwood 1893, 53).

Calderwood's enquiries convinced him that comparative brain research on anatomical structure, on the localization of brain function, and on physiological mechanism failed to provide explanations for human rational life. Reflective activity that issues in *self-directed activity*—that is, rational and moral conduct—does not lie within the explanatory modes of physiology. It leaves open to consideration the reasonable hypothesis that "rational phenomena altogether transcend the functions of organism," admitting, of course, that the brain is the organ of the mind. As closely allied with animal life as human life is, it is also necessary to acknowledge that the diversities apparent in rational life are beyond those that are apparent in the life of animals; hence, the contrasts between physical and rational life are profoundly demarcated.

> On the physical side, variations lead to new species; on the mental side, variations warrant no such distinctive classifications. Rational life is one, whatever its variations. . . . Physiological differences are insufficient to disturb this evidence for the unity of the race. . . . We are now contemplating a single order of life . . . the laws of whose development are different from those applicable to lower orders of life. (1893, 62–64)

Calderwood proceeded to argue that there is no analogy between the muscular movements that follow sensory impressions and the rational activity that follows the same impressions:

> The one is continuous under the same laws, passing through the nerve-cells to the nerve fibers, and continuing onwards to the muscles. The mental activity is *discontinuous*. . . . It comes to receive these new impressions in harmony with its own generalizations in the past. Here is the contrast between man and animal. . . . The man remarks that the movement which has arrested attention is that of a bird, that the bird is a bullfinch; and desiring to protect the bird, he calls back his dog, and drives away the cat. In this course of action, nerve-cells and nerve fibers are called into use, just as before, and these work just as they operate in every organism. . . . Everything of this kind is physical . . . just as are the movements of the cat and of the dog. The forms of reflective exercize are, however, *discontinuous*, because proceeding from a different cause. . . . In marking that . . . the action of intelligence is interposed by the man within his own consciousness; that the reflective exercize is not even "movement" in any sense analogous with that recognized in activity of nerve-fiber, we observe that our rational life is distinct from our physical. . . . There are thus two distinct phases of activity; so distinct that one is not continuous with the other, in respect of energy and movement, though continuous in time. (1893, 273–74, 276)

Calderwood thus concluded that the evolution of the physical organism is not capable of explaining fully the working of human rational consciousness, and it is this rational power that reveals the vast change that has overtaken the world.

James Martineau (1805–1900), the Unitarian philosopher who served as professor and principal of Manchester New College, was a persistent and influential philosophical critic of the materialist doctrines of mind, will, and ethics. He began as an empiricist in the tradition of Locke and Mill, but reflection on inner, psychic experience led him to stress the unique and autonomous character of knowing and willing.

The crux of Martineau's critique of materialism lay in his reflections on causation. Scientific naturalism held that cause and effect are homogeneous phenomena, standing in serial relation and necessary connection according to some law. It was a view of causation that entailed a doctrine of determinism, including that of the human will. Martineau, on the contrary, conceived of cause as a genuinely heterogeneous, productive human force, the source of the real origination of the effect. The only cause that we truly know, he argued, is our own will, and the meaning of causality is denoted by what we know as will, that is, a power capable of originating phenomena. In a letter to W. B. Carpenter dealing with matters of physiological psychology, Martineau wrote:

> I distinguish between the muscular *sensations* (which occur during the execution of an act), and the muscular *nisus* (which sets the act on foot). The former alone would, in my opinion, no more give us the knowledge of *power*, than any other sensory impressions. The latter would give it, even if the sensory nerves were paralysed. Will effectuated and will impeded, be the intermediate instruments sentient or insentient, would suffice, I think to occasion the dynamic antithesis of power within and power without. Take away the inward *nisus* of the Will; let the motory nerves be set in action by galvanism instead; and however perfectly the sensory nerves retain their function, I conceive that all dynamic ideas are out of reach.
>
> In short, we exercize power within, and plant it out believingly in the world. We have no means, independent of this translation, of perceiving, observing, or inductively inferring it in the external scene. Mere motion would not help us, even though it hurt us or gratified us. The experiences to which you appeal are not mere sensory experiences; they are a counter-ploy against the muscular *nisus*. (J. E. Carpenter 1905, 464–65)

In an essay entitled "The Place of Mind in Nature and Intuition in Man" (1872), Martineau elaborated on his concept of causality and brought to the fore his recent debates with Huxley, Tyndall, and Clifford in meetings of the Metaphysical Society. The essay received considerable attention and respect. James Knowles, the editor of the *Contemporary Review*, told Herbert Spencer in an after-dinner conversation at Huxley's that "the general opinion is that you gentlemen are getting the worst of it" in the contest with Martineau (J. E. Carpenter 1905, 466). In fact, both Spencer and Tyndall responded to Martineau's several forays, scoring some telling counterpoints of their own (Spencer 1872; Tyndall 1875). Martineau persisted, writing two additional works, "Religion as Affected by Modern Materialism" (1874) and *Modern Materialism: Its Attitude towards Theology* (1876), largely devoted to detailed analyses of the unresolved metaphysical problems in the writings of Tyndall and of materialism generally. Martineau did not, however, take Spencer's response to these issues as a serious threat, and he reserved his most telling attack on Spencer, as we will see, for his critical analysis of evolutionary ethics in *Types of Ethical Theory* (1885).

In his reply to Tyndall, Martineau argued that since, for the materialist, "causal power other than will is an unknown quantity[,] . . . teleology and causality are incorporated in one." Mechanical necessity, rather than the negation of teleology, is its mode and persistence. But it is foolish to insist, as do the materialists, that discovering the physical cause of change is to prove that it was never contemplated: "If man is only a sample of the universal determinism, yet forms purposes, contrives for their accomplishment, and executes them, definite causality and prospective thought can work together, and the field which is occupied by the one is not pre-occupied against the other" (Martineau 1875, 70–71).

What else, Tyndall had asked, is there in an account of saline crystals, ice-stars, fern fronds, and human birth than matter? Martineau answerd: "the *movements* of matter, with their disposing and formative *power*," which, "in *dealing with* molecules and cells *are not* molecules and cells." Some conception, Martineau argued, over and above "pure matter" is required to explain vital life (Martineau 1875, 73). Tyndall had drolly joked about Martineau's conjuring of "a vegetative soul," but Martineau responded that Tyndall's alternative of a "formative power" remained unexplained. "Whilst it lies in wait behind the scenes—before the time for the deposit of the crystal or the germination of the acorn—*where* is it? behind what molecules does it hide? through what space is it invisibly present?" (Martineau 1875, 74). The "power" that Tyndall pursued through nature becomes, in fact, increasingly opaque to any intellectual comprehension.

In his response to Martineau, Tyndall spoke of the inorganic, vegetable, and animal realms as constituting a unity, wherein he envisioned "life as immanent everywhere." However, he proceeded to emphasize that he was anxious not "to shut out the idea that the life here spoken of may not be a subordinate part and function of a higher life." Indeed, he spoke not only of a single power, immanent through the whole, but of one "higher" to which the laws of nature "do but give functional expression." The notion puzzled Martineau. May we legitimately think of this idea, Martineau asked, "of a life 'higher' than what is supreme in the world—higher therefore than the human?" The reason for the question is, of course, that for a scale of height above that of the human we know only, by analogy, as a transcendent Mind and Will. Since Tyndall refuses to predicate Mind or Will to his "higher life," Martineau asks, "on *what* scale, then, is it 'higher'?" (1875, 76).

Martineau's line of attack on the metaphysical conundrums of the popularizers of scientific materialism was taken up by his friend, the eminent physiologist W. B. Carpenter, in the preface to the fourth edition of his *Principles of Mental Physiology* (1876). One would presume that the confidence with which the materialists advanced the claims of human automatism reflected some newly discovered scientific facts. But Carpenter found nothing in the most recent research to change his conviction of the fundamental distinction between animal automatism and what is peculiar to human life, namely, "the distinct purposive intervention of the self-conscious ego which we designate Will" (W.B. Carpenter 1876, xxvii).

Carpenter's own work had given extensive attention to the fact that automatism plays a very large role in the life of every human being. And this fact, he felt, was what later persuaded Huxley to give up his belief that "volition counts for something." Carpenter had shown that humans continually make adjustments of muscular movements under circumstances that forbid the intervention of conscious will. Huxley similarly discovered that human "volition" could point to a purely automatic causation, and gave considerable attention to the case of a French sergeant to prove his point. As a consequence of a wound in the head received in battle, the Frenchman frequently passed into a state resembling that of artificially induced hypnotism, a suspension of the directing power of the will. The Frenchman's actions were, in this condition, determined automatically by suggestion. But Huxley inferred from this and other instances that the same is true in our normal state of consciousness, namely, that what we call will is only the symbol in consciousness of a material change that would equally take place without it.

Carpenter perceived in Huxley's example of the French sergeant a contrary conclusion since, for Carpenter, it was imperative to recognize the difference between the normal and abnormal states of human subjects. Because the abnormal state consists in the suspension of volitional power, it makes all the difference in our judgment regarding moral responsibility. We would hold the Frenchman "'responsible' for any theft he might commit when in full possession of his wits," and yet the same action performed in an automatic condition would be excusable, due to the absence of self-control. Huxley's human examples of automatism were, in Carpenter's judgment, "readily explicable by the principle of *secondary* or *acquired* Automatism," which in the case of the lower animals would be *primary* and *original*. An example would be Huxley's chosen illustration of Goltz's experiments with the frog. As Carpenter pointed out, the certain automatic actions of a frog might resemble those a human might execute volitionally; the point being that the frog possesses by inheritance what the human learns only by intentional training:

> The fullest recognition of Automatism in the performance of Goltz's frog does not in the least invalidate the testimony of my own Consciousness, that when, being called upon to balance my body under some unaccustomed circumstances (as in crossing a stream on

a narrow plank, or over a series of stepping-stones), I give my whole attention to that act, the movements of my body are executed under my intentional direction. Again, the fact that various actions have become so familiar to me by habit as to be performed Automatically, affords no contradiction to the testimony of my own Consciousness, that when I was first trained . . . to execute them, my Will issued the mandates which were carried into effect by my muscles. I cannot believe that a piece of delicate handiwork, such as a minute dissection, or the painting of a miniature—requiring constant visual guidance, and trained exactness of muscular response—can be executed without a distinct Volitional direction of each movement. (1876, xxviii)

Carpenter concluded that, while acknowledging that a great deal of automatic activity without the intervention of consciousness takes place in the cerebrum that would usually be accounted as the effects of volition, "in all such cases *the action takes place on the lines previously laid down by Volitional direction*" (1876, xxix). And with regard to ethics, the fact is that if right and wrong are the products, like sugar and vitriol, whose laws science can be expected to discover, it is "as irrational to feel indignation at base and cowardly actions as it would be to feel angry about their chemical affinities." The same would hold, of course, on the automatist hypothesis, of our moral approval of noble acts of self-sacrifice (xxxix).

The philosophy of sensationalism, with its implicit materialism and denial of an autonomous self and free will, was also the target of philosophical realists. One of these was W. G. Ward, whose papers delivered before the Metaphysical Society entitled "On Memory as an Intuitive Faculty" and "Can Experience Prove the Uniformity of Nature?" were widely regarded as impressive critiques of some of the empiricists' fundamental principles. Ward's Roman Catholic colleagues Henry Manning and J. D. Dalgairns also entered the lists with Martineau and Carpenter in the Society's debates of the early 1870s. Manning, the Catholic archbishop of Westminster, responded to Huxley's "Has a Frog a Soul?" with a paper on "What Is the Relation of the Will to Thought?" (Manning 1871). Manning argued that far from the brain's being commensurate with the self, the self through the will educates the brain. It does this through the acts of intention, attention, and intensity.

A more incisive philosophical defense of the reality and independence of mind and will was offered by J. B. Dalgairns (1818–1876), a Roman Catholic priest of the Oratorians associated with the important Brompton Oratory, London. Dalgairns was well grounded in contemporary German as well as British philosophy; he was also dubious of the capacity of the older scholasticism to deal persuasively with current intellectual questions. In his paper

"On the Theory of a Human Soul," Dalgairns proposed an alternative to the sensationalists' explanation of the relation between sense, intellect, and will. But in doing so he also rejected intuitionist epistemology which, he believed, failed to do justice to the role of sensation. He agreed with J. S. Mill "that our direct knowledge of the outer world is phenomenal" (Dalgairns 1871, 41). Empiricist epistemology failed, however, to understand the distinctive role of human consciousness.

Dalgairns proceeded to demonstrate that the concept of mind proposed by Mill and his empiricist disciples had forced them, often unawares, into an idealist theory of knowledge. Dalgairns called it "Bishop Berkeley minus God." Mill's conception of mind as merely "a series of feelings aware of itself, as past and future" compelled him to assert for the mind a far greater power and independence than his physiology or logic would allow. Mill was too acute to see that sense "can never prove the reality of an outer world, unless the mind adds an act of perception which affirms it." But this is to acknowledge that the mind has an originating power that runs contrary to the logic of Mill's theory. To say that a substantive external world is conceivably not real independent of our sense-data "is simply the affirmation of the creation of an outer world by the mind." For even if we grant that the external world is an illusion,

> surely the mental faculty which can thus, taking sense as its fulcrum, make a spring into chaos, and return laden with nothing less than a world of its own creation, peopled with spirits and many-coloured objects of matter, is a god, and not a labeller of sense-materials. The upshot of the theory is that the independence of mind has returned upon us in a most unexpected shape. (1871, 34)

Dalgairns then proceeded to show that the scientific sensationalist's refuge in nescience is an act of mind that demonstrates its independence. For "what can be more independent than the very declaration of nescience by which we pronounce that we do not know things as they are in reality?" In fact, we clearly do know two things—"our thought and reality—or else we could not pronounce them to be unlike." Even if the reality were only a sensation, still, Dalgairns argued, a person's "thought is clearly not the sensation, for it is a judgment on the sensation." That judgment is not only a denial of its identity with the sensation but a declaration of its independence. We know nothing adequately of what the sensation is in itself. We are in truth "behind the scenes. . . . We know the phenomenon, the act and the agent. We know that this is our act, and that we are the actors" (1871, 34). Here, in the act of judgment, Dalgairns concluded, we stand on the edge of the abyss that distinguishes matter and spirit while conjoining them.

From the Idealist side, the most sustained defense of the independence and distinctiveness of the human mind and will was undertaken by Oxford philosopher T. H. Green (1836–1882) in his Oxford lectures in the late 1870s. They were first published as articles in the journal *Mind* and then, posthumously, as *Prolegomena to Ethics* in 1883. The thrust of Green's argument was to refute the growing evolutionary idea that ethics can be explained in naturalistic and genetic terms, that is, circumscribed to a subfield of natural science. He began his discussion of ethics with the fact of the natural or animal impulse in humans of *wants* which, in the ethical sphere, correspond to our animal *sensations* in the field of knowledge.

Green distinguished, however, between a mere want and a wanted object. The transition from one to the other "implies the presence of the want to a subject which distinguishes itself from it and is constant throughout successive stages of the want" (Green 1883, 91). This implies a subsistent self or consciousness that can compare various wants and satisfactions and that is *other* than their succession in that it supervenes over their succession. It is, in other words, a "consciousness which yields . . . the conception of something that *should be* as distinct from that which *is*" (91–92). This implies, of course, actions in which the determining causes are *motives*, for motives imply "an idea of an end, which a self-conscious subject presents to itself, and which it strives and tends to realize." A motive is not something independent of the person that then acts upon her or him as an outside agent. For upon any human want there "supervenes the presentation of the want by a self-conscious subject to himself, and with it the idea of a self-satisfaction to be attained"—that is, motives derive from a person's self-conception. Motives are not, in any ordinary sense, *natural* if naturalness implies simply determination by antecedent events (93–94).

For Green, persons are free agents in that they originate their own motives. Moral action is always a union of circumstances and character. The latter is the unity of our temporarily sequential wants, which raises them to the sphere of morality. Circumstances, on the other hand, are not what they would be qua circumstances, that is, independent of character. "They are not like forces converging on an inert body which does not itself modify the direction of the resulting motion. Thus even a circumstance in itself and in its antecedents so strictly physical as hunger . . . has in effect a quality not determined by natural antecedents" (100–101).

The details of Green's moral theory are not our concern here. It is evident in what we have seen, however, that his fundamental aim was to distinguish the moral and spiritual life of humanity from the natural life from which it emerges and, to a large extent, to which it remains interlinked. Persons are, nonetheless, those restless spirits who transcend their natural bounds through self-mastery and in pursuit of a spiritual ideal in art, morality, and religion.

The Later Critiques: James Ward to William James

Cambridge philosopher and psychologist James Ward sought to expose the assumptions and incoherences of mental materialism in his Gifford Lectures, which were published as *Naturalism and Agnosticism* in 1899. The book served its purpose so effectively that it was said that "the object of its attack ceased to exist" (Lambrecht 1926, 137). Ward's critique focused on the inconsistent and incoherent responses of British empiricist epistemology and psychology to Cartesian psychophysical dualism—especially by those Victorian scientists who espoused forms of psychophysical parallelism. The problems were particularly evident, Ward believed, in the writings of W. K. Clifford and T. H. Huxley.

Psychophysical parallelism and its accompaniment, conscious automatism, were the doctrines defended by those scientific naturalists sensitive to the dangers of a crude ontological materialism. We have seen that both Clifford and Huxley disclaimed knowledge of either material or mental substance and held to a doctrine of parallelism as the most scientific inference that could be drawn from the facts. The doctrine affirmed a dissimilarity of matter and mind, yet one involving a perfect parallelism or point-for-point correspondence. Ward found no such correspondence between the two modes of activity. "If, while one watches 'the lark soaring and singing in the blinding sky,' the other peers into his head as he watches, where is the parallelism" or correspondence? (J. Ward 1915, 306; see also Orr 1906, 74–77). Parallels, after all, are lines that never meet. Ward saw this dualism of mind and matter as inevitably resulting in either a vague, agnostic hypothesis called monism or, more often as in the case of Huxley, in the subordination of the psychic or mental to the physical. In either case, there does not appear to be a genuine causal interaction.

Ward, like Henry Calderwood, highlighted Huxley's equivocations, saying at one time that there is no evidence that consciousness may cause molecular changes in the brain, on other occasions affirming that human volition is efficacious in the course of events, and then finally opting for the view that psychic experience does not react upon the physical life but is, rather, functionally dependent on the latter. Ward pointed to Huxley's 1892 correction of his earlier belief regarding volition. I speak of volition, wrote Huxley, "or to speak more accurately, the physical state of which our volition is the expression" (T. H. Huxley 1893b, 163). Huxley did not, Ward pointed out, speak of the obverse—namely, the physical state that is the expression of our volition, whereby the latter "might 'count for something' in the course of events" (J. Ward 1915, 349).

Ward suggested that the naturalist's view of volitions as shadows or symbols of molecular processes in the brain entails the judgment that intellectual activity also is illusory, determined simply by mechanical neural connections: "Logical processes become in truth but the concomitants of physiological processes" (1915, 336). Why is this not determinism? Huxley replied that he takes the conception of necessity to have a logical, not a physical foundation. But if our mental conditions are but "the symbols in consciousness of the changes that take place automatically in the organism," then logical necessitation is, like volition, an illusion (1915, 337). Even if one were to agree that the course of events *is* entirely the result of initial physical conditions, and not that it logically *must* be, the mechanical character of all brain processes is, nevertheless, for Huxley a fact as inevitable as a natural law.

Huxley had insisted, notwithstanding, that we are free inasmuch as in many respects we can do as we like. But Ward contended that Huxley's words do not mean at all what they appear to mean. They do not refer to purposes carried out by an efficient agent. Rather, "they simply indicate a special class of pleasures, the pleasures that sometimes accompany motor reflexes. This is all . . . they can mean, if conscious automatism be true" (1915, 339). Thus, our consciousness of moral and artistic aims and efforts are illusory, they "are not the source of their supposed teleological characteristics" (1915, 349).

Ward proceeded to demonstrate that conscious automatism remains the position of Huxley, Clifford, and Tyndall until, that is, all three begin to discourse on ethics. Then they fall back on an agnostic psychophysical parallelism. For example, in his exposition of the true agnostic posture, Huxley wrote that "in itself it is of little moment whether we express the phenomena of matter in terms of spirit, or the phenomena of spirit in terms of matter" (T. H. Huxley 1893b, 164). Huxley followed "a sort of book-keeping by double entry"—a characteristic of conscious automatism but, in Ward's estimation, "a palpable contradiction" (J. Ward 1915, 351).

A number of other defenders of freedom pointed up the incoherence between the empiricists' sensationist epistemology and their psychological and moral assertions. They saw the problem as especially exemplified in George Romanes's *Mental Evolution in Man* (1888). The book was closely analyzed by Scottish theologian and scientist James Iverach and by Aubrey Moore in his essay "Mental Evolution of Man." Many of the defenders of physiological psychology treated feelings and volitions as though they existed apart from the creature experiencing them—atomic neural feelings producing consciousness, rather than a conscious subject who holds the feelings together in some kind of unity.

Iverach argued, with T. H. Green and James Ward, that the self stands over against the objects of experience, which are themselves referred to this self-conscious unifying center. He thought that Romanes had affirmed the same when, for instance, he declared that "every stimulus supplied from without, every movement originating from within, carries with it the character of belonging to that which feels or moves" (Romanes 1888, 197). Iverach found, however, that Romanes's conception of the unified self was inconsistent with the psychological assumptions that he derived from John Locke. For example, Romanes classified simple ideas as percepts, general ideas as concepts, and added "recepts," a vague *tertium quid* between them. Romanes concluded from this classification that the mind is wholly passive at the level of perception and reception and active only at the stratum of conceptual thought. Iverach saw this as inconsistent with Romanes's comments about the unifying center "which feels and moves" (200).

Romanes's error, continued Iverach, was his confusing the self with an abstract idea. He failed to recognize that he has himself the highest self-consciousness "when he is occupied so completely with the study of external objects as to forget the inner self-consciousness altogether." Self-consciousness does not coincide only with the emergence of general ideas. Nor, Iverach insisted, is it possible to separate action and feeling from conception in so sharp a manner. What motivated Romanes to do so is that, following Locke, he saw in the power of forming abstract ideas the dividing line, the Rubicon, between man and brute. Iverach argued, however, that abstract thought is not the only relevant distinction, since human self-consciousness begins at a much earlier stage with the feeling and acting agent, before the stage of introspection even begins (Iverach 1894, 170–71). The fact is that the feelings, emotions, and appetites of the human self take on complex meanings that differentiate even them from the experiences of animals.

Following Darwin, Romanes had set out a catalogue of animal emotions—surprise, fear, jealousy, sympathy, shame, revenge—that he claimed resemble, or are the same as, those referred to by the same word in human experience. But are they the same? Iverach thought not, for while the signs of fear or shame may be the same in animal and human, yet "in the case of man the feelings are taken up into the web of conscious rational experience." A feeling is never an unrelated occasion; "it is the response of the living being to the stimulus." What a particular feeling or emotion is depends "on the experience and wisdom of the being who experiences it" (1894, 157–58). Due to the human capacity for self-transcendence, human emotional life has a wider, deeper, more complex quality. The simplest human feelings are apprehended by a most complex consciousness. While the physical signs may thus be the same, they mask subjective feelings that are poles apart in their meanings. For this reason, comparative psychology faces real pitfalls in Iverach's estimation. The special danger is, of course, anthropomorphism. Because the person who makes the comparison is rational, he or she likely will read rational behavior into what animal activity he or she observes. Physiological psychologist C. Lloyd Morgan later made the same point in critical detail.

In his book on mental evolution, Romanes sought to show that intelligence in animals is the same in *kind* as intelligence in humans, although he admitted to a difference in degree. For Romanes "difference of kind" meant difference of *origin* and was "the only real distinction that can be drawn between the terms 'difference of kind' and 'difference of degree'" (Iverach 1894, 160; see also A. L. Moore 1890b, 55, 60; Jones 1899, 56–65). As a good Darwinian, Romanes held that a distinction between one species and another never can be one of kind because it never can be a "difference of origin." All forms of animal life have one origin. Iverach pointed out, however, that this is the view of theology as well. Theology does "not distinguish between man and lower animals by a difference of origin; for all derived existence must trace its origin to God" (Iverach 1894, 161).

Iverach proposed, however, that another form of classification is required if the real differences that do exist are to be satisfied. What may amount to a real difference of kind between animal and human life may "be determined by a consideration, not of the origin and history of a being, but by a consideration of its present nature, character, and action." Biologists, after all, do not deny a difference of species between, say, a salmon and an elephant, or an ape and a man. Iverach did not care what language Romanes might have used to distinguish between one species and another so long as it did the job: "We shall not quarrel with [Romanes] about phrases." If Romanes "will give us a word which will express the difference between species and species, we shall take it; but till then we shall say . . . that a difference in degree may become so great as ultimately to amount to a difference in kind" (1894, 162).

Iverach associated self-consciousness with the most basic human feeling and action, while, we have seen, Romanes considered an agent's abstract thought as alone separating him or her from the brute world. But even disregarding this important question, Iverach contended that in either case the difference is very great indeed, locate it where one will. Further, Iverach asserted that it does not seem possible to explain such a difference by anything but itself. We may say, with Romanes, that "the foundations are laid in the fact that the organism is one connected whole." But so, Iverach submitted, "we might say that the foundations of water are laid in oxygen and hydrogen, and the foundations of life are laid in the chemical properties of matter." But the fact remains that "water and life have properties which cannot be explained by the characteristics of the foundations. So it appears to be with self-consciousness. It is unique" (1894, 172). That, Iverach contended, is, for a theological anthropology, all that matters. Though inconsistent and stuck with an odd and unhelpful distinction between differences of degree and kind, Romanes often appeared to be in accord with Iverach's point.

Another significant figure in this story is C. Lloyd Morgan (1852–1936), an English biologist and philosopher. Morgan was the most incisive critic of Romanes's comparative psychology but was, with Romanes, an ultra-Darwinian. Furthermore, he followed Romanes in championing a monism that served as the foundation for a spiritual philosophy supporting both free will and theism. Romanes, Morgan, and William James were, perhaps, the most eminent of the thinkers who, in the period 1890–1910, testified to the concurrence between a Darwinian approach to the evolution of mind and a reaction against materialism, necessitarianism, and atheism (see Richards 1987).

Morgan studied with T. H. Huxley at the Royal College of Science and was profoundly influenced by him. He also served as Romanes's literary executor, seeing through the press Romanes's final two volumes, *Darwin and after Darwin* (1893–1897) and the essays that constitute *Mind and Motion and Monism* (1895). Morgan succeeded to the chair of geology and zoology at University College, Bristol, in 1884 and remained at that institution until his retirement in 1919. His early work was in geology, while his later years were preoccupied with philosophy, the most important work in the latter field being his Gifford Lectures delivered at St. Andrews and published as *Emergent Evolution* (1923) and *Life, Mind, and Spirit* (1926). His enduring contribution to scholarship, however, was in the field of animal and comparative psychology, which resulted in studies such as *Animal Life and Intelligence* (1890–1891), *Habit and Instinct* (1896), and *Animal Behaviour* (1900).

The details of Morgan's attack on Romanes's comparative psychology need not concern us. His basic point was the contention that when we attribute conscious states to others, animals or humans, we project upon them an image of our own consciousness. To attribute certain subjective psychological states to animals is an especially risky business, and Morgan thought that it hardly warranted the name of science. He proposed that a *science* of animal psychology must represent a more limited and modest task, for example, a comparative examination of the adjustive behaviors of animals. The attributions by Romanes and Darwin of certain psychological states to animals essentially amounted to mere anthropomorphic conjecture.

Morgan's critique had another motive, however, and that was to reinforce what he believed the evidence did demonstrate, namely, that animal and human minds differ in essential ways. Animals possess intelligence but not reason. They learn by associative trial and error, by the chance hitting on a solution, but they cannot discern abstract relationships, analogies, ratios, and so forth, or draw their logical implications. For Morgan, intelligence (instinct) is associated with "the inferences formed in the field of perception," while the word *reason* must be reserved for that supervention of conceptual analysis that is lacking in the activity of animals. While there is no breach of continuity between the two forms of cognition, reason "constitutes a new departure" that is rendered possible through, as Friedrich Max Müller had claimed, the acquisition of language. In language we see abstract thought, hence logical analysis in germ (C. L. Morgan 1890–1891a, 373–75).

With regard to the conjoining of ultra-Darwinism with a spiritualist tele-ology, Morgan's most significant contribution was his formulation—arrived at concurrently with the American psychologist James Mark Baldwin (1861–1934)—of the theory of "organic selection." While compatible with ultra-Darwinism—for example, with the theory of August Weismann—it nevertheless resembles Lamarckianism. Morgan proposed that animals possess, in addition to congenitally definite structures, a certain amount of innate plasticity or modifiability. Over several generations these learned behaviors, "though not transmitted to the germ, nevertheless afford the opportunity for the occurrence of germinal variations of like nature." That is, those animals with innate plasticity equal to a changing environment will survive, and these modifications will then be given full scope generation after generation. Hence, "any congenital variations similar in direction to these modifications will tend to support them and to favor the individuals in which they occur. Thus will arise a congenital predisposition to the modification in question." The Lamarckian transmissionists assumed that modifications as such were unlimited, whereas Morgan suggested "that the modification *as such* is not inherited, but is the condition under which congenital variations are favored and given time to get a hold on the organism, and are thus enabled by degrees to reach the fully adaptive level" (C. L. Morgan 1890–1891a, 739–40).

According to Morgan, the principle of "organic selection" thus allows for acceptance of the facts adduced by the Lamarckians but understood in strict neo-Darwinian terms. Morgan's principle was hailed by Darwinians, for example by Alfred Wallace, as putting to rest all remaining objections to natural selection. Here is another case of ultra-Darwinism open to certain forms of theistic metaphysics (see Richards 1987, 375–405).

Along with the philosopher Samuel Alexander, Morgan became known as a principal British proponent of "emergent evolution." He was especially careful to distinguish his theory from various forms of "vitalism" and from the *elan vital* of Henri Bergson's "creative evolution." Morgan insisted that his emergent doctrine actually describes scientifically, that is, naturalistically, what happens in evolution in terms of its critical turning points or breaks, while avoiding an appeal either to "mysticism" or to "mechanism." What is distinctive about emergent evolution—fully incorporating Darwinian principles—is that the new features that emerge cannot be predicted from the stages through which they emerge, though in retrospect they usually can be scientifically described. For example, the appearance of organic life from the inorganic, or the emergence of consciousness, or of reason, could not have been anticipated. Morgan was especially concerned to counter mechanistic reductionism and insisted that there is more in the newly emergent advance than is contained or explicable solely in its parts or elements. Our unique human consciousness and reason are not latent in the inorganic germs.

Morgan believed that reality was, finally, explainable from two perspectives. One is that of natural evolution through the application of scientific method. The other is metaphysical and is concerned, for example, with ultimate or final causation. "Push any physical or scientific inquiry deep enough, and you get the general reply, 'That's the way things are constituted.' And man the metaphysician will still want to know what is the cause of this constitution" (C. L. Morgan 1897–1898, 245–46). For Morgan, metaphysics concerns itself with those aspects of reality that lie beyond the scope of science. Examples would be Morgan's own panpsychic doctrine, but also the theistic hypothesis, and our concern here: the unity of the self and human freedom.

In the early years of the twentieth century in Britain, the evaluation of physiological psychology, as it pertained to traditional theology, was best articulated by the Anglo-Catholic priest Philip N. Waggett, whom we encountered in chapter 5. He fully endorsed the work of the mental physiologists as it applied to the study of psychology. He felt that it would free the study of human psychology from the long-standing hostility of the physical sciences. Waggett wanted both to relate and to distinguish the reality of human consciousness and the physiologist's work that studies how consciousness is connected to its bodily frame.

Waggett pointed out how we often are rightly alarmed when, for example, a person speaks of his heart's being full of grief because of a sense of sin and then the brain physiologist proceeds to explain the sentiment sufficiently by reference to the facts of nervous impulse and the reflex action associated with consciousness. The neurophysiologist not only assumes that the physical basis of conscious states offers an adequate interpretation. He or she also often describes the workings of the brain in psychological language that, for example, seems to imply a consciousness of afferent or inner impulses. Our consciousness is not, however, this richly endowed. "What consciousness reports," Waggett reminded the physiologist, "is not afferent impulse." Consciousness reports our feelings, our judgments about things, and our motives—things such as remorse, repentance, and hope. Waggett wrote, "We know these other facts, the grey matter and the ganglia, by inductive science; by the observation of other brains than our own, by dissecting the tissues and nerve tracts of other organisms. . . . Of physiological *ideas* one is conscious as of other ideas, but one is not conscious in that sense of physiological processes" (Waggett 1905, 203–4).

While Waggett insisted on the crucial importance of the new knowledge of how material changes profoundly condition consciousness, he urged that we not confuse physiology and psychology. Though grounded in matter, human thought remains distinct from matter and its processes. The study of nerve processes will not bridge the gulf between matter and thought. Waggett suggested that our memory and our moral judgments illustrate his point:

How does the man condemn his present moral apprehension by the standard which was his own yesterday? And the physiologist is ready to answer: All these mental connections have a material basis. You undertook a certain action at a former period under a certain stimulus coming from the sensory organs to the brain. The brain worked out suitable motor impulses to meet the case; and these received a certain measure of success and satisfaction. And both the reception of the sensory afferent impulses and the production of the energising efferent impulses left their impressions upon nervous tissues. There the action left its record in subtle changes of structure or state; and this record is memory. (1905, 206–7)

This does appear to "lift the veil" from processes such as memory or moral judgment—until, that is, the question asserts itself: "But who read the records? Who compared them? Did the old record read the new one, or the new record the old?" Waggett suggested that to reduce memory to a succession of atomic nervous events "is something like saying that in a phonograph the record on the second half of the cylinder was able to recognize its own likeness to, or difference from, the record on the first part of the cylinder." No, the most extensive and transparent collection of physiological facts and explanations cannot, Waggett concluded, discover, that is, fully explain the unity of personal consciousness upon which all the physical events, so to speak, transpire (1905, 207). The two accounts—physical and spiritual—of human consciousness and volition need not be seen as mutually exclusive alternatives. They are, in fact, two languages, two renderings of one reality arrived at by different paths.

Perhaps the most influential Darwinian defender of the mind as, in some respect, distinct from and operative upon the brain, of human free will, and the reality of a spiritual world, was the American William James (1842–1910). His influence on this British debate was considerable. As early as 1879 James published in *Mind* an article entitled "Are We Automata?" Its argument later appeared in a fuller form as chapter 5 of his very influential *Principles of Psychology* (1890). In the article James argued, like James Ward and the others we have examined, against scientific positivism and a materialist reductionism. He defended the active, autonomous, goal-directed function of human consciousness. Consciousness, in James's vivid expression, "is a *fighter for ends*." He likened human consciousness to "the loading of dice," in that consciousness brings "a more or less constant pressure to bear in favor of *those* of its performances which make for the most permanent interests of the brain's owner" (James 1890, 141, 140). Freedom thus consists in the mind's capacity for selective attention and interest. James argued, on evolutionary principles, that consciousness could not be a superfluous epiphenomenon, otherwise what would be the survival advantage of possessing both brain and rational mind?

James's psychology became, in turn, the groundwork for his reflections on metaphysics, morals, and religion. He often used Darwinian principles to give a scientific foundation for these reflections. A major thrust of his work on the science of mind was directed at countering the metaphysical prejudices of materialism and in defending a spiritual world. In "Are We Automata?" he summed up for his philosophical *confreres* a complaint that was increasingly felt: "It is really monstrous," James wrote, "to see the *prestige* of 'Science' invoked for a materialistic conclusion, reached by methods which, were they only used for spiritualistic ends, would be hooted as unscientific in the extreme" (James 1879, 21).

Herbert Spencer and the Evolutionary Foundation of Morals

In the last third of the nineteenth century, British scientists and humanists were called upon to respond to the widely held conviction that if the religious roots of Western civilization were weakened or allowed to die its moral limbs would soon languish and waste away. "Can morality persist without religion?" was a widely debated question. Darwin had called upon researchers on the human species and its history to establish their studies on a scientific basis and to apply "the laws of nature" to the study of human life. Evolutionary anthropologists J. F. M'Lennan, John Lubbock, and E. B. Tylor already had begun this work. Thinkers such as Herbert Spencer, Leslie Stephen, W. K. Clifford, and Henry Sidgwick now turned to the study of ethics in an effort to establish the sanctions of morality on scientific grounds, that is, to replace the seemingly discredited moral sanctions of theology. Spencer, Stephen, and Sidgwick all undertook large works in this cause, although Sidgwick's conclusions were characteristically more ambivalent and open ended. The others suffered no such incertitude, and while their efforts in ethical theorizing often proved amateurish, they represented an important and influential position in the last decades of the century.

When Herbert Spencer died in 1903 his influence lingered on for a while, especially in America. But as we have learned, his scientific and philosophical theories had for some time been discredited in Britain. This has, unfortunately, tempted many twentieth-century scholars to brush aside Spencer with brief, often ridiculing comments. This reveals, however, a great failure to appreciate Spencer's extraordinary influence on scientists, on political economists, on philosophers, and on theology during the entire latter third of the nineteenth century. Alexander Bain, Alfred R. Wallace, Huxley, Darwin, William James, and Emile Durkheim, to name but a few worthies, held him in high regard at some point in their careers, and acknowledged his influence. For example, after reading Spencer's *Principles of Biology*, Darwin confessed that Spencer was "a dozen times my superior" (F. Darwin 1887, 56).

Spencer's importance for our purpose in this chapter lies in the fact that his life's work, brought to completion in his massive *Synthetic Philosophy*, was to establish a scientific and thoroughly biological basis for morals. It was his conviction that the religious foundations of culture were becoming increasingly discredited, and his work challenged that traditional source of moral authority. In 1879 he explained what had been his aim since he first began to write: "[My] ultimate purpose, lying behind all proximate purposes, has been that of finding for the principles of right and wrong in conduct at large, a scientific basis. . . . Now that the moral injunctions are losing the authority given by their supposed sacred origin, the secularization of morals is becoming imperative" (Spencer 1879, iii–iv).

A "right rule of life, individual and social" was, then, the impetus and aim of Spencer's elaborate effort to find the laws that determine the evolution of social life. In his first book, *Social Statics* (1851), he wrote:

A belief, as yet fitful and partial, is beginning to spread amongst men, that here [in morality] also there is an indissoluble bond between cause and consequence, an inexorable destiny, a "law which altereth not." . . . In the moral as in the material world, accumulated evidence is gradually generating the conviction that events are not at bottom fortuitous; but that they are wrought out in a certain inevitable way by changing forces. (Spencer 1851, 40–41)

Spencer's ethical prepossessions informed his progressive, optimistic vision of the evolutionary process, a vision derived largely from the religious ideology of his Dissenting upbringing (see Peel 1971, esp. 102–11). The *Social Statics* is saturated with a necessitarian optimism in which human nature progresses inexorably toward a moral perfection that, for Spencer, meant a complete adaptation to a social condition in which the maladaptations of ignorance and moral evil are finally effaced (Spencer 1851, 65). He described this inevitable process of moral change in distinct evolutionary terms as a movement from nonadaptation to adaptation. He called it "the evanescence of evil":

> All evil results from the non-adaptation of constitution to conditions. This is true of everything that lives. . . . Equally true is it that evil perpetually tends to disappear. In virtue of an essential principle of life, this non-adaptation of an organism to its conditions is ever being rectified; and modification of one or both, continues until the adaptation is complete. Whatever possesses vitality, from the elementary cell up to man himself, inclusive, obeys this law. (1851, 59–60)

Spencer found in Lamarck a conception of biological evolution that involved both adaptation to the environment and the inheritance of acquired characteristics, ideas that fit well with his own belief in the inevitable social development of humanity. As early as "The Development Hypothesis" (1852), Spencer had argued that a naturalistic account of the transformation of species makes more sense than the biblical accounts of special creation. Following the work of the German Karl Ernst von Baer, he compared the development of species to the growth of the simple, undifferentiated embryo into the complex, highly differentiated adult. Ontogeny thus recapitulates phylogeny; the evolution of savage man into civil man corresponds to the development of the child into the adult. Spencer's Lamarckian conception of the evolutionary struggle for survival facilitated his attack on all forms of state welfare, such as the Poor Laws, since these policies, he believed, prevented people from adapting themselves to their conditions through their own effort. Only in this way would their progress become "organic" in the race as a whole. Policies of social welfare remove the vital incentive for individual adaptation to the social state. The healthy merits of struggle did not mean that there would be, in the state of civilization, a "war of all against all," since Spencer saw the struggle for existence as characteristic of the early stages of social evolution. In civilized society he observed a movement from egoism to altruism:

Though, during barbarism and the earlier stages of civilization war has the effect of exterminating the weaker societies, and of weeding out the weaker members of the stronger societies. . . . [As] there arises higher societies, implying individual characters fitted for closer co-operation, the destructive activities exercised by such higher societies have injurious re-active effects on the moral natures of their members—injurious effects which outweigh the benefits resulting from extirpation of inferior races. (Spencer 1873, 199–200)

So it is that persistent cooperative and altruistic social behavior involves a hereditary tendency to become cumulative in future generations through the law of inheritance of acquired characteristics. As we know, in the latter years of the century, Spencer's Lamarckian ideas came under increasing fire by the "ultra-Darwinists." This involved him in an exchange with the German biologist August Weismann in the pages of the *Contemporary Review*. Spencer marshaled case upon case to demonstrate that natural selection was not sufficient to explain evolution. While from the hindsight of our present knowledge Weismann is seen to have been the winner, Spencer was thought to have made a very persuasive case at the time. He argued that if the inheritance of acquired characteristics presents some difficulties, so, in very large measure, does the mechanism of natural selection. One theory is no more compelling than the other (see Richards 1987, 293–94).

The emergence of greater altruistic moral behavior could be explained, Spencer believed, on purely naturalistic, evolutionary grounds. Morality originates as a rather crude example of an egoistic utilitarian calculus: I must act in a certain way toward my neighbor if I expect similar treatment in return. But Spencer did not believe that morality remains at the level of utility; rather, it evolves into a nonrational altruistic intuition. In a letter to J. S. Mill, Spencer described his Lamarckian conception of moral evolution:

I believe that the experiences of utility, organized and consolidated through all past generations of the human race, have been producing corresponding modifications, which, by continued transmission and accumulation, have become in us certain faculties of moral intuition—certain emotions responding to right and wrong conduct, which have no apparent basis in the individual experiences of utility. (Bain 1868, 722)

For Spencer, the goal of human moral development was the achievement of a freedom that allows each person to exercise his or her fullest capacities without infringing on the freedom of others. He believed that a society that manifests equal freedom among its citizens is the happiest. The greatest happiness—and what defines good and evil—is the maximizing of the whole society's adaptation to its circumstances. Therefore, the greatest happiness entails altruistic behavior, cooperation, and a shared division of labor. Indeed, altruism, or justice, is the prerequisite of the greatest happiness. Spencer argued that when a society fails to produce an adequate number of altruistic persons, it will degenerate and result in a loss of individual satisfactions among its members (Spencer 1876, 235). Because Spencer saw these moral ends as also the ends of biological evolution, his defense of Lamarckianism was crucial. Darwin's evolutionary theory was, of course, quite the opposite. The end (if one can call it that) of evolution is not happiness or justice but survival. There is no teleology, no necessary moral direction to Darwin's evolutionary process, since Darwin offered no moral criterion of "fitness." For Spencer, however, adaptation in the more complex societies would eventuate not in struggle and competition but in cooperation.

Spencer's stress on environmental (rather than hereditary) factors and the inheritance of acquired characteristics brought him into conflict with his friend T. H. Huxley. Regarding the Lamarckian features of Spencer's perception of evolution, Huxley wrote, "You appear to me to suppose that external conditions modify machinery as if by transferring a flour-mill into a forest you could make it into a saw-mill" (L. Huxley 1903, 2:126).

Huxley long had opposed the extreme laissez-faire social policies espoused by Spencer. This first became evident in his defense of state-sponsored education for the poorer classes in "Administrative Nihilism" in 1871. Huxley's permanent break with Spencer came, however, with the publication of his later article "The Struggle for Existence: A Programme" (1888), which was written shortly after his youngest daughter, the talented Marian, died following a period of mental breakdown. Her death in 1887 broke the aging Huxley, who thereafter was haunted by sadness and melancholy. Earlier he had championed a kind of Leibnitzian optimism about nature's justice. He could speak, for example, of science as the "priestess" whose mission it is to spread the faith in the fixed order of nature. This ensures that social disintegration follows immorality as surely as physical illness follows physical abuse. At that time, in a letter to his friend Charles Kingsley, Huxley wrote that "the absolute justice of the system of things is as clear to me as any scientific fact. The gravitation of sin to sorrow is as certain as that of the earth to the sun, and more so—for experimental proof of the fact is within reach of us all" (L. Huxley 1903, 1:236). By 1887 he had given up this naïve theodicy of Job's friends. With "The Struggle for Existence in Society," Huxley's romantic conception of nature was not only abandoned, but it was passionately renounced.

Huxley's new conviction was Humean: Nature was directed neither by Ormuzd, the Good, nor by Ahriman, the Evil one; it was entirely amoral and indifferent to human life and striving. The message of Mill's posthumously published essay "Nature" (1874) had retained its force. And Huxley was able to reiterate Mill's point that the word *nature* has two quite different meanings. It can signify "the entire system of things," or it can mean "things as they would be, apart from human intervention." "In the first of these senses," explained Mill, "the doctrine that man ought to follow nature is unmeaning; since man has no power to do anything else than follow nature; all his actions are done through, and in obedience to, some or many of nature's physical or mental laws." However, in the other sense of the term, the doctrine that man ought to follow nature—that is, ought to make the natural course of things the model of his voluntary actions—"is equally irrational and immoral" (Mill 1874, 1958, 44, G. Nakhnikian edition).

In "The Struggle for Existence," Huxley bitterly attacked the evolutionary optimists who declared that the frightening struggle for existence tends to a final good, "and that the suffering of the ancestor is paid for by the increased perfection of the progeny." It was not clear to an outraged Huxley "what compensation the *Eohippus* gets for his sorrows in the fact that, some millions of years afterwards, one of his descendants wins the Derby." For Huxley, evolution does not signify "a constant tendency to increased perfection." Rather, it entails constant adaptation of organisms to new conditions, and "it depends on the nature of those conditions whether the direction of the modifications effected shall be upward or downward" (T. H. Huxley 1888, 163).

Huxley suspected that his essay would put Spencer in a white rage (L. Huxley 1903, 2:199). In fact, Spencer responded that he had nothing to object to in Huxley's essay and further pointed out that he too had shocked colleagues by insisting on the amoral character of nature. Even so, the intellectual breach between the two friends had begun, only to become unbridgeable with the delivery of Huxley's Romanes Lecture on "Evolution and Ethics" in 1894. With this lecture, Huxley clearly broke rank with both Darwin and Spencer and also with the Russian philosopher Peter Kropotkin's (1842–1921) ideas about a human "social instinct." With his characteristic unpredictability, Huxley spoke of his lecture as "an effort to put the Christian doctrine that Satan is the Prince of this world on a scientific foundation" (L. Huxley 1903, 2:359).

Huxley had written earlier that primitive man suffered less than civilized man since, like the animals, he gratified all his desires, innocent of either right or wrong. Unlike Darwin and Spencer, Huxley regarded human instinct as basically antisocial and social peer pressure as only partially overcoming these antisocial vestiges. "Since each person held fast a full share of the desire for unlimited self-gratification," Huxley judged that "the struggle for existence within society, could only be gradually eliminated" (T. H. Huxley 1901, 9, 35). Thus, he saw human ethics and human instinct locked in continual warfare with one another: "The effort of ethical man to work towards a moral end by no means has abolished, perhaps has hardly modified, the deep-seated organic impulses which impel the natural man to follow his non-natural course" (1888, 166).

Huxley's conception of humanity's "organic impulses" was the basis for his proposing a secular idea of original sin, one that might challenge the Christian doctrine of the fall. For Huxley—as for Hegel and some late Victorian British theologians—the consciousness of sin is a rise from an amoral but destructive innocence, not a fall from an idyllic state. Huxley, the secular Calvinist, now proclaimed humanity's "innate desire to enjoy the pleasures and escape the pains of life . . . without the least reference to the welfare of the society into which they are born." This "innate desire" is our inheritance from our primal ancestors, and it is "the reality at the bottom of the doctrine of original sin." And while it had proved an essential impulse of survival in the state of nature outside, it is "the sure agent of the destruction of society if allowed free play within" (1901, 27).

As humanity passes from the natural, Hobbesian "war of all against all" to social life, the earlier serviceable qualities are seen as defects and are called sins (1901, 52). So it is, Huxley proceeded, that social progress requires a severe checking of the cosmic process by what may be called the ethical process, whose end is the survival of those who are ethically the best (81). In an often quoted admonition, Huxley exhorted his auditors to "understand, once for all, that the ethical progress of society depends, not on imitating the cosmic process still less in running away from it, but in combating it" (83).

With Spencer especially in mind, Huxley conceded that how our moral sensibilities, as well as our evil tendencies, have arisen may be discerned from a study of cosmic evolution. Yet evolution in itself is not competent "to furnish any better reason why what we call good is preferable to what we call evil than we had before" (80). It was the failure of men like Spencer to recognize this point that is, Huxley believed, the root of the "fanatical individualism" that attempts to apply the analogy of cosmic nature to society (82).

Huxley's assertion of a radical dualism between nature and civil society was, however, vulnerable on at least two counts. First, his notion of the "ethically best" was left extremely vague and was, on his own admission, based on certain moral and aesthetic intuitions not easily understood by his critics. Second, his splitting of natural processes and human cultural activity seemed to imply that humanity had lifted itself out of nature, a view that contradicted his earlier vigorous assertions, for example, those made in the essay

"On the Hypothesis That Animals Are Automata" (1874). As we saw earlier, Spencer was quick to call attention to Huxley's incoherences, especially what he saw as the implied assumption that there exists something in us which is not a product of the cosmic process, a return, in Spencer's estimation, to the old theological dualism (Duncan 1911, 336). If Huxley was not reverting to theology in matters of metaphysical and moral knowledge, he was, on his own admission, espousing a rather ill-founded idealism.

Spencer further drew attention to the fact that the two men were working with different conceptions of evolution. In the context of his discussion of ethics, Huxley viewed evolution in strictly Darwinian terms, that is, through the mechanism of natural selection and survival of the fittest. Spencer was, of course, a Lamarckian and regarded natural selection as instrumental only in the prehuman phase of evolution. Therefore, Spencer could argue that the human mind is capable of putting "a check upon that part of the cosmic process which consists in the unqualified struggle for existence" (Duncan 1911, 336).

Irrespective of this fundamental difference over the mechanisms of evolution, Huxley had come to differ with Spencer on the fundamental question of human nature and its implications for a philosophy of history. Spencer, to the end, remained sanguine about discovering those laws of social evolution that not only would reveal the direction of the social process but the "inevitability" of its moral progress and the extirpation of evil and immorality. In the third and last volume of the *Principles of Sociology* Spencer did appear to retract his utopianism and to embrace a more modest optimism. "Evolution," he now admitted, "does not imply a latent tendency to improve, everywhere in operation." But his retraction was only apparent, for he proceeded in these late reflections to prophecy the coming of a "higher stage" of humanity. "Long studies," Spencer concluded, "have not caused me to recede from the belief expressed nearly fifty years ago that—'The ultimate man will be . . . that manner of man who, in spontaneously fulfilling his own nature, incidentally performs the functions of a social unit; and yet is only enabled so to perform his own nature by all others doing the like'" (Spencer 1896, 599–601).

In retrospect, the Huxley of "Evolution and Ethics" certainly conveyed the deeper ambiguities of the *fin de siècle* and of our own time. Freud, for one, joined with Huxley in warning that "the principal task of civilization, its actual *raison d'être*, is to defend us against nature" (Freud 1928, 20). Spencer's confidence in the evolutionary process was largely shared, however, by Leslie Stephen and by other late Victorian worthies, and it remains alluring, for example, in the hopes of some proponents of contemporary sociobiology (see Passmore 1971 for the durability of this view).

Leslie Stephen published his *Science of Ethics* in 1882. It was the offspring of a twenty-year quest "to find reasons why men wish to be good even when they do not fear an after-life" (Annan 1951, 201–2). He had high hopes for the book, but they were soon dashed. Stephen not only rejected all ethical theories grounded on transcendental sanctions but also those based on purely theoretical reasoning, such as he found in Henry Sidgwick's *The Method of Ethics* (1874). Stephen's purpose was to shape ethics into a science, one founded on observations of how humans have, in fact, acted. This entailed, as Spencer also had insisted, the application of evolutionary principles to the study of moral questions, for this would reveal not only the ways in which morality had developed over time but also the laws at work in the process itself.

Stephen was confident that history would reveal that morality serves to further the health, well-being, and survival of the "social tissue" or social organism. Furthermore, this would be achieved through the process of natural selection, whereby those moral principles that proved more effective in furthering the social organism would prevail over those less effective. Since the well-being of society must coincide with the greatest happiness of the greatest number of members of the organism, utilitarianism can be shown to have a scientific basis, that is, if its earlier, atomistic understanding of society is superseded by a more adequate social model.

According to Stephen, morality is transmitted, in Lamarckian fashion, through the "social tissue" largely by means of the family that inculcates in its children those qualities that ensure the health and survival of the race. Though continually modified to meet new exigencies, morality is, nevertheless, crucial to the welfare and the survival of the social organism. Stephen conjoins virtue with social utility or usefulness (not merely expediency), that is, with survival value. Intemperance, for example, could be shown scientifically to be socially dysfunctional, while courage, justice, and fellow feeling could be shown to be essential to the commonweal.

Stephen's trust that the *general* health (survival) of a society is congruent with the general happiness of the people reveals his true faith. It is this same coincidence of social survival and personal happiness that T. H. Huxley found so suspect in Spencer's ethical theory. Others also saw this as the Achilles' heel of Stephen's apologia for a scientific morality. The argument against Stephen was basic: Ethics deals with obligations, with the "ought" of behavior; science simply tells us how, in fact, human beings have behaved and do behave. Stephen, however, spoke of *conscience* as "the utterance of the public spirit of the race, ordering us to obey the primary conditions of its welfare" (L. Stephen 1882, 350–51). But if we define morality as nature's inculcation of those social habits that prove to have survival value, the definition of morality lacks its essential feature—namely, conscience, the conscious sense of obligation and not simply nature's innate sanction. As Huxley came to see, conscience entails undertaking actions that may not prove conducive to racial survival.

The late Victorian critics of evolutionary ethics all made this one crucial point: There is no logical connection between morality and the evolutionary process. Henry Sidgwick proved to be foremost among these critics of Spencer and of Stephen's *The Science of Ethics*. He pointed out, simply, that Stephen held two incompatible standards and goals of ethical conduct. The first was his belief that it is reasonable for the individual to aim at maximizing the general happiness. The other was the preservation of the "social tissue." Stephen had acknowledged that he sought to justify evolutionary ethics as both "happiness giving" and "life preserving" and that if these ends diverged he would "get into considerable difficulties." Yet he also considered it sufficient to claim that "the very principle of evolution implies that there must be at least an approximate coincidence, and there is no apparent *a priori* reason why the coincidence should not be indefinitely close." This, the critics noted, begged the question. Sidgwick thought it "much too short a cut to Optimism," since evolution can decide nothing "as to the issue between Optimism and Pessimism." Evolution is innocently silent as to "whether life on the whole has a balance of inevitable pain" (Sidgwick 1882, 581–82).

Sidgwick further reverted to Stephen's admission that "'if the preservation of the race meant a continuance of misery,' he could not reasonably take preservation as his criterion of morality." But Stephen chose the evolutionist criterion in preference to the utilitarian, and so his ethical system was logically bound to include an adequate refutation of pessimism, which he failed to provide. Sidgwick suggested that Stephen was able to weasel on this demand by a nifty use of such terms as "social welfare," "wellbeing," and "health," rather than merely using the term "preservation." These former terms, of course, clearly implied that the existence preserved was a desirable existence. Sidgwick's crucial point was that Stephen failed to establish his case scientifically (1882, 581–82; see also Sidgwick 1876, 54, 59).

While purporting to be a scientific treatise, it was shown that Stephen's book lacked not only the empirical data to support his claims but also that critical, analytical method that his "scientific" pretensions required. Stephen's book, it turns out, was an essay expressing his opinions and his fondest hopes for humanity. Stephen's biographer, Noel Annan, asks what sort of satisfaction Stephen may have derived from his defense of an evolutionary ethics. "It was," he replies, "in making the social sciences do the work of religion." For Stephen, "evolution is an Immanent God or Process at work within the world" (Annan 1951, 219). Stephen the believer found comfort and hope in his faith that morality had discovered a firm sanction in evolution.

A significant error of evolutionary ethics, commonly alluded to by its late Victorian critics, is the fallacy of explaining a reality by giving an account of the preceding factors or stages out of which it arose. This genetic account fails to explain adequately the *difference* in a new phenomenon when compared with its antecedents. This was a central theme of James Martineau's ongoing critique of all forms of evolutionary ethics. For Martineau, evolution consists in the continued emergence of something new that is an "increment of being" upon prior stages. And when evolution reaches the stage of human consciousness, it moves beyond the sphere of problems that can be expressed wholly in terms of matter in motion. It represents a new departure "where two conflicting impulses dispute possession of us, and clamour for our decision of the alternative[,] . . . where we know ourselves, not as the *theatre*, but as the *cause* of the decision. . . . Here we are introduced to the consciousness of the Free-will, and the dawn of the Moral idea" (Martineau 1885, 368). As Martineau was wont to argue, the scientific naturalists did not establish a catena of causality that linked matter and the conscious mind without animating matter in some anthropomorphic way. John Tyndall admitted as much implicitly. But most of his colleagues lacked the courage of their German counterpart, the zoologist Ernst Haeckel, who finally confessed, "You must bespeak a soul within your atoms, or you will never get it out of them" (Martineau 1885, 370).

In *Types of Ethical Theory* (1885), Martineau resorted again and again to his complaint that the evolutionists *theorize* in one language and *feel* in another and thereby "retain ideal conceptions of a scale of good . . . for which their doctrine can find no corresponding place." This is no accident, for by "naturalising ethics" the evolutionists have "ethicised Nature" (1885, 391–93). Here Martineau drew attention to what G. E. Moore, in *Principia Ethica* (1903), was soon to call the "naturalistic fallacy"—also a crux of Henry Sidgwick's numerous forays against evolutionary ethics.

Herbert Spencer had often acknowledged that his evolutionary ethics were useless for the individual in any practical sense, since the two ends of life—survival and happiness—do not coincide in any particular case here and now. Spencer always insisted that actions conducive to life must, on the whole, be conducive to happiness, *which is the ultimate end.* The question of whose happiness resolves itself into the general happiness. But it was clear to Sidgwick and others that this end is merely projective. A further weakness of Spencer's evolutionary ethics was, then, its projective utopianism. Sidgwick suggested that, on the basis of our present state of knowledge, Spencer's evolutionary optimism "should be kept as a theological doctrine, or, if you like, a philosophical postulate" and not be confused with "the process of scientific inference to the future from the past." It is, after all, a too common inclination of the optimist "to believe that what is coming is good because it is coming, no less than what is good is coming because it is good" (Sidgwick 1899, 267–69).

Even before Spencer's later volumes of his *Principles of Ethics* (1892–93) were completed, the socialist British Labour Party was launched and militarism was revived in Europe—two objects of his greatest antipathy. These and other unexpected events cast a dark shadow over Spencer in his last years. He had preached that wars had been necessary but now were a passé means of human improvement, and that progress was assured through "the quiet pressure of a spreading industrial civilization on a barbarism which slowly dwindles" (Spencer 1877, 2:664). He was mercifully spared the horrors of World War I.

In the latter years of the nineteenth century the critics of evolutionary ethics were judged successful in demonstrating its significant weaknesses and the irony of its moral "intuitionism." But these critics pressed further to show the moral inadequacy of scientific naturalism as such. Huxley's telling critique of Spencer, linked with his own admission of the insufficiency of an evolutionary ethics, set him up as the test case. On examination, Huxley too seemed to be at a loss to explain morality on the grounds of a scientific naturalism or to grasp the implications of his own ethical intuitions.

The appearance of self-conscious rational beings only seemed to have intensified Huxley's view of the prehuman "cosmic" struggle for existence. But while the instinctive desires of the ape or tiger are limited, the desires of the rational human being are unlimited and, all too often, insatiable. In becoming rational the cosmic process has, it appeared, become more cunningly evil. One could argue that dumb nature better reveals the rudiments of Huxley's ethical ideal. Imposing his own form of anthropomorphism on the cosmic process, Huxley saw the law of self-sacrifice and community cooperation in the work of the ant and the bee. Man, it would appear, had fallen below the level of insect life. Reflecting on Huxley's noble but dubious moral speculations, the theologian James Iverach felt obliged to conclude that humanity's moral grandeur and its moral misery required a deeper examination and explanation than Huxley and the evolutionary ethicists were able to supply (Iverach 1894, 183–85).

CHAPTER 7

The New Science of Religion

Christianity's Relation to Other Faiths

He who knows one [religion] knows none.

Friedrich Max Müller [after Goethe]

Theologians all to expose—
'tis the *mission* of Primitive Man.

E. B. Tylor

It has been a matter of controversy . . . whether evolutionary theory demonstrates the need for a new religion to include the new idea of an evolving Universe or whether nothing more is needed than a transformed—or for the first time clearly understood—Christianity.

John Passmore

The Background

The decade of the 1860s in Britain also represented the opening of a new era in the study of the world's religions, with significant bearings on Christian theology. Here history and its cognate disciplines of philology and archaeology and the new disciplines of sociology and anthropology were to play especially important roles. The years after 1860 are, moreover, associated with the widespread application of evolutionary ideas to the study of society and human culture, hence with the dissemination of influential new theories of religious origins and development by J. F. M'Lennan (1827–1881), E. B. Tylor (1832–1917), W. Robertson Smith (1846–1894), James George Frazer (1854–1941), Herbert Spencer (1820-1903), and Friedrich Max Müller

(1823–1900). The works of these writers revolutionized thinking about the nature of religion and, in the case of Christianity, prompted various reconceptions of some of its traditional ideas and claims.

In the minds of most early Victorian Englishmen, an enormous gulf existed between the revealed truth of Christianity and the crude, superstitious mythologies of the heathen cultures. In the fifty years following 1860, the relationship between Christianity and the world's other religions became a matter of the most serious scholarly debate. There were, of course, some advanced thinkers of England in the decades prior to 1860 who were somewhat knowledgeable about the non-Christian religions and more charitable toward them. Most theologians and churchmen, however, considered Christianity a uniquely revealed divine truth and saw other religions as productions of the human imagination, often in its darker aspects.

The shock and challenge represented by the new thinking is reflected in a passage by Rowland Williams (1817–1870) that opened his contribution to the provocative *Essays and Reviews* (1861). The passage achieved considerable notoriety. "We cannot," Williams wrote, "encourage a remorseless criticism of Gentile histories [such as the historian George Grote had recently undertaken] and escape its contagion when we approach Hebrew annals; nor acknowledge a Providence in Jewry without owning that it may have comprehended sanctities elsewhere." Williams went on to acknowledge that if we examine fairly "the religions of India and Arabia, or even those of primeval Hellas and Latium, we find they appealed to the better side of our nature, and their essential strength lay in the elements of good which they contained, rather than in any satanic corruption." What Williams proposed was a widening of the idea of divine revelation, "not removing the footsteps of the Eternal from Palestine, but tracing them on other shores" (R. Williams 1860, 51; see also R. Williams 1856).

A decade earlier the Anglican theologian F. D. Maurice (1805–1872) had explored the significance of the world's great faiths in his reflection on a Christian philosophy of history, as had the biblical scholar and classicist Benjamin Jowett in his study of the Pauline epistles. These men were forerunners of a new way of thinking, although Williams and Maurice did not live to see the radical direction of the debate and the potential threat it posed to Christian claims.

F. D. Maurice's reflections were stimulated by a flood of recent literary and historical information that shed new and often more favorable light on the "heathen" faiths. These included Thomas Carlyle's (1795–1881) essay on Muhammad, a new edition of the *History of British India*, Elphinstone's *History of India*, and several recent volumes of *Researches* published by the Royal Asiatic Society that contained articles on the Hindu Vedas, the Puranas, and the Vedanta. A. P. Stanley later pointed out, correctly, that Maurice's *The Religions of the World and Their Relation to Christianity* (1847) could not have been written earlier, since it was an appreciative response to "what is due to other forms of thought" and is now "felt throughout our whole system" (Stanley 1865, 257).

Maurice's book revealed a deep sensitivity to the issues raised by Christianity's traditional claims to absoluteness and finality in the light of those elements of temporal relativity and acculturation he now perceived as undeniably part of Christianity's historical life. In fact, he anticipated the questions that would be posed by the German *Religionsgeschichtliche Schule* fifty years later:

> Might not particular soils be adapted to particular religions? Might not the effort to transport one into another involve the necessity of mischievous forcing and terminate in inevitable disappointment? Might not a better day be at hand in which all religions alike should be found to have done their work of partial good, of greater evil, and when something much more comprehensive and satisfactory should supersede them? (Maurice 1861, 3)

Maurice sought to take seriously the anthropological (and Hegelian) view that the evolution of religious systems is rooted in a primordial human faith and hope that is adapted through time to peculiar climes and races, as well as the implications of this view for Christianity. He recognized, for example, the special gifts that Islam, Hinduism, and Buddhism offer to Christianity as a needed corrective, and he explored how these elements might be preserved and made effectual. However, he wished to show as well that Christianity, rightly understood, does full justice to those characteristic principles possessed by these other faiths. Furthermore, Christianity in its fullness can supply all that is lacking in these other religions. Maurice concluded that Christianity, indeed, displays those notes of a universal faith and therefore "proves itself to be *not* a human system, but *the* Revelation, which human beings require" (1861, 239–40).

Maurice's book marked something of a juncture in the Victorian reconception of Christianity's relation to other faiths. It was a significant move away from a pervasive religious triumphalism. Maurice's facts were often faulty, in spite of his efforts to consult some of the best sources available to him. He made no distinction, for example, between the major schools of Theravada and Mahayana Buddhism in discussing its doctrine, and he associated the early Vedic religion with monotheism. Nevertheless, Maurice's genuine empathy and his critique of Western Christian parochialism were impressive. More significant, perhaps, is the searching, if inconclusive, way he raised the questions of finality and cultural relativity and the challenge they posed. Both Maurice's and Williams's understanding of Christianity's relation to other religious faiths—buttressed in the years following by a renascent Logos Christology and neo-Hegelian philosophy—became a dominant, perhaps the normative, theological position on this question in the latter decades of the century.

Benjamin Jowett's position was a more radical one. His serious interest in the non-Christian religions emerged between 1855 and 1859, the dates of the first and second editions of his commentaries on the Pauline epistles. Jowett had been involved in the establishment of the Indian Institute and the chair of Sanskrit at Oxford. The holder of the chair, Friedrich Max Müller, became a close friend, and the two men supported one another during times when both suffered for their advanced academic and religious views. Müller stimulated Jowett's interest in comparative religion, and the latter, in turn, raised their mutual friend Tennyson's curiosity about the Oriental faiths. Jowett sent the poet Müller's translation of the *Vedas* and his *Comparative Mythology* (1859), various works on the history of India, and Alfred Lyall's *Asiatic Studies*. Jowett was, it appears, the principal stimulus of Tennyson's poems on Oriental themes, including the "Ancient Sage" and "Akbar's Dream" (Livingston 1989, 157–68).

Jowett's earliest sustained reflection on the "heathen" religions in relation to Christianity appeared in a long essay entitled "Natural Religion," inserted into his commentary *The Epistles of St. Paul*. The impress of Müller's work was clearly evident in this essay. Jowett rejected the prevailing idea of a primordial revelation, in which the pagan religions were seen as gradual corruptions of the primal truth. Rather, according to Jowett, "the worship of nature in its many forms is now acknowledged to be deeply rooted in the age, country, people, which gave them birth." Moreover, the study of languages has shown "the connexion of the oldest forms of religion with the structure of the human mind itself." Jowett was not surprised then to find profound truth in the doctrines of the heathen legislators and the founders of the Eastern religions—all "raised above the level of humanity." "What shall we say of these things?" he asked (Jowett 1859, 385).

In Jowett's estimation, the contemporary Christian church was about to face the same change that the fathers of Alexandria faced as they became aware that heathenism was not purely evil or even antagonistic to the gospel. He surmised that "no one who looks at the religions of the world, stretching from east to west, through so many cycles of human history, can avoid seeing in them a sort of order and design. They are like so many steps in the education of mankind." Jowett did not blink at what he perceived to be the consequences of this new science of religion. Not only must Christians acknowledge the fact of law in the spiritual evolution of the race, he wrote, but the parallels with the heathen religions also will "alter our point of view in respect of many of the details . . . of Christian truth" itself (1859, 386).

Jowett's theological reconception is marked by three features that will stand out as characteristic of liberal theology's thinking on the subject for the next fifty years. The first is his evolutionary preconceptions about the laws of religious growth and the progressive divine education of the human race. This he shared with Rowland Williams and others, and it often entailed some notion or other of Christianity's "fulfillment" or "crowning" of the other ancient creeds. Second, and not always resting easily with the idea of "fulfill-ment," is Jowett's admission, indeed, his too naïve perception of comparisons and parallels among the great religious traditions. This simplifying tendency later led to unforeseeable and insecure conclusions in liberal Christian apolo-getics. A third characteristic of Jowett's thinking, which also became a feature of more radical forms of theology, is his easygoing relinquishing of the Bible's singular revelatory authority. To the "lessons of Scripture" Jowett added the tests of the broadest historical and religious experience.

Williams, Maurice, and Jowett represent the boldest and most advanced thinking on the subject of the non-Christian religions among the mid-Victorian theologians. However, in view of what was soon to fully blossom in Britain as the "science of religion," they were precritical and amateurish. None of the three had firsthand experience of Hinduism, Buddhism, or Islam. Neither did they have the professionals' grasp of the languages and texts of these religions.

The New Context after 1860

The new scientific and comparative study of religion, which came to frui-tion in the second half of the nineteenth century, was one of the important intellectual accomplishments of modernity, and Britain played a leading role in this new endeavor. In *The Origin of Species* Darwin predicted that other fields would soon be open to "far more important researches" in the study of human life and institutions through the evolutionary principles employed in his book (C. Darwin 1917, 428). In fact, it took at most a decade. Writing to the anthropologist E. B. Tylor in 1871 on the publication of the latter's *Primitive Culture*, Darwin commented on how wonderful it was that Tylor had traced "animism from the lower races up to the religious belief of the highest races." He confessed that it made him "look at religion from a new point of view" (F. Darwin 1887, 151). Darwin was not alone.

Tylor's and Herbert Spencer's evolutionary ideas were, initially, innocent of Darwin, but *The Origin of Species* gave weight both to *Primitive Culture* and to Spencer's evolutionary *First Principles* (1862). By the end of the 1860s, through the impress of Darwin's work and the popularization of evolution in Comte and Spencer, all of human history and culture—including religion—was being examined afresh in terms of its origin and development.

This evolutionary frame of mind, joined with the remarkable infusion of new knowledge of foreign faiths in Britain's far-flung empire, stimulated the rapid growth of the scientific and comparative study of religion in Britain. Its beginnings are associated with Friedrich Max Müller's London lectures of 1870, published as *An Introduction to the Science of Religion* (1873). Müller distrusted Darwinian evolutionary naturalism, but his own convictions about the human spirit and cultural progress were rooted in German Romanticism and the Hegelian philosophy of history. It was, in fact, Hegel's vision of spiritual process that gave a religious character to British philosophy between 1870 and 1900. One can see this as early as 1860 in the writings of Benjamin Jowett and Frederick Temple, and it became more prominent in the works of T. H. Green and his disciples, including Edward Caird and some of the contributors to *Lux Mundi* (1889).

Müller's *Introduction to the Science of Religion* was informed by these evolutionary ideas. A related theme of the lectures is Müller's protest against the ignorant and prejudiced treatment of other religions by Christian historians and theologians. "Every doctrine," he reproved, "is interpreted in the worst sense that it will bear; every act of worship that differs from their own way of serving God is held up to ridicule and contempt." Of special concern to Müller was the fact that "by unduly depreciating all other religions," Christianity is uprooted from its sacred context in the spiritual history of the world. This disparagement has "woefully narrowed the sundry times and divers manners in which, in times past, God spoke unto the fathers by the prophets," protested Müller, and it sees other nations as "mere outcasts, forsaken and forgotten of their Father." Müller called this Christian attitude the worst kind of "godless heresy" (Müller 1873a, 148).

In an era when European scholars were slowly learning to do justice to ancient and even primal political and social institutions, it was time, Müller admonished his audience, to do the same in the field of religion. It was now possible "to speak freely and fearlessly" of the fact that the study of the world's religions teaches "that there is no religion which does not contain some grains of truth," and that we must now "see in the history of the ancient religions . . . the *Divine education of the human race*" (1873a, 158).

A number of publications and activities undertaken concurrently or shortly following Müller's apology underscore the growing interest in the science of religion and the fact that Müller was not alone in establishing its foundations. John Lubbock's (1834–1913) *The Origin of Civilization and the Primitive Condition of Man* (1870) and E. B. Tylor's *Primitive Culture* (1871) were the groundwork of the Victorian anthropological study of religion. In 1875 Cornelius Petrus Tiele (1830–1902), the Dutch Egyptologist, published his important article "Religion" in the ninth edition of the *Encyclopaedia Britannica*. It immediately became the standard summary of the comparative-historical method. Tiele's widely consulted *Outlines of the History of Religions to the Spread of the Universal Religions* also appeared in an English translation in 1877. The following year the Hibbert Lectures were established; by the turn of the century they had produced a series of highly influential books on the history of religions, issued in inexpensive, uniform editions. A letter sent to the Hibbert trustees by an impressive group of liberal Christians, including A. P. Stanley, W. B. Carpenter, John Caird, and James Martineau, had urged that a lectureship be initiated through whose auspices "the various Faiths of mankind might receive capable and exhaustive treatment." The series included "Lectures on the Origin and Growth of Religion," illustrating the religions of India (Müller, 1878), ancient Egypt (Peter Renouf, 1879), Indian Buddhism (T. W. Rhys Davids, 1881), the religion of Mexico and Peru (Albert Réville, 1884), ancient Babylonia (A. H. Sayce, 1887), and so on.

By the end of the 1870s two notable publication ventures—one scholarly, the other popular—were inaugurated. Through his own tireless efforts, Müller secured the translations of primary texts that became the fifty volumes of *The Sacred Books of the East*, a work undertaken by an entire generation of scholars (1879–1904). The project made accessible for the first time a mine of textual riches of Brahmanism, Jainism, Buddhism, Zoroastrianism, Confucianism, and Islam. In 1877 the Society for the Promotion of Christian Knowledge initiated a series of popular primers entitled *Non-Christian Religious Systems*, which ran to eleven volumes. What was characteristic of this and similar projects—which by 1910 became a flood tide—was the fact that most volumes were well informed and fair minded.

One effect of all this new interest was, of course, the fomenting of new thinking about Christianity's place "in the Divine education of the human race." "It is not surprising," the now elderly Tractarian priest R. W. Church admitted, "that these mysterious utterances breaking in on us . . . from the dawn of time, should have awakened a very deep interest. . . . They seem to require us to revise our judgments and widen our thoughts" (Church 1880, 382). Increasing numbers of High Churchmen, liberals, and Nonconformists alike were, or soon would be, required to assimilate these new facts and theories into their theological reflections.

The British Pioneers in the New "Science of Religion": Some Suggestive Theological Implications

Before examining the variety of religious and theological responses to the new science of religion, it will be helpful to give some account of the new archaeological, philological, and ethnological discoveries and the influential theories they generated. This will provide a sense of the rather volatile intellectual context in which the debate about Christianity's relation to the world religions was taking place. The purpose here is not a thorough summary of the contributions of the influential British scholars and theorists such as Müller, Tylor, W. Robertson Smith, James George Frazer, and Andrew Lang. Rather, it is to call attention to the research and theories of these scholars that had a significant bearing on traditional Christian assumptions and beliefs.

Among the British comparative philologists and anthropologists, Müller was, with Smith, closest to Christianity in personal allegiance and sympathy. Though Müller's views were opposed and censured by churchmen, he was a friend and colleague of influential ecclesiastics and a Church of England communicant. We have seen that he was sensitive about the implications of the science of religion for Christianity, although these matters were to prove more ambiguous and problematic to the theologians than to Müller himself.

What Müller called for was a deep empathy for all religions and a disinterested study of them, including one's own. This meant bracketing distinctions such as "true" and "false" or "revealed" and "natural": "If people regard their religion as revealed, it is to them a revealed religion, and has to be treated as such by every impartial historian" (Müller 1880, 74). Müller also opposed the idea of degeneration and the correlative notion of a singular "original" revelation that had in time been corrupted. For Müller, religion is a human a priori, and "whenever there are traces of human life there are traces of Religion" (1873a, 65). He found the origin and essence of religion in the unique human sense of the infinite and believed that this uniqueness gives us the clue to the grandeur and oneness of the human story—hence the need for a deep empathy and impartiality: "However imperfect, however childish a religion may be, it always places the human soul in the presence of God; and however imperfect and however childish the conception of God may be, it always represents the highest ideal of perfection which the human soul, for the time being, can reach and grasp" (1873a, 263).

Müller's humanistic idealism, coupled with his eloquence and sympathy, were deeply attractive to many among the British educated class. And he was a close friend of Queen Victoria and particularly of Prince Albert. At the same time, his open, pluralistic views were threatening traditional ideas of

Christianity's uniqueness and finality. This was especially true of his sponsorship of the comparative method. Its challenge to Christian convictions is evident in the following appeal, so typical of Müller:

> He must be a man of little faith who would fear to subject his own religion to the same critical tests to which the historian subjects all other religions. We need not surely crave a tender or merciful treatment for that faith which we hold to be the only true one. . . . In the Science of Religion we can decline no comparisons, nor claim any immunities for Christianity, as little as the missionary can when wrestling with the subtle Brahman, or the fanatical Mussulman, or the plain-speaking Zulu. (1881, 13–14)

Müller's comment about "the only true one" was disquieting, since he often commented that "the points on which the great religions differ are far less numerous, and certainly far less important, than are the points on which they all agree" (Müller 1901, 335). The comparative study of religion, he insisted, "would enable us to gain a truer insight into the peculiar character of Christianity," but this would result from "showing what it *shares in common* with other religions" as well as "what distinguishes it from all its peers" (Müller 1873a, 37; italics added). Müller was apparently oblivious to what for many Christians was the ambiguity of such statements as the following: "I make no secret that true Christianity—I mean the religion of Christ—seems to me to become more and more exalted the more we know, and *the more we appreciate, the treasures of truth* hidden in the despised religions of the world" (Müller 1873a, 37). For some theists, these shared "treasures of truth" did indeed deepen their sense of the grandeur of God and of Christianity. For others, they raised serious questions about Christian claims.

Müller spoke of Christianity as "pre-eminent" among the world's faiths, yet it was not historical or dogmatic Christianity of which he spoke but the ethical ideal taught by Jesus. In his notable lecture "On Missions," delivered at Westminster Abbey in 1873 at the invitation of the dean, Arthur Stanley, Müller identified "creedalism" and party strife as the curse of Christian missionary work and called for a Christianity not creedal or sectarian, not preached but "lived in the spirit." When one contemplates the mystery and majesty of God, Müller asked, "[what] are all those formulas but the stammerings of children?" (Müller 1873b, 50–51). For Müller, true Christianity is found in the love of God and love of man, but this for him is the ideal that all religions—as reflections of a natural, divine revelation—seek.

If God is loving, he would not, Müller insisted, reveal himself to us and not have made other revelations to his other children as well. This argument was echoed with equal force and simplicity almost a century later by the liberal Christian historian Arnold Toynbee in his *Christianity among the Religions of the World* (1958) and by a growing chorus of Christian theologians in the latter decades of the twentieth century. Müller shared with other neo-Kantians the epistemological conviction that each religion is, so to speak, God's countenance as *perceived* by his devotees. God is experienced *really* but *selectively*, as is required by each community's spiritual capacity or equipment. This too became a common theme in late twentieth-century dialogues between Christians and those of other faiths and is espoused most influentially by the British philosopher John Hick in his many books, especially *An Interpretation of Religion* (1989).

It is hard to gauge exactly Müller's influence on changing religious attitudes among the educated British public. It is clear, however, that his popular writings and lectures on behalf of the science of religion gained considerable sympathy for the religious treasures of the East and contributed to the liberalizing of religious attitudes in Britain in the years following 1870 (Müller 1902, 135).

Müller's role in the reconception of Christianity's encounter with other faiths went beyond his pioneering efforts on behalf of the comparative method and his theory of a primordial religious sentiment common to humankind. He was also an early opponent of the anthropological school whose working suppositions were naturalistic. To many of the mid- and late Victorians this was the greater threat to Christian belief. The anthropologists John Lubbock, E. B. Tylor, J. F. M'Lennan, and Andrew Lang all were—at least for a time— evolutionary naturalists and Darwinians. They conceived of primitive man as moving from animal brutality up the evolutionary ladder through childish superstition to higher stages of ethical belief or agnostic rationalism. The presence of primordial myths and folklore in the present was attributed to the persistence of "survivals"—like fossils—in the institutions of the present.

Müller strongly contended against this vision of humankind and religion, and he sought to discredit it. The idea of humanity emerging from a state of animal brutality would not, he insisted, hold up to the evidence of philology, which he believed to be more secure than all the evidence of ethnology. There was, he wrote, "no valid foundation for the study of the religion of savages except the study of their languages" (1873a, 56). Against Darwinian opposition, he maintained that "language is our Rubicon, and no brute will dare to cross it." Naturalistic explanations of language could, in Müller's estimation, account for only a small portion of primitive linguistic roots. He held fast to the idea of basic "phonetic types," which he took to be "ultimate facts" given "by the hand of God" (Chaudhuri 1974, 257). While most anthropologists had refused, or had failed, to master Sanskrit and the other critical languages, Müller increasingly took account of ethnological data, using it in a series of studies to confute the anthropologists' theories. He criticized, for example, the vagueness and ambiguity of their use of such terms as *fetishism, animism,* and *totemism,* and chided them for their linguistic ignorance and dependence on the biased reports of missionaries and travelers.

Müller's telling criticisms, conjoined with his idealism, were grist for those Christian apologists who were quick to join in the attack on what they considered the fantastic theories of a reductionistic naturalism that they associated with the anthropological school. The fact that a scholar of Müller's preeminent rank could hold his own against the ethnological claims of an E. B. Tylor or an Andrew Lang (1844–1912), and especially the folklorist and anti-Christian popularizer Edward Clodd (1840–1930), gave sufficient ammunition to Christian apologists. As it turned out, Müller was both more complex and inconsistent than his defenders were aware. He later came to display sophistication in ethnological matters and conceded that anthropology and philology must work closely in tandem. Much of his work can also be read in evolutionary terms. It is worth noting that in the 1860s E. B. Tylor resorted to Müller's researches in developing his own evolutionary scheme and commended Müller for pursuing his own work on the basis of Lyell's evolutionary principles.

The aspect of Müller's scholarship that has least endured, and the one, unfortunately, with which he is often most associated, is his grand theory of solar mythology. A sketch of the theory will suffice, since it is central to our theme only because some of Müller's disciples used solar mythology in the tacit service of Christian apologetic.

As a comparative philologist Müller was struck, as were others, by the parallels in the names of many of the gods of Indo-European mythology, and Müller wished to explain them. As the European groups migrated from the original Indic civilization, their languages and their mythologies splintered into many offshoots. In time the original meanings of the words for the Vedic gods were forgotten and stories arose to explain the words. Mythology was then the unintended poetic or metaphoric product of this original and ongoing linguistic process. Müller called the emergence of mythology a "disease of language":

> Whenever any word, that was at first used not metaphorically, is used without a clear conception of the steps that led from its original to its metaphorical meaning, there is danger of mythology; whenever those steps are forgotten and artificial steps put in their places, we have mythology, or if I may say so, we have diseased language. (Müller 1885, 392–93)

Müller was convinced that all Aryan mythology was traceable to a com-mon source in the observation of natural phenomena, especially the solar drama that revolved around the sun, the dawn, and the sky. He saw the solar drama of sunrise and sunset, the struggle between light and darkness, as the subject of most mythology. He perceived the theme in the myth of the death of Herakles, in the tale of William Tell, and in most of the stories about the hero who dies in his youth. Balder, Sigurd, Achilles all were "first suggested by the Sun, dying in its youthful vigor, either at the end of the day, conquered by the powers of darkness, or at the end of the sunny season, stung by the thorn of winter" (Müller 1856, 140). Müller's obsession with solar mythology was the source of a long-standing feud with his critics, especially with Andrew Lang. His pansolarism also led to humorous but often unfair parodies of Müller's position in which, for example, Napoleon, Julius Caesar, Cortez, and Müller himself were "solarized" (see Tylor 1891, 319–20). In the final analysis, how-ever, these criticisms missed the real mark, since, for Müller, the relation of mythology and religion was not essential. Indeed, the mythopoesis repre-sents a "degeneration" that obscures profound and primordial religious truth, namely, the perception of the infinite beyond and yet through the phenom-enon of nature. For Müller, mythology merely conceals the soul of religion.

There were, however, themes in the solar myth that pointed to latent Christian ideas. These were given much attention by some of Müller's dis-ciples, especially by George William Cox (1827–1902) and Abram Smythe Palmer. Cox was the author of a *Manual of Mythology* (1867), *The Mythology of the Aryan Nations* (1870), and *An Introduction to the Science of Comparative Mythology and Folklore* (1881). In these works he popularized the idea that all Aryan myths are analogous, their narrative elements pointing to the arche-typal struggle between the sun and night—a struggle that Cox christianized: "The story of the sun starting in weakness and ending in victory, waging a long warfare against darkness, clouds, storms, and scattering them all in the end, is the story of all patient self-sacrifice, of all Christian devotion" (Cox 1870, 168).

Cox loosely lumped together the tales of Roland, the biblical David, Beowulf, Cinderella, and Hansel and Gretel together as telling the same solar drama of night and dawn, of winter and coming spring. Nevertheless, as Richard Dorson points out, Cox revealed more sophistication than did Müller in his structural comparisons of myth and "was moving onto the sounder ground of type and motif analysis" (Dorson 1968, 176). Typology and motif research increased in scholarly favor and shortly became a major force in biblical scholarship and also in the service of Christian apologetic.

E. B. Tylor is recognized as one of the "fathers" of the study of anthropol-ogy. While his own research brought together a rich fund of anthropological data, it was interwoven with considerable religious speculation. Furthermore, Tylor's scientific work was fueled by the typical Victorian rationalist's reforming purpose; he spoke of the science of culture as "essentially a reformer's science" (Tylor 1871, 410). Tylor was raised a Quaker, and he shared the English Nonconformists' antipathy to Catholicism. He was indifferent to the life and significance of religious ritual and the social dimensions of religious cult. Religion for Tylor was intellectual and moral, and so was his reformation.

Tylor shared a faith in progress with the Enlightenment, the philosopher Auguste Comte (1798–1857), and historian T. H. Buckle (1821–1862). The obstacle to progress was not "priestcraft" alone but the less obvious and more insidious impediment of irrational cultural "survivals." While Tylor's contribution to the science of religion is usually associated with his theory of animism, the real threat that his work posed for Christianity was his unilinear evolutionism and its attendant doctrine of survivals, those relics of a primitive time that Tylor saw as carried forward into later stages of society as irrational habit and mere superstition. While Tylor's own attitude toward Christianity might appear at times to be positive—he saw a rational and moral Christian monotheism as the enlightened historical development out of religious barbarism and delusion—his own deep faith rested elsewhere. When he wrote that it is a "painful office of ethnography to expose the remains of crude old cultures which have passed into harmful superstition, and to make these out for destruction" (1871, 410), attentive readers did not miss his meaning. While some Christian beliefs and practices may at one time have been warranted, Tylor viewed much of Christian belief and practice as irrational and useless vestiges of a bygone age.

Tylor was an evolutionist in the sense that he viewed human culture as progressing from lower to higher forms of life in a natural and largely unbroken sequence. His massing of extensive ethnographic data from all over the world not only accentuated the linkages between primitive and civilized societies; it also implied a *law of progression* that governed the historical process itself. Let us consider his doctrine of animism, or "belief in spiritual Beings," his minimum definition of religion. For Tylor, animism is not simply religion's most primordial form; it is the foundation of all subsequent religion. While animism characterizes tribes "very low in the scale of humanity," it also develops continuously, in modified forms, "into the midst of high modern culture." It is then the "groundwork" of all religion, "from that of savages up to that of civilized man" (1889, 426), taking the ascending forms of ancestor worship, fetishism, totemism, polytheism, and, finally, monotheism.

Tylor's purpose was not only to refute degenerationism and to neutralize notions of religious diffusion. He wanted to silence the argument of the theologians who insisted that human spiritual life was distinct from material life, since it was not governed by the same natural laws of progressivism (see Stocking 1987, 160ff.). The history of mankind, Tylor insisted, is part and parcel of the history of nature in that our thoughts and actions accord with laws as definite as those that govern the motion of the tides and the life of plants and animals. Tylor's clear implication was, of course, that humankind's spiritual evolution is guided neither by special, divine interventions, nor by the diffusion of the Christian message by missionary effort.

While animism may give support to the notion of a sequential religious evolution from fetishism to the "one Supreme Being," Tylor also perceived a parallel and more potent process at work, one that would direct the world on a steadier and continuous course of progress. This was the development of scientific method:

> Through all these gradations of opinion, we may thus see fought out, in one stage after another, the long-waged contest between the theory of animation which accounts for each phenomenon of nature by giving it everywhere a life like our own, and a slowly-growing natural science which in one department after another substitutes for independent voluntary action the working out of systematic law. (1866, 83)

"It was," G. Stocking remarks, "as though primitive man, in an attempt to create science, had accidentally created religion instead, and mankind had spent the rest of evolutionary time trying to rectify the error" (Stocking 1987, 192).

The concept of survivals was critical to Tylor's theory of religion and also was in conflict with Christian belief. Since religious beliefs and behavior are found universally among primitive peoples, Tylor deduced that religion belongs to a very early stage of the evolutionary process. Thus, those irrational and seemingly functionless beliefs and practices of the European and Latin peasantry—so at variance with those of the present "educated classes"—suggested to Tylor that they are residues of a more primitive cultural life. These survivals also confirmed Tylor's belief in evolutionary development, since development does not always move at the same pace. In higher culture there often remain retarded elements that reflect its ancient past. And Tylor saw in the late Victorian interest in spiritualism and psychic research a current vestige of primitive superstition. He scornfully (and humorously) denounced a contemporary British medium as "a Red Indian or a Tatar shaman in a dress coat" (Tylor 1869, 528).

Tylor spoke of survivals as *mere* survivals, that is, as vestiges of bygone, primitive belief. While a scholar such as Andrew Lang could see in myths masks of profound truth, Tylor saw them only as "antiquarian relics," conceptions "now fallen into absurdity from having been carried on into a new

state of society, where the original sense has been discarded" (1891, 94). A
historian thus can speak of Tylor's war on survivals as comparable to "the
fervour of George Fox denouncing the steeple-houses," since he approached
theology "with the air of one about to cleanse the temple of the Lord"
(Burrow 1966, 256). Here Tylor's kinship with the new, more radical evolutionary naturalism is clear.

The theological significance of *Primitive Culture* was not lost on reflective
Victorians. Darwin saw it as strengthening the case against the degenerationists, such as the Duke of Argyll. Edward Clodd, president of the Folk-
Lore Society, rationalist freethinker, and dogged critic of the theologians,
spoke in his *Memoirs* of the powerful role that *Primitive Culture* had played
in his own rejection of biblical revelation. Clodd came to view all Christian
beliefs and practices as survivals of heathen ideas—a theme that he drove
home relentlessly in his many popular books.

Tylor's evolutionism occasionally proved to be theologically useful. In
some cases—for example, in the writings of the liberal Anglican comparativist F. B. Jevons (1858–1936)—it was enlisted in the service of schemes of progressive revelation and the psychic unity of the race. More often, however,
Tylor's work had a prejudicial and malign effect on theology and religious
belief. Many readers put down *Primitive Culture* clearly aware of Tylor's cardinal point: "Rather than God having created man in His image, man had,
through evolutionary time, created God in his" (Stocking 1987, 195).

W. Robertson Smith was the first British biblical scholar to take serious account of the work of the social anthropologists, especially that of his
friend J. F. M'Lennan, and to incorporate their evolutionary framework
and such concepts as totemism and survivals into his biblical researches.
Smith's enormous contribution to Old Testament scholarship was twofold: first, through his own learned studies; second, by serving as a con-
duit for the ideas of Continental biblical scholars such as Julius Wellhausen
(1844–1918) and Abraham Kuenen (1828–1891). Smith was a son of the
manse, his father a minister of the Free Church of Scotland at Kieg. He
was educated at Aberdeen University and at New College, the theological
hall of the Free Church in Edinburgh. He was ordained in 1870. That same
year, he was appointed to the chair of Oriental languages and exegesis of the
Old Testament at the Free Church College in Aberdeen. His publications
soon were considered dangerous, and between 1875 and 1881 he suffered
through a series of investigations and trials by his church, finally being suspended from his professional duties. He served as editor of the renowned
ninth edition of the *Encyclopaedia Britannica*, was appointed to the faculty
at Cambridge, where he successively became Reader and then Professor of
Arabic, and was named university Librarian in 1886. Smith has been called

the founder of the comparative sociology of religion, and his work had a profound influence on Emile Durkheim, James George Frazer, and Sigmund Freud, the latter uncritically accepting but also distorting his ideas. Smith also influenced eminent twentieth-century British anthropologists, including Edward Evans-Pritchard and Mary Douglas.

Smith's major work is *Lectures on the Religion of the Semites: The Fundamental Institutions* (1889). The central theme is the social character of religion, and all of the subthemes of the volume—sacrifice, totemism, ritual—illustrate that leitmotiv. Smith argued that a person does not "choose his religion or frame it for himself"; rather, it comes "as part of the general scheme of social obligations and ordinances laid upon him, as a matter of course, by his position in the family and in the nation" (W. R. Smith 1894, 28). Countering the views of Müller, Tylor, and his friend and protégé James George Frazer, Smith rejected the notion that the essence of religion rests in the beliefs or behavior of individuals. He maintained, rather, that rites, as collective representations, are the root of all religion—that in the beginning was the *social act*.

For Smith, religion not only mirrors social organization and social relations, it projects them onto the natural and supernatural world. Consequently, ritual precedes myth or doctrine both temporally and essentially. Myth may then be explained as the attempt to rationalize rituals whose purpose may be wholly latent. "Religion in primitive times was not," Smith insists, "a system of belief with practical applications: it was a body of fixed traditional practices, to which every member of society conformed as a matter of course" (1894, 20). This insight was Smith's great contribution to Durkheim and to social anthropology in the twentieth century.

Allied to the fundamentally social and ritualistic character of religion, Smith developed his theories regarding the practice of totemism, that is, the worship of sacred animals, which he took over largely from J. F. M'Lennan. Smith's theories about totemism and a necessary "totemistic stage" of religious evolution are among his most conjectural and least convincing ideas, although through the popular works of Frazer, Stanley A. Cook (1873–1949), F. B. Jevons, and Sigmund Freud they remained current—while further distorted—and influential for some time.

Totemism, according to Smith, simply expresses the organic solidarity between the gods and their worshipers through the material totemic representation:

> In the totem stage of society each kinship or stock of savages believes itself to be physically akin to some natural kind of animate or inanimate things, most generally to some kind of animal. Every animal of

> this kind is looked upon as a brother, is treated with the same respect
> as a human clansman, and is believed to aid his human relations by a
> variety of friendly services. (1894, 124)

The god, who is father of the clan, and the kinsmen are thus bound together through blood relations in one natural community through the institution of totemism.

Totemism steered Smith into a lengthy discussion of sacrifice, which takes up half of his book. The Semitic tribal clans, according to Smith, periodically expressed the unity of their members and their god and ensured their vitality by slaying the totem animal and consuming its flesh and blood. Tylor earlier had argued that primitive sacrifice is characterized by crude gift-giving (the *do ut des*, "I give in order that you will give"). Smith rejected this idea as fundamentally less basic, and introduced his thesis that the crucial idea in ancient Semitic animal sacrifice is "not that of a gift made over to the god, but of an act of communion, in which the god and his worshippers unite by partaking together of the flesh and blood of a sacred victim" (1894, 226–27). The anthropologist Edmund Leach rightly underscores the fact that "for Smith the crux lay in the performance itself. . . . Sacrifice is not just *thought* of as a communion; it *is* a communion" (Leach 1985, 241). The sacred power is actually ingested, taken on.

Smith's theory of sacrifice has not stood up well against the ethnographic data. There is no evidence of its primordiality, there is slight evidence in totemistic societies of the group ceremonially eating their totems, and there are plenty of cases where primitive sacrifice clearly is unrelated to communion. More recent studies, while recognizing the complex levels of meaning in ancient sacrifice, do stress especially the theme of expiation or atonement in Semitic sacrificial rites. Smith's misconceptions acknowledged, there is little doubt that he was correct in seeing the institution of sacrifice, and its interpretation, as the central problem of ancient religion. Moreover, his concentration on sacrifice focused scholarly attention on the fundamental role of social ritual in any proper understanding of the phenomenon of religion.

Smith shared the Victorian anthropologists' evolutionary scheme and, consequently, their need to account for the persistence of savage thought and behavior—hence their appeal to the doctrine of survivals. These working assumptions resulted in ambiguities and contradictions in Smith's own work. He believed in the slow yet divine education of the human race and viewed Protestant Christianity as representing the acme of the process. However, Smith's hero, Martin Luther, and modern Protestant moral individualism did not easily square with his preoccupation with the social and ritualistic roots of religion. His own personal convictions, which included Christianity's absoluteness or finality, also appeared to escape his general, and relativistic, principle that religions mirror the structure of their society. The innovative prophet does, after all, break through the cultural grid. It would appear then, for Smith, that Christianity both is and is not—as it served his scholarly and theological purposes—continuous with the evolutionary process. Here the doctrine of survivals served him well.

Smith's ambiguity or ambivalence is especially observable in his uncertain treatment of sacrifice and the Christian Eucharist or Holy Communion. In the *Lectures*, he adopted a geological image to establish his evolutionary procedure:

> The record of the religious thought of mankind resembles the geological record of the earth's crust; the old and the new are preserved side by side, or rather layer upon layer. The classification of ritual formations in their proper sequence is the first step toward their explanation, and that explanation itself must take the form, not of speculative theory, but of a rational life-history. (1894, 24)

Smith then applied the scheme to the study of Christian sacrifice and fixed the links connecting past and present forms and their explanatory roles: "Thus, when we wish thoroughly to study the New Testament doctrine of sacrifice, we are carried back step by step till we reach a point where we have to ask what sacrifice meant, not only to the old Hebrews alone, but to the whole circle of nations of which they formed a part" (3).

Smith included in his discussion of sacrifice a lecture on the "Annual Death of the God," introducing a theme that was to be taken up not only by Frazer and Freud but later by S. H. Hooke (1874–1968), professor of Old Testament at London University, and his colleagues in the British myth and ritual school. In a passage on the slaying of the high god-king—which received considerable notoriety and was removed from the second edition— Smith spoke of the "foreshadowing" of the Christian God-man's sacrifice in terrible and odious ancient rites. Yet the passage also reflects his concern to distance the Christian idea from the pagan features in which "the germs of better things are effectively hidden out of sight":

> That the God-man dies for His people, and that His death is their life, is an idea which was in some degree foreshadowed by the oldest mythical sacrifices. It was foreshadowed, indeed, in a very crude and materialistic form, and without any of those ethical ideas which the Christian doctrine of the atonement derives from a profounder sense of sin and divine justice. And yet the voluntary death of the divine

victim which we have seen to be a conception not foreign to ancient sacrificial ritual, contained the germ of the deepest thought in the Christian doctrine. (Smith 1889, 393)

Smith's evolutionism proved to be something like recent notions of "punctuated equilibria," rather than orthodox scientific "uniformitarianism." He was able to affirm "catastrophic" discontinuities (innovative prophecy) within a generally slow evolutionary continuity. Moreover, "survivals" were able to explain the presence of more savage ideas and behavior—the mere vestiges of a more brutish age.

Smith's position became popular in the following decade among those who, though committed to evolutionary anthropology, were also Christian apologists. The works of men such as F. B. Jevons and J. Estlin Carpenter (1844–1927), the Unitarian scholar at Manchester College, Oxford, are examples. It proved, however, a rather unstable position and was discredited, along with evolutionary anthropology, after 1914. Exploring Smith's discussion of sacrifice, a student of Smith's work detects his ambivalence and unease: "While he [Smith] wants to consider Christian origins anthropologically, he still must separate his own religious faith from the same type of critical scrutiny that he levels against ancient faiths" (Beidelman 1974, 58). This was a deepening problem for many scholars with Christian commitments until, as we will see, it reached a resolution of sorts—or a deadend, depending on one's viewpoint—in the crisis introduced by the work of the German *Religionsgeschichtliche Schule* and the historian and theologian Ernst Troeltsch (1865–1923) at the turn of the century.

The ambivalence in a position such as Smith's is palpable. There were those—for example, Anglican and Catholic modernists such as the classical archaeologist Percy Gardner (1846–1937) and the theologian George Tyrrell (1861–1909)—for whom the "foreshadowings" of Christian thought and ritual in primitive and antique faiths enhanced their sense of the former's universality and experiential truth. But others saw in Smith's comparative method the great dissolvent of all claims to Christianity's uniqueness and finality. They found it hard to distinguish between Smith's discrete comparisons and the more overt rationalism and reductionism of a Frazer, or the popularizing of an Edward Clodd.

James George Frazer undoubtedly was the most famous and, outside the professional field of anthropology, the most influential British evolutionary anthropologist and historian of religion in the late Victorian era. Like his friend and mentor W. Robertson Smith, he was raised in the bosom of the conservative Free Church of Scotland; however, at Glasgow University he early adopted a rationalist outlook, and the religion of his childhood withered away. He took a second baccalaureate degree at Trinity College, Cambridge, and became a Fellow there in 1879, remaining for sixty years. Through the urging of Smith, Frazer came to write the articles on "Taboo" and "Totem" for the ninth edition of the *Encyclopaedia Britannica*, and this launched the classicist into the new fields of the anthropological and comparative study of religion.

Frazer's influential work, *The Golden Bough*, appeared in two volumes in 1890. This was followed by a three-volume edition in 1900, and between 1911 and 1915 the work expanded to twelve volumes. It was the first two editions, however, that proved most influential. What *The Golden Bough* did was apply late Victorian rationalism and evolutionism to the reinterpretation of Greco-Roman religion. Frazer demonstrated that the real but often ignored savagery and irrationality of the religion of the classical age resembled that of rude "primitives." His comparative evolutionism drew the further conclusion that the religions of more recent times reveal as well the vestiges of those older primitive beliefs and practices, forcing on his readers the conclusion that the course of religious evolution is a continuous one and is similar among all societies.

In carrying out his comparative and evolutionary program, Frazer made three important contributions to religious scholarship. He proposed a theory of magic whereby he sought to distinguish magic from both religion and science. He further popularized the theme of the dying and rising god or goddess and, related to this, the concept of divine kingship. These latter two themes proved attractive and of wide interest, and Frazer's influence was acknowledged by the next generation of British classicists—Jane Harrison (1850–1928), Francis Cornford (1874–1943), A. B. Cook (1868–1952), and Gilbert Murray (1866–1957)—and others, including biblical scholars, who followed the lead taken by scholars associated with the myth-ritual school.

Frazer was an indefatigable collector and classifier of primitive and archaic religious data. He was, and perhaps remains, one of the most famous practitioners of comparative religion. His numerous comments on the method reveal his evolutionary and comparativist preconceptions. The method, he wrote, regards

the religions of the world . . . not as systems of truth or falsehood to be demonstrated or refuted, but as phenomena of consciousness to be studied like any other aspect of human nature. . . . Now when . . . we examine side by side the religions of different races and ages, we find that, while they differ from each other in many particulars, the resemblances between them are numerous and fundamental, and that they mutually illustrate and explain each other. (Frazer 1894, 802)

In Frazer's estimation, the work of the comparativist does not, however, rest in such a purely comparative or antiquarian interest. He could not resist raising the question of truth, and, while warning against the genetic fallacy, he more often was unable to resist committing the fallacy himself: "We can hardly help suspecting that our own cherished doctrines may have originated in the similar superstitions of our rude forefathers; and the suspicion inevitably shakes the confidence with which we hitherto regarded these articles of faith" (Frazer 1913, 4).

Frazer was sensitive to this shaking of confidence, since "society has been built and cemented to a great extent on a foundation of religion" (1913, 5). Nevertheless, he held, the candid historian should not dissemble but prosecute his duty unflinchingly. Frazer was convinced that a great proportion of the religious beliefs and practices of the race are "false and foolish." The comparative study of religion is, therefore, also a demand for the radical reconsideration of the foundations of both theology and ethics. Yet he perceived his own melancholy but necessary task of criticism as preliminary, "only dragging the guns into position." It would be for others to build up "the old structures so rudely shattered" (1911, xxv–xxvi).

Frazer's description of the phenomena and the principles of magic—for example, his distinctions between homoeopathic or imitative magic, based on the law of similarity, and contagious magic, based on contact—have proven illuminating and useful. Yet his contention that magic is older than religion lacks ethnographic evidence. Moreover, this was not an issue that was especially challenging for the claims of Christian doctrine. Rather, it was his extensive work on magic as it related specifically to the themes of the divine god-king and the dying and rising god or goddess that cut closer to the theological bone.

In *The Magic Art and the Evolution of Kings*, Frazer developed the theme of the man-god, that is, the priest-king, who serves as a divine mediator and possesses magical powers. This he related to the pervasive ritual slaying of the priest-king and to the theme of reinvigoration and resurrection in *The Dying God*, in *Adonis, Attis, Osiris*, and in *Spirits of the Corn and of the Wild*, the fourth, fifth, and sixth volumes of *The Golden Bough*. What was shocking and discomforting to many was the largely implicit connections or analogies between Frazer's discussion of these pagan themes of the man-god—the substitute or representative, the sacrificial death, the resurrection—and Christian belief. Frazer described the religious (as distinct from the magical) man-god as being "of an order different from and superior to man [who] becomes incarnate, for a longer or shorter time, in a human body, manifesting his super-human power and knowledge by miracles wrought and prophecies uttered through the medium of a fleshly tabernacle in which he had deigned to take his abode" (Frazer 1911, 244).

Frazer's long discussion of the figure of the hero-god who dies and is revived or resurrected artfully concluded with a note on the crucifixion of Jesus Christ. The god's death and resurrection is, in each case, accompanied by elaborate ritual observances that represent the actions of the god mimetically. Frazer's description of the ceremony associated with the resurrection of Attis is vivid, and the language reminiscent of a more familiar narrative:

> When night had fallen, the sorrow of the worshippers was turned to joy. For suddenly a light shone in the darkness: the tomb was opened; the god had risen from the dead; and as a priest touched the lips of the weeping mourners with balm, he softly whispered in their ears the glad tidings of salvation. The resurrection of the god was hailed by his disciples as a promise that they too would issue triumphant from the corruption of the grave. (1911, V, 272)

While Frazer recognized that the differences between the pagan and Christian themes are significant, he nevertheless often suggested or implied a relationship or an analogy, as in his discussion of the themes of redemption, renewed life, and baptism (1911, V, 70, 72–73, 109, 249). In commenting, for example, on the role of sacramental sacrifices in history and in Robertson Smith's research, he wrote:

> The peculiarity of these sacrifices is that in them the victim slain is an animal or man whom the worshippers regard as divine, and of whose flesh and blood they sometimes partake, either actually or symbolically, as a solemn form of communion with the deity. The conception of such a sacrifice and the observance of such a communion are, of course, familiar to us in the Christian doctrine of the Atonement and the Christian sacrament of the Eucharist. . . . But the religious ideas and observances of this type are world-wide, and that they originated, not in an advanced, but in a low stage of society and in a very crude stage of thought is not open to question. . . . Among the many questions which it raises, the one which will naturally interest Christians most deeply is, how are we to explain the analogy which it reveals between the Christian Atonement and Eucharist on the one side, and the mystical or sacramental sacrifices of the heathen religions on the other? (Frazer 1927, 288–89)

Frazer's answer is unequivocal: Present Christian belief and rite are primitive survivals.

In Frazer's evolutionary scheme two things are transparent. One is the implicit, if not always explicit, contention that Christianity is the outgrowth of the primitive legends of Oriental vegetation cults he had amassed in *The Golden Bough*. The second is his belief that the spread and influence of these archetypal magico-religious myths and rituals in the Christian West were retrograde and gradually to be superseded by the emergence of science and rationality introduced by modernity.

Frazer's vast accumulation of evidence of humanity's religious belief and ritualistic behavior influenced the work of numerous scholars who also embraced his rationalist preconceptions: British writers such as A. E. Crawley (1869–1924), Grant Allen (1848–1899), E. S. Hartland (1848–1927), and the French archaeologist Saloman Reinach (1858–1932). Also, at a time when philosophy, psychology, and literature were newly exploring the rich veins of the nonrational in human experience, Frazer's *Golden Bough* proved to be a well-stocked lode of information and suggestion. The English classicist Jane Harrison, the psychotherapist Carl Jung (1875–1961), the philosopher Henri Bergson (1859–1941), and the poets W. B. Yeats (1869–1939) and T. S. Eliot (1888–1965) were only a few of the new generation of scholars and writers who found in Frazer's vast work a valuable source of ideas.

At the same time, Frazer's professional colleagues in anthropology and folklore were not as impressed with his prodigious achievement. Their primary reservation, and what proved to be a most damaging criticism, was their conclusion that Frazer forced his myriad illustrations into a procrustean bed of theory that simply could not withstand careful ethnographic scrutiny. George Laurence Gomme (1853–1916), president of the Folk-Lore Society from 1890 to 1894), joined a group of professionals, including Andrew Lang, the Jewish biblical scholar Moses Gaster (1856–1939), and the comparativist F. B. Jevons in reviewing *The Golden Bough* for *Folk-Lore*. Gomme summarized nicely their common complaint:

> Everything seems to be sacrificed to the one object of bringing the comparative results of the Latin and European customs into effective line. Too much is thus sacrificed for one study. There are many European customs which do not really belong to the subject, but which are nevertheless necessary to prove the desired results by Mr. Frazer's method. (Gomme 1901, 225)

Gaster complained that "the net is spread so wide, that even the most improbable is drawn into it and has to serve as an argument to prove a theory" (Gaster 1901, 226). Andrew Lang's criticism of Frazer's comparative work focused specifically on the connections he drew between the death and revival of the pagan hero-gods and the New Testament accounts of Christ's scourging, death, resurrection, and the eucharistic celebration. In a notable essay in the *Fortnightly Review*, Lang demonstrated that Frazer's effort was little more than a collocation of disparate traditions from Western Asia that possessed only specious resemblances. Lang judged the claim of kinship between the feast of Purim, the Saturnalia, and the crucifixion of Jesus to be only wild conjecture (Lang 1899).

Frazer's critics did not only concentrate on his extravagant comparisons. Gomme pointed out that Frazer's theory of survivals was not consistent with those of Lang, Hartland, and Clodd, and that their disagreements indicated that the theory of survivals itself was in a questionable state. Both Lang and Jevons wrote impressive criticisms of Frazer's theory of a prereligious stage of magic, criticisms that essentially discredited the whole idea (Lang 1898; Jevons 1901).

Andrew Lang is the one other influential British writer associated with the emergent "science of religion" that requires our attention here. A Scottish anthropologist and folklorist, Lang was educated at St. Andrews, Glasgow, and Oxford. He then embarked on a professional literary career that was amazing in the variety of its output, which included journalism, poetry, histories, novels, fairy tales, and sport, as well as studies of folktale and religion. Since he often wrote on topical matters, much of Lang's work on religion was not enduring. His role was, rather, that of a penetrating critic of other scholars' conjectures and presumptions. He thoroughly enjoyed polemic.

For our purposes, Lang's appeal lies in his counteracting and, in some instances, annihilating the theories concerning the origin and nature of religion, speculations that often had come to enjoy considerable esteem and influence. Lang's probing, nondogmatic yet compelling studies helped to produce a more open, less rationalistic approach to the study of religion, although Lang himself remained a skeptic. He was no defender of the theologians, and while they were critical of aspects of his work, they also found much of his writing congenial. Lang remained independent of all parties, and his critiques of Müller, Frazer, Tylor, and others were often considered definitive.

In addition to serving as president of the Folk-Lore Society in 1888 and 1889, Lang also served as president of the Society for Psychical Research in 1911. In *The Making of Religion* (1898) he marshaled a repertoire of examples from primitive religion of seers whose reports confirmed the findings of the Society. Yet his interest in psychical phenomena was essentially scientific, and he found most spiritualists fraudulent. Like Henry Sidgwick, he remained an open-minded enquirer. Lang thus is a good representative of the move away from Victorian positivism at the end of the nineteenth century.

Lang's importance with regard to the theological significance of the new science is linked to his criticism of Frazer, Müller, and Tylor. In *Modern Mythology* (1897) Lang summarized his long dispute with Müller on the subject of nature mythology. He showed that Müller's benign pansolar theory simply could not account for the brutal and irrational dimensions of much of the world's mythic traditions, which included, but greatly surpassed, the themes that the pansolarists found in the Indo-European traditions (Lang 1890, 139). While Lang believed that religious myth could be accounted for by the human tendency to personify nature, and that the mythopoeic represented a time when the human and natural worlds were not sharply separated, he also envisioned myth as a key to the real condition of the human intellect. In this, and in his opposition to positivistic reductionism, he reflected an attitude more in common with twentieth-century anthropological work on myth.

Earlier in his career Lang had been a proponent of Tylor's evolutionary theory of animism. But later, while studying totemism among Australian primitive tribes, he was confronted with evidence of gods whose characteristics could only be defined as those of a Supreme Being, a god unrelated to other inferior gods. These "High Gods" possessed the attributes of a creator god; they were moral, fatherly, omnipotent, and omniscient. Lang soon discovered corroborative evidence among other primitive tribes and, in his essay "High Gods of Low Races," he defended his thesis that many primitive races have, in addition to animistic beliefs about souls and disembodied spirits, some conception of a Supreme Being, and that, contrary to evolutionary supposition, such a belief could not have arisen later from animistic ideas of ghosts or spirits (Lang 1900, 2). Lang was loath to speculate on the origin of High Gods. "It is about as easy," he conjectured, "for me to believe that they were not left without a witness, as to believe that this God of theirs was evolved out of the maleficent ghost of a dirty mischievous medicine-man" (170).

It was also clear to Lang that belief in a High God is usually *corrupted* by animistic mythology. "Animism," he wrote, "is full of the seeds of religious degeneration" (1900, 264). While he clearly denied that a hypothesis such as original sin was required to explain religious degradation, his own description of the corrupting role of animism sounds not unlike what theologians had meant by the Adamic doctrine: "That god thrives best who is most suited to his environment. Whether an easy-going, hungry ghost-god with a liking for his family, or a moral Creator not to be bribed, is better suited to an environment of not especially scrupulous savages, any man can decide." Such is the process by which animism supplants theism: "Beyond all doubt savages who find themselves under the watchful eye of a moral deity whom they cannot 'square' will desert him as soon as they have evolved a practical ghost-god, useful for family purposes, whom they *can* 'square'" (206). Lang was certain that "higher" and "lower" religions are to be found coexisting throughout human history. He did not consider it necessary to argue either that the higher evolves out of the lower or that the lower necessarily is a degenerate form of the higher. He did, however, see considerable significance in the difference between what is cosmic and what is local in religion.

Lang's claims about High Gods among "low races" was not widely accepted by his anthropological colleagues in Britain. His work on this theme did, however, have a powerful influence on, among others, the German anthropologist Wilhelm Schmidt (1868–1954). Schmidt's twelve-volume *Der Ursprung der Gottesidee* (1912–1955) is one of the more impressive arguments for the pervasive character of belief in a Supreme Being in tribal societies, which Schmidt associated with a primal monotheism. Lang's most durable contribution, however, was his thorough questioning of an invariable progressive evolution of religious belief and cult. He argued, tellingly, that religious change often is for the worse rather than for the better. The history of religion, more often than not, represents a *degeneration*. "So far, then," Lang conceded, "the nature of things and of the reasoning faculty does not seem to give the lie to the old Degeneration theory" (Lang 1900, 267).

Lang's defense of "degeneration" from an original, purer religion gave comfort and a helping hand to the theologians. Earlier writers such as W. E. Gladstone (1869) had meant by degeneration the falling away into paganism from God's original, special revelation to Israel. Lang, on the contrary, rejected the biblical doctrine of an original supernatural revelation. He was simply arguing, rather like an old-fashioned deist, that the religious sentiment was universal and was purest at its source. It is interesting to note, nonetheless, that on anthropological evidence alone, Lang came to conclusions not dissimilar to those arrived at more speculatively by Müller, namely, the conviction about sublime High Gods among primitive peoples. In arriving at this conclusion Lang appears, however, to have weakened his claim that persistent irrational elements in later myth can be explained as the survivals of savagery (see Dorson 1968, 171). Such, it was becoming plain, were the ironies and the contradictions that characterized the growing but increasingly complex and untidy science of religion. It was, for this new science, a time of prodigious scholarship and advance, but also a time of growing uncertainty about fashionable theories.

Despite the increasingly sophisticated critiques of the grand theories of Tylor, Frazer, and others, the theory of primitive survivals persisted into the latter decades of the century. Borrowing heavily from Tylor and lesser lights, its proponents portrayed Christianity simply as a survival of primitive savagery and illusion, a syncretistic and relativistic phenomenon in the process of historical evolution or, more likely, extinction. There was a heady feeling among a cadre of rationalistic anthropologists and classicists that a new era had arrived in the study of humanity with momentous consequences for social institutions resulting from the new scientific study of religion. This can be seen in the work of professionals such as the classicist A. E. Crawley (Crawley 1908) and the anthropologist E. S. Hartland (Hartland 1913), as well as popularizers like Edward Clodd (Clodd 1875).

The Consolidation of the Science of Religion in Britain and Its Influence on Christian Theology

The major works of the anthropologists, classicists, and comparativists after 1870 were accompanied by an array of handbooks and manuals on the history of religions directed to the general public. In addition to the eleven-volume set from the Society for the Promotion of Christian Knowledge, there appeared a series, the *Non-Biblical Systems of Religion* (1887) in Nesbit's Theological Library; *Religious Systems of the World* (1880); seven booklets comprising *The World's Religions Series* (1904–1905); and *Religions Ancient and Modern* (1905) in twenty-one volumes at a cost of one shilling each. Jesuit scholar C. C. Martindale devoted great energy to the cause of disseminating accurate information about the non-Christian religions to the Roman Catholic public, including a five-volume series of *Lectures on the History of Religion* at a shilling a volume. By the 1890s, some of the non-Christian religious organizations in Britain also were roused to activity in circulating popular, appealing accounts of their traditions and beliefs. *The Wisdom of the East Series*, in eight volumes, was inaugurated in 1904. In 1908 the Buddhist Society of Great Britain and Ireland was formed in London. It published a popular series of pamphlets, *The Message of Buddhism to the West*, as well as the *Buddhist Review*. In the summer of 1908 the Orient Exhibition, held in London, included a new feature: a "Hall of Religions" with exhibits and public lectures on the non-Christian faiths.

The year 1908 turned out to be a significant date in Britain for the comparative study of religion. In addition to the events already mentioned, the Wilde Lectureship in Natural and Comparative Religion was inaugurated at Oxford. The classicist Lewis Farnell was the first incumbent. (The first British chair or professorship in comparative religion had been established in 1904 at the University of Manchester.) Also in 1908 the Third International Congress of the History of Religions was held at Oxford. Most significantly, the year marked the appearance of the first volume of the twelve-volume *Encyclopaedia of Religion and Ethics* (1908–1921), edited by the Scot James Hastings (1852–1922). Almost nine hundred scholars were engaged in its production, and for several decades it represented the very best in European religious scholarship. What is notable for our purposes is that the *ERE*, as it came to be called, was intended to be an encyclopaedia of *comparative religion*. Its aim, according to Hastings, was to give an account of Religion and Ethics in all ages and in all countries of the world. Every separate religious belief and practice [e.g., theodicy, eschatology] and every separate philosophical and ethical idea or custom were to be treated in separate articles and each of them by a man who has made that particular custom or idea his special study (Hastings 1908, V, preface).

The *ERE* became an indispensable resource and, more importantly, played a critical role in shaping scholarly thinking about religion and about Christianity's place among the world's faiths.

Britain was late in producing a journal exclusively devoted to the history or comparative study of religion, but by the turn of the century a number of religious journals, normally devoted to specialized topics, took particular interest in the newer developments in the scientific study of religion. This was especially true of the *Expository Times* (1889 to present), also edited by James Hastings; the *Critical Review* (1891–1904), superseded by the *Review of Philosophy and Theology* (1905); the *Quest* (1909); the *Hibbert Journal* (1902); and the *Moslem World* (1911). Some of the older, established journals, such as the *Quarterly Review*, addressed, often with considerable vigor, the issues raised by the likes of Tylor and Frazer. However, much of the best discussion of the issues raised by the comparative study of religion appeared in the great secular journals, such as the *Nineteenth Century*, the *Contemporary Review*, and the *Fortnightly Review*.

In the 1880s and 1890s there appeared in English translation several works by eminent Continental scholars that set out the major principles and the theoretical frameworks of what was, by then, variously called the science of religion or the comparative study of religion. These books were significant for a number of reasons. First, they were a response to "a strong desire," widely felt (Chantepie de la Saussaye 1891, ix), for English translations of these scholarly works that had, in a systematic way, laid the foundations of the new science. Along with Müller's 1873 *Introduction to the Science of Religion* and the *ERE*, these works, perhaps more than any others, contributed to the acceptance in Britain of a new way of looking at religion and especially at the world's faiths in their relation to Christianity. This new perception was accompanied by a general sense that the older forms of Christian apologetic were no longer adequate. The importance of these books can be attributed in part to their illumination of the theological problematic; they represented a clear commitment to the scientific study of religion conjoined with an effort to relate this approach satisfactorily to a Christian allegiance.

The first of these scholarly handbooks was the translation of Albert Réville's (1826–1906) *Prolégomène de l'histoire des religions* in 1884. Réville was the first incumbent (1879) in the chair of the history of religions in the Collège de France. He strongly objected to the idea—still advanced in Britain—of a "primal" revelation followed by various stages of religious degeneration. The further we go back in time, when early humans approached mere animal life, Réville found it "infinitely hard to imagine that in the beginning of this slow and painful development, man, yet plunged in absolute ignorance, was in possession of sublime religious doctrines such as the most pure inspiration has been able to offer to cultivated societies, rich in accumulated experience" (Réville 1884, 40). While Réville believed—with the German theologian Friedrich Schleiermacher—that humans were *naturally* religious, he also adopted a thorough evolutionary view. However, his evolutionism was not theologically taboo for the likely reason that his elaborate developmental scheme concluded with a portrayal of Christianity as the most sublime of the universal, monotheistic faiths.

In 1887, P. D. Chantepie de la Saussaye (1848–1920), professor at Amsterdam, published the first volume of his two-volume *Lehrbuch der Religionsgeschichte*. This volume was published in London in 1891 as *Manual of the Science of Religion*, and for a time it was the indispensable handbook in English. Beyond outlining the principles of the new science, as distinct from theology, Chantepie introduced a comparative, descriptive approach that came to be called the *phenomenology of religion*. He did this by bringing together in subsections of his book distinct types of religious phenomena from the history of religions. There were, for example, sections on sacred times, places, and persons; on forms of worship from magic and divination to sacrifice and prayer; on types of religious communities, and so on. The book was the fullest individual attempt to trace types of human religious belief and behavior that were analogous to those found in Christianity.

Chantepie, like Müller, criticized the theories of Tylor, Spencer, and others, and he was able to ease the minds of Christian readers by insisting that the study of the science of religion could only enhance the understanding and appreciation of Christianity itself. Echoing Müller, he urged the theologians to begin the study of the new science, for, as he assured them, "it is certainly time that the eye which has been sharpened through a comparative study of religion, can better realize the religious idea of Christianity" itself. The history of Christianity, he insisted, "can only be rightly understood when one has studied the non-Christian religions from which Christianity borrows so much or to which it stands in sharp opposition" (Chantepie de la Saussaye 1891, 10).

In Chantepie's artless appeal there was present, of course, the very ambiguity about Christianity's uniqueness and finality that was troublesome to many believers. The book, nonetheless, was cordially received for underlining a cardinal point made by a writer for the *Critical Review*: "More than ever it is apparent that the religions of the past must be systematically studied, not regarded as merely exploded superstitions . . . but in some degree as the working, however obscurely, of the divine life in the heart of man" (Stewart 1891, 403). The *Critical Review* represented advanced thinking on matters theological and biblical, and by the 1890s this reviewer's response to Chantepie's work was widely shared by many educated believers.

It is generally acknowledged that the Dutch scholar Cornelis P. Tiele (1830–1902) shared with Müller the distinction of being called the "founder" of the new science of comparative religion. As early as 1877, J. Estlin Carpenter, a Unitarian scholar, had published an English translation of Tiele's *Outlines of the History of Religions*. Tiele's Gifford Lectures on the *Elements of the Science of Religion* (two volumes) were published in England in 1897–1898 and were also well received. Tiele was greatly respected for his meticulous scholarship, his wide knowledge, and his scrupulous impartiality. Yet, as in the case of Müller and Chantepie, the relationship between his descriptive disinterestedness and his Christian convictions did not go undetected. This is especially clear in *Elements of the Science of Religion*, and it may well explain its positive reception in Britain. Tiele set out to assure his readers that, as a man of science, he saw all religious forms as objects of investigation. It was not, he urged, his vocation to champion any one form of religion as best or the only true form. He would leave that to the apologist (Tiele 1897, 9–10). That said, Tiele nevertheless proceeded to insist that scientific impartiality and religious conviction are not incompatible. Quite the contrary, together they may facilitate special religious insight. Tiele proposed that the science of religion must be seen, then, as not superseding but, rather, as uniting all the studies that have religion as their object, including theology:

> It is an error to suppose that one cannot take up such an impartial scientific position without being a sceptic[,] . . . that a man is incapable of appreciating other forms of religion if he is warmly attached to the Church or religious community. . . . I at least, do not love the religious community to which I belong the less because I strive to appreciate, by the light of science, what is truly religious in other forms. (11)

Having defended disinterested research, Tiele proceeded to develop an elaborate scheme of progressive religious evolution in which each historical form represents a stage in religious development, essentially from the lower nature religions to the higher ethical religions, Christianity representing for Tiele the highest development of religion in its ethical and universal form. Tiele associated Christianity's superiority with its ethical conception of the Fatherhood of God and the universalism of its doctrine of reconciliation. And while he acknowledged that such a claim is a matter of faith, he immediately pulled back to insist that even from a "purely scientific and impartial position" he would hold that "the appearance of Christianity inaugurated an entirely new epoch in the development of religion . . . and that religious development will henceforth consist in an ever higher realization of the principles of that religion" (1897, 211–12).

Tiele's reference to the future development of religion no doubt conveyed to many of his Christian auditors the same equivocality regarding Christianity's absoluteness and finality that one finds in Müller and Chantepie. Earlier in his Gifford Lectures, Tiele had asked whether Christianity, the highest of the universal, ethical religions, is also "the highest conceivable." With some considerable equivocation he nonetheless insisted that from the bosom of Christianity, "which contains the eternal principles of true religion . . . *others will yet be born* which will do better and more complete justice to these principles, and which will then perhaps exhibit a somewhat different character from the religions we have termed ethical or supernaturalistic" (1897, 148–49; italics added).

All of these leaders of the new science of religion—Müller, Réville, Chantepie, Tiele—were liberal Christians. Their messages were in many respects similar and, when closely examined, their treatises include statements that are ambiguous, if not contradictory, and that very likely struck many Christian scholars as theologically dubious. Christianity, these liberal scholars insisted, was the highest development of religion, and yet other great faiths also contained profound truths wholly lost to Christianity, truths that would enrich it. Furthermore, Christianity represented for these men *the highest present form of universal, ethical monotheism*. But should we not, they appeared to ask, look to those future developments that will more fully manifest the divine mind and will? The claims of their science and their Christian faith appear in an uneasy alliance.

By the 1880s, the burden of this dual commitment was nowhere more acutely felt than in the field of biblical studies. The older doctrines of biblical inspiration and authority had separated the Bible off from every other book and had placed it in splendid but unhistorical isolation. The impact of developments in geology, in German higher criticism, in evolutionary theory, and now the new science of religion made such an isolationism impossible. The Bible, including the New Testament, was increasingly to be studied in relation to its ancient Near Eastern and Greco-Roman environments.

This shift is apparent in James Hastings's *Dictionary of the Bible* (1898), which included contributions by scholars—F. B. Jevons, A. S. Peake (1865–1929), F. C. Burkitt (1864–1935), and A. H. Sayce (1845–1933)—who supported a comparativist approach, and their articles in the *Dictionary* reflect that method. The Old Testament expert W. O. E. Oesterley (1866–1950) also appropriated the comparative approach, as is evident in his exploration of the various conceptions of *sin, saviour,* and *salvation* in his *Evolution of the Messianic Idea* (1908).

In the 1880s and 1890s in Britain there also developed a growing interest in the more benign, if esoteric, philosophical teachings of Hinduism and Buddhism in particular. While the numbers of persons who embraced one or another of the Oriental faiths remained small, the popular dissemination of information about these religions was culturally significant. This new curiosity often tended to ignore the more startling and, for Europeans, morally repulsive aspects of, for example, some popular Indian rites. Books such as Edwin Arnold's very successful *The Light of Asia* (1879) romanticized the Eastern religions. These idealizations were, in turn, frequently challenged by knowledgeable Christian scholars, such as Monier Monier-Williams, Boden Professor of Sanskrit at Oxford, who spent considerable time in India, and by Reginald S. Copleston, the bishop of Colombo, Ceylon (Monier-Williams 1890; Coplestone 1888; 1890). Yet the popularization of the Eastern religions and the dissemination of books on comparative religion raised new religious questions in the minds of the public.

The attitudes toward Christianity in its relation to other religions, and the apologetic strategies that were shaped roughly in the period 1870–1910, were many and diverse. There were, however, some that came to represent a distinct standpoint or position.

Types of Religious Response to the Science of Religion, 1870–1910

In 1909 the New Testament scholar William Sanday wrote about the new science of religion as it was affecting Christian thinking, and he suggested that theology "had still many delicate tasks remaining to be accomplished" in this field (Sanday 1909, 18). Some, of course, followed traditional ways of thinking on this urgent question. But new perspectives and theological formulations were gaining ground among increasing numbers of respected Christian clergy and scholars as well as secular writers.

Traditional Exclusivism

It is not surprising that a traditional exclusivist position continued to be defended in Britain. Its champions held that the non-Christian world faiths were either crude superstition and idolatry—a degeneration from the original divine revelation—or, at best, reflections of truths fit for a lesser stage of human civilization. It is not surprising that these biblically conservative apologists wholly rejected the position of the new *Religionsgeschichtliche*

Schule, namely, that the New Testament reflects the beginnings of a syncretistic degeneration of the primitive Christian message itself. They continued to see the Bible as the unique and essentially inerrant word of God.

Many of the British missionaries in India and the Far East were products of the Evangelical revival of the early nineteenth century, or of the later Evangelical awakening associated with the American Dwight L. Moody. Moody had been the force behind the Student Volunteer Movement, and his work had brought scores of British recruits to the mission field. Not a few of these Church of England and Nonconformist Evangelicals considered the "heathens" to be doomed unless they confessed Christ as their atoning Savior, and many saw popular Hinduism and Buddhism—with which some had years of contact—as the work of "the Evil One." Unlike the theologians back home, of course, they observed firsthand the effects of the caste system; the practice of widow burning; wild, bloody sacrifices; and the extremes of asceticism.

In late Victorian Britain there were, as well, both Evangelical and High Church Anglicans and Nonconformists who, without any firsthand knowledge, wrote apologetic treatises that continued to portray the great living world religions as false and degenerate, representing lower stages of human spiritual life. Illustrative of this position early in the era were J. R. T. Eaton's Bampton Lectures in 1872 on *The Permanence of Christianity*. After expatiating at length on the permanence and finality of Christianity, Eaton concluded that "other religions have been local, temporary, limited, fitted for definite stages of culture, partial in their hold upon particular truths. . . . They have accordingly developed tribes and nations to a fixed line and point of progress, and then their course seems stayed. They have no further message to the soul of man" (Eaton 1872, 275).

Eaton did not examine the non-Christian religions in any detail. This was not the case in John Wordsworth's (1843–1911) Bampton Lectures a decade later, entitled *The One Religion* (1881). A High Churchman and tutor of Brasenose College, Oxford, Wordsworth thought of his lectures as "a contribution to the comparative study of religion from a Christian point of view." The new knowledge of other faiths now available, and the misconceptions to which Christians were liable from only partial knowledge, prompted Wordsworth to undertake his own "fresh discussion" of the subject. The lectures describe in some detail a wide range of religions, concentrating especially on Buddhism and Islam. Wordsworth made admirable use of the researches of experts, including Müller, Monier-Williams, and T. W. Rhys Davids. He insisted that the non-Christian religions under review must "be approached with sympathy and reverence" (Wordsworth 1881, 119).

Unfortunately, Wordsworth altogether failed to carry through on his own counsel. Only the most untutored reader would not recognize immediately that Wordsworth's handling of other faiths was neither sympathetic, accurate, nor fair-minded. Assuming the exclusivity and superiority of Christianity at every point, he measured all other religions by his own Christian presuppositions, described the non-Christian religions in the most pejorative language, and painted them in their worst light. Wordsworth's discussion of sacred writings and the claims of revelation is characteristic. He acknowledged that the non-Christian religions hold their sacred scriptures in the highest esteem but that they also "treat them with a superstitious and exaggerated reverence":

> The Vedas are thought to be the eternal voice of the Divine Being. The Koran is similarly regarded as the uncreated word of God; while the Granth of the Sikhs, which no Westerner can read with patience, is actually worshipped. But how formal, how unreal, is the use of these books . . . compared, for instance, with our own use of the Psalter. (Wordsworth 1881, 119–20)

Wordsworth's treatment of the Buddha and Muhammad and their messages is disparaging, even despising. "Buddha," he wrote, "makes absurd pretensions to knowledge and virtue, and on the day of his death outbrags a rival teacher as to his successful attainment of a useless and selfish apathy" (1881, 124). As for Islam:

> God is represented as perfect power, but not as perfect goodness; as arbitrary will . . . but not as holy love. Consequently, the worship of God is almost entirely of an external character, consisting of ceremonies, formal repetitions and recitations, washings, pilgrimages, fastings, alms giving, and the like. These have a tendency . . . to become mere mechanical acts. . . . The law is not difficult to keep. . . . Further, in its ethical character Islam is a gloomy religion. It has no true heart-felt love of God. (244–46)

Wordsworth's exclusivism, which perceived Christianity as the only authentic, divine truth, standing over against degenerate "heathen" error, had other advocates among Evangelicals and High Churchmen, but it was a position that was losing favor among the educated British clergy and laity, both within the established Church and among the Nonconformists.

Christianity and the Theory of Degeneration

Not all of the conservative Christian apologists dismissed the findings of the new science of religion. Rather, they often used selective findings in the service of their Christian apologetic, especially against the Tylorian belief in the progressive evolutionary development of religion. These apologists sought to show that Tylor's doctrine ran counter to the new ethnographic evidence. This evidence was read as being in accord not only with the biblical teaching that humanity was descended from one original pair (monogenism) but also in support of their belief in a primal "monotheism." The evidence also was used to read the history of the non-Christian religions as the story of the *degeneration* of religion from God's primal revelation to his people, Israel. The theory of degeneration continued, within a limited circle, to provide a reasonable explanation for the extraordinary diversity of the world's peoples and cultures while maintaining the traditional belief in the unity of the race. Furthermore, the unity—which implied a substratum of primal knowledge—explained the presence (the "survival") of some "high" beliefs among savage peoples. To the supporters of degenerationism, the doctrine of a unilinear progressive evolution appeared to call into question the biblical anthropology that spoke of Adam's fall and original sin, as well as the drama of Christ's unique and necessary redemption.

As early as the middle decades of the nineteenth century the themes of primordial revelation, degeneration, and survivals were familiar ones in British works on Christianity and the non-Christian faiths, for example, in Charles Hardwick's *Christ and Other Masters* (1855) and later in Prime Minister W. E. Gladstone's *Juventus Mundi* (1869). Anglican canon F. C. Cook's *The Origin of Religion and Language* (1884) follows in this tradition and was written to demonstrate that the documents of Indo-Aryan and Iranian religion had a common source, a primal revelation, that reflected belief in one personal God. Cook sought to show that later religious development was one of decline and degradation. The book sparked a brief debate between the degenerationists and the Tylorians. It revealed that the theory of degeneration continued to have its advocates and that it could be reconciled with belief in evolutionary development.

The theory of degeneration was given unexpected support and a renewed credibility late in the century through Andrew Lang's *The Making of Religion*. His influence can be observed in the work of the learned Scottish theologian James Iverach (Iverach 1898). And as late as 1912, the Anglican missionary-apologist William St. Clair Tisdall, in *Christianity and Other Faiths*, continued to advance the theory of an original pure monotheism and its consequent degeneration. "Except for Israel," he asserted, "the story of religion is a melancholy story of steady progress downward" (Tisdall 1912, 44). However, developments at the end of the century in biblical scholarship and in anthropology made it increasingly difficult to support the ideas of an *original* monotheism and degeneration.

The Appropriation of the Science of Religion in the Service of Theological Reconception

The appropriation of the work of a number of the leading comparativists was paralleled by the use of the history of religions in both biblical studies and theological apologetics in the years immediately preceding and following the turn to the twentieth century.

Classicist and Anglican Modernist Percy Gardner (1846–1937) was one of a small group of scholars of Christian origins, including Edwin Hatch (1835–1889) and Kirsopp Lake (1872–1946), who embraced the work of the new history of religions school (what the Germans now called the *Religionsgeschichtliche Schule*) and the comparative method. As we have seen, in the period 1890–1910 in Britain a long and often acrimonious debate flourished over which alleged events in the New Testament and the creeds were historical and which were legendary, mythical, or symbolic. In the midst of this dispute, Percy Gardner published an article on "The Descent into Hades" in response to what he perceived as a growing consensus that belief in Christ's descent into hell was "removed from the field of historic fact to that of pious imagination." The historian's task, Gardner wished to suggest, should not end, however, with such a judgment. It now became imperative "to investigate [the account of the descent] according to the methods of anthropology and comparative religion, to search for its origin in previous beliefs, and for its relation to Jewish and Gentile mythology" (Gardner 1895, 362–63).

Gardner's proposal is instructive, for it represents one path that was taken by some Christian scholars who now embraced the scientific study of religion. It also reveals some of the unconventional theological implications of such an approach:

> The result has been the discovery of a great probability that the Christian doctrine of the Descent into Hades, together with the imagery in which the future world was presented to the early Christian imagination, was derived, neither from a Christian nor a Jewish, nor even a Hellenic source, but from the mystic lore of Dionysus and Orpheus. And however much the doctrine was Christianised, it never wholly shook off, especially among the unlearned, a certain barbarism which belongs to its origin. In this case it seems that Christianity transplanted ideas and beliefs which had already come into being before its advent. This would not, of course, be the case with all doctrines. But certainly it would be the case with many. (1895, 376)

Gardner clearly saw the Orphic teaching as a pagan "survival" and a blight upon Christianity. As we will see, theologians sympathetic to Gardner's history of religion approach called for a purging of those elements that represented Christianity's Hellenistic inheritance of metaphysics and mystery cults.

Like Gardner, Edwin Hatch, an Oxford New Testament specialist, Reader in ecclesiastical history, and a devoted parish priest, was committed to the methods pursued by the history of religions school. He likened the work of the biblical scholar to that of a geologist and evolutionist. He laid down two fundamental hermeneutical principles in his important book *The Influence of Greek Ideas and Usages on Christianity* (1889):

> 1) It is impossible to separate the religious phenomenon [of a race] from the other phenomena, in the same way that you can separate a vein of silver from the rock in which it is embedded. . . . We may concentrate our attention chiefly upon them, but they still remain part of the whole complex life of the time. . . .
>
> 2) No permanent change takes place in the religious beliefs or usages of a race which is not rooted in the existing beliefs and usages of that race. . . . A religious change is, like a physiological change, of the nature of assimilation by, and absorption into, existing elements. (Hatch 1889a, 3–4)

Christianity, Hatch sought to show, emerged out of the fertile environment of Hellenistic Judaism and especially the Greek mystery cults, their usages, and their metaphysical doctrines. "I venture to claim," he wrote,

> to have shown that a large part of what are sometimes called Christian doctrines, and many usages which have prevailed and continue to prevail in the Christian Church are in reality Greek theories and Greek usages. . . . The question which forces itself upon our attention . . . is the question of the relation of these Greek elements in Christianity to the nature of Christianity itself. Its importance can hardly be overestimated. (1889a, 350–51; see also Hatch 1889b)

Hatch's work made several claims that challenged traditional opinion. Some of these were explicit, others more implicit but, for some, equally provocative. He was plainly demonstrating that New Testament Christianity did not emerge isolated and *sui generis* but, rather, had grown and flourished by assimilating pagan elements from its environment. Christianity was, Hatch insisted, a complex "syncretistic" religion, the product of late Judaism,

Oriental eschatology, the Greek mysteries, Gnosticism, and so forth. This, again, challenged older views of Christianity's claim to uniqueness. Is historical Christianity a relativistic phenomenon in the process of development and transmutation?

Of course, Hatch was also asking whether these pagan survivals in Christianity represented the true nature of Christianity itself. His own view was that they did not, and that, on the contrary, the Christian message should be pruned of these nonessential Hellenistic beliefs in which early Christianity had become enveloped. The true kernel should be freed from its nonessential cultural husk. Here was a call for a reconception of essential Christianity that challenged long-held convictions about the nature and authority of some doctrines seemingly fixed in the New Testament texts. The question was: What was to be left of the New Testament if it were to be shorn of those features that it assimilated from late Jewish eschatology and Greek thought and culture?

Gardner's and Hatch's positions on pagan survivals and the need to free Christianity of these elements were shared by other influential historians of religion who also held liberal theological views. One was Allen Menzies (1845–1916), professor of biblical criticism at St. Andrews and author of the popular *History of Religion* (1895), a handbook that remained in print for a quarter of a century. Influenced especially by Tylor and Lang, Menzies accepted the current anthropological doctrine of survivals, and he was not loath to acknowledge the corrosive effect of survivals on historic Christianity. He believed, however, that Christianity possessed the necessary vitality to throw off these extraneous relics, "for," as he wrote, "when the forms of knowledge in which religion has clothed itself are found to be mistaken, religion has power to leave them behind and to adopt other forms" (Menzies 1895, 62).

The challenge posed by Christian scholars such as Hatch, Gardner, and Menzies might have had little effect if they had not received the increasing support of other esteemed biblical scholars who were willing to defend their methods if not all of their conclusions. Such support was given by the highly respected and moderate Old Testament scholar S. R. Driver. As early as 1886, Driver had published an essay, "The Cosmology of Genesis," in which he acknowledged the syncretistic nature of the sources of the Genesis account of creation, and that its narrative incorporated elements of Assyrian, Phoenician, and Babylonian traditions. William Sanday also was insistent that there was "really a gain from these newer views and from the habits of thought" the new scholars had brought with them (Sanday 1908, 8). The endorsement of these trusted experts was evidence of how far, in thirty years, the new methods, and even the results, of the science of religion had penetrated mainstream British theological scholarship. An unease remained, however, as to whether this new science truly was the handmaiden of a new Christian apologetic or its greatest threat. W. O. E. Oesterley, professor of Hebrew and Old Testament exegesis at Kings College, London, pointed out the ambivalence: "According to the one, Christianity is not what it claims to be because it is the lineal descendant of primitive forms of belief; according to the other, primitive forms of belief contained elements of truth because the evolution of these truths shows that they form part of the Christian faith" (Oesterley 1908, 275).

In the years between the late 1880s and 1910, theologians and churchmen representing a broad ecclesiastical spectrum were selectively appropriating the methods and the results of the history and comparative study of religions in the cause of Christian apologetics. This use of the new science was prominent in the writings of the foremost Christian apologists of the period, including W. B. Carpenter (1841–1918), the Anglican bishop of Ripon and founder of Ripon College, a center of liberal theology; Scottish philosopher Edward Caird; liberal Anglican J. R. Illingworth; and the Congregationalist A. M. Fairbairn (1838–1912), principal of Mansfield College, Oxford (W. B. Carpenter 1899, xxi; Caird 1899, 1–83; Illingworth 1889; Fairbairn 1902, ch. 6). In 1880 the Anglican Evangelical Monier Monier-Williams was already commending the comparative method as essential to the apologetic task (Monier-Williams 1887, 233). By the time of the meeting of the historic Edinburgh World Missionary Conference in 1910, there was a near consensus that denunciation of other religions had done incalculable harm to the missionary endeavor, and that (a) a sympathetic understanding of the beliefs and practices of the foreign religions and (b) the use of the methods and enduring results of the comparative approach were necessary to the success of apologetics and to missionary work abroad.

Many of the new Christian apologists were, by now, specialists in a non-Christian religion and knowledgeable about—indeed, in Britain, leaders in—the comparative study of religion. These included F. B. Jevons, Anglican principal of Hatfield College, Durham University, and author of the popular *An Introduction to the History of Religion* (1896); the Unitarian J. Estlin Carpenter, editor of four volumes in the Pali Text Society series; J. H. Moulton (1863–1917), a Wesleyan Methodist, friend of Frazer, authority on Persian Zoroastrianism, and a learned comparativist; Allan Menzies, author of the previously mentioned handbook *History of Religion* (1895); and the Indologist J. N. Farquhar (1861–1929), author of *Gita and Gospel* (1903) and the influential *The Crown of Hinduism* (1913).

A second feature characteristic of the work of these scholar-apologists, and philosophical writers such as Caird and Illingworth, was their confidence in dealing not only appreciatively but also critically with the methods and conclusions of the new science of religion. T. W. Rhys Davids, the Pali and Buddhist scholar, and C. C. Martindale, the Roman Catholic apologist, are illustrative of this group. Rhys Davids was scornful of the loose kind of comparisons, torn out of context, that characterized much of the work of Frazer and his followers. Coincidences of belief or rite, he insisted, provide no proof of direct relationship or borrowing, or of validity (Rhys Davids 1882, 2ff.). Martindale likewise scolded the professional anthropologists for their philosophically "coarse mistake" of asserting "causal connection where we see external similarity, or identity of idea where there is coincidence of phenomenon." The comparativists too often isolated this or that phenomenon, dismembering it from its historical context, whereas a religion must be taken as a living whole (Martindale 1911, I, 14–15; for similar criticisms see Fairbairn 1902, 204; Banks 1890, 4ff.; Macalister 1899; Illingworth 1889).

That said, Martindale looked positively on the remarkable evidence that Frazer had marshaled on the theme of the dying and rising god. He saw in this vast data the evidence of an archetypal human exigence and yearning, one that was to find its fulfillment in the Catholic Mass. It was Frazer, after all, who remarked that "the blow struck at Golgotha set a thousand expectant strings vibrating in unison wherever men heard the old, old story of the dying and rising god." And, as Martindale pointed out, it was the presence of the Catholic rite of the dying and rising God that facilitated the spread of Christianity (Martindale 1905, 6). Therefore, Martindale considered it useless to engage in "barren refutation" of what Christianity finds false in theories such as Frazer's, since the apologist can use the work of the comparativists "to support the very position they assail." Martindale recognized in pagan antiquity a fertile field, "full of facts, not yet caught up into the sphere of Christian apologetic" (7–8).

What the science of religion had shown is that religion is natural to humankind, universal, and enduring, and not merely a phase of human history as the rationalists had claimed. These were among the cardinal points of Carpenter's Bampton Lectures for 1899, entitled *The Permanent Elements of Religion*. Carpenter rejected the old defenses of religion based on philosophical proofs. Rather, he held, it is when one undertakes the study of the origins and growth of religion that the abiding strength and permanence of religion truly is appreciated. More than that, Carpenter was certain that the history of religions "may afford a test of fitness which may create a strong presumption in favour of or against the permanent value of one religion or another." He then spelled out those elements that humans imperatively demand of a religion and, not surprisingly, found those features most adequately developed in Christianity. Using the language of biological evolution, Carpenter concluded that Christianity possesses those "elements which are indestructible" and that it "has the power of survival in [its] capacity of adjusting [itself] to the shifting conditions of the world" (Carpenter 1899, xxii–xxv). What the comparative study of religion—pursued within an assumed evolutionary framework—made possible for the new apologetic was, according to the popular author J. A. Macculloch, the claim that Christianity can be seen as the "fulfillment" of the religious aspirations and progressive evolution of the race. Therefore, Christianity does not dismiss all other religions as false; indeed, it readily admits their genuine, if limited, contributions (Macculloch 1908, 69; see also Macculloch 1902 and 1904).

The growing recognition by anthropologists that religion is a universal phenomenon and is natural to humankind supported the classic theological claim that God did not leave himself without a witness in his creation. The new apologists thus repeatedly cited the teaching of the Alexandrian church fathers whose central theme had been the immanence of the Divine Logos within both nature and human history. This theme became the central motif in the writings of Anglican and Roman Catholic apologists of the period. It is summarized in the words of the Jesuit theologian George Tyrrell in his review of Andrew Lang's *The Making of Religion*, where he argued that comparative religion serves the cause of Christianity by "bringing out the unity of type" between the natural, ethnic religions and Catholicism (Tyrrell 1898, 363). However, this theme was also prominent in the work of the Congregationalist A. M. Fairbairn, the Methodist J. H. Moulton, and the Evangelical Scot J. N. Farquhar. Since religion is natural to the race, it is not surprising that the non-Christian religions reveal ideas, rites, and beliefs analogous to those found in Christianity. Illingworth's statement of the point is representative:

> The history of the pre-Christian religions is like that of pre-Christian philosophy, a long preparation for the Gospel. . . . And from this point of view the many pagan adumbrations of Christian doctrine, similarities of practice, coincidences of ritual, fall naturally into place. . . . In the present day they are capable of disturbing minds, when unexpectedly presented before them. But all this is unphilosophical, for in the light of evolution the occurrence of such analogies is a thing to be expected; while to the eye of faith they do but emphasize the claim of Christianity to be universal, by showing that it contains in spiritual summary the religious thoughts and practices and ways of prayer and worship, not of one people only, but of all the races of men. (Illingworth 1904, 151)

The science of religion not only confirmed the unity of the race and religion as a natural, universal dimension of human life; it also established the progressive, evolutionary development of religion. The latter greatly appealed to the new generation of Christian apologists, especially to those with more progressive theological leanings. What they found in the rational developmentalism of Tylor and Frazer was support for their own understanding of a progressive revelation and for viewing Christianity as the fulfillment of the developmental process. J. W. Burrow has called attention to how these Victorian theories of social evolution were able to provide "a way of being both relativist and not relativist; of admitting that many diverse modes of organizing and interpreting social life might have something to be said for them ... while continuing to maintain the absolute validity of one such mode" (Burrow 1966, 263). Burrow is referring to the Comtean positivism of Tylor and Spencer, but his point can be applied as well to the Christian thinkers who conjoined the idea of evolutionary development with the Logos theology of the Greek fathers.

The theologians of the era used a variety of images to convey the idea of a teleological development. J. Estlin Carpenter perceived the religions as parts of a vast cathedral. "Yet, as you climb from crypt to pinnacle and spire, you find that the builders have builded more wisely than they knew. Even the plan that was outgrown pointed the way to a nobler work" (J. E. Carpenter 1890, 37). More often the imagery was taken from biological science. Albert Réville, in his popular handbook, spoke of *the principle of development* "in virtue of which everything begins in the form of a germ, of rudiments full of promise and of marvelous ductility, but as yet very incomplete" (Réville 1884, 65). J. A. Macculloch, in his *Comparative Theology*, employed an analogy from comparative anatomy: The human body is kin with the animal creation, yet it "is still the noblest work of God ... so near and so like the animals around him, yet far removed from them and very unlike them." In like manner, Christianity shares a kinship with other religions and yet remains a distinct and unique development (Macculloch 1902, 10–11; see also Menzies 1895, and Jevons 1896 and 1906).

These ideas received their most sophisticated philosophical defense in Edward Caird's neo-Hegelian Gifford Lectures in 1890–1891 and 1891–1892 on *The Evolution of Religion*. Caird proposed that the "guiding principle" informing the new science of religion is the idea of the unity of man "as manifesting itself in an organic process of development" (Caird 1899, 21). The multifarious historical expressions of religion are to be seen, then, as "correlated phases of one life," and in their historical succession they "can be shown to be the necessary stages of one process of evolution" (25). The "germination principle" of the entire religious progression is not to be found, however, in each early stage of religion taken separately but, rather, in the transitions whereby one religion develops out of another and, more especially, in the final form of religion. This mature form enables "us to cast the light of the present upon the past, and to explain man's first uncertain efforts to name and realize the divine." According to Caird, the history of religions is "just religion *progressively defining itself*," its essence or truth only fully manifest in its most mature form (47).

Caird judged Christianity to be that final or "absolute" religion, since its essence is the idea of a divine incarnation and progressive divine immanence in the world. In Christianity, God is known neither as external object nor as pure subjective consciousness but as the unitary ground of the object (the not-self) and the subject (or self). In the development of the idea of God to its absolute expression in Christianity one can discern, then, "a direction of progress from multiplicity to unity, from the natural to the spiritual, from the particular to the universal" (1899, 62).

J. R. Illingworth was as certain as was Caird that the science of religion had reached some established results that were in perfect harmony with Christian belief. Beyond confirming the natural universality of religion, the new science had shown that there is a progressive tendency observable in the religions of the world. For Illingworth, however, religious progress is far from uniform or constant. It is always threatened by degeneracy:

> Individuals elevate, masses degrade religion. There is no progress by insensible modifications. . . . What is needed is a Buddha or Zarathustra to create. And so religion is handed on, from one great teacher to another, never rising above the level of its founder or last reformer, till another founder or reformer comes; while in the interval it is materialized, vulgarized, degraded. (Illingworth 1904, 149)

Illingworth spoke of the pre-Christian religions as partial revelations, grasping only one or another aspect or truth of the religious consciousness. They thus need completion or fulfillment. Illingworth too found in the doctrine of the incarnation of the Divine Logos Christianity's answer and distinct claim. In Illingworth's estimation, neither Islam nor Buddhism—to his mind the only living competitors of Christianity—is able to satisfactorily unite the tendencies of theism and pantheism, or divine transcendence and immanence.

With this new reconception of the ancient argument for Christianity's fulfillment of the non-Christian religions, the late Victorian apologists were putting the argument of popular critics of Christianity such as Edward Clodd or J. M. Robertson on its head. These apologists were insisting that the coincidence of Christianity with pagan religions—so thoroughly demonstrated by the most recent anthropological and classical scholarship—also showed the universality and truth of Christianity as answering to, purifying, heightening, and making permanent the diverse hopes and longings of the race. Christianity proves itself, they argued, not by being absolutely different from, nor even vastly superior to, the non-Christian religions; rather, its truth lies in confirming their deepest sentiments and beliefs. Consummation, not displacement, became the prevailing term.

The reconceived theme of fulfillment achieved its most thorough and influential treatment in J. N. Farquhar's *The Crown of Hinduism* (1913). While conservative Evangelical missionaries never were to accept the concept of fulfillment and its evolutionary implications, Farquhar's idea achieved something close to a normative status in liberal missionary thinking for a quarter of a century or longer. Farquhar had used the concept of fulfillment for years prior to the publication of *The Crown of Hinduism*, but that book was the most thorough comparison of the main features of Hinduism (the caste system, the family, karma, Vedanta, etc.) with Christian teaching. What Farquhar meant by fulfillment is, perhaps, most succinctly stated in a report he made to the conference of the World Student Christian Federation at Oxford in 1909:

> The method I refer to . . . consists in setting forth Christianity as the fulfilment of all that is aimed at in Hinduism, as the satisfaction of the spiritual yearnings of her people, as the crown and climax of the crudest forms of her worship as well as those lofty spiritual movements which have often appeared in Hinduism but have always ended in weakness. . . . [The method] sets forth every part of Hinduism as springing from some real religious instinct and having a value of its own. . . . Yet it sets Christ as supreme over all, and proclaims Him to be the consummator of religion. The theory thus satisfies the science of religion to the uttermost, while conserving the supremacy of Christ. (Farquhar 1909a, 72)

While Farquhar's "fulfillment" meant the replacement of the "lower" by the "higher," it also implied the increasingly shared conviction that genuine truths exist in the non-Christian religions. There is, nevertheless, an ambiguity in Farquhar's idea that Christianity brings to fruition already existing truths. It is present, for example, in the following statement: "Hinduism must die into Christianity, in order that the best her philosophers, saints, and ascetics have longed and prayed for may live" (Farquhar 1909b, 824;

on Farquhar, see Sharpe 1965). Other Christian thinkers—particularly *some* Anglican Modernists—were soon to take the idea of fulfillment further. They were to suggest a form of eclectic sharing of truths or to propose a genuine pluralism of religions.

Christianity and Religious Pluralism

Progressive theologians and clergy represented a significant voice in British religious life in the early years of the twentieth century. Among these progressives were Anglican Modernists whose forum later became the *Modern Churchman* (first published in 1912). Generally, they welcomed the results of the science of religion as illustrating and confirming important truths of Christianity. However, they often went further. This is evident in A. R. Lilley's (1860–1948) characterization of the Modernist position on other faiths. Lilley was the Anglican vicar of St. Mary's, Paddington Green, London, and later archdeacon of Ludlow. He was sympathetic to Roman Catholic modernism. "The Modernists," he wrote in 1908, "see in these alien religions yet other revelations of God. . . . But they see in them also the same revelation, the same power of God working through so many different types of racial character, the Eternal Word dispensing His Light wherever light is found" (Lilley 1908, 17).

For many of the Modernists, the notion of Christianity's "absoluteness" needed to be rethought since, as the Anglican Modernist H. D. A. Major (1871–1961) suggested, we no longer "have the facilities that we once thought we had for . . . the demonstration of absolute truth in this domain" (Major 1909, 5–6). Major has rightly been called the "apostle" of English Modernism. For him, and many Modernists, the practical question in religion was "not whether such and such a religious idea seems to be or can be demonstrated as absolutely true, but whether it seems to be the truest of its rivals and above all what is its real value in life" (32). In Major's judgment the best current theological teaching was in accord with the science of religion on a number of points about which, a short time before, there had been very sharp differences. Among these agreements was the conviction that there "no longer was support for the distinction made between *natural* and *revealed* religion" (33). According to Major and other Modernists, each religion is true and has served a useful purpose in human evolution. It is false, however, if it remains when that stage of evolution is past. "It is then in the true sense . . . a survival of a lower form of religion which has been or should be superseded by a higher." Major and many of his Modernist colleagues agreed with Edwin Hatch and Percy Gardner that not only the pagan religions but Christianity itself contained "survivals" that were "liable to prove a constant menace to the life of religion" (37).

While each religion is in one sense unique, all religions are manifestations in different ways of the same Spirit. The genus religion includes many species. Perhaps the most radical idea subscribed to by many liberal and Modernist theologians and clergy was one that was also central to the *Religionsgeschichtliche Schule* and systematized by the German theologian Ernst Troeltsch (1865–1923), whose writings were becoming known in Britain. Troeltsch held that all religions, including Christianity, are indissolubly connected with their cultural environment and that one's religion is largely shaped by forces that lie beyond the group religion to either control or direct. A religion's normativity, essence, and "truth" cannot be derived by appeal to isolated events or beliefs but by the religion's "historical totality." While Christianity must be entirely open to and compared with the non-Christian religions, this does not lead to a complete value relativism. Among the many religious worldviews, Troeltsch—as well as many Modernists—saw only "a few great orientations." He saw two powerfully different options, the personal and the impersonal. He wrote, "It is necessary to make a choice between redemption through meditation on Transcendent Being or non-Being and redemption through faithful trusting participation in the person-like character of God, the ground of all life. . . . This is a choice that depends on religious conviction, not scientific demonstration" (Troeltsch 1971, 112). Troeltsch and the Anglican Modernists saw greater profundity in the Christian personalistic religion. However, another crucial test of a religious "truth," both agreed, is its ability to adapt itself to environmental change. Most Modernist churchmen were convinced, with their more orthodox brethren, that Christianity did possess the truth and the power to pass these tests.

Some British missionary-apologists went beyond their Modernist colleagues at home and embraced a thoroughgoing pluralism and even syncretism, although their numbers were not large. The influential British missionary C. F. Andrews, of the Cambridge Mission to Delhi, insisted that there is an "experience of Christ-life outside the Church of the baptized," and came to reject all Christian proselytism (Andrews 1909, 3). K. J. Saunders, a Church Missionary Society missionary in Ceylon and an expert on Buddhism, perceived little difference, if any, between Buddhism and Christianity. In Buddhism he saw "very much of the spirit of Christ" and considered Buddhism God's gift to Asia. When asked in what did Christianity's originality and finality consist, he answered that it was not to be found in the originality of its teachings, for "Gotama and Laotze taught a very Christ-like gospel . . . six centuries before Christ." Saunders believed that the uniqueness of Christianity lay, rather, in the historic fact that it "sums up and gives perfect and poignant expression to processes that are operative everywhere, and to truths that are eternal. . . . Christianity is *final*, because these truths, as we discover more and more, are the very warp and woof of our universe" (Saunders 1922, 187).

While Saunders was part of a small minority of the missionary apologists whose views were criticized, even repudiated, by other liberal missionaries, what was shared—outside the circle of an older evangelical orthodoxy—was an appeal to Christianity on the grounds of an experimental or experiential test. This had become the bedrock of most authoritative claims regarding Christianity's truth and finality: its ability to take into itself and to sum up the spiritual needs and aspirations of diverse races and to adapt itself to humanity's growing knowledge and experience. Higher criticism and the science of religion had made dubious the older claims to authority and finality, for example, the proof from miracles, appeals to an inerrant Bible, or exclusivist claims for a special revelation. The tests were intrinsic worth, staying power, and achievement.

The theme of Christianity's proven fitness was not, however, distinctive only of liberal and modernist apologetic. It is the crux of Bishop B. F. Westcott's *The Gospel of Life* (1892), an influential book in which Westcott compared Christianity to other faiths. "The ultimate criterion, the adequate verification, of Revelation to man," Westcott argued, "lies in its proved fitness for furthering, and at last for accomplishing his destiny." It is that religion, he continued,

> which has this fitness in its highest conceivable degree universally from its very nature; that which is shewn to be most capable of aiding us in our endeavour to attain to the highest ideal of knowledge, feeling, action, under every variety of circumstance, that is the view which corresponds most completely with our nature . . . which must be the absolute interpretation of the Divine will for man. (Westcott 1892, 304–5)

Westcott was convinced that Christianity most perfectly fit this character.

In 1908, at the end of our period, the eminent biblical scholar Samuel R. Driver was invited to preach a sermon before the meeting of the Third Congress of the History of Religions. Driver's theme and conclusion are a reiteration of what, by now, had become a rather standard theme: Christianity welcomes the scientific, comparative study of religion; those features that best reveal humanity's religious life are features that it shares with Christianity, and they are the key witness to the truth of Christianity itself. Those universally shared spiritual instincts are, Driver told the Congress, "rooted in human nature and have a real claim to be satisfied." It is the science of religion, he concluded, that "has thus created a strong presumption that the religion which satisfies them most completely is the highest and the truest" (Driver 1908, 41).

By 1910 a significant number of prominent Christian scholars and theologians were not only open to but also knowledgeable about the methods and the results of the new scientific study of religion, and many found them useful in their own research and writing. At the same time, it was also clear that these scholars were well aware of the limitations and the questionable claims in the work of scholars such as Tylor, Frazer, and even Smith. Nonetheless, the genuine insights and results of this new social-scientific examination of religion were now broadly approved. For example, many respected biblical scholars now included the best of this work in their own repertoire of tools. Many of these same scholars did, however, also remain confident about their ability to show that Christianity summed up and fulfilled the spiritual needs of the world's diverse human family.

Christian scholars and theologians following World War I were not as sanguine. A number of factors contributed to this changed climate that called into question many of the late Victorian assumptions. First, the new century saw a rising tide of resurgent nationalism and xenophobia in India, the Far East, and Africa—a development that was closely tied to religious renewal in these cultures. Now the claims for Christianity's fulfillment of humanity's religious aspirations would encounter more resistance, if not hostility. Second, the war had profoundly challenged belief in a spiritual progress of humanity and its institutions. The division of religions into "higher" and "lower" was exploded when it was shown how deeply it reflected Western assumptions. The very concept of "fulfillment" now was regarded by many as pretentious and patronizing of other faiths. Third, the chastened postwar culture was fertile soil for a critique of liberal theology in general.

The new religious challenges on the Continent after 1918 were existentialism and neo-orthodox theology, led by the Swiss-German theologian Karl Barth (1886–1968) and reflecting the influence of the newly rediscovered Danish philosopher Søren Kierkegaard (1813–1855). While the impact of such thinkers on British religion and theology was significant at the time, it was by no means dominant. The great and abiding importance of the continental neo-orthodox or dialectical theology for British theology was its critique of an optimistic modernity and the dangers of an easy, knee-jerk accommodation of historical Christianity to prevailing but all too often unstable cultural and intellectual vogues. However, in their often sweeping denunciations of the so-called rationalism, scientism, and optimism of the eighteenth and nineteenth centuries, the dialectical theologians and the influential existentialist writers too often simply failed to pursue seriously an engagement with the compelling questions posed by developments in twentieth-century science, philosophy, and historical studies. Often these developments addressed issues central to Christian theological traditions and belief. It has been said, correctly, I believe, that British theology, during the decades (1920–1950) when existentialism and neo-orthodoxy flourished, maintained a more truly dialectical relationship with the important challenges posed by the new knowledge emerging in a wide range of the sciences and in biblical and historical scholarship. This became even more evident in the latter half of the twentieth century, which saw a renewed encounter between British theology and developments in the natural sciences, historical work, and the comparative study of the world religions. The real achievements of theology during the late Victorian era, while corrected as necessary, were not, on the whole, rejected but rather were recognized as critical landmarks in the challenging new contexts of the twentieth century.

Some Concluding Remarks

In 1912 a group of young Oxford friends published a volume of essays entitled *Foundations*. What the authors claimed to share was the fact that they were "modern," not "Victorian," for they had not been shaped by the religious presuppositions of the precritical times before the 1860s. The foundations of those "Victorian" religious assumptions were, they believed, largely discredited. The time had now arrived, as editor B. H. Streeter proposed, when a new generation of religious thinkers "should set themselves to a careful reexamination and, if need be, re-statement of the foundations of their belief in the light of the knowledge and thought of the day" (Streeter 1912, vii). If the evidence marshaled in the chapters of this book is convincing, that work of reexamination and restatement had begun and was carried out during the fifty years prior to the appearance of *Foundations*. This is not to say, of course, that questions posed in 1912 did not require exploration in view of this new context. Rather, as this study has sought to demonstrate, many of the crucial issues concerning biblical and creedal interpretation and authority, the achievements of science and especially of Darwinian evolution, and the questions posed by the emerging social sciences and their implications for traditional religious anthropology and for the special claims of Christianity resulted in significant reconceptions of doctrine and belief, especially in the years 1880–1910.

The period was, then, a time of openness, exploration, and resistance to purely dogmatic solutions, whether theological or scientific. Anthropologists, psychologists, and philosophers, such as R. R. Marett, James Ward, and William James, were now opening up new spiritual interpretations of the world. There also was a flowering of new religious surrogates for traditional belief, seen, for example, in the popularity of psychical research and Eastern philosophy and in the search for spiritual resources in the literary imagination itself. But while these did not prove long-lived in Britain, the theological developments of the period remained vital and enduring in their influence on later British theology.

Some have insisted that the reign of Edward VII (1901–1910) represents a decisive ending of an era and the beginning of what we now call Modernism, an ethos and a sensibility considered sharply antagonistic to everything "Victorian." In the fields of art and literature, such a momentous transition may well have taken place. Roger Fry's 1910 London exhibition "Monet and the Post-Impressionists" may represent a break with the artistic past. But literary and artistic Modernism did not emerge from the same intellectual or cultural sources as did theological and religious modernism. And their identification has proved to be the source of confusion in recent discussions of religion. Aesthetic modernism represents, in Lionel Trilling's words, "a bitter line of hostility toward civilization," a sense of alienation, despair, and the radical negation and breaking up of traditional forms. What can be called theological modernism represented, on the contrary, an ever renewed effort to reconcile the religious tradition of the past with the modern critical spirit and the advances in science and philosophy. It was not a wholesale disenchantment with the past but, rather, a holding of the past religious tradition and modern criticism in dialectical tension. In Britain in the late Victorian decades it was characterized by a genuine openness to the most revolutionary advances in the sciences and critical historical scholarship; a growing recognition of religious pluralism and its implications, without yielding to an easy relativism; an agnostic temper of mind, without embracing agnosticism; a repudiation of an older natural theology and biblical "evidence" while, at the same time, resisting the claims of an often-combative scientific naturalism. It seldom wholly repudiated belief in the unity of truth. The balance and tension of this effort at reconciliation was not, of course, always maintained, though generally it was the guiding ideal. It is expressed in Matthew Arnold's comments about Dean Arthur Stanley, "who, shuttering his mind against no ideas brought by the spirit of his time, sets these ideas, in the sphere of the religious life, in their right prominence . . . and who, under pressure of new thoughts keeps the centre of the religious life where it should be" (Arnold 1968, 69–70).

In the sphere of religious thought, the late Victorian writers here studied set an agenda of issues that were to remain at the center of British theological discussion through most of the twentieth century. While the late Victorian writers did not resolve these questions, they nonetheless recognized what they were, they asked the right questions, and they boldly charted the way. Many of our religious questions remain those first wrestled with in the latter decades of the nineteenth century. This remains a significant accomplishment and a challenging legacy.

References

Abbott, E., and L. Campbell. 1897. *The Life and Letters of Benjamin Jowett*. London.

Abbott, E. A. 1906. *Silanus the Christian*. London.

Andrews, C. F. 1909. "A Missionary's Experience." In *India Interpretation*.

Annan, N. 1951. *Leslie Stephen*. London.

Anon. 1863. "Lyell on the Geological Evidence of the Antiquity of Man." *Anthropological Review* 1.

Argyll, the Duke of. 1867. *The Reign of Law*. London.

———. 1887. *The Unity of Nature*. New York.

———. 1896. *The Philosophy of Belief, or Law in Christian Theology*. London.

Arnold, M. 1968. "Dr. Stanley's Lectures on the Jewish Church." In vol. 3 of *Complete Prose Works of Matthew Arnold*. Ann Arbor.

———. 1970. "Review of Objections of 'Literature and Dogma.'" In vol. 7 of *Complete Prose Works of Matthew Arnold*. Ann Arbor.

Avis, Paul 1988. *Gore: Construction and Conflict*. Worthing, UK.

Babbage, A. 1837. *Ninth Bridgewater Treatise*. Cambridge.

Bain, A. 1868. *Mental and Moral Science*. London.

Balfour, A. 1879. *A Defence of Philosophic Doubt*. London.

———. 1895. *The Foundations of Belief*. London.

———. 1905. *Essays and Addresses*. Edinburgh.

———. 1909. *Papers Read before the Synthetic Society 1896–1908*. Privately printed.

Banks, J. S. 1890. *Christianity and the Science of Religion*. London.

Bartholomew, M., 1973. "Lyell and Evolution: An Account of the Response to the Prospect of an Evolutionary Ancestry of Man." *British Journal for the History of Science* 6.

Beidelman, T. O. 1974. *W. Robertson Smith and the Sociological Study of Religion*. Chicago.

Bowler, P. 1977. "Darwinism and the Argument from Design: Suggestions for a Reevaluation." *Journal of the History of Biology* 10.

———. 1983. *The Eclipse of Darwinism*. Baltimore.

———. 1988. *The Non-Darwinian Revolution*. Baltimore.

Brooke, J. H. 1977. "Natural Theology and the Plurality of Worlds: Observations on the Brewster-Whewell Debate." *Annals of Science* 34.

———. 1979. "The Natural Theology of the Geologists: Some Theological Strata." In *Images of the Earth*. Edited by L. J. Jordanova and R. S. Porter. Chalfont St. Giles.

———. 1985. "The Relations between Darwin's Science and His Religion." In *Darwinism and Divinity*. Edited by J. Durant. Oxford.

———. 1989a. "Science and the Fortunes of Natural Theology." *Zygon* 24.

———. 1989b. "Scientific Thought and Its Meaning for Religion: The Impact of French Science on British Natural Theology, 1827–1859." *Revue de Synthèse* 4.

———. 1991. *Science and Religion: Some Historical Perspectives*. Cambridge.

———. 1994. "Between Science and Theology: The Defence of Teleology in the Interpretation of Nature." *Journal of the History of Modern Theology* 1.

Brougham, H. 1839. *Dissertations on Subjects of Science concerned with Natural Theology: Being the Concluding Volumes of the New Edition of Paley's Works*. London.

Brown, F. B. 1986. "The Evolution of Darwin's Theism." *Journal of the History of Biology* 19.

Buckland, W. 1820. *Vindiciae Geologicae*. Oxford.

———. 1836. *Geology and Mineralogy Considered with Reference to Natural Theology*. Vol. 1. London.

Budd, S. 1977. *Varieties of Unbelief: Atheists and Agnostics in English Society 1850–1960*. London.

Burrow, J. W. 1966. *Evolution and Society: A Study in Victorian Social Theory*. Cambridge.

Bynum, W. 1974. *Time's Noblest Offspring: The Problem of Man in the British Natural Historical Sciences*. PhD diss., Cambridge University.

Caird, E. 1899. *The Evolution of Religion*. Vol. 1. 3rd ed. Glasgow.

Calderwood, H. 1871. "The Present Relationship of Physical Science to Mental Philosophy." *Contemporary Review* 16 (January).

———. 1893. *Evolution and Man's Place in Nature*. London.

Cannon, W. 1960. "The Problem of Miracles in the 1830s." *Victorian Studies* 4.

———. 1961. "The Basis of Darwin's Achievement." *Victorian Studies* 5.

———. 1978. *Science in Culture: The Early Victorian Period*. Cambridge.

Carpenter, J. E. 1890. *The Place of the History of Religion in Theological Study*. Oxford.

———. 1905. *James Martineau, Theologian and Teacher*. London.

Carpenter, W. B. 1852. "On the Relation of Mind and Matter." *British and Foreign Medico-Chirugical Review* 10.

———. 1876. "On the Fallacies of Testimony in Religion to the Supernatural." *Contemporary Review* 27 (January).

———. 1888. *Nature and Man: Essays Scientific and Philosophical*. London.

———. 1899. *The Permanent Elements of Religion*. London.

Carré, M. H. 1949. *Phases of Thought in England*. Oxford.

Chadwick, O. 1966. *The Victorian Church*. Vol. 1. London.

———. 1967. *The Mind of the Oxford Movement*. Stanford, CA.

———. 1970. *The Victorian Church*. Vol. 2. London.

Chambers, R. 1844. *Vestiges of the Natural History of Creation*. London.

Chantepie de la Saussaye, P. D. 1891. *Manual of the Science of Religion*. London.

Chaudhuri, N. C. 1974. *Scholar Extraordinary: The Life of Professor the Rt. Hon. Friedrich Max Müller, P.C.* New York.

Chronicle of Convocation. 1914. London.

Church, R. W. 1880. *The Gifts of Civilization*. London.

———. 1891. *The Oxford Movement: Twelve Years 1833–1845*. London.

Clarke, J. 1734. *A Further Examination of Dr. Clarke's Notions of Space*. London.

Clifford, W. K. 1874. "Body and Mind." *Fortnightly Review*, ns, 16 (December).

———. 1877. "The Ethics of Belief." *Contemporary Review* 29.

Clodd, E. 1875. *The Childhood of Religion*. London.

Colenso, J. W. 1862/1963. *The Pentateuch and the Book of Joshua Critically Examined*. Repr. New York.

Conybeare, W. D. 1834. *Christian Observer*. London.

Conybeare, W. J. 1853. "Church Parties, Past and Present." *Edinburgh Review* 98.

Cooter, R. 1984. *The Cultural Meaning of Popular Science: Phrenology and the Organization of Consent in Nineteenth Century Britain*. Cambridge.

Copleston, R. 1888. "Buddhism." *Nineteenth Century* 24 (July).

———. 1890. "Buddhism." *Quarterly Review* 170 (April).

Cox, G. W. 1870. *The Mythology of the Aryan Nations*. Vol. 1. London.

Crawley, A. E. 1908. *The Tree of Life*. London.

Cronin, H. 1991. *The Ant and the Peacock*. Cambridge.

Curteis, G. 1885. *The Scientific Obstacles to Christian Belief.* London.

Dalgairns, J. B. 1871. "On the Theory of the Human Soul." *Contemporary Review* 16 (December).

Darwin, C. 1859. *On the Origin of Species by Means of Natural Selection, or the Preservation of Favored Species in the Struggle for Life.* London.

———. 1871. *The Descent of Man.* 2 vols. London.

———. 1874. *The Descent of Man.* 2 vols. 2nd rev. London.

———. 1886. *The Descent of Man.* 2nd ed. New York.

———. 1917. *The Origin of Species.* 6th ed. London.

———. 1952. "Sketch." In *Evolution by Natural Selection.* Edited by G. De Beer. Cambridge.

———. 1969. *The Autobiography of Charles Darwin.* Edited by N. Barlow. London.

Darwin, F. 1887. *The Life and Letters of Charles Darwin.* Vol. 2. London.

Daston, L. J. 1982. "The Theory of the Will versus the Science of Mind." In *The Problematic Sciences: Psychology in the Nineteenth Century.* Edited by W. Woodward and M. Ash. New York.

Davies, J. L. 1879. "Belief in Christ: Its Relation to Miracles and Evolution." *Contemporary Review* 34 (March).

Dawson, W. J. 1892. *Christian World,* 31 (March).

De Beer, G. R. 1952. "Sketch." In *Evolution by Natural Selection.* Cambridge.

———. 1960. "Darwin's Notebooks on Transmutation of Species." *Bulletin of the British Museum,* Natural History, Series 2.

De Guistino, D. 1975. *Conquest of Mind: Phrenology and Victorian Social Thought.* London.

Desmond, A. 1989. *The Politics of Evolution: Morphology, Medicine, and Reform in Radical London.* Chicago.

Desmond, A., and J. Moore 1991. *Darwin.* London.

Dorson, R. 1968. *The British Folklorists.* Chicago.

Driver, S. R. 1905. *The Book of Genesis.* Oxford.

———. 1908. *Christianity and Other Religions.* London.

Drummond, H. 1884. *Natural Law in the Spiritual World.* London.

———. 1886. *Natural Law in the Spiritual World.* New York.

———. 1894. *The Ascent of Man.* London.

Duncan, D. 1911. *Life and Letters of Herbert Spencer.* London.

Durant, J. 1977. *The Meaning of Evolution: Post-Darwinian Debate on the Significance for Man of the Theory of Evolution.* PhD diss., Cambridge University.

———. 1985. "The Ascent of Nature in Darwin's *Descent of Man.*" In *The Darwinian Heritage.* Edited by D. Kohn. Princeton.

Eaton, J. R. T. 1872. *The Permanence of Christianity*. London.

Eliot, G. 1865. "The Influence of Rationalism." *Fortnightly Review* 1.

Ellegard, A. 1958. *Darwin and the General Reader: The Reception of Darwin's Theory of Evolution in the British Periodical Press, 1859–1872*. Gothenburg, Sweden.

Ellis, I. 1980. *Seven against Christ: A Study of Essays and Reviews*. Leiden.

Evans, J. 1859. "On the Occurrence of Flint Implements in Undisturbed Beds of Granite, Sands, and Clay." *Archaeologia* 38.

Fairbairn, A. M. 1893. *The Place of Christ in Modern Theology*. London.

———. 1902. *The Philosophy of the Christian Religion*. London.

Farquhar, J. N. 1909a. *Report of the Conference of the World's Student Christian Federation Held at Oxford*. Oxford.

———. 1909b. "Brahma Samaj." In vol. 2 of *The Encyclopedia of Religion and Ethics*. Edinburgh.

Fleming, J. 1822. *Philosophy of Zoology*. Edinburgh.

Forbes, G. H. 1861. *Some Remarks on the Essay of the Late Rev. Baden Powell, on "The Study of the Evidences of Christianity."* Oxford.

Forsyth, P. T. 1909. *The Person and Place of Jesus Christ*. London.

Frazer, J. G. 1894. "William Robertson Smith." *Fortnightly Review*, ns, 55 (June).

———. 1911. *The Golden Bough*. Vol. 5. 3rd ed. London.

———. 1913. *The Belief in Immortality*. Vol. 1. 3rd ed. London.

———. 1927. *Man, God, and Immortality*. London.

Freud, S. 1928. *The Future of an Illusion*. Translated by D. Robson-Scott. New York.

G. A. C. 1912–1921. *Dictionary of National Biography*. Oxford.

Gardner, P. 1895. "The Descent into Hades." *Contemporary Review* 67 (March).

Gaster, M. 1901. "The Golden Bough." *Folk-Lore* 12.

Gauld, A. 1968. *The Founders of Psychical Research*. London.

Gillespie, N. C. 1979. *Charles Darwin and the Problem of Creation*. Chicago.

Gladstone, W. E. 1869. *Juventus Mundi*. London.

Gomme, G. L. 1901. "The Golden Bough." *Folk-Lore* 12.

Gore, C., ed. 1887. *The Clergy and the Creeds*. London.

———. 1889. *Lux Mundi*. London.

———. 1890a. "The Holy Spirit and Inspiration." In *Lux Mundi*. 2nd ed. London.

———. 1890b. "On the Christian Doctrine of Sin." In *Lux Mundi*. 2nd ed. London.

———. 1895. *Dissertations*. London.

——. 1900. *The Epistle to the Romans*. Vol. 2. London.

——. 1904. "The Holy Spirit and Inspiration." In *Lux Mundi*. 15th ed. London.

——. 1905. *The Permanent Creed and the Christian Idea of Sin*. London.

——. 1912. "Christianity and Miracles." In *Report of the Church Congress, Middlesbrough*. London.

Green, T. H. 1883. *Prolegomena to Ethics*. Edited by A.C. Bradley. Oxford.

Greene, J. C. 1959. *The Death of Adam*. Ames, IA.

——. 1981. *Science, Ideology, and World View*. Berkeley, CA.

Gregory, F. 1992. *Nature Lost: Natural Science and the German Theological Traditions of the Nineteenth Century*. Cambridge, MA.

Griffith-Jones, E. 1899. *A Study of the Doctrine of Redemption in the Light of the Theory of Evolution*. London.

Grove, W. R. 1867. *The Correlation of Physical Forces, Followed by a Discourse on Continuity*. London.

Gruber, H. E., and P. H. Barrett. 1974. *Darwin on Man: A Psychological Study of Scientific Creativity*. New York.

Gruber, J. W. 1960. *A Conscience in Conflict: The Life of St. George Jackson Mivart*. New York.

——. 1965. "Brixham Cave and the Antiquity of Man." In *Context and Meaning in Cultural Anthropology*. Edited by Melford E. Spiro. New York.

Hamilton, W. 1852. "On the Philosophy of the Unconditioned." In *Discussions on Philosophy and Literature, Education and University Reform*. Edinburgh.

Hansard. 1840. *Parliamentary Debates*. London

Hare, J. C. Letter in Bodleian Library MS Eng. Lett. E86, f104.

Harper, G. H. 1933. *Cardinal Newman and William Froude*. Baltimore.

Hartland, E. S. 1913. "The Debt of Free Thought to Anthropology." In *The Rationalist Press Association Annual*. London.

Harvey, V. 1985. "The Ethics of Belief Reconsidered." In *The Ethics of Belief Debate*. Edited by G. D. McCarthy. Atlanta.

Hastings, J. 1908. "Preface." *Encyclopedia of Religion and Ethics* 1. Edinburgh.

Hatch, E. 1889a. *The Influence of Greek Ideas and Usages on the Christian Church*. London.

——. 1889b. "From Metaphysics to History." *Contemporary Review* 55.

Hensen, H. H. 1912. *The Creed in the Pulpit*. London.

Herschel, J. 1836. Letter to Charles Lyell, 20 February, Lyell Collection, American Philosophical Collection Library, Philadelphia.

Hodge, M. J. S. 1991. "The History of the Earth, Life, and Man: Whewell and Palaetiological Science." In *William Whewell: A Composite Portrait*. Edited by M. Fisch and S. Schaffer. Oxford.

Hügel, Baron F. von. 1931. *The Reality of God, and Religion and Agnosticism.* Edited by Edmund G. Gardner. London.

Hume, D. 1947. *Dialogues concerning Natural Religion.* Edited by N. K. Smith. New York.

Hutton, R. H. 1885. "The Metaphysical Society: A Reminiscence." *Nineteenth Century* 18.

Huxley, L. 1903. *Life and Letters of T. H. Huxley.* Vols. 1 and 2. London.

Huxley, T. H. 1869. "On the Physical Basis of Life." *Fortnightly Review*, ns, 5 (February).

———. 1876. "The Evidence of the Miracle of the Resurrection." Paper presented to the Metaphysical Society, 11 January. Privately printed.

———. 1879. *Hume.* London.

———. 1884. "Agnosticism: A Symposium." In *The Agnostic Annual.* Edited by Charles Watts. London.

———. 1888. "The Struggle for Existence: A Programme." *Nineteenth Century* 23 (February).

———. 1892a. "Agnosticism." In *Controverted Questions.* London.

———. 1892b. "An Apologetic Irenicon." *Fortnightly Review*, ns, 52 (November).

———. 1893–94a. [1883] "Evidence as to Man's Place in Nature." In *Collected Essays.* Vol. 7. London.

———. 1893–94b. *Darwiniana* 9. London.

———. 1894. "Evolution and Ethics." In *Collected Essays.* Vol. 9. London.

———. 1901. *Collected Essays.* Vol. 9. London.

Illingworth, J. R. 1889. "The Incarnation in Relation to Development." In *Lux Mundi.* 1st ed. Edited by C. Gore. London.

———. 1895. *Personality Human and Divine.* London.

———. 1904. "The Problem of Pain." In *Lux Mundi.* 15th ed. Edited by C. Gore. London.

———. 1915. *The Gospel Miracles.* London.

Inge, W. R. 1919. "Bishop Gore and the Church of England." In *Outspoken Essays.* London.

Irvine, W. 1959. *Apes, Angels, and Victorians: Darwin, Huxley, and Evolution.* New York.

Iverach, J. 1894. *Christianity and Evolution.* London.

———. 1898. Review of *The Making of Religion. Critical Review* 8.

Jacyna, L. S. 1981. "The Physiology of Mind, the Unity of Nature, and the Moral Order in Victorian Thought." *British Journal for the History of Science* 14.

James, W. 1879. "Are We Automata?" *Mind* 4.

——. 1890. *Principles of Psychology*. Vol. 1. New York.

Jevons, F. B. 1896. *An Introduction to the History of Religion*. London.

——. 1901. "The Golden Bough." *Folk-Lore* 12.

——. 1906. *Religion in Evolution*. London.

Johnson, D. 1999. *The Changing Shape of English Nonconformity, 1825–1925*. Oxford.

Jones, E. G. 1899. *The Ascent through Christ: A Study of the Doctrine of Redemption in the Light of the Theory of Evolution*. London.

Jowett, B. 1859. "Natural Religion." In *The Epistles of St. Paul*. Vol. 2. London.

——. 1861. "On the Interpretation of Scripture." In *Essays and Reviews*. London.

——. 1895. *College Sermons*. ed. W.H. Fremantle. Oxford.

Kent, J. 1977. "A Late Nineteenth-Century Nonconformist Renaissance." in *Renaissance and Renewel in Christian History*. Edited by D. Baker. Oxford.

Kingsley, C. 1871. "The Natural Theology of the Future." *Macmillan's Magazine* 23.

Kingsley, Mrs., ed. 1876. In *Charles Kingsley: His Letters and Memories of His Life*. Vol. 2. London.

Kippenberg, H. G. 2002. *Discovering Religious History in the Modern Age*. Princeton, NJ.

Kirby, W. 1835. *On the Power, Wisdom, and Goodness of God as Manifested in the Creation of Animals and in Their History, Habitats, and Instincts*. Vol. 2. London.

Kirby, W., and W. Spence. 1823. *An Introduction to Entomology*. Vol. 2. 3rd ed. London.

Knox, R. 1914. *Some Loose Stones*. London.

Kohn, D. 1989. "Darwin's Ambiguity: The Secularization of Biological Meaning." *British Journal for the History of Science* 22.

Lambrecht, S. P. 1926. "James Ward's Critique of Naturalism." *Monist* 36.

Lang, A. 1890. "Mythology." In *Encyclopedia Britannica*. Vol. 9. London

——. 1898. *The Making of Religion*. London.

——. 1899. "Mr. Frazer's Theory of Totemism." *Fortnightly Review*, ns, 65 (June).

——. 1900. *The Making of Religion*. 2nd ed. London.

Leach, E. 1985. "The Anthropology of Religion." In *Nineteenth Century Religious Thought in the West*. Edited by Ninian Smart et al. Cambridge.

Lecky, W. E. H. 1870. *History of the Rise and Influence of the Spirit of Rationalism in Europe*. Vol. 1. London.

Lewes, G. H. 1853. *Comte's Philosophy of the Sciences*. London.

———. 1867. "The Reign of Law." *Fortnightly Review,* ns, 2 (July).

Liddon, H. P. 1893. *Life of Edward Bouverie Pusey.* Vols. 1 and 2. London.

Lightman, B. 1987. *The Origins of Agnosticism: Victorian Unbelief and the Limits of Knowledge.* Baltimore.

———. 1989. "Ideology, Evolution and Late-Victorian Agnostic Popularizers." In *History, Humanity, and Evolution.* Edited by James Moore. Cambridge.

Lilley, A. L. 1908. *Modernism: A Record and Review.* London.

Livingston, J. C. 1974. "The Ethics of Belief: An Essay on the Victorian Religious Conscience." *AAR Studies in Religion* 9. Missoula, MT.

———. 1985. "British Agnosticism." In vol. 2 of *Nineteenth Century Religious Thought in the West.* Edited by Ninian Smart et al. Cambridge.

———. 1989. "Tennyson, Jowett, and the Chinese Buddhist Pilgrims." *Victorian Poetry* 27.

Livingstone, D. N. 1987. *Darwin's Forgotten Defenders: The Encounter between Evangelical Theology and Evolutionary Thought.* Grand Rapids.

Lodge, O. 1903. *Papers of the Synthetic Society, 1896–1908.* Edited and privately printed in 1909 by the Rt. Hon. Arthur James Balfour. London.

Lubbock, J. 1865. *Pre-historic Times.* London.

Lyell, C. 1859. *Report of the British Association for the Advancement of Science.* Vol. 29. London.

———. 1863. *The Geological Evidence of the Antiquity of Man.* London.

———. 1872. *Principles of Geology.* Vol. 2. London.

———. 1970. *Species Journal.* Edited by L. G. Wilson. New Haven, CT.

Lyell, Mrs. C. K. M., ed. 1881. *Life, Letters, and Journals of Sir Charles Lyell.* Vols. 1 and 2. London.

Lyttleton, A. T. 1899. *The Place of Miracles in Religion.* London.

Macalister, A. 1899. "Anthropology and Christianity." *London Quarterly Review* 92 (July).

Macculloch, J. A. 1902. *Comparative Theology.* Churchman's Library Series. London.

———. 1904. *Religion: Its Origin and Forms.* London.

———. 1908. *Religion and the Modern Mind.* London.

Mahieu, D. L. 1976. *The Mind of William Paley: A Philosopher and His Age.* Lincoln, NE.

Major, H. D. A. 1909. *The Science of Religion and Its Bearing upon Christian Claims.* London.

Manning, H. 1871. "The Relation of the Will to Thought." *Contemporary Review* 16 (February).

Mansel, H. L. 1856. *A Lecture on the Philosophy of Kant.* Oxford.

———. 1859. *The Limits of Religious Thought Examined.* London.

——. 1861. "On Miracles as Evidence of Christianity." In *Aids to Faith*. Edited by W. Thomson. London.

——. 1866. *The Philosophy of the Conditioned*. London.

——. 1873. *Letters, Lecture, Reviews*. London.

Marchant, J., ed. 1916. *Alfred Russel Wallace: Letters and Reminiscences*. Vol. 1. London.

Marett, R. R. 1936. Remarks in *Custom Is King: Essays Presented to R.R. Marett*. Edited by L. H. D. Buxton. London.

Martindale, C. C. 1905. "Adonia." *Month* 110.

——. 1911. *Lectures on the History of Religions*. Vol. 1. London.

Martineau, J. 1875. *Religion as Affected by Modern Materialsm*. London.

——. *Modern Materialism: Its Attitude towards Theology*. London.

——. 1885. *Types of Ethical Theory*. Oxford.

——. 1888. *A Study of Religion*. Vol. 2. Oxford.

Matheson, G. 1885. *Evolution and Revelation*. Edinburgh.

Maudsley, H. 1883. *Body and Will*. London.

Maurice, F. D. 1842. *The Kingdom of Christ*. Vol. 2. London.

——. 1861. [1874] *The Religions of the World*. 4th ed. London.

McCosh, J. 1850. *The Method of the Divine Government, Physical and Moral*. Edinburgh.

——. 1871. *Christianity and Positivism*. New York.

McCosh, J., and G. Dickie. 1857. *Typical Forms and Special Ends in Creation*. New York.

McTaggart, J. E. 1903. *Papers Read before the Synthetic Society*. Edited and privately printed by A. Balfour. London.

Menzies, A. 1895. *History of Religion*. London.

Mill, J. S. 1865a. *An Examination of Sir William Hamilton's Philosophy*. London.

——. 1865b. *A System of Logic*. Vol. 2. London.

——. 1958. [1874] "Nature." In *John Stuart Mill: "Nature" and "Utility of Religion."* Edited by G. Nakhnikian. New York.

——. 1969. "Theism." In vol. 10 of *Collected Works*. Edited by J. M. Robson. Toronto.

Mivart, St. G. J. 1871a. "Darwin's *Descent of Man*." *Quarterly Review* 131.

——. 1871b. *On the Genesis of Species*. London.

——. 1872. "Evolution and Its Consequences: A Reply to Mr. Huxley." *Contemporary Review* 19 (January).

——. 1876. *Lessons from Nature*. London.

Monier-Williams, M. 1887. *Modern India and the Indians*. 4th ed. London.

——. 1890. *Buddhism*. London.

Moore, A. L. 1883. "Recent Advances in Natural Science." *Report of the Church Congress, Reading*. London.

———. 1889. *Science and the Faith: Essays on Apologetic Subjects*. London.

———. 1890a. "Memoirs." In *Essays Scientific and Philosophical*. London.

———. 1890b. "Evolution and the Fall." In *Essays Scientific and Philosophical*. London.

———. 1892. "Darwinism and Christian Faith." In *Science and the Faith: Essays on Apologetic Subjects*. London.

———. 1904. "The Christian Doctrine of God." In *Lux Mundi*. 15th ed. London.

Moore, J. R. 1979. *The Post-Darwinian Controversies: A Study of the Protestant Struggle to Come to Terms with Darwin in Great Britain and America*. Cambridge.

———. 1983. "Evangelicals and Evolution: Henry Drummond, Herbert Spencer, and the Naturalization of the Spiritual World." *Scottish Journal of Theology* 38.

Morell, J. D. 1856. "Modern English Psychology." *British and Foreign Medico-Chirugical Review* 17.

Morgan, C. L. 1890–1891a. *Animal Life and Intelligence*. London.

———. 1890–1891b. "On Modification and Variation." *Science* 4.

———. 1897–1898. "Causation, Physical and Metaphysical." *Monist* 7.

Morgan, R. 1989. *The Religion of the Incarnation: Anglican Essays in Commemoration of Lux Mundi*. Bristol.

Mozley, J. B. 1865. Bampton Lectures *On Miracles*. Oxford.

———. 1885. *Letters of the Rev. J. B. Mozley*. London.

Max Müller, F. 1856. *Comparative Mythology*. London.

———. 1864. *Lectures on the Science of Language*. 4th ed. London.

———. 1873a. *Introduction to the Science of Religion*. London.

———. 1873b. *On Missions*. London.

———. 1880. *Lectures on the Origin and Growth of Religion*. London.

———. 1881. *Selected Essays*. London.

———. 1885. *Lectures on the Science of Language*. Second Series. London.

———. 1901. *Last Essays*. Vol. 2. London.

———. 1902. *Life and Letters of the Rt. Hon. Friedrich Max Müller*. Vol. 2. Edited by Georgina Max Müller. London.

Neill, S. 1966. *The Interpretation of the New Testament 1861–1961*. Oxford.

Newman, J. H. 1870/1985. *An Essay in Aid of a Grammar of Assent*. Edited by I. T. Ker. Repr. Oxford.

Oesterley, W. O. E. 1908. *The Evolution of the Messianic Idea: A Study in Comparative Religion*. London.

Orr, J. 1906. *God's Image in Man*. 2nd ed. London.

Ospovat, D. 1981. *The Development of Darwin's Theory: Natural History, Natural Theology, and Natural Selection, 1838–1859*. Cambridge.

Owen, R. 1838. MSS, Hunterian Lectures for 1838. Royal College of Surgeons, London.

————. 1868. *On the Anatomy of Vertebrates*. Vol. 3. London.

Paley, W. 1802. *Natural Theology*. London.

————. 1825. *The Works of William Paley*. Vol. 3. London.

Pals, D. 1982. *The Victorian Lives of Jesus*. Harrisburg, PA.

Passmore, J. 1971. *The Perfectability of Man*. New York.

Pattison, M. 1885. *Memoirs*. London.

Peel, J. D. Y. 1971. *Herbert Spencer: The Evolution of a Sociologist*. London.

Peterson, H. 1932. *Huxley: Prophet of Science*. New York.

Pope, W. B. 1879. *A Compendium of Christian Thought*. Vol. 1. London.

Powell, B. 1838. *The Connexion of Natural and Divine Truth*. Oxford.

————. 1860. "On the Study of the Evidences of Christianity." In *Essays and Reviews*. London.

Pringle-Pattison, A. S. 1917. *The Idea of God in the Light of Recent Philosophy*. Oxford.

Pritchard, E. E. 1965. *Theories of Primitive Religion*. Oxford.

Prothero, R. E. 1893. *The Life and Correspondence of Arthur Penrhyn Stanley*. Vol. 2. London.

Raby, P. 2001. *Alfred Russel Wallace: A Life*. Princeton, NJ.

Rashdall, H. 1897. "Professor Sidgwick on the Ethics of Religious Conformity: A Reply." *International Journal of Ethics*.

————. 1902a. *Contentio Veritatis*. London.

————. 1902b. "Personality." In *Papers Read before the Synthetic Society*. Edited by A. J. Balfour. 1909. London.

————. 1905. "The Nature of Christ's Resurrection." In *Papers Read before the Synthetic Society*. Edited by A. J. Balfour. 1909. London.

————. 1910. *Philosophy and Religion*. New York.

Rawlinson, A. E. J. 1915. *Dogma, Fact and Experience*. London.

Reade, W. 1872. *The Martyrdom of Man*. London.

Reardon, B. M. G. 1971. *From Coleridge to Gore: A Century of Religious Thought in Britain*. London.

Réville, A. 1884. *Prolegomena of the History of Religions*. London.

Rhys Davids, T. W. 1882. *Lectures on the Origin and Growth of Religion, as Illustrated by Some Points in the History of Indian Buddhism*. London.

Richards, R. J. 1987. *Darwin and the Emergence of Evolutionary Theories of Mind and Behavior*. Chicago.

Rogers, J. G. 1851. *Christianity and Its Evidences*. London.

Roget, P. M. 1839. *Animal and Vegetable Physiology Considered with Reference to Natural Theology*. 2nd American ed. Philadelphia.

Romanes, G. 1881. "The Scientific Evidence of Organic Evolution." *Fortnightly Review*, ns, 36 (December).

———. 1883. *Mental Evolution in Animals*. London.

———. 1886. "Mr. Mivart on the Rights of Reason." *Fortnightly Review*, ns, 45 (March).

———. 1888. *Mental Evolution in Man*. London.

———. 1889–1890. "Is There Evidence of Design in Nature?" In vol. 1 of *Proceedings of the Aristotelian Society*.

———. 1895. *Mind and Motion and Monism*. Edited by C. Lloyd Morgan. London.

———. 1896a. *The Life and Letters of George John Romanes*. Edited by Ethel Romanes. London.

———. 1896b. *Thoughts on Religion*. 7th ed. Edited by Charles Gore. London.

———. 1897. *Darwin and after Darwin*. Vol. 3. London.

Row, C. A. 1879. *Christian Evidences Viewed in Relation to Modern Thought*. 2nd ed. London.

Rudwick, M. J. S. 1976. *The Meaning of Fossils*. 2nd ed. New York.

Rupke, A. 1983. *The Great Chain of History: William Buckland and the English School of Geology, 1814–1849*. Oxford.

Russell, G. W. E. 1902. *The Household of Faith*. London.

Ryder, H. I. D. 1875. "Miracles: Objections against Their Possibility and Antecedent Probability." *Dublin Review*, ns, 24 (April).

Sanday, W. 1905. *Outlines of the Life of Christ*. Edinburgh.

———. 1908. *Christianity and Other Religions*. London.

———. 1909. *The New Marcion*. London.

———. 1911. "The Meaning of Miracle." In *Miracles*. Edited by H. S. Holland. London.

———. 1912. "Historical Evidence for Miracles." *Report of the Church Congress, Middlebrough*. London.

———. 1914. *Bishop Gore's Challenge to Criticism*. London.

Sanday, W., and A. C. Headlam. 1897. *Critical and Exegetical Commentary on the Epistle to the Romans*. 3rd ed. New York.

Sanday, W., and N. P. Williams. 1916. *Form and Content in the Christian Tradition*. Oxford.

Saunders, K. J. 1922. "Christianity and Asia." *Modern Churchman* 12.

Secord, J. 2000. *Victorian Sensation*. Chicago.

Sedgwick, A. 1834. "Address to the Geological Society." In vol. 1 of *Proceedings of the Geological Society of London*. London.

——. 1860. "Objections to Mr. Darwin's Theory of the Origin of Species." *The Spectator*, 24 March. London.

Seth, J. 1894. "The Roots of Agnosticism." *The New World* 3.

Sharpe, E. J. 1965. *Not to Destroy but to Fulfil: The Contribution of J. N. Farquhar to Protestant Missionary Thought in India before 1914*. Lund.

Shea, V., and W. Whitla, eds. 2000. *Essays and Reviews: The 1860 Text and Its Reading*. Charlottesville, VA.

Shermer, M. 2002. *In Darwin's Shadow: The Life and Science of Alfred Russel Wallace, A Biographical Study on the Psychology of History*. Oxford.

Sidgwick, H. 1870. *The Ethics of Conformity and Subscription*. London.

——. 1871. "The Verification of Beliefs." *Contemporary Review* 17 (July).

——. 1876. "The Theory of Evolution and Its Application in Practice." In vol. 1 of *Mind*.

——. 1882. "The Incoherence of Empirical Philosophy." In vol. 7 of *Mind*.

——. 1888. "Presidential Address." *Presidential Address to the Society of Psychical Research*. Glasgow.

——. 1899. "The Relation of Ethics to Sociology." *International Journal of Ethics*.

Smith, R. 1977. "The Human Significance of Biology: Carpenter, Darwin, and the Vera Causa." In *Nature and the Victorian Imagination*. Edited by U. C. Knoepflmacher and G. B. Tennyson. Berkeley, CA.

Smith, W. R. 1889. *Lectures on the Religion of the Semites*. London.

——. 1894. *Lectures on the Religion of the Semites*. 2nd ed. London.

Spencer, H. 1851. *Social Statics*. London.

——. 1862. *First Principles of a New System of Philosophy*. London.

——. 1872. "Mr. Martineau on Evolution." *Contemporary Review* 20 (June).

——. 1873. *The Study of Sociology*. Vol. 1. London.

——. 1876. *The Principles of Ethics*. Vol. 1. London.

——. 1877. *Principles of Sociology*. Vol. 2. New York.

——. 1879. *The Data of Ethics*. Vol. 1. London.

——. 1882. *First Principles*. New York.

——. 1896. *The Study of Sociology*. Vol. 3. London.

Stanley, A. P. 1845. *The Life and Correspondence of Thomas Arnold*. Vol. 2. London.

——. 1865. "Theology in the Nineteenth Century." *Frasers Magazine* 71 (February).

Stephen, J. F. 1872. "On Certitude in Religious Assent." *Frasers Magazine*, ns, 5 (January).

————. 1875. "Remarks on the Proof of Miracles." Paper presented before the Metaphysical Society, 9 November. Privately printed.

Stephen, L. 1873. *Essays on Freethinking and Plainspeaking*. London.

————. 1877. "Newman's Theory of Belief." *Fortnightly Review*, ns, 22 (November–December).

————. 1882. *The Science of Ethics*. London.

————. 1893. *An Agnostic's Apology and Other Essays*. London.

Stephenson, A. M. G. 1965–1966. "William Sanday." *Modern Churchman*, ns, 9.

Stewart, A. 1891. *Critical Review* 1.

Stewart, B., and P. G. Tait. 1875. *The Unseen Universe; or, Physical Speculations on a Future State*. London.

Stocking, G. 1987. *Victorian Anthropology*. New York.

Streeter, B. H. 1912. *Foundations: A Statement of Christian Belief in Terms of Modern Thought*. London.

————. 1914. *Restatement and Reunion*. London.

Sumner, J. B. 1816. *A Treatise on the Records of Creation*. Vol. 2. London.

Temple, F. 1884. *The Relations between Religion and Science: Eight Lectures Preached before the University of Oxford*. New York.

Tennant, F. R. 1902. *The Origin and Propagation of Sin*. Cambridge.

————. 1909. "The Influence of Darwinism upon Theology." *Quarterly Review* 211.

————. 1912. *The Concept of Sin*. Cambridge.

————. 1925. *Miracle and Its Philosophical Presuppositions*. Cambridge.

————. 1930. *Philosophical Theology*. Vol. 2. Cambridge.

Thompson, J. M. 1911. *Miracles in the New Testament*. London.

————. 1912. *Through Facts to Faith*. London.

Tiele, C. P. 1897. *Elements of the Science of Religion*. Edinburgh.

Tisdall, W. St. C. 1912. *Christianity and Other Faiths*. London.

Troeltsch, E. 1971. *The Absoluteness of Christianity and the History of Religions*. 2nd ed. Translated by D. Reid. Richmond, VA.

Tulloch, John. 1862. *Beginning of Life*. London.

Turner, Frank. 1993. *Contesting Cultural Authority: Essay in Victorian Intellectual Life*. Cambridge.

Tylor, E. B. 1866. "The Religion of Savages." In *Fortnightly Review* 6 (August).

————. 1869. "The Survival of Savage Thought in Modern Civilization." In Vol. 5 of *Proceedings of the Royal Institution*. London.

————. 1871. *Primitive Culture*. Vol. 2. London.

————. 1889. *Primitive Culture*. Vol. 1. New York.

————. 1891. *Primitive Culture*. Vol. 1. 3rd ed. London.

Tyndall, J. 1874/1902. *Fragments of Science*. Vol. 2. Repr. New York.

———. 1875. "Materialism and Its Opponents." *Fortnightly Review*, ns, 18 (November).

———. 1892. *Fragments of Science*. Vol. 2. London.

Tyrrell, G. 1898. "The Making of Religion." *Month* 92.

———. 1900. Untitled paper. February, in *Papers Read before the Synthetic Society 1896–1908*. Edited by A. J. Balfour. 1909. London.

———. 1903. "The Finite God." In *Papers Read before the Synthetic Society 1896–1908*. Edited by A. J. Balfour. 1909. London.

———. 1914. "Divine Fecundity." In *Essays on Faith and Immortality*. London.

Vorzimmer, P. 1970. *Charles Darwin: The Years of Controversy*. Philadelphia.

Waggett, P. N. 1900. "Evolution and the Fall of Man." *Pilot* 1.

———. 1905. *The Scientific Temper in Religion*. London.

Wainwright, G. 1988. *Keeping the Faith: Essays to Mark the Centenary of Lux Mundi*. Philadelphia.

Wallace, A. R. 1864. *Journal of the Anthropological Society of London*. Vol. 2. London.

———. 1869. "Sir Charles Lyell on Geological Climates and 'The Origin of Species.'" *Quarterly Review* 126 (April).

———. 1870. "The Limits of Natural Selection as Applied to Man." In *Contributions to the Theory of Natural Selection*. London.

———. 1875. *On Miracles and Modern Spiritualism*. London.

———. 1891. *Natural Selection and Tropical Nature*. London.

———. 1905. *My Life: A Record of Events and Opinions*. Vol. 2. London.

Ward, J. 1911. *The Realm of Ends or Pluralism and Theism*. Cambridge.

———. 1915. [1899] *Naturalism and Agnosticism*. 4th ed. 2 vols. London.

Ward, W. G. 1878. "The Reasonable Basis of Certitude." *Nineteenth Century* 3 (March).

Webb, B. 1926. *My Apprenticeship*. London.

Westcott, B. F. 1884. *The Gospel of the Resurrection*. 5th ed. London.

———. 1892. *The Gospel of Life*. London.

Whewell, W. 1836. *Astronomy and General Physics Considered in Reference to Natural Theology*. London.

———. 1840. *The Philosophy of the Inductive Sciences*. Vol. 2. London.

Williams, R. 1856. *A Dialogue of the Knowledge of the Supreme Lord, in Which Are Composed the Claims of Christianity and Hinduism*. London.

———. 1861. "Bunsen's Biblical Researches." *Essays and Reviews*. 6th ed. London.

Williams, T. C. 1990. *The Idea of the Miraculous*. London.

Wilson, J. M. 1891. *Report of the Church Congress, Rhyl*. London.

———. 1896. "The Bearing of the Theory of Evolution on Christian Doctrine." *Report of the Church Congress, Shrewsbury*. London.

———. 1903. *Problems of Religion and Science*. London.

Wordsworth, J. 1881. *The One Religion*. New York.

Yeo, R. 1979. "William Whewell: Natural Theology and the Philosophy of Science in Mid-Nineteenth Century Britain." *Annals of Science* 36.

Young, R. M. 1970. *Mind, Brain, and Adaptation in the Nineteenth Century: Cerebral Localization and Its Biological Context from Gall to Ferrier*. Oxford.

———. 1985. *Darwin's Metaphor: Nature's Place in Victorian Culture*. Cambridge.

Index